Emmanuel Levinas and the Limits to Ethics

Emmanuel Levinas and the Limits to Ethics highlights how radically different Jewish ethics is from Christian ethics, and the profound affinities that subsist between Jewish ethics and philosophical and political liberalism.

The philosophy of Emmanuel Levinas has captured the imagination of a global constituency who take his absolutizing of ethical demands and his assigning primacy to ethics over all other branches of inquiry in his mapping of Western philosophy to be indicative of a major reordering of both personal and cultural identity. It is this reordering, they believe, that would restore greater wholeness and value to human life. In this book, Aryeh Botwinick takes issue with both the theoretical analysis in which Levinas engages and the practical ethical import that he draws from it.

Arguing that what Levinas has to say about both skepticism and negative theology can be used to reroute his argument away from the avowed aims of his thought, this book will be of great interest to students and scholars of Jewish Studies, Ethics, Political Theory and Philosophy.

Aryeh Botwinick is Professor of Political Science at Temple University specializing in political theory. He studies the relationship between monotheism and skepticism considered both as a structure of argument and as an ethical content. Previous publications include *Skepticism, Belief and the Modern: Maimonides to Nietzsche* (1997) and *Michael Oakeshott's Skepticism* (2011).

Routledge Jewish Studies Series
Series Editor: Oliver Leaman, University of Kentucky

Studies, which are interpreted to cover the disciplines of history, sociology, anthropology, culture, politics, philosophy, theology, religion, as they relate to Jewish affairs. The remit includes texts which have as their primary focus issues, ideas, personalities and events of relevance to Jews, Jewish life and the concepts which have characterised Jewish culture both in the past and today. The series is interested in receiving appropriate scripts or proposals.

MEDIEVAL JEWISH PHILOSOPHY
An Introduction
Lavinia Cohn-Sherbok and Dan Cohn-Sherbok

FACING THE OTHER
The Ethics of Emmanuel Levinas
Edited by Seán Hand

MOSES MAIMONIDES
Oliver Leaman

A USER'S GUIDE TO FRANZ ROSENZWEIG'S STAR OF REDEMPTION
Norbert Samuelson

ON LIBERTY
Jewish Philosophical Perspectives
Edited by Daniel Frank

REFERRING TO GOD
Jewish and Christian Philosophical and Theological Perspectives
Edited by Paul Helm

JUDAISM, PHILOSOPHY, CULTURE
Selected Studies by E. I. J. Rosenthal
Erwin Rosenthal

PHILOSOPHY OF THE TALMUD
Hyam Maccoby

FROM SYNAGOGUE TO CHURCH: THE TRADITIONAL DESIGN
Its Beginning, its Definition, its End
John Wilkinson

THE HIDDEN PHILOSOPHY OF HANNAH ARENDT
Margaret Betz Hull

DECONSTRUCTING THE BIBLE
Abraham ibn Ezra's Introduction to the Torah
Irene Lancaster

THE IMAGE OF THE BLACK IN JEWISH CULTURE
A History of the Other
Abraham Melamed

FROM FALASHAS TO ETHIOPIAN JEWS
The External Influences for Change, c. 1860–1960
Daniel Summerfield

PHILOSOPHY IN A TIME OF CRISIS
Don Isaac Abravanel: Defender of the Faith
Seymour Feldman

JEWS, MUSLIMS AND MASS MEDIA
Mediating the "Other"
Edited by Tudor Parfitt and Yulia Egorova

THE JEWS OF ETHIOPIA
The Birth of an Elite
Edited by Tudor Parfitt and Emanuela Trevisan Semi

ART IN ZION
The Genesis of Modern National Art in Jewish Palestine
Dalia Manor

HEBREW LANGUAGE AND JEWISH THOUGHT
David Patterson

CONTEMPORARY JEWISH PHILOSOPHY
An Introduction
Irene Kajon

ANTISEMITISM AND MODERNITY
Innovation and Continuity
Hyam Maccoby

JEWS AND INDIA
Perceptions and Image
Yulia Egorova

JEWISH MYSTICISM AND MAGIC
An Anthropological Perspective
Maureen Bloom

MAIMONIDES' GUIDE FOR THE PERPLEXED
Silence and Salvation
Donald McCallum

MUSCULAR JUDAISM
The Jewish Body and the Politics of Regeneration
Todd Samuel Presner

JEWISH CULTURAL NATIONALISM
Origins and Influences
David Aberbach

THE JEWISH–CHINESE NEXUS
A Meeting of Civilizations
Edited by M. Avrum Ehrlich

GERMAN–JEWISH POPULAR CULTURE BEFORE THE HOLOCAUST
Kafka's Kitsch
David A. Brenner

THE JEWS AS A CHOSEN PEOPLE
Tradition and Transformation
S. Leyla Gürkan

PHILOSOPHY AND RABBINIC CULTURE
Jewish Interpretation and Controversy in Medieval Languedoc
Gregg Stern

JEWISH BLOOD
Reality and Metaphor in History, Religion and Culture
Edited by Mitchell B. Hart

JEWISH EDUCATION AND HISTORY
Continuity, Crisis and Change
Moshe Aberbach; Edited and translated by David Aberbach

JEWS AND JUDAISM IN MODERN CHINA
M. Avrum Ehrlich

POLITICAL THEOLOGIES IN THE HOLY LAND
Israeli Messianism and its Critics
David Ohana

COLLABORATION WITH THE NAZIS
Public Discourse after the Holocaust
Edited by Roni Stauber

THE GLOBAL IMPACT OF THE PROTOCOLS OF THE ELDERS OF ZION
A Century-Old Myth
Edited by Esther Webman

THE HOLOCAUST AND REPRESENTATIONS OF JEWS
History and Identity in the Museum
K. Hannah Holtschneider

WAR AND PEACE IN JEWISH TRADITION
From the Biblical World to the Present
Edited by Yigal Levin and Amnon Shapira

JESUS AMONG THE JEWS
Representation and Thought
Edited by Neta Stahl

GOD, JEWS AND THE MEDIA
Religion and Israel's Media
Yoel Cohen

RABBINIC THEOLOGY AND JEWISH INTELLECTUAL HISTORY
The Great Rabbi Loew of Prague
Meir Seidler

ISRAELI HOLOCAUST RESEARCH
Birth and Evolution
Boaz Cohen

MODERN GNOSIS AND ZIONISM
The Crisis of Culture, Life Philosophy and Jewish National Thought
Yotam Hotam

THE EUROPEAN JEWS, PATRIOTISM AND THE LIBERAL STATE 1789–1939
A Study of Literature and Social Psychology
David Aberbach

JEWISH WOMEN'S TORAH STUDY
Orthodox Religious Education and Modernity
Ilan Fuchs

EMMANUEL LEVINAS AND THE LIMITS TO ETHICS
A Critique and a Re-Appropriation
Aryeh Botwinick

Emmanuel Levinas and the Limits to Ethics
A Critique and a Re-Appropriation

Aryeh Botwinick

LONDON AND NEW YORK

First published 2014
by Routledge
2 Park Square, Milton Park, Abingdon, Oxfordshire OX14 4RN

And published by Routledge
711 Third Avenue, New York, NY 10017

First issued in paperback 2016

Routledge is an imprint of the Taylor & Francis Group, an informa business

© 2014 Aryeh Botwinick

The right of Aryeh Botwinick to be identified as author of this work has been asserted by him in accordance with sections 77 and 78 of the Copyright, Designs and Patents Act 1988.

All rights reserved. No part of this book may be reprinted or reproduced or utilised in any form or by any electronic, mechanical or other means, now known or hereafter invented, including photocopying and recording, or in any information storage or retrieval system, without permission in writing from the publishers.

Trademark notice: Product or corporate names may be trademarks or registered trademarks, and are used only for identification and explanation without intent to infringe.

British Library Cataloguing in Publication Data
A catalogue record for this book is available from the British Library

Library of Congress Cataloging in Publication Data
Botwinick, Aryeh.
 Emmanuel Lévinas and the limits to ethics : a critique and a re-appropriation / Aryeh Botwinick.
 pages cm. – (Routledge Jewish studies series)
 Includes bibliographical references and index.
 1. Lévinas, Emmanuel. 2. Jewish ethics. I. Title.
 B2430.L484B67 2013
 296.3'6–dc23
 2013020379

ISBN 13: 978-1-138-21766-9 (pbk)
ISBN 13: 978-0-415-84331-7 (hbk)

Typeset in Times
by Taylor & Francis Books

Dedicated to the Memory of the Ponevezer Rav
HaRav Yosef Kahaneman ZT"L
Who in his Lifetime Fully and Gloriously Exemplified
the Principles of a Rabbinic Ethics

Contents

Preface xii

1 **Introduction** 1
  Notes   10

2 **The routes to the ethical** 11
  Ethics and the totality vs. infinity distinction   11
  The primacy of the ethical   12
  The idea of the infinite in Levinas   15
  Levinas and Descartes   19
  Totality and infinity   23
  Notes   25

3 **The Talmud and liberalism** 27
  The Talmud: theorizing ethics from the perspective of the same   27
  Privileging the relationship to the self over the Other in Levinas   31
  Machiavelli, Hobbes and liberalism in Levinasian perspective   33
  Notes   36

4 **Theory and ideology in Levinas** 38
  *Religion/secularism and theory/ideology from within the
     context of Levinas' thought   38*
  Monotheism and skepticism   40
  Maimonides and horizontal transcendence   41
  *The relationship between the Other and Others in Maimonides and
     Levinas   43*
  Notes   44

5 **Levinas and his contemporaries** 46
  Buber and Levinas   46
  Derrida and Levinas   50
  Plato, Derrida and Levinas   53

x Contents

    Ricoeur and Levinas 56
    Parfit and Levinas 58
    Ethics and a generalized agnosticism 63
    Parfit, Freud and Levinas 65
    Epistemology, ethics, circularity and a generalized agnosticism 67
    A generalized agnosticism, Sellars and McDowell 69
    Theory and ideology 71
    Theory and its limits 73
    Notes 84

6 **An ethics of theory vs. an ethics of ideology**   88
    Aristotle's ethics as an exemplar of an ethics of theory 88
    The mishnah in Avot *4:4 and the Theory of the Mean 91*
    Hillel and the moral ontology of the Rabbis 96
    Rabbinic and Maimonidean ethics contrasted with Levinasian ethics 98
    Alasdair MacIntyre and the project of devising an alternative to modernity 103
    Plato's Greater Hippias, *the relationship between theory and ideology, and Levinas 104*
    The Rabbis and the internalized, metaphorical Other 109
    Rabbi Akiva and the totality vs. infinity distinction 111
    Rabbi Akiva's series of statements in the third chapter of Pirkei Avot *116*
    Hillel as a theological precursor of Rabbi Akiva 118
    Notes 122

7 **Nietzsche and Levinas**   126
    Nietzsche, the Rabbis and Levinas 126
    Theory and practice in Rabbinic Judaism 134
    Notes 138

8 **Plato and Levinas**   140
    Monotheistic religion and Plato 140
    Plato's Cratylus *and* Theaetetus, *skepticism and totality and infinity 141*
    Polytheism and monotheism; convergent and divergent thought 157
    Circularity, the political and dialogue in Plato 159
    Notes 162

9 **Can there be an ethics that is otherwise than being?**   164
    The phenomenological background to Otherwise than Being *164*

Popper as a skeptical philosopher of science malgre lui   *167*
Levinas and Jeanne Delhomme   170
*Levinas and his phenomenological predecessors Husserl and
   Heidegger   171*
Levinas' ethics as a Christian ethics   174
*Levinas' skepticism juxtaposed to that of Quine and Reb Chaim of
   Brisk   176*
*What does the fate of skepticism in philosophy license Levinas to
   argue about ethics?   180*
The tension between "diagnosis" and "resolution" in Levinas   183
Notes   185

10 The tension between Levinas' ethics and his political theory   188
The tension   188
*Being gripped by the human Other as the pre-theoretical moment that
   renders theorizing possible   189*
The priority and primacy of human freedom   193
Affirmation of the Other and self-affirmation   200
Plato and Levinas: words and things   202
Rabbinic tradition subverts Levinasian teaching   205
*A monotheistic ethics: the mishnah of Ben Zoma (*Avot *4:1) as a
   case in point   215*
Notes   225

Index   228

Preface

One of the major practical goals of Levinas' philosophy seems to be to refocus Western consciousness on the primacy of ethics. The proliferation of violence and the suspension of ethical factors and considerations appear to be one of the great casualties of modern secularism, with its cultivation of technological and instrumental modes of thought. In order to make the case for the primacy of the ethical, Levinas has recourse to phenomenology, which assigns priority to the postulates and correlates of consciousness as the authentic building blocks of philosophy. In two major systematic works – *Totality and Infinity: An Essay on Exteriority* (Original French Edition, 1961) and *Otherwise than Being or Beyond Essence* (Second French Edition, 1978) – Levinas connects with infinity (in the first work) and with the persecuting glance of the Other (in the second work) as the correlates of his consciousness, enabling him to establish his case for ethics as first philosophy, preceding ontology and epistemology. Moreover, Levinas is convinced that his reading of ethics resonates with that of the Rabbis, whom he cites copiously by way of support in both books.

In the course of making his argument in the two works, Levinas shows a keen appreciation for two central teachings of the Western intellectual tradition – negative theology and skepticism. He believes that both of these doctrines buttress his phenomenological reading of ethics. In contrast to Levinas, I argue that both negative theology and skepticism work to undermine his theorizing of ethics and point to a completely different understanding of both where it comes from (where it theologically and philosophically originates) and what its role in the intrapsychic and interpersonal economies can be theorized as being. In addition, I also argue that the conceptualization of our obligations to the Other in Judaism conforms much more closely to my model of ethical theorizing than to Levinas'.

I am indebted to my editor at Routledge, Joe Whiting, for his encouragement and support in preparing this volume for publication. Oliver Leaman, the editor of the series in which this book appears, has been a good friend and very valuable conversation partner for me over the years, from whom I have learned (and continue to learn) a great deal. Kathryn Rylance at Routledge has been extremely helpful in expediting the progress of this book toward publication. Routledge's two anonymous referees have offered me the best kind of criticism that an author can hope for. While generally sympathetic to my argument, they have pointed out important ways in which I could make it better. I hope that I have lived up to their vision of the book.

This book is dedicated to the memory of the Ponevezer Rav, Rav Yosef Kahaneman, who invited me at the age of thirteen to come study at his yeshiva in Bnei Brak, which turned out to be one of the watershed experiences of my life. Rav Kahaneman, who lost everything in the Holocaust and rebuilt it all in the Land of Israel, very searingly impressed himself upon my consciousness as the Rabbinic Jew par excellence, and that image has remained intact with the passage of time.

I am indebted to Peter Hanley, the manager of the Instructional Support Center at Temple University, for his expert help in ironing out various technical computer issues for me.

My student Bob Comis helped me in the early stages of the preparation of the manuscript by converting an assortment of separate files into a smoothly readable, uniform computer file.

My wife Sara has been a constant conversation partner in discussing the arguments of this book. My teenage sons, Shmuel Kalman and Michoel Yosef, have been deepening and enlarging my ethical horizons, which has helped to make me more receptive to Emmanuel Levinas' ethics, and to its limits.

I am indebted to my student Michael Cesal for his excellent job in compiling the index.

Finally, I am grateful to Temple University for granting me a number of Summer Research Fellowships over the course of the past ten years that have facilitated the research for, and the writing of, this book.

1 Introduction

Emmanuel Levinas' philosophy seems to have captured the imagination of a global constituency who take his absolutizing of ethical demands and his assigning primacy to ethics over all other branches of inquiry in his mapping of Western philosophy to be indicative of a major reordering of both personal and cultural identity that would be necessary in order to restore greater wholeness and value to human life. In this book, I take issue with both the theoretical analysis that Levinas engages in and the practical ethical import that he draws from it. Both the premises and structure of argument that Levinas works with and his vision of ethics as a whole seem to me to be highly questionable. This book is devoted to an interrogation of those premises and that structure and to an elaboration of an alternative vision of ethics.

To make his critical case against Western philosophy that enables him to create the space in which to push ethics into a position of primacy, Levinas continually invokes arguments from Greek philosophy, especially from Plato. In elaborating his alternative understanding of ethics from that which currently prevails in modern secular society, Levinas copiously cites from Rabbinic texts, seeing them as offering inspiring models and corroboration for his own version of ethics. In this book, I engage in sustained analyses of both Platonic and Rabbinic texts by trying to illustrate how they yield support for critiques and alternative readings that diverge very dramatically from those advocated by Levinas.

Fortunately, Levinas has approached his themes from a number of different and not easily reconcilable directions, and in multiple texts. As with a number of other key philosophers of the Western tradition, such as Plato, Maimonides and Adam Smith, there is a problem of "the two Levinases." In his earlier work, *Totality and Infinity*,[1] the categorical pivot upon which both his critique and my reconstruction turn is a distinction that resonates very well with the Western philosophical tradition as it developed from Plato to Nietzsche. The uses to which he puts this distinction in support of an extremely altruistic and self-denying conception of ethics are also vulnerable to attack, but at least the distinction itself properly reinterpreted can serve as its own corrective and lead into understandings of ethics that dovetail much better with classical liberal and Rabbinic readings of ethics than the ethical views advanced by

Levinas. There are striking phenomenological descriptions of ethical relationships from a Levinasian perspective in this earlier work as well, but they are not organically connected to the analytical framework that informs it. The analytical framework by itself (which I deal with extensively in this book) conjures up enough antagonistic images and possibilities to cast a heavy aura of suspicion and mistrust upon the phenomenological descriptions, especially as they are elaborated upon in the later work, *Otherwise than Being*.[2]

In *Otherwise than Being*, the totality vs. infinity distinction becomes much more secondary than it was in the earlier work, and most of the argument is given over to making a systematic phenomenological case for the extreme ethical vision that Levinas argues for in a more nuanced way earlier. In *Otherwise than Being*, we are in an ethical universe dominated by impossibility, where only the morally and rationally defiant conception of ethics advanced by Levinas can be construed as the ethical norm. Despite Levinas' persistent fascination with both negative theology (the idea that since the Divine vocabulary is inherently, irredeemably metaphorical, we can only say what God is not, but never what He is) and skepticism, in *Otherwise than Being* he theorizes and advocates an ethics anchored in certainty, rather than an ethics grounded in skepticism.

The tensions and contradictions that subsist between Levinas' two major works – *Totality and Infinity* and *Otherwise than Being* – can be rendered biographically and historically more comprehensible if one takes into account the fact that at the time Levinas was writing and publishing *Otherwise than Being* his most loyal and devoted constituencies were religious lay Catholics strongly committed to their religion and Catholic theologians. It is not surprising that even partially unconsciously Levinas starts appropriating their central categories and priorities in the hope of achieving more effective communication and solidifying his relationship with them. In the 1980's and beyond, he was beginning to be appreciated by a larger and more diverse audience, including many Jews, and he toned down the absolutist strains of his earlier, more purely Christian ethics by elaborating further upon the concept of the "third party" (how a large and pluralistic political community impinges upon his earlier formulations of ethical perfectionism) and persevering with ongoing Talmudic readings, which at least overtly seek to take their ethical bearings from Rabbinic texts.[3]

In contradistinction to the Levinas of *Otherwise than Being*, negative theology itself can be viewed as an offshoot and continuation of skepticism. It represents the consummation of a rationalist quest for the most ultimate factor that can be invoked in human explanatory schemata. Since God is conceived of as being utterly transcendental, subsisting in an infinite dimension of space-time, it is not possible, by definition, to pierce behind or beyond Him in searching for a final explanation. "God" is the name we come up with for the ultimate explanatory factor responsible for everything that we encounter in the world. This ultimacy, however, is achieved only by sacrificing intelligibility because it leaves the matter of how the infinite intersects with the finite thoroughly unaccounted for. If, *per impossibile*, this relationship could be worked out, then the infinite regress that confronted us at the start of our explanatory quest would be restarted, and our postulation of God would have proven to have been entirely futile.

From a Levinasian perspective, skepticism resides upon the same paradox-ridden terrain as negative theology. The "saying" of skepticism never meshes with the "said" of skepticism. The "saying" of skepticism consists in an impulse to question everything based upon the underdetermination of words by things, the awareness that more than one string of words can encompass a seemingly common "thing" and, because of "underdetermination," the ontological status of the thing itself that is being described remains endlessly deferred. The "said" of skepticism refers to a realization of this impulse to question through an act of verbalization, which, because it does not include itself in its gesture of blanket questioning, remains fundamentally inconsistent. Once skepticism is leveled to the status of its official targets (so that the skeptic includes his own adherence to skepticism within his ambit of interrogation), the doctrine that he is subscribing to can no longer be called skepticism, but is more appropriately classifiable as a generalized agnosticism, a reflexive inclusion of skepticism itself among its objects of interrogation.

Skepticism itself is underdetermined by the phenomenon of underdetermination that it seeks to explain. For example, "underdetermination" can be accounted for by a category such as mysticism, which emphasizes the unknowability of objects based upon strictly linear, discursive modes of analysis and description. Skepticism construed as "underdetermination" gives rise to a paradox of explanation. Given the principle of underdetermination, which states that "things" by themselves cannot exert a final constraint upon the "words" that we apply to circumscribe them, every explanation can be immediately reclassified as a redescription, which merely re-inaugurates the quest for explanation. From the skeptical angle of vision of "underdetermination," the failure of the project of explanation is guaranteed by (is encoded in) the very giving of an explanation. Every description invites (and often requires) an explanation. This is one of the major roles of theories or hypotheses in the sciences. Once an explanation is provided, however, given the principle of "underdetermination," it becomes a new description (or redescription). As a description, it requires an explanation – and so the round continues indefinitely, without offering any possibility of breaking out of it.

Levinas' category of "infinity" suitably reinterpreted can be related to this whole discussion concerning the affinities between negative theology and skepticism. Negative theology is inherently contradictory. God is able to serve as the final factor in explanation only because He does not explain anything. Because He subsists in an infinite domain that is infinitely distant from the human world, He brings the explanatory quest to a halt. He becomes the final explanatory datum only because His infinite distance ensures that He cannot explain anything. God is a contradiction. Analogously, skepticism works only because it refuses to take its skeptical definitional protocols into account by resisting skeptical questioning of itself. Both God and skepticism are sustainable only if contradiction is domesticated and naturalized. The generalized agnosticism that skepticism devolves into suggests that no version of human understanding is ever the last word, that the work of investigators in all fields of knowledge in any given generation is hostage to the work of future generations of investigators throughout all subsequent generations. What I have just described consists in an unpacking of the metaphor of infinity as horizontal rather than as vertical transcendence, with each generation of investigators contributing to rejecting, refining, revising, transforming or confirming, in an altered intellectual environment, the work of its predecessors. In the course of time, this openness to future developments might lead to a widespread reception of multivalued logics, which would have the effect of normalizing contradiction.

Given Levinas' continuing adherence in virtually all of his writings to both negative theology and skepticism, the appropriate ethical extension of and complement to his thought would seem to be an ethics grounded in skepticism, not one formed in certainty. The central tension in Levinas' work is between his laying the groundwork for an ethics that is otherwise than certainty and his actual pursuit of an ethics of certainty. In this book, by exploring (among other issues) the argumentative resources residing in the category of infinity (such as horizontal transcendence), I demonstrate how being attentive to this groundwork enables us to fashion an ethics that is faithful to some of the key skeptical inspirations that animate Levinas' thought.

There are a number of key polarities that are central to my argument: theory/ideology; religion/secularism; and Judaism/Christianity. What distinguishes theory from ideology is its willingness to turn inward in relation to itself the critical canon that it initially directs toward external targets of thought. Skepticism, construed as a generalized agnosticism that confers legitimacy and cogency upon the notion of horizontal transcendence, is a theoretical concept. Extreme versions of skepticism, which refuse to reflexively apply protocols of consistency to their own teachings, should be consigned to the domain of ideology. Belief in any statement or creed that is untempered by an awareness of the vulnerability of that statement or creed to issues of underdetermination of words by things or meaning by text is evocative of ideology, rather than theory. Uncritical, wholesale acceptance of either belief or skepticism situates one as an adherent of ideology, rather than theory.

From this perspective, it would be grossly superficial and misleading to differentiate between religion and secularism by saying that religion revolves around belief and that secularism is characterized by skepticism. Neither belief nor skepticism are sustainable in their pristine forms. Belief is susceptible to skeptical interrogation – and skepticism requires mitigation and reformulation in light of the protocols of consistency. Moreover, monotheistic belief, at least, is riddled by paradox and contradiction, whose structures resemble the paradox and contradiction affecting skepticism. Given the monotheistic backdrop to Western religion, there is a secular aura that has overhung it from its inception. In effect, the religion/secularism dichotomy is called into question by the theory/ideology duality. From a strictly theoretical standpoint, religion and secularism can both be appropriately denominated as either religious or secular.

To the extent that Judaism and Christianity are both monotheistic religions, paradox and contradiction gnaw at the very conceptualization of God to which they both give allegiance. The differences between them emerge in their starkest form in terms of the pivotal role that Christianity assigns to Jesus as the Redeemer and Savior of all of humankind. Judaism very rigorously upholds an unbridgeable distance separating man from God. This structure of allegiance, coupled with the paradox and contradiction affecting the notion of the monotheistic God, ensures that all of the moves that one undertakes within either religion – both those affecting the organization and content of the religion itself and those using it as a guidepost for conducting one's worldly transactions – will never be purged of uncertainty. Christianity with its doctrine of the Incarnation, with Jesus as the Son of God harboring a component of Divinity within Himself, and conceived of as redeeming humankind of all of its transgressions past, present and future through His Crucifixion, closes the yawning distances that remain unsealed in Judaism and introduces striking elements of certainty into the human story. The version of "infinity" in Levinas' corpus that I am calling "horizontal transcendence" remains close to the Jewish script, whereas the systematically phenomenological ethics of *Otherwise than Being* evokes and dramatizes Christian certainty.

This book also takes the initiative in arguing that an egoistically-grounded, liberal ethics is *ethically* superior to Levinasian ethics. In addition, I offer a revised and detailed systematic exposition of what Jewish ethics looks like that is dramatically different from that offered by Levinas. I attempt to theorize in this book new ways of conceiving how skepticism actually feeds into and supports ethics and how, in fact, it can be regarded as a type of ethics itself.

In fixing the framework for the whole argument, I would like to establish a baseline picture of what a Rabbinic ethics looks like. A natural textual candidate for this purpose seems to me to be Nahmanides' (Rabbi Moses ben Naḥman Girondi [1194 – 1270]) very short and intensely personal ethical regimen (known to generations of Jews as the *Iggeret HaRamban* – literally, the "Letter of the Ramban")[4] that he lays down for his son to follow in order to help him lead an optimally religious existence. What makes this document especially instructive and revealing is the strong emotional bond between father and son exuded by the *Iggeret*, which does not allow the father much space for deep personal reflection, but only for a restatement of the obvious – the body of ideas, the whole religious and ethical sensibility, that he and his son take for granted and upon which the father can spontaneously expound.

What makes the *Iggeret* a paradigmatically Rabbinic text is the extent to which *Anavah* (Hebrew: "humility") rather than *Chesed* (Hebrew: "kindness" or "loving-kindness") emerges as the primary, foundational Rabbinic virtue. Nahmanides writes:

Accustom yourself to speak gently to all people at all times. This will protect you from anger – a most serious character flaw which causes one to sin. ... Once you have distanced yourself from anger, the quality of humility will enter your heart. This sterling quality is the finest of all admirable traits, as Scripture writes: On the heels of humility comes the fear of God (Proverbs 22:4). ... When your actions display genuine humility – when you stand meekly before man, and fearfully before God; when you stand wary of sin – then the spirit of God's presence will rest upon you, as will the splendor of His glory; you will live the life of the World to Come. ... Let all men seem greater than you in your eyes: If another is more wise or wealthy than yourself, you must show him respect. And if he is poor, and you are richer or wiser than he, consider that he may be more righteous than yourself: If he sins it is the result of error, while your transgression is deliberate.[5]

In these passages, the tone seems superficially Levinasian, but the content appears to be diametrically opposed to Levinas' teaching. Nahmanides seems to be advocating total subordination to the Other – placing him on a pedestal while completely debasing oneself. In Nahmanides' advice to his son about how to conduct his life, the display of kindness and generosity to the Other (*Chesed*) knows no bounds. It becomes almost axiomatic that the Other is more righteous, more worthy, more deserving than oneself. What drives all of this self-abasement, however, is the cultivation of the value that Nahmanides, under the tutelage of the Rabbis in the Talmud, considers the supreme personal virtue, namely, humility (*Anavah*). Nahmanides inverts Levinas. He turns Levinas on his head. We should subordinate ourselves to Others in our manner of speaking and relating to them in order to cultivate personal humility. For Nahmanides, subordinating ourselves to the Other is itself subordinate and instrumental toward the cultivation of a personal virtue, namely, humility. The Other is being used to augment the virtue and greatness of the self. The moral and religious focus is on the self. According to Nahmanides, we are not being bidden to be humble in order to more appropriately relate to the Other. We need rather to be subservient to the Other in order to cultivate a proper and enduring humility. Through doing (in this case being kind and generous toward others) we become (humble). The focus from start to finish in Nahmanides' discourse remains on the self.

Further corroboration of the idea that Rabbinic ethics never leaves the plane of the Same[6] can be found in the fact that an organizing principle of this ethics is Raba's statement that *Adam Karov Aitsel Atzmo V'Ain Adam Masim Atzmo Rasha* – "Every man is considered a relative to himself, and no one can incriminate himself."[7] The way Rashi (Rabbi Shlomo Yitzchaki [1040 – 1105], the great medieval Jewish Biblical and Talmudic commentator) spells out the legal import of Raba's dictum in the Babylonian Talmud, *Sanhedrin* 9b and *Yebamoth* 25b is as follows: since the Rabbis postulate a person as being a relative to himself, and the Torah prohibits relatives from giving testimony about each other, then a person's testimony incriminating himself is regarded as invalid. But this is only true with regard to matters of *Issur V'Heter*, where Jewish law prohibits a certain practice pertaining to religious requirements, and a person says that he committed it. With regard to *Dinei Mamonot* – civil matters – if a person acknowledges that he owes someone one hundred dollars, he is required to pay it based upon his own testimony (*Hodoat Piv K'Meah Adim Dami* – his own admission is equivalent to the testimony of one hundred witnesses). In the case of a civil dispute, the wrong is still rectifiable if the person pays the money that he agrees he owes, so that in civil matters he is not incriminating himself by his admission.

Generalizing the legal principle of *Ain Adam Masim Atzmo Rasha* into a moral principle suggests that a person does and should give himself the benefit of every doubt that he is acting in an upright way. The ambiguity of motives, the conceptual indeterminacy of the factors that the motives are about and the requirement to continually resituate oneself to inaugurate new beginnings in the field of action all point to the need to tease out the most favorable translations of one's previous actions. As one moves ceaselessly forward, one must use the insights gleaned from his later experience to reconfigure his earlier experience. Past and future subsist in a seamless web of mutual rearticulation without a final picture of either past or future ever congealing. The resources of the Same extend infinitely without a space emerging for assigning priority to the Other in Levinas' sense. The self's ongoing reoccupation of the threshold of selfhood remains its lifelong focus and challenge. The perfectionist ethic of Christianity which Levinas implicitly follows is preceded in Judaism by an ethic postulating a trajectory of diminishing imperfections resulting from unrelieved acts of doing, without a moment ever emerging when we are clearly and definitively out of the woods.

The primacy of doing over being is registered in two famous verses in the Psalms: "The beginning of wisdom is the fear of Hashem – good understanding to all their practitioners [literally, doers] ... Praiseworthy is the man who fears Hashem, who intensely desires His commandments."[8] In the first verse, there is an abrupt, and therefore also nearly imperceptible, transition between a very lofty state of being, namely, fear of God (*Yirat Hashem*) and doing (*Asiya*). *Yirat Hashem* is immediately translated by the Psalmist into the doing of *Mitzvot* (conformity to Divine commandments). The next verse more directly and emphatically stresses the same theme: *Yirat Hashem* is manifested in doing, that is, in *Mitzvot* – not in an inner state of being.

Doing precedes, and endlessly staves off the possibility of, being. We never get to being, including being totally subordinated to and persecuted by the Other. We are always only in the throes of doing, and need to sustain the desiderata and preconditions of *that*. Fear of God, as the highest state of being (or, according to Moses Maimonides [1135 – 1204], the second highest state, coming after love of God)[9] is collapsed by the Psalmist into an endless series of actions that preempt and expose the illusory character of any state of being. God can *be* – but we human beings can only *do* – or, stated more precisely, on a metaphysical level, for God being and doing coalesce, whereas for us, interpreting the categories in their usual way, the gap between them remains unbridgeable.

The Rabbis adopt a diametrically opposed point of view to that which they criticize in *Ain Adam Masim Atzmo Rasha*, or its more personalized variation, *Al Tehi Rasha Bifnei Atzmecha* – Do not judge yourself to be a wicked person.[10] The Babylonian Talmud, in *Shabbath* 128a, says: *Kul Yisrael Bnai Melachim Haim* – "All of Israel are royal children." This flamboyantly metaphorical statement can obviously be unpacked in many different ways that highlight the Jews' special covenantal relationship with God. In light of our previous discussion, we can add an additional gloss. There is a regal character pertaining to our actions deriving from our radical insufficiency as human beings. Our actions can only beget – and be redeemed by – further actions without our entering upon a secure plateau that can sustain our state of being. The sovereignty of doing is an inescapable result of human limitation. It is in our moment of enduring withdrawal to a plane of endless doing that we most acutely exhibit our God-like character, since, in the Biblical account, God's supreme creativity is manifested in His own withdrawal to make room for what is other than Himself, namely, the world.

Rashi's commentary at the top of the Talmudic page in *Shabbath* 127b underscores the centrality of *Chesed* in order to have a proper appreciation of those *Mitzvot* that have nothing to do with *Bein Adam L'Chaveiro* – relations between one human being and the next – but are rather the keenest expression of the dimension of *Bein Adam L'Makom* – relations between human beings and God. To reconcile a discrepancy in the numbering patterns of two Tannaitic sources, the Talmud (according to Rashi) wants to say that *V'Iyun Tefilah Haynu B'Clal Gemilut Chasadim D'Chetiv "Gomel Nafsho Ish Chesed"* – Meditation in prayer (through focusing on the meaning of the words that one is reciting) is included in the practice of loving deeds – to one's own soul – as it is written, "the man of love doeth good to his own soul" [Proverbs 11:17].[11]

The remarkable thing about this passage is that the vocabulary of *Chesed* is being applied to *Mitzvot* that very clearly exemplify the domain of *Bein Adam L'Makom* – human beings in relation to God – i.e. concentration in prayer. How can we theorize where *Chesed* belongs in the sphere of human being–God relations? Apparently, the theological vocabulary referring to God as the ultimate, infinite Other of monotheistic religion is irredeemably metaphorical. With regard to God, metaphors can only be translated into other metaphors, with no realistic substratum being available to us where we can finally, breathlessly, drop anchor. The most that we can do (which is the strategy that the Rabbis usually avail themselves of) is to say that the traits and dispositions that the Torah attributes to God metaphorically inscribe the norms that we should strive to conform to in our regular human behavior. If God is described as kind and compassionate, we should try to be kind and compassionate toward our fellow human beings.

However, the content of Divine description is not exhausted by human emulation. If what rationally drives our quest for God is the search for final explanation – and the only way that the postulation of God can help us achieve finality in our explanatory quest is by His being conceived of as Infinite (i.e. above and beyond anything we can imagine) – then just as God's infinity blocks literalization of His attributes, so too it simultaneously blocks deliteralization. If, because of the infinite distance that separates us from God, we cannot know who God is, we also, by the same token, cannot know who He isn't. In some manner that we cannot fathom, He might display all of the traditional attributes in a literal sense (omnipotence; omniscience; all-benevolence) and still be the *infinite* God. Given how the human ratiocinative process leading to God blocks and thwarts itself at every turn – it cannot utter either a resounding "yes" or a full-throated "no" – conformity to any monotheistic religious system requires from us a gigantic commitment of *Chesed* – of sheer goodwill and overflowing generosity – to fashion a way of life out of materials that defy our understanding from beginning to end.

Given what I have just said, namely, that the breakdown of reason might not apply to God – His infinity (infinite reason) prevents us from saying anything about Him – the next available candidate toward which one can direct this pattern of reasoning is the human epistemological realm. This is the skepticism with which Levinas has been obsessed throughout his career. The constitutive principle of philosophical skepticism is the underdetermination of words by things. More than one string of words can be made to consistently fit any given object. If one then seeks to salvage realism by pointing out that skepticism is inconsistent – to be consistent, the skeptic would have to skeptically question skepticism alongside all of the official targets that one has mobilized skepticism to attack – then the path that one needs to pursue at this point remains systematically unclear. One can say that the movement of recoil mandated by an awareness of the inconsistency of skepticism leads to a rehabilitation of all of those objects of thought previously called into question by skepticism in their full pristine realism. Or, one can say that, given the surplus of words in relation to things, the urge to question also legitimately returns in its full force and that we are now caught in a gesture of inexorable oscillation between affirmation and negation with regard to the things of this world. The generosity that the Talmud in *Shabbath* tells us is necessary to navigate our communication with God in prayer turns out to be the crucial leaven upon our negotiation and management of the everyday world, as well as of all the specialized worlds of inquiry and practice flourishing within it. Preternatural love is what enables us to keep the world afloat within our preferred domains of uncertainty and is simply not available as a pre-ontological connection with the Other who, much like us, can be presumed to confront dilemmas relating to uncertainty.

In this book, I invoke Levinas not only as a target of criticism, but also as an ally in helping me make my critique of his conception of ethics and my articulation of an alternative vision of ethics. What Levinas has to say about both skepticism and negative theology can be used to reroute his argument away from the avowed aims of his thought. His distinction between the "saying" and the "said" of skepticism – and his uncompromising view concerning the Otherness of God – point in the direction of a radical reconfiguration of his own thinking concerning ethics. In this book, I try to pick up the intimations of, and expound upon, this other Levinas that resides within Levinas.

Notes

1 Emmanuel Levinas, *Totality and Infinity: An Essay on Exteriority*. Trans. Alphonso Lingis. (Pittsburgh: Duquesne University Press, 1969). The original French edition was published in 1961.
2 Emmanuel Levinas, *Otherwise than Being or Beyond Essence*. Trans. Alphonso Lingis. (The Hague: Martinus Nijhoff, 1981). The second French edition was published in 1978.
3 I am grateful to Zeev Harvey for emphasizing these factors to me in personal conversation.
4 From the time that it was written in approximately 1267 until today, the *Iggeret HaRamban* has been reprinted innumerable times. The edition that I am using in the text is by Avrohom Chaim Feuer and is called *Iggeret HaRamban: A Letter for the Ages* (Brooklyn: Mesorah Publications, 2007).
5 Ibid., pp. 17, 19.
6 In his essay, "Philosophy and the Idea of the Infinite," Levinas uses the terminology of the Same and the Other. He is inspired in his usage of this dichotomy by Plato's earlier invocations of it in the *Sophist*, the *Timaeus* and the *Theaetetus*. See Adriaan T. Peperzak, *To the Other: An Introduction to the Philosophy of Emmanuel Levinas* (West Lafayette: Purdue University Press, 1993), p. 99.
7 *Hebrew-English Edition of the Babylonian Talmud: Sanhedrin*. Chapters I-VI trans. Jacob Shachter. (London: Soncino Press, 1987), 9b. The identical statement is found in the Babylonian Talmud, *Sanhedrin* 25a and *Yebamoth* 25b. The second half of Raba's statement is found in the Babylonian Talmud, *Ketuboth* 18b.
8 Psalms 111:10; 112:1. The translation comes from *The ArtScroll Tehillim*. Trans. Hillel Danziger with Nosson Scherman. (Brooklyn: Mesorah Publications, 1988), p. 246.
9 Maimonides, *Mishneh Torah* (hereafter *The Code*), Book 1: The Book of Knowledge, Laws of Repentance. Trans. Moses Hyamson. (Jerusalem: Feldheim, 1974), Chapter 10. See my article, "In Defense of *Teshuvah* – A Modern Approach to an Ancient Concept," *Judaism*, Volume 26, Number 4 (Fall 1977), pp. 475 – 480, especially pp. 478 – 480.
10 *Pirkei Avot* 2:18
11 *Hebrew-English Edition of the Babylonian Talmud: Shabbath*. Trans. H. Freedman. (London: Soncino Press, 1987), 127b, FN.

2 The routes to the ethical

Ethics and the totality vs. infinity distinction

Emmanuel Levinas (partially unwittingly) offers us a hermeneutical key for reconceiving what is at stake in the Western intellectual tradition. Certain recurring conundrums of Western philosophy lead him to assign primacy to ethics above all other modes of inquiry and categorization within philosophy, as well as to affirm the pursuit of infinity and denigrate the preoccupation with totality in all spheres of human theoretical and practical activity. In Levinas' intellectual landscape, the totality vs. infinity distinction constitutes a prime analytical tool for heightening the primacy of the ethical within the multiple arenas of human thought, action and relationships. In this book, I argue that the notion of the primacy of the ethical is not equal to the conceptual and analytical tasks that Levinas wants to thrust upon it – but that the distinction between totality and infinity itself goes a long way toward engaging those tasks without either entailing or even requiring a series of moves that catapult us beyond ontology or traditional philosophy, which are integral to Levinas' concept of the primacy of the ethical. The means of Levinas' argument overshadow or overpower his end – so that a proper explication of the totality vs. infinity distinction helps to clarify why the primacy of the ethical cannot be argued for in Levinas' sense.

With a revised context in place for locating the totality vs. infinity distinction, we are in a position to appreciate the ways in which it enables us to reconceptualize the Western intellectual tradition. "Totality vs. infinity" helps to capture the religious dimension of secularism – the ways in which modern liberalism, for example, still nurtures and promotes a religious project. This distinction also facilitates our rediagnosing the relationship between key figures in the development of modernity, such as the one subsisting between Niccolò Machiavelli (1469–1527) and Thomas Hobbes (1588–1679).

In what follows, I will first try to clarify what Levinas means by the primacy of the ethical and explain the role of this concept in his thought. I will explore why it cannot do what he wants it to do – and how the totality vs. infinity distinction properly elucidated, which operates within being and does not emanate from or extend beyond being, goes a long way toward achieving results that Levinas hoped to derive from the primacy of the ethical. I will then try to sketch in short compass, without going into details, how this distinction allows us (or even compels us) to reconceive the project of modernity and, more specifically, how Machiavelli's theorizing of power translates into the political doctrines of modern liberalism.

The primacy of the ethical

In his essay, "Philosophy and the Idea of the Infinite," Levinas uses the Platonic terminology of the Same and the Other (as developed in the *Sophist*, the *Timaeus* and the *Theaetetus*) to level a broad indictment against Western philosophy. He condemns it for being "indissolubly bound up with the adventure that includes every Other in the Same."[1] What Levinas means by this is that through conceptualization – that is, recourse to language (language as "the house of being" in the Heideggerian sense) – the Otherness of what lies outside or beyond human beings is subdued and domesticated to conform to the ordering mechanisms of language. In Levinas' formulation (which is simultaneously evocative of Hobbes and of Nietzsche), "reason, which reduces the other, is appropriation and power."[2]

The Same thus overwhelms the Other. In addition (and here the argument begins to more emphatically echo Plato, especially the Third Man Argument in the *Parmenides*), the Same is not even able to preserve its viability as the Same. The problem with the Same consists of several interrelated components. It situates the relationship between theory and fact; language and world; and words and objects in such a way so as to virtually guarantee the underdetermination of the former by the latter. The reason why the original delineation of the problem cannot be reformulated – so that we describe what is at stake in our recourse to concepts and language as a matter of straightforward reportage or reflection of what confronts us in the world – is that the choice of organizing frameworks itself remains underdetermined by factors outside itself. Again, whether the vocabulary of choice or constraint is appropriate at this juncture is also underdetermined by factors outside of the elements that constitute the choice situation itself. The vocabulary of underdetermination itself remains underdetermined, which in a negative sense provides Levinas with an opening wedge for considering alternatives that are "otherwise than being" (the master category of the Same), namely, genuinely unassimilable human Otherness and God.

The paradox and irreconcilable tension upon which Levinas' theorizing rests is that it is only by manifesting the full panoply of powers of the Same that he is able to make room for the Other. A central presupposition of Levinas' thought is that the Same always triumphs over the Other. As a result, the questionings of the Same always triumph over the certainties of the Same. In our idiom, the thesis of the underdetermination of theory by fact (language by reality) is exposed as being itself underdetermined. This skeptical questioning of skepticism is what enables Levinas in a negative sense to point to what might lie beyond being. To make his argument for what is "otherwise than being," Levinas needs to invoke precisely what the conclusion of the argument seeks to rule out: the primacy of the Same over the Other.

In being a captive of this dilemma, Levinas' argument resembles Maimonides' case for negative theology in *The Guide of the Perplexed*.[3] In order to show that none of the attributes that monotheistic theology traditionally ascribes to God can be applied literally, Maimonides needs to presuppose the subsistence of that very God Himself, so that the endless disownings of the literal significations of attributes can take place. Analogously, to make his case for the Other, Levinas has to persistently exploit the argumentative resources residing in the Same. He needs the Same in order to be able to call forth the Other.

Levinas emphasizes again and again that he is making a philosophical case about the limitations of philosophy, the indirect payoff of which for him is that it creates a clearing for God and the human Other. But if Levinas' argument is largely negative in character (emphasizing what reason cannot accomplish), then there are two things that we must immediately notice about it. The first thing is that the category "otherwise than being" can be almost anything at all. Being, as an overarching category designed to integrate all aspects of worldly experience within itself, can be contrasted with almost any set of phenomena that are too fine or too quirky or too poignant to be susceptible to such a wholesale processing response. Being, in the sense that Levinas employs the term, can just as appropriately be contrasted with the shapes of colors on the horizon or an intimate, bonded relationship with the earth as it is in Levinas' case with the nudity of the face of the Other, imposing an impossible ethical demand upon us that comes before being. The second thing is that, on an intuitive basis, perhaps, we can appreciate the greater gravity attaching itself to ethical imperatives above esthetic considerations and the need to feel a greater degree of communion with the environment. But Levinas claims not to be relying upon intuition – but to be fashioning a philosophical argument consisting of reasoned defenses of the positions he is advancing. From a strictly analytical perspective, there is an irreducible element of arbitrariness in Levinas' choice of the Other as the focal category to contrast with being. The fact that being is not self-justifying does not create a prima facie case for any humanly-centered category as the appropriate complement or support or background factor for being.

Michael Theunissen, in his book *The Other*,[4] establishes an ideal typology for theorizing about the Other by contrasting two broad approaches, which Fred Dallmayr summarizes in the following way: "Transcendental phenomenology, abbreviated as 'transcendentalism' and the 'philosophy of dialogue' or 'dialogism.' While, starting from the premise of the ego, the first position seeks access to inter-subjectivity by construing the other basically as an 'other I' or *alter ego*, the second position derives ego or self in some manner from an original encounter with a 'Thou.'"[5] Theunissen associates transcendental phenomenology with Edmund Husserl and Martin Heidegger, and regards Martin Buber as a key exponent of dialogism. Levinas is a severe critic of the

Husserlian and Heideggerian varieties of phenomenology and is clearly trying to fashion a version of Buberian dialogism that has a richer philosophical amplitude than Buber himself was able to provide.

In addition, Levinas has a strong theological motive for wanting to affirm the Other as a precondition for the formation of the self. From Levinas' perspective, God needs to be mediated through the Other in conformity with the imperatives of negative theology. A more direct theological/theoretical route to God – for example, one that straightforwardly sought to describe His nature and His difference from things human – would, in spite of itself, assimilate Him to the world by virtue of the humanly delimited descriptions and analogies that it would be compelled to employ. To declare God to be totally different from us – to utilize a human vocabulary to register and denote that difference, however negatively, is to be engaging in what our theological strictures seek to rule out: a human delimitation of the nature of God. From this perspective, a recourse to the Other becomes the most extreme of philosophical gestures: It absolves us of the need to engage in the inconsistent gesture of *speaking* about our inability to speak about God. Indeed, it obviates our resorting to language altogether with regard to describing the nature of God. The existence of multiple Others on the human scene is a forceful reminder of the insufficiency of the Same, despite all its efforts and pretensions to continual conceptual and material self-aggrandizement.

What is problematic in this sort of approach is that dialogism in a logically inexorable sense merges into transcendental phenomenology. Levinas' retort to Jacques Derrida's reproach of him just confirms Derrida's critique. Derrida quoted "a Greek who said, 'If one has to philosophize, one has to philosophize; if one does not have to philosophize, one still has to philosophize (to say it and think it). One always has to philosophize.'"[6] To this Levinas responds by saying, "*Not to philosophize would not be 'to philosophize still.'*"[7] However, to resist philosophizing – to declare its writ terminated – is just another move in the philosophical game. To affirm the primacy of the Other – to assign priority to ethics above ontology – is to be registering certain philosophical understandings concerning the limitations of reason and the moves that remain possible under such circumstances. Levinas' attack on Heidegger's transcendental phenomenology can with equal justice be leveled against Levinas himself. Levinas addresses to Heidegger the critique that "Being *is not* a being. It is a Neuter which orders thought and beings."[8] Correspondingly, we can say to Levinas: "The Other is not a person. It is a Neuter which orders thought and beings."

Levinas' analysis of the Other gets impaled on the horns of a dilemma. If, on the one hand, the feelings of extreme vulnerability that Levinas describes as leading to a total assumption of responsibility even for one's persecutors is to be taken as a straightforward empirical account of a universal human experience, then Levinas as a phenomenologist would have to be the first to acknowledge that the brute experience without conceptual overlay is the most ideal construct of all – that the human world is constituted precisely by a series of conceptual frameworks that delineate and define experience for us. If, on the other hand, Levinas takes an idealist approach to the experience of vulnerability – that it results from the postulation of a particular conceptual framework among theoretically available alternatives for comprehending this particular segment of experience – then the role of the Same or identity in shaping a world in which the Other is highlighted as a dominant force is even more brazenly affirmed. Whether Levinas' organizing perspective is classified as empiricist or idealist – or as some subtle synthesis between the two – he faces what appears to be an insuperable challenge in making sense of it in ways other than that which states that the Same extends its sway over experience by coming up with new ways of processing and classifying it in terms congenial to itself: "My responsibility for the Other ... *testifies* to Infinity"[9] because of a certain conceptual framework that I bring to bear in construing my relationship to the Other and not because of some magic residing in Otherness.

The idea of the infinite in Levinas

The idea of the "infinite" in Levinas follows a Maimonidean trajectory – and is invoked for reasons parallel to Maimonides' emphasizing this constitutive element in God's "make-up" as being integral to Biblical and Rabbinic conceptualizations of Him. As long as God is theorized as finite, He does not bring the explanatory quest to a halt. One can always attempt to penetrate to what lies above and beyond Him that is responsible for the phenomenon that one is examining. The idea of "infinity" is introduced to render God on a literal level conceptually inaccessible to us and therefore the factor beyond which, by definition, one can no longer inquire. God achieves ultimacy – and His total Otherness from things human is guaranteed – once the metaphor of "infinity" is conjoined with the whole panoply of attributes (e.g. omnipotence, omniscience, etc.) that Biblical religion ascribes to Him.

One can discern a parallel movement of argument taking place in Levinas. "The Other," he says, "who provokes this ethical movement in consciousness and who disturbs the good conscience of the Same's coincidence with itself compromises a surplus which is inadequate to intentionality. Because of this inassimilable surplus, we have called the relation that binds the I to the Other (*Autrui*) *the idea of the infinite.*"[10] In order to properly affirm and respect the Otherness of the Other, we cannot resort to purely egoistically determined psychological processes that yield to us our sense of the Other, which then become the basis for the moral judgments that we make concerning him/her. At some point, there is a need to break out of the circuit of the self to both grasp our notion of the Other and to affirm the moral priority that Levinas claims he/she has over us. The metaphor of "infinity" (encapsulating as it does unfathomable and irreducible distance) becomes the appropriate symbolic vehicle for both fixing the genuine "Otherness" of the Other and for dramatizing the priority that his/her claims exert upon us.

Once we acknowledge that the idea of infinity is introduced by Levinas as a metaphor for rhetorically working his way around the limits of logic and language to be able to embrace both the authentic Otherness and the moral superiority of the Other, we notice that (just as with Maimonides) the idea of infinity obfuscates and mystifies more than it clarifies. In Maimonides, God's infinity enables us to achieve ultimacy in our explanatory quest, but only by sacrificing intelligibility. If God's ultimacy were indeed to bring our search for explanations to a satisfactory arrest, we would have to be able to show what by definitional postulation we are debarred from doing, namely, how the infinite intersects with the finite. If, *per impossibile*, we would be able to do this, however, it would only restart (give a new impetus to) the explanatory quest, because then God would cease to be the final factor in explanation.

Similar vicissitudes of argument bedevil Levinas' strategy. If it is the metaphor of the "infinite" that gives us our idea of the human Other and accentuates the notion of his moral priority over us, how do we rescue an intelligibly relatable Other from the metaphorical thicket of "infinity"? The moment we begin to pursue our usual moral deliberations in trying to determine how to act, the metaphor of "infinity," with its inscrutability and unchartable and irrecoverable distances, becomes unactionable and untranslatable. With regard to our moral quandaries and dilemmas centering on the issue of how to escape the taint of self in our moral theorizing and deliberating, we find ourselves in precisely the same location that we were in before the metaphor of "infinity" was introduced. Levinas at this point in his exposition confronts a choice between two equally unpalatable alternatives. While fully acknowledging the metaphorical character of the "infinite," he can declare that it is an indispensable category for accounting for ethical judgment and deliberation. Levinas appears to be pursuing this approach in the following passage: "The Other resists my attempt at investiture, not because of the extent and obscurity of the theme that it offers to my consideration, but because of the refusal to enter into a theme, to submit to a regard, through the eminence of its epiphany."[11] In other words, the metaphor of "infinity" helps to fix for me my relationship to the Other. But, in this case, if one needs to invoke the humanly delineated metaphor of "the infinite" in order to gain conceptual and moral access to the Other, this constitutes the weightiest declaration of the triumph of the Same imaginable.

Alternatively, Levinas could be opting for a remapping of the philosophical landscape, with the idea of infinity (its unintelligibility unrelieved, so that it is only its rhetorical adaptation for human ethical uses that lies in the foreground) being invested with obdurate, if cognitively inaccessible, reality and primacy, so that it overshadows key standard categories in the lexicon of philosophy. In the following excerpt, Levinas seems to have opted for this way of dealing with infinity: "In this way, we rediscover the Cartesian itinerary, which moves from the Cogito to the World by passing through the idea of the infinite. In a more general way, the priority of the idea of the infinite is asserted over the idea of being and ontology."[12]

The routes to the ethical 17

Levinas seeks to accommodate the "surplus which is inadequate to intentionality" – a conceptualization of the Other as genuinely Other – either by rigorously extending the domain of metaphor or by rezoning reality to make room for new categories and new priorities. The first approach is counterproductive (and recognized by Levinas as such) because the proliferation of metaphors is one of the major ways through which the empire of the Same is extended. The second approach is ineffective because it can only be understood as a variation on the first approach. By making sense of our relationship to the Other under the aegis of the category of infinity, Levinas is not deciphering the notion of infinity for us (which would be logically impossible; infinity can only be described in negative terms by inventorying what it is not), but trading upon some of its metaphorical connotations in order to buttress his understanding of the primacy of the ethical. Just as Maimonides' theorizing of Biblical monotheism invokes a notion of the infinite that is neither analytically nor emotionally "sublimatable" to a set of higher, more overarching terms or reducible to a set of familiar categories that would enable us to immediately domesticate it, – so, too, Levinas' reference to the infinite in making sense of our relationship to the Other cannot be extrapolated to a more general, inclusive level that would give us a more secure grip on the infinite, nor can it be collapsed to a set of familiar ways of making sense of and conceiving of the Other. "Infinity," in both Maimonides' and Levinas' hands, reflects back to us limits to reason from which we must now seek to find our bearings.

Levinas appears resolutely inconsistent in his romance with the infinite. If (as Levinas admits) the infinite constitutes a metaphor for envisioning human relations, then it would not be contradictory if, in our efforts to make sense of how we theorize and existentially grasp Otherness, we could come up with an approach that would in fact be rooted in the perspective and limitations of the Same and still be able to account for how behavior that was faithful to the mandate of Otherness was generated – an approach that would even appear compelling to the individual ethical practitioner. As a metaphor – and not as itself an ethical, epistemological or theological imperative – "infinity" does not constrain us in terms of how ethics actually operates. We are free to explore and imagine other routes to Otherness aside from infinity that would support or converge upon the notion of Otherness as conjured up by the metaphor of infinity.

Levinas, however, does not say this. He argues instead that "the idea of the infinite consists in grasping the ungraspable while nevertheless guaranteeing its status as ungraspable."[13] This statement, of course, is overtly, and even flamboyantly, contradictory. Once one grasps the ungraspable (i.e. the infinite), it ceases to be ungraspable. "Guaranteeing its status as ungraspable" after one has grasped it simply means refusing to treat "infinity" as a metaphor, but instead as a realistic feature of the interpersonal world. "Infinity" in Levinas' hands becomes an institutionalized contradiction. We persistently need to both know and not know what "infinity" signifies. The most persuasive way to approach it is in the spirit of a generalized agnosticism, which leaves the door open to the proliferation of logics that would map contradiction as an acceptable accompaniment to our perception of how reality is unfolding.

If in his head-on tackling of the issue of being able to show the primacy of ethics Levinas comes up with the idea of "infinity" which eventuates in contradiction, then he has at his disposal a very economical route for defending the primacy of ethics beyond introducing the theme of infinity. A skeptic – a disbeliever in ethics and, *a fortiori*, the primacy of ethics – would also end up willy-nilly supporting the Levinasian position. Since skepticism is an inconsistent and contradictory philosophical thesis – to be consistently skeptical would require one to include skepticism itself among his array of skeptical targets – one can only embrace skepticism at the cost of embracing contradiction. Since admitting one contradiction into the body of statements that one takes to be true preempts one from foreclosing any other contradictions, no statement or concept (however contradictory in character) can ever be excluded.[14] As a result, "infinity," with all of its paradoxes and contradictions, would also have to be admitted. From a Levinasian perspective, one could say that both skepticism and ethics become possible because they are both predicated upon contradiction.

To state the argument in general terms, we could say that, as we saw earlier, skepticism is irrefutable – so that contradiction is unavoidable. Karl Popper's proof then extends the argument to show that contradiction is also uncontainable.[15] God on the one side and skepticism on the other always ensure that there is at least one contradiction to which everyone adheres. This confirms and reinforces the uncontainability of contradiction.

The upshot of my analysis is that the structures of the arguments in Levinas' two major attempts to follow through on his phenomenological project of fixing the identity of ethics as first philosophy run parallel to each other. In *Totality and Infinity*, it is the category of infinity that shoulders the burden of being the conceptual fulcrum from which the absolute demands of the Other are directed toward us. In *Otherwise than Being*, it is the Face, or even the very existence of the Other, that signifies the primacy of the Other (ethics in the grandest sense) over all other modes of human interaction and cognition. Neither a realistic nor a metaphorical construal of these notions can ground the thesis of ethics as primary philosophy. However, appropriately scaled down to everyday human uses – with infinity understood as ongoing horizontal movement across time rather than as vertical deliverance or transcendence, and the Face as referring to an awareness of the Other that captivates us and momentarily reorients us, but does not permanently rivet and transform our lives – both infinity and the Face can help to significantly illuminate questions and quandaries that emerge within the field of ethics. In addition to theorizing a wholly different approach to understanding where Judaism stands in relation to basic questions of ethics than that of Levinas, this book as a whole is devoted to a "de-apocalypticizing" of basic Levinasian categories to a more intermediate human level.

Levinas and Descartes

Levinas is very enamored of Descartes' ontological proof of God's existence put forward in the *Meditations*[16] as a philosophical strategy enabling him to make his case for the primacy of ethics. This is the way Levinas seeks to appropriate Descartes' deployment of the idea of the infinite:

> After the certainty of the *Cogito*, present to itself in the Second Meditation, the Third Meditation announces that "in some way I have in me the notion of the infinite earlier than the finite – to wit, the notion of God before that of myself." ... The putting into us of an un-includable idea overturns that presence to self which consciousness is, forcing its way through the barrier and checkpoint, eluding the obligation to accept or adopt all that enters from the outside. It is then an idea signifying with a signifyingness prior to presence, to all presence, prior to every origin in consciousness and thus an-archical, accessible in its trace. It signifies with a signifyingness from the first older than its exhibition, not exhausting itself in exhibiting itself, not drawing its meaning from its manifestation, and thus breaking with the coinciding of being with appearance in which, for Western philosophy, meaning or rationality lie, breaking with synopsis.[17]

How does the notion of the infinite – the idea of God – get transformed into a proof of God's existence? Following Anthony Kenny, we might schematize the Ontological Argument as follows:

(1) God's existence is possible.
(2) God is by definition all-powerful and independent.
(3) God can exist by His own power.
(4) What can exist by its own power, does exist.
(5) God exists.[18]

Kenny argues that Descartes' God resembles Alexius Meinong's Pure Object, which "stands between being and nonbeing."[19] The problem with Meinong's Pure Object and Descartes' possible God is that we are unable to provide criteria of identity for them. As Willard Van Orman Quine rhetorically asks: "What sense can be found in talking of entities which cannot meaningfully be said to be identical with themselves and distinct from one another?"[20]

Kenny's reading of Descartes' Ontological Argument concerning the existence of God in the light of Quine's critique of Meinong's Pure Object represents only one possible way of making sense of Descartes. The unintelligibility that Kenny imputes to Descartes' exposition of the statement that "God exists" is dependent upon the unavailability of a referent concerning whom Descartes' statement could apply. However, Descartes' Ontological Argument can be understood as making the case for the possibility of invoking precisely such a referent – and that his linguistic determination of this referent confers all of the reality that is needed or is possible for such an entity. Construing Descartes' version of the Ontological Argument on Kenny's model yields a different formulation of the argument from that found in its original expositor – St. Anselm of Canterbury. If Descartes' argument about God is understood as following straightforwardly the linguistic path mapped out by St. Anselm, then Kenny's strictures concerning his argument would not apply.[21]

In order to see this more clearly, let us consider the following: A major strategy for fixing the import of Descartes' ontological proof might be an avowedly skeptical one – invoking the principle of the underdetermination of theory by fact. The existence of the world is compatible both with the thesis of Divine existence and creation, and with more narrowly configured scientific hypotheses. On the basis of the facts going to compose the world, there is no way that either organized perspective can be conclusively corroborated or discredited. However, the thesis of underdetermination only succeeds in accomplishing a negative result. It restores parity between scientific accounts of nature and theological ones by arguing that none of these accounts can be ruled out on the basis of the facts. The thesis only enshrines skepticism. It no more succeeds in proving infinity than it succeeds in establishing a thoroughly naturalistic universe of finite duration.

There is internal evidence to support a reading of Descartes as a consistent, that is to say, a generalized-agnostic, skeptic. Viewing Descartes as an heir to late-medieval nominalism[22] and negative theology gives one the impetus to read his reformulation of the Ontological Argument and the *cogito ergo sum* passage in tandem with it as attempted resolutions for the problem posed by skepticism. I would like to use the *cogito* passage to resolve an ambiguity lurking in his presentation of the Ontological Argument.

St. Anselm – the original propounder of the Ontological Argument in the 11th century – uses negative theology as the premise from which to launch this argument: "Anselm ... does not define God as the most perfect being that there is, but as a being than whom no more perfect is even conceivable. This represents the final development of the monotheistic conception."[23] Descartes inaugurates his version of the Ontological Argument with the premise that "the idea of a supremely perfect being necessarily includes the attribute of existence."[24] On the surface, it looks as if Descartes is deriving God's existence from a positive premise about the nature of God. Is there any evidence to suggest that the appropriate way to read Descartes is in accordance with the model provided by St. Anselm – that existence is somehow an inference from a negative-theological conception of God emphasizing what God is not (that all human forms of perfection are not God) rather than what He is?

I would suggest that there is convincing internal evidence. There is a parallel structure to the *cogito* passage and the Ontological Argument in Descartes. The core data for the *cogito* passage are human argumentative/philosophical practices that tacitly take for granted a persistent human reasoner pressing forward with his argumentative moves despite the skeptical counter-thrusts that tilt the argument away from any positive resolution.

Analogously, the core data for the Ontological Argument, which tries to bridge the gap between the premise that God's existence is possible and the conclusion that God exists, are human linguistic practices that carve out a niche for God. In both cases, what exist are formatted sequences of human action (making reference to God in His relationship to human beings and the world; charting the paths that a person travels in trying to make the case for one position or another) which are registered (and at least to some extent reified) in a set of linguistic categories and social practices. While neither God nor the argumentative point one is seeking to make are successfully negotiated in our God and argumentative discourses, the ongoing practices themselves at least yield evidence of enduring human preoccupations that belie attempts at an irrevocable discrediting of God and philosophy.

The parallel structure between the *cogito* passage and the Ontological Argument conceived in this way evokes negative theology. Negative theology deliteralizes the attributes that we ascribe to God and thereby restores theological focus to the human activity that conceptualizes and speculates about those attributes. Similarly, in the *cogito* passage (and if one reads the Ontological Argument in its light, also in the Ontological Argument), Descartes devalues the substantive emphasis on engagement with epistemological or more broadly philosophical truth – and God – in favor of a critically foreshortened focus on the procedural and methodological presuppositions of our philosophical and theological statements. From the organizing perspective that I am proposing, the implicit philosophical import of Descartes' approach is to nominalistically deflate and deflect human philosophical and theological preoccupations away from what they substantively argue for to a reflexive inventorying of what they disclose to us about human rational limitations and strategies for grappling with them, and sustaining inquiry (in however attenuated a form) within their bounds.

In a positive vein, it is ironic that Levinas, whose proclaimed self-image is that of a philosopher incidentally making or pointing to a clearing for God rather than that of a theologian directly addressing issues of God's accessibility and intelligibility, should, on a formal level, duplicate the structure of negative-theological argument. What centrally drives negative theologians such as Maimonides to conceive of God in non-humanly accessible terms (with the actual vocabulary used to describe God being viewed as irredeemably metaphorical) is the quest to bring the search for primary reasons and causes to a halt. By positing God – who is utterly different from all things human – as the ultimate explanatory factor, common ground between the items needing to be explained and the factor doing the explaining is exploded, and the restless inquiry for a more primary explanation has no place to go. The formal structure of Levinas' argument duplicates that of negative theology. The appropriate context to make sense of being are the impossible ethical demands emanating from the Other. What restores repose to metaphysical inquiry is the invocation of the ethical dimension of human life, whose starting-point (rather than culmination-point) is finality: human beings conceived of as unbreachable ends, demanding, rather than supplying, reasons. Levinas has given us a metaphorical version of immanence. The monotheistic God is not in the world, but his metaphorical stand-in – the ethical standpoint that originates in the finality of a kingdom of human ends, rather than human beings' laboriously striving toward finality through sustaining protracted levels of argument – is transposed by Levinas into the heart of the human world. Since any location of the monotheistic God within the human world has to be construed metaphorically, the location of a metaphorical surrogate for God within our common world is negatively theologically considered on a par with the "immanentizing" of the literal God. The superimposition of a metaphor upon a metaphor (ethics for God) does not render the search for immanence any less poignant or self-defeating.

The collapse of literalism into metaphor in the delineation of the monotheistic God can already be noticed as occurring within the Biblical canon itself. For example, Chapter 113 of the Psalms (which is incorporated in the Jewish liturgy as the first chapter of the *Hallel*, a prayer recited on Jewish festivals to praise and give thanks to God) harbors as one of its major motifs a surprising theological deflation. Instead of focusing directly on God, the name of God is substituted for God as the object of veneration and adulation. The chapter reads as follows:

> Halleluyah! Give praise, you servants of God; praise the Name of God! Blessed be the Name of God, from this time and forever. From the rising of the sun to its setting, God's Name is praised. High above all nations is God, above the heavens is His glory. Who is like God, our God. Who is enthroned on high – yet deigns to look upon the heaven and the earth? He raises the needy from the dust, from the trash heaps He lifts the destitute. To seat them with nobles, with the nobles of His people. He transforms the barren wife into a glad mother of children. Halleluyah![25]

The chapter's diction appears to be contradictory. It seems to slide imperceptibly from talking about God's Name (which carries the implicit suggestion that God Himself is unapproachable by us) to talking about God – as if He were an accessible target for our worship and discourse. However, if we examine the context in which the transition to God occurs, we see that the diction of the chapter is entirely smooth and consistent. God is "above the heavens" in "His glory." He is "enthroned on high – yet deigns to look upon the heaven and the earth." The God who is invoked by the Psalmist cannot be identified with any physical location – not even the heavens. This spatial dislocation of God suggests that even when He is referred to without the designation "Name," all He is or ever can be for the Psalmist is a Name – a carrier of a set of connotations without a set of corresponding denotations – a Subject of limitless epithets that can never be cashed in or referentially pinned down.

Both the negative and positive aspects of Levinas' theorizing of the primacy of the ethical suggest that he has provided us with a mesmerizing rhetoric of religious thought and practice rather than a philosophical defense of a category "otherwise than being". Levinas has given us an augmented intra-human frame of reference for speaking about God without having effectively transformed human rational limitation into a new positive premise for validating God's existence or presence in the world.

Totality and infinity

A transition to the totality vs. infinity vocabulary as superseding the primacy of the ethical conceptualizations is provided by Levinas himself in the course of adducing background argumentation concerning why the concepts of being and the Same, taken by themselves, are inadequate. In *Otherwise than Being*, Levinas establishes a significant linkage between skepticism and his attempts to burst the traditional Western philosophical vocabulary. He says that the "return of the diachrony refusing the present makes up the invincible force of skepticism."[26] The continual return of skepticism throughout the history of Western philosophy is symptomatic of the failure of synchronous modes of thought – the epitome of assertions of the Same – to resolve philosophical perplexity. Synchronous philosophical positions invariably give rise to their skeptical antitheses, but a commitment to synchrony forecloses our achieving a coherent formulation of skepticism. To *formulate* skeptical arguments or doctrines founders on the charge of inconsistency because to be consistently skeptical requires one to be skeptical of skepticism, as well as of competing and alternative doctrines. A way out of this dilemma would appear to consist in introducing some version of diachrony that would enable us to factor out – to posit as analytically distinct – the activity of skeptical questioning from the resulting inconsistent formulations. One way in which this could be done would be to invoke multivalued logics that map the suspension of the Law of the Excluded Middle, so that we legitimate a third possibility: instead of having just the contrasting options of skepticism and non-skepticism, when we formulate the tenets of skepticism themselves we encode the paradoxical case of their being predicated upon non-skepticism.[27] What defeats the philosophical surge toward synchrony are just the limitations built into language itself – which require us to affirm diachronous rhythms or patterns of expression in order to achieve maximum coherence. This awareness leads Levinas to say in a striking formulation that "language is already skepticism."[28]

A generalized agnosticism comes in at two points to enhance the persuasiveness of this position. By itself, a generalized agnosticism seems like the most consistent version of skepticism, since it encodes being skeptical about skepticism. In addition, it paves the way for the legitimation of multivalued logics because it refuses to categorically embrace any vision of reality generated from within any of the sciences or domains of inquiry established to promote understanding of human beings and the world. Metaphysical space is thus created for the reception of multivalued logics as a tool for better understanding ourselves and the world.

It is interesting to note the structural dynamics of Levinas' argument, which looks both initially promising and helps to account for the ultimate quandaries in which he finds himself. Levinas deliberately shuns the friend/enemy distinction as elaborated upon by the ancients (e.g. the "Polemarchus" section in Plato's *Republic*; the discussion of friendship in Aristotle's *Ethics*) and opts for the Same/Other distinction, whose original home (as we have seen) is also in Plato. Part of what ostensibly motivates the shift between the two sets of categories is the notion that friendship is morally tainted by its dependence upon its conceptual opposite number – enmity – for intelligibility and coherence. As long as we stay on the level of friendship, the discordant resonances of enmity are still there to haunt us and to induce ambivalences concerning the attainability of genuine friendship. Shifting the categorial focus of discourse to the Other enables us to divest ourselves of these discordances and ambivalences by fixing as the dialectical opposite number to the Other not the moral-ethical category of enmity, but the epistemological idea of the Same. There is an additional dimension to Levinas' artfulness. By collapsing the substantive moral-ethical distinction of friend/enemy into the prefatory epistemological distinction between Same and Other he has diverted our attention away from a hopelessly entangled realm of moral complexity to a preliminary level of epistemological investigation.

The irony, of course, is that by making his situation as a moral philosopher initially better he has made it ultimately worse. The ways in which the category of the Other is ultimately tainted by the category of the Same render the category of the Other much more problematic in an ethical sense than the ways in which conceptual strands of enmity get entangled within our notions of friendship. The conceptual notion of the Same vitiates the worldly specification and translation of the category of the Other in a much more complete way than the category of enmity calls into question the workability of a satisfactory realization of the possibilities of friendship.

If we take Levinas' position on the pervasiveness of skepticism seriously, then we need to deliteralize his notion of the Other and recognize that its content does not substantively add anything beyond what is already suggested by the notion of infinity. In contrast to what superficial readings might suggest, the Other does not constitute a conceptually unmediated trace that is supposed to emanate from and reflect "otherwise than being." The harbinger – the vehicle or the conduit – for affirming the trace of God in the human world is the concept of infinity itself (in resistance to or rejection of totality) – and its pervasiveness (as we shall see in the next chapter) in modern Western theorizing. An illuminating way to read Levinas is in a strongly negative-theological vein that couples negative theology with a negative hermeneutics. The notion of the Other comes to block the conceptual self-aggrandizement of the Same – it summarizes how dilemmas of self-referentialism rule out thought's total conquest of experience in a burst of rampant skepticism – rather than literally and positively affirming the role of the Other in orienting and shaping the self. To achieve maximum coherence, a negative hermeneutics needs to be applied to Levinas' concept of the Other – emphasizing what it preempts, not what it affirms.

The idea of totality is evocative of the possibility of assigning a positive, non-logically-vulnerable content to concepts. The notion of infinity suggests, by contrast, that in our inquiries and theoretical pursuits and in the practical programs of action that they sanction we can only proceed negatively – with thought working critically to block the projection of final positive content onto the concepts and theoretical categories that we fashion. After we skeptically attack or criticize them and expose their logical and other vulnerabilities, our skepticism itself cannot be viably contained within particular concepts, but needs instead to be diachronically stretched out in the form of a generalized agnosticism, which, because it does not allow us to embrace anything in a conclusive fashion, leaves the door open, in a strictly negative sense, for what might lie beyond being. Infinity conjures up the negative import of analysis and theorizing.

If Levinas' theoretical exertions are not effective in achieving the primacy of ethics over epistemology, perhaps an alternative route starting from the self – the Same (Identity, rather than Difference) – might work if the argument is oriented in a negative-theological direction, emphasizing the limitations of reason rather than being built up through a series of cumulative positive stages. Contra Levinas, one could point to how, from a strictly negative-theological perspective, one gets from the self to the Other through the medium of the category of generosity (and its relationship to epistemological limitation). Negative theology highlights the sheerly arbitrary character of all of our descriptions of God. Given the infinite distance that separates us from Him, none of our statements can be taken to literally refer to Him. "Arbitrariness" connotes that we are bereft of a decision-making rule that will provide us with a principled basis for making selections among alternative formulations concerning the nature of God. From a negative-theological perspective, they all equally miss the mark.

At this point, ethics can be mobilized to rescue epistemology. Acting spontaneously, generously – as it were, arbitrarily – to help other people without a discernible causal factor or element of self-interest driving us to do so represents the peak of ethical behavior. Kindness, compassion and benevolence all bespeak the transformation of a lack of reason for action into the highest principle of action. Solicitousness for the Other can be derived from the equations of incompleteness characterizing the Same.

Notes

1 Peperzak, *To the Other*, p. 99.
2 Ibid., p. 98.
3 Maimonides, *The Guide of the Perplexed*. Trans. Shlomo Pines. (Chicago: University of Chicago Press, 1963). See the discussion of this work in my book, *Skepticism, Belief, and the Modern: Maimonides to Nietzsche* (Ithaca: Cornell University Press, 1997).

4 Michael Theunissen, *The Other: Studies in the Social Ontology of Husserl, Heidegger, Sartre, and Buber.* Trans. Christopher Macann. (Cambridge: MIT Press, 1984).
5 Fred R. Dallmayr, *Critical Encounters: Between Philosophy and Politics* (Notre Dame: University of Notre Dame Press, 1987) p. 211.
6 Jacques Derrida, *Writing and Difference.* Trans. Alan Bass. (Chicago: University of Chicago Press, 1978) p. 152.
7 Emmanuel Levinas, *Basic Philosophical Writings.* Ed. Adriaan T. Peperzak, Simon Critchley and Robert Bernasconi. (Bloomington: Indiana University Press, 1996), p. 148; italics in original.
8 Peperzak; *To the Other,* p. 102; italics in original.
9 Levinas, *Basic Philosophical Writings,* p. 103; italics in original.
10 Ibid., p. 19; italics in original.
11 Ibid., p. 12.
12 Ibid.
13 Ibid., p. 19.
14 Compare Karl Popper: "If two contradictory statements are admitted, any statement whatever must be admitted; for from a couple of contradictory statements any statement whatever can be validly inferred." Karl R. Popper, *Conjectures and Refutations: The Growth of Scientific Knowledge.* Second Revised Edition. (London: Routledge and Kegan Paul, 1965), p. 317.
15 Ibid., pp. 317–322.
16 Rene Descartes, *Meditations on First Philosophy.* Trans. Laurence J. Lafleur. Second Revised Edition. (Indianapolis: Bobbs-Merrill, 1960), Third Meditation, pp. 43–50.
17 Levinas, *Basic Philosophical Writings,* pp. 136–137.
18 Anthony Kenny, *Descartes: A Study of his Philosophy* (New York: Random House, 1968), pp. 160–161.
19 Alexis Meinong, "The Theory of Objects," in Kenny, *Descartes,* p. 155.
20 W. V. Quine, *From a Logical Point of View* (New York: Harper & Row, 1961), p. 4; cited in Kenny, *Descartes,* p. 169.
21 See the discussion of St. Anselm's Ontological Argument in my book, *Michael Oakeshott's Skepticism* (Princeton: Princeton University Press, 2011), pp. 84–88.
22 See Hans Blumenberg, *The Legitimacy of the Modern Age.* Trans. Robert M. Wallace. (Cambridge: MIT Press, 1983), Chapter 3.
23 John Hick, "Ontological Argument for the Existence of God." *Encyclopedia of Philosophy.* Ed. Donald M. Borchert. Volume 7. Second Edition. (Detroit: Macmillan Reference USA, 2006), p. 16.
24 Ibid.
25 *The Complete ArtScroll Siddur.* Trans. Nosson Scherman; Ed. Nosson Scherman and Meir Zlotowitz. (Brooklyn: Mesorah Publications, 1984), p. 633.
26 Levinas, *Otherwise than Being,* p. 169.
27 W. V. Quine, *Philosophy of Logic* (Englewood Cliffs: Prentice-Hall, 1970), p. 85.
28 Levinas, *Otherwise than Being,* p. 170.

3 The Talmud and liberalism

The Talmud: theorizing ethics from the perspective of the same

The following are some Talmudic examples of how it is possible to theorize ethical postulates without departing from the metaphysical terrain of the Same. The touchstone of what is regarded as ethics would be the pragmatic consensus of human communities concerning how human beings should behave:

1. R. Joshua b. Levi's statement in *Sotah* 38b – "Every *kohen* [priest] who pronounces the benediction is himself blessed, but if he does not pronounce it he is not blessed; as it is said, 'I will bless them that bless thee.' (Genesis 12:3)"[1] – exemplifies the Rabbinic understanding of how the exertions and initiatives of the self compensate for the problematic ontological, epistemological and ethical status of the Other. A *Kohen*'s blessing of the Other (in this case, the community of his fellow Jews – the *Yisraelim*) becomes from a Jewish theological perspective ontologically interchangeable with the Other's blessing of him – i.e. his becoming blessed. So whether the physical existence of the Other can be validated or not – and whether his ethical status can be affirmed – becomes of secondary importance in light of the theological insight that the *Kohen*'s blessing of the Israelites accomplishes the same goal as the Israelites' blessing of the *Kohen*. By being able to muster the psychological resources to overcome the fear, jealousy and resentment that actually/potentially interfere with the *Kohen*'s blessing of the Israelites, the *Kohen* manifests the fact/takes concrete steps to ensure that he himself is blessed. The *Kohen* accomplishes through his own intervention what the Israelites' intervention (which was not called for – and is therefore not forthcoming) would have brought about.

The obliqueness and indirection of the whole process of blessing is insinuated by the Torah in its description of the *Chanukat Hamishkan* (the inauguration of the tabernacle in the desert), where a key component of the investiture of the *Kohanim* (the "priests") with their special role, which entitles them to bless the rest of the Jewish community, consists in the Israelites (the non-*Kohanim*; the non-Levites) placing their hands in a position of blessing upon the Levites (which includes the future *Kohanim* who come from the tribe of Levi): "And thou shalt bring the Levites before the Eternal; and the children of Israel shall lay their hands upon the Levites" (Numbers 8:10). The Israelites who are the objects of the *Kohanim*'s blessings during the regular services in the Sanctuary and Temple themselves become the source of the *Kohanim*'s special status, which entitles them to confer the blessings upon the remainder of the community. This Biblical projection of blessing as a kind of round in which the roles of conferrer of blessing and object of blessing can be exchanged is evocative of the endlessly displaced character' of the activity of "blessing." It is not just that the *Kohanim* have to come on to the Israelites to be blessed – and the Israelites have to come on to the *Kohanim* to be blessed. The process of displacement is manifested on each and every occasion of blessing. When the *Kohen* blesses the Israelites, he is actively ensuring his own blessed state. And the same is true when the Israelites invest the *Kohanim* with blessedness. They too are ensuring their own blessedness.

In terms of fixing the larger prototype for this conception of blessedness and ethics as not departing from the metaphysical terrain of the Same, it is interesting to note that the Talmud in *Sotah* 38b juxtaposes another statement by Rabbi Joshua b. Levi to the one I have just cited concerning how the *Kohen* who recites the benediction is himself blessed. This other statement reads as follows: "Whence is it that the Holy One, blessed be He, desires the priestly benediction? As it is said, 'So shall they put My name upon the children of Israel; and I will bless them'" (Numbers 6:27).[2] Rashi, in explicating this statement in the Talmud, says that "The verse makes the matter dependent upon them to make this blessing [the occasion for] the placing of His name upon His nation. And [the verse] did not make it a necessity of Israel, but a necessity of God."[3] Given the monotheistic constraints on the possibility of relating to Him, God, as it were, requires some subsection of the Jewish community (in this case, the *Kohanim*) to seize the initiative in blessing all other Jews in order for *His* blessing to devolve upon them.

R. Joshua b. Levi's formulation as interpreted by Rashi is all of a piece with the Rabbinic construal of the verse, "This month shall be unto you the beginning of months; it shall be the first month of the year to you" (Exodus 12:2). Dwelling upon the phrase "unto you," the Rabbis infer that the fixing of the calendar – the determination of when each month starts based upon the rising of the new moon – is assigned to an earthly Jewish court. All of the holy days of Judaism with their myriad requirements and restrictions thus derive from the rulings of a Jewish court under whose jurisdiction these rulings come. The Heavenly Court, as it were, simply ratifies and follows the fixing of the calendar and the consequent fixing of the dates of the holidays that the earthly Jewish court adopts, confirming the rotations of the moon as faithfully reported by witnesses.[4] "God's doing," in the cases of both the blessing of the Jewish community and the determination of the calendar, is displaced upon human doing in order for God's doing to be acknowledged as efficacious and as, in fact, occurring. This pattern is recapitulated in the case of the *Kohanim*'s blessing of the Israelites and the Israelites' blessing of the

Kohanim, where blessing is reconfigured as most affecting the more palpably real Same or self that is conferring the blessing – rather than the more shadowy recipient or Other. The setting that needs to be most zealously delineated and delimited is the active one where recitation of the blessing occurs (to show how blessing is already manifest in the structure of that setting taken by itself) in order to serve as a placeholder for the broader and looser rhetoric of blessing as encompassing other people to take hold.

Negative theology serves as the background model for this conception of blessing and ethics that focuses upon the Same or the self. In negative theology, God is the necessarily absent Partner in the human being–God relationship. If He were present in a way that human beings could grasp, He would not be the Absolutely One God. What makes him Supremely One is that he cannot be inserted into any comparative (human) context with regard to any of His attributes – including His Oneness. The upshot of the theological constraint exerted by the monotheistic understanding of God is that all religious activities take place in a literally un-partnered sense. The monotheist studies God's Word, the ways of God and even prays to God without being able to physically or conceptually pinpoint whom he is relating to. A central informing motif of negative theology is that the studying and praying activities that the monotheistic religious believer and practitioner engages in – as well as his other religious enactments – transform him into the highest caliber of religious believer and practitioner regardless of the fact that he cannot literally (in any particular manner) identify who the Object of or Partner to his relationship is. It is the doing – the engagement in all of the *Mitzvo*t (commandments) that he performs – that elevates and exalts his religious status – not his imbibing of sacred blessings literally derived from the Divine Source. In a certain strategic sense, one could say that negative theology is predicated upon the metaphysical and psychological equivalence between the individual monotheistic believer and practitioner investing fully his energies of will by performing God's commandments and the literal immersions of the non-monotheistic believer and practitioner in relating to his palpably accessible God. It is the multiple deeds of the monotheistic believer that are crucial to cultivating and fixing his status, not the literally discernible effects he has upon (and the responses he receives from) a palpable God.

As a text (or series of texts), monotheism insinuates the dispensability of the literally conceived Divine Partner for the emergence of a religious personality and a religious way of life. Ethics can be directly patterned along monotheistic lines. As we have seen in the case of blessing, one can be blessed by both meaningfully receiving a blessing and by meaningfully conferring one. The effects on the self are almost identical in either case. In relation to almost any ethical attribute – for example, kindness and compassion – one can become more kind and compassionate through being the beneficiary of and reflecting upon and responding to someone else's kind and compassionate behavior toward oneself. Or, one can become more kind and compassionate by exhibiting this very type of behavior toward someone else. The results in either case are fairly equivalent. In order to make room for the human Other – just as in the case of the Divine Other – one does not have to step outside of the boundaries of the self to be able to appropriately organize his life around the prospects of the human Other and the Divine Other.

2. Another example of how extreme solicitude for the Other can be cultivated on the metaphysical and theological terrain of the Same is suggested by the following formulation by Maimonides in his *Code*:

> The Sages of old were wont to let the slave partake of every dish that they themselves ate and to give the meal of the cattle and of the slaves precedence over their own. Is it not said: "As the eyes of slaves unto the hand of their master, as the eyes of a female servant unto the hand of her mistress" (Psalms 123:2)? ... .
>
> Furthermore, whoever has compassion will receive compassion, as it is said: "And He will show thee mercy, and have compassion upon thee, and multiply thee" (Deuteronomy 13:18).[5]

The last paragraph I have cited from Maimonides' *Code* (together with its Biblical prooftext) is found verbatim a second time in the *Code* in its *Laws Concerning Gifts to the Poor*, Chapter 10, Paragraph 2. Maimonides' formulation has its source in a statement found in the Babylonian Talmud, *Shabbath* 151b: "It was taught, R. Gamliel Beribbi said: 'And He shall give thee mercy, and have compassion upon thee, and multiply thee' (Deuteronomy 13:18): he who is merciful to others, mercy is shown to him by heaven, while he who is not merciful to others, mercy is not shown to him by Heaven."[6] The basis for this exegesis is the repetition of the verb form of the Hebrew word for mercy and compassion – "*V' Richamecha*" – in juxtaposition to the noun form of the same word – "*Rachamim*" – as if to suggest that in the manner in which a person treats others, so will he be treated by Heaven ("*B'Midah Sh'adam Moded, Modedin Lo*" – "In the measure that a person metes out to others, so is it meted out to him").[7]

One subtle but revealing discrepancy between the Talmudic text and Maimonides' paraphrase of it consists in Maimonides' omission of the words "by Heaven" in his two restatements of R. Gamliel Beribbi's insight. Maimonides simply says that "whoever has compassion will receive compassion" without referring to Heaven directly as the bestower of said compassion. Perhaps, in a negative-theological vein that is not able to assign literal credence to any of the verbs and attributes ascribed to God, Maimonides wants us to see the human agent's display of compassion toward others as itself symptomatic of the receipt of the highest degree of compassion from God. Doing – taking the initiative on one's own of being compassionate to others – is the optimal register or reflection of one's having been compassionately nurtured and related-to. The dyadic display of compassion – between man and man, and between God and man – is here reduced to a monadic efflorescence of compassion. When a human being is compassionate, it is evocative of God's compassion toward him to enable him to be compassionate toward Others. Since "we are enjoined to imitate ... the attributes of the Holy One, blessed be He," our compassion toward others finds its consummate expression in the next person's ability to be compassionate toward other human beings, who, in turn, register the compassionate impact of the Other by their own positive impact upon Others. Without ever leaving the plane of the self, with the negative-theological model of human goodness that Maimonides projects, we are able to imagine an ethically empowered world taking root in the interstices of a skeptically severed and segmented universe.

This reading of Maimonides receives a certain degree of corroboration from a central case that he deals with in Chapter 9, Paragraph 8 of the *Laws Concerning Slaves* that I cited earlier: "The Sages of old were wont to let the slave partake of every dish that they themselves ate of and to give the meal of the cattle and of the slaves precedence over their own. Is it not said: 'As the eyes of slaves unto the hand of their master, as the eyes of a female servant unto the hand of her mistress, so are our eyes unto Hashem, our God, until He will favor us' (Psalms 123:2)?" The verse that Maimonides cites from the Psalms already establishes an equivalence between how a person treats his male and female slaves (his social inferiors) and the treatment that will be/is meted out toward him by God. If we are compassionate toward our slaves – "As the eyes of slaves unto the hand of their master, etc" – so will be/are our eyes turned toward God and we will find favor in His eyes. The giving establishes the basis for – and almost is – the receiving. The greatest gift we can receive is the ability to give. When we give, it is symptomatic of our having been given of the grace and bounty of God in an emotional, existential sense that enables us to enact the position of the giver.

Privileging the relationship to the self over the Other in Levinas

To revert back temporarily to Michael Theunissen's terminology, once the merging of dialogism into transcendental phenomenology is recognized as occurring, we might as well acknowledge that human rational limitations prevent us from securely exiting discourse about the Same into discourse about the Other. The most we can do in a negative-theological vein is to creatively transform our limitations into vantage points from which to launch new interventions into the world, whose outcomes remain as unpredictable and as metaphysically and morally ambiguous as our earlier "unredeemed" interactions with the world. The route from "causality" to "responsibility"[8] can be plotted along the lines sketched out from Maimonides and the Rabbis, and not only in accordance with Levinas' projected movement beyond ontology. There is also an ethical motive informing our staying within the precincts of skepticism in negotiating this transition. The critical role of human fallibility and the need to continually compensate and seek correctives for it is better sustained by staying on the skeptical plane of the Same than postulating a pre-ontological role for the Other. By way of corroborating this point, it is worth noting that Levinas privileges the relationship to the self in contrast to the relationship with the Other. The self is tractable; the Other is not:

> Between the one I am and the other for whom I am responsible there gapes open a difference, without a basis in community ... Proximity is a difference, a non-coinciding, an arrhythmia in time, a diachrony refractory to thematization, refractory to the reminiscence that synchronizes the phases of a past. The unnarratable other loses his face as a neighbor in narration. The relationship with him is indescribable in the literal sense of the term, unconvertible into a history, irreducible to the simultaneousness of writing, the eternal present of a writing that records or presents results.[9]

The Other is "unnarratable." He/she can only be engaged diachronically. However, the self apparently is narratable and can be appropriated synchronically. Such a reading is resisted by Levinas himself in some powerful passages. For example, he says: "An alternating rhythm of the said and the unsaid, and the unsaid being unsaid in its turn, will have to be substituted for the unity of discourse. There is here a breakup of the omnipotence of the logos, that of system and simultaneity."[10] One could also argue that if, as Levinas has stated, "language is skepticism," then the self that is mediated largely through language is the Other (or at least one of the dominant Others of our lives).

The advantage of assigning primacy to the concept of power (as Hobbes, for example, does) that remains squarely within the arena of the Same over Levinas' category of the Other is that the notion of power enables Hobbes to appreciate the extent to which our relationship to ourselves is as complex, oblique and intractable as our relationship to the Other. The nature of human beings – self and Other – becomes as destabilized and conceptually unhinged as the nature of God discussed earlier. Hobbes might have designed his category of "the passions" negatively – to emphasize that we are governed by factors that have nothing to do with reason, with what is conceptually delimitable and inter-subjectively transparent. The primacy of the passions over reason in Hobbes might be symptomatic of a vast conceptual emptiness concerning the nature of human beings, which is parallel to the vast conceptual emptiness surrounding the nature of God in monotheistic theology. "Passion" for Hobbes signifies "not-reason" and not an autonomous content of its own. The pursuit of pleasure and the avoidance of pain with which Hobbes identifies "passion" are equally empty, tautologous categories, the content of which can only be filled in retrospectively on the basis of the investment of human energies that eventuate in ideas, events, structures and relationships that can be established and/or identified as harbingers of pleasure or sources of pain. "Pleasure" and "pain" – just like the term "passion" itself – reconnect us with an inchoate field of action, whose energies need to be channeled and structured before more precise quantitative and qualitative readings of human motivation are obtainable.

Juxtaposing Hobbes with Levinas helps us to see how the vocabularies of epistemology and ethics are equally metaphorical – and that the relationship between them is reciprocal and interactionist, with each set of terms being used to illuminate the other and no set of terms being susceptible to literalist deflation. The self, in the end, is as enigmatic as the Other – and for analogous reasons.

Machiavelli, Hobbes and liberalism in Levinasian perspective

Machiavelli's implied embrace of the totality vs. infinity distinction in his theorizing of power facilitates the birth of modernity. Machiavelli theorizes power in such a way that the more fully it is displaced, the more effective it becomes. Where "appearance" does the job of "reality" – the "reputation" for power substitutes for the "reality" of power and "deterrence" accomplishes the identical result as actual military mobilization and engagement – then one is "truly powerful." His model political animal is the fox rather than the lion – where stratagem substitutes for brute force.[11] The lion is a devotee of "totality" – and the fox represents "infinity," that is, infinite substitutions for an unrealizable brute force.

According to Machiavelli, the tests to apply whether power has been maximized or undermined in a particular situation are a series of counterfactual probings. If one had acted differently from the way one did on a particular occasion, would one have reached the same outcome with more or less violence? Would fewer or more lives have been spared? It is the invocation of counterfactual tests that determines the degree of power at the disposal of a state. The Machiavellian paradox consists in showing how power is "present" the more fully it is "absent."[12]

One of the things that Hobbes and subsequent social contract theorists learned from Machiavelli is that state-making consists in minimizing overt uses of power. This insight is institutionalized in classical liberal theory in the imagery and argument of the social contract, where the assertion of power is depicted as a pre-political, pre-civil act. What marks the fashioning of civil society is the containment of power in its unbridled, menacing forms.

The assigning of primacy to "process" and "procedure" above "substance" in the liberal state – the formally subordinate, instrumentalized role that the public sphere plays in relation to the private sphere and the design of governmental institutions that facilitates the pursuit of "the priority of the right over the good" – seem to be responsive to the Machiavellian understanding that the more power is dispersed and deferred, the more enduring it becomes.

The conception of power that animates Machiavelli's thought can be viewed as his response to the dilemmas of self-referentialism haunting formulations of skepticism in Western thought. Contained, limited skepticism opens up onto scenes of unmitigated, open-ended skepticism via the medium of a shift from validationist to vindicationist paradigms of doing philosophy.[13] What makes sense in terms of a set of premises internally applied becomes skeptically vulnerable once one invokes an external questioning of the categories employed in the premises. Thus, even limited knowledge statements and claims can be skeptically challenged. The skeptical critique of these statements alerts us to the traces of un-rationalized, unredeemed power in our theoretical formulations. A key meta-theoretical vulnerability of a skeptical-critical perspective is that in order for skeptical canons to be applied consistently, they must end up engulfing and consuming themselves. One needs to be skeptical of skepticism as well as of its theoretical alternatives and competitors. If a "not-fully-successfully-executed" skeptical critique of our concepts and theories issues forth in a recognition of the tremendous role played by power considerations of various sorts in our structuring of the world, then the "trick" becomes to theorize power in such a way that echoes of this "not-fully-achieved" devolution of skepticism onto power are erased. Machiavelli theorizes power in such a way that all vestiges – all remainders and reminders – of the issue of self-referentialism have been "folded" onto our envisioning of power. He conceives of power as involving endless deferral. The foundationless character of reason displaces onto power, and power in turn displaces onto an endless displacement of itself. We might describe what I just summarized as the Machiavellian encapsulation of the Levinasian notion of "infinity." As with Levinas, it is issues of skepticism that alert us to the traces of the infinite.

We might say that "power" in Machiavelli registers the same sort of ambiguity that "the Other" does in Levinas' thought. Power stands poised somewhere in between tautology and objective description. On the one hand, to refer to power as shaping the outcome of a situation is just a way of redescribing that whatever happened, happened. Power becomes a kind of neutral conceptual currency into which the self-images and official proclamations of participants in events can be discounted. On the other hand, though, the vocabulary of power seems to partake of the character of objective description precisely in terms of what it rules out – the inflated pretensions of the agents directly involved in events. Analogously, the notion of the Other in Levinas seems to be situated somewhere in between a further conceptual artifact claimed by autonomy (the Same) and a potential manifestation (an experience, expression, reminder or conjuring-up) of heteronomy (being grasped by the Other).

Alternatively, we could say that if Levinas is not succeeding at what he is trying to do – if the Other cannot be successfully theorized without extending the empire of the Same – then what he is doing (which is not necessarily the same as what he thinks he is doing or what he theorizes himself as doing) is engaging in a series of power moves, which he denominates as responsiveness to the Other. Levinas would then find himself in Machiavellian territory. The Other would have to be at least partially seen as fixed by a series of power moves.

The conceptualization of power that Machiavelli bequeaths to Hobbes engenders a theorizing of the liberal state as the custodian of a movement toward horizontal transcendence – of time stretching endlessly forward to infinity. Liberal democracy has been described in the writings of Immanuel Kant and John Rawls as that form of state that institutionalizes "the priority of the right over the good."[14] The state is officially debarred from embracing a conception of the good of its own, but must instead assign priority to individuals and groups in the private sphere to elaborate and pursue conceptions of the good of their own, constrained by what their "noumenal" or ideal selves would choose. From Rawls' perspective, these "noumenal selves" choose organizational principles for the basic structure of society that reflect their own self-respect and their own preoccupation with cultivating their highest selves – i.e. they select as their optimal societal framework Rawls' individualist, contractarian society. The state's role is to be instrumental to the individuals and groups that will compose the private sphere in exercising their primary right to their separateness (including their right to formulate separate and divergent visions of the good) and to the whole panoply of rights that this more basic right spawns – and to renounce any independent visions of the good of its own except those that support the basic neutral social structure. Thomas Nagel and others have argued that this stance of subordination of the public sphere in relation to the private sphere is itself grounded in some conception of the good that identifies the good with neutrality.[15] Nagel does not offer us a very ample discussion of what the background conception of the good animating the liberal state's policies and priorities is. I would submit that, at least in metaphysical terms, we could describe it as the pursuit of horizontal transcendence as the political, this-worldly unpacking of the metaphor of infinity. The liberal state is structured in such a way as to ensure endless deferral of such issues as sovereignty, truth and justice. The public sphere defers to the private sphere, which in turn has its wants and demands processed by multiple tiers and branches of government, which contribute to both dispersing and deferring a concerted stand on any of the overarching issues affecting the life of the community. The diffusion of decision-making across generations also contributes to dispersal and deferral.

Translating this image of the liberal state into a more narrowly epistemological idiom, we might say that the liberal state resists embracing a more positive conception of the good because of its implicit grounding in skepticism. The problem with skepticism is that it is an unsustainable philosophical thesis. To be consistently skeptical requires one to be skeptical of one's own skepticism – and thus to disengage from the very position one is seeking to define and defend. The version of skepticism that is able to accommodate these scruples is a generalized agnosticism – which interweaves skepticism of itself into its formulation of skepticism. A generalized agnosticism in turn requires what I am calling "horizontal transcendence." If every present crystallization of meaning and reference needs to be displaced onto future crystallizations, since we need to take into account the possibility that the returns are not fully in with regard to our theoretical formulations, and if "vertical transcendence" is ruled out by skepticism and/or negative theology, then "horizontal transcendence" would constitute a most plausible candidate for carrying the conceptual weight of a consistent skepticism. Horizontal transcendence is integral to a liberal politics. The future is needed as a continual balancing and corrective mechanism to the past – a kind of institutionalization of a pattern of reverse causation. Every present moment in human existence remains radically incomplete – with later events, occurrences and discoveries being required to render more precise (more filled-in with content) our present understandings and formulations themselves. A generalized agnosticism establishes the future as an indispensable resource for rendering our statements (in the present) more perspicuous and more objective.

Hobbes' projection of the Leviathan-state as a progressively developing society that persists into the indefinite future harbors the motif of a generalized agnosticism.[16] His widespread skepticism, which can only be sustained as a generalized agnosticism, guides him to postulate a non-disruptive future as a continuing resource for filling-in with content a not-fully-realized or specified present. In Levinas' arresting formulation, "the awaiting of the Messiah is the duration of time itself."[17] Hobbes cements the link between a negatively-constituted political society and a generalized agnosticism.

"Infinity," which is the value implicit in Machiavelli's conception of power as endless deferral, turns out to be the most promising candidate for the category of "supreme good" underlying liberalism's embrace of the priority of the right over the good. The normative basis for liberal-democratic politics might be conceived of as a nurturance of time to enable the play of contingency to be redeployed again and again without succumbing to either premature abstraction or closure, or under-responding by failing to notice and capitalize upon the range of possibilities residing within current constellations of forces. The political in a technical, non-metaphysical sense has to do with keeping the prospect of successive presents endlessly alive.

I have already alluded to the fact that monotheistic religion negatively theologically construed is skeptical. Levinas helps us to see how the converse of this thesis is equally true: Western skepticism is religious. The upshot of these two mutual interpenetrations – of the religious by the skeptical or secular, and the skeptical or secular by the religious – is that the whole dichotomy needs to be transcended. Levinas provides us with a vocabulary for being able to discern the abiding traces of negative theology in Western skepticism and political theory and practice. The eroding of the religion/skepticism dichotomy carries in its train a questioning of the theory/ideology dichotomy because it dramatizes for us how protagonists on either side of the great divide between religion and skepticism cannot simply dismiss their opponents as purveyors of ideology. It is to a fuller examination of the dualities of religion/secularism and theory/ideology from within the context of Levinas' thought – and stretching outside it – that we now turn.

Notes

1 *Hebrew-English Edition of the Babylonian Talmud: Sotah*. Trans. A. Cohen. (London: Soncino Press, 1985).

2   Ibid.
3   My translation.
4   Babylonian Talmud, *Rosh Hashanah* 22a.
5   Maimonides, *The Code*, Book 12: The Book of Acquisition: Laws Concerning Slaves. Trans. Isaac Klein. (New Haven: Yale University Press, 1951), Chapter 9, Paragraph 8, pp. 281–282.
6   *Hebrew-English Edition of the Babylonian Talmud: Shabbath*. Trans. H. Freedman. (London: Soncino Press, 1987).
7   Babylonian Talmud, *Megillah* 12b; *Sotah* 8b.
8   Levinas, *Basic Philosophical Writings*, p. 94.
9   Levinas, *Otherwise than Being*, p. 166.
10 Levinas, *Basic Philosophical Writings*, p. 148.
11 Niccolò Machiavelli, *The Prince*. Trans. George Bull. (Baltimore: Penguin Books, 1961), Chapter 18, p. 99.
12 For further discussion of Machiavellian minimalism and its influence on Hobbes and the subsequent social contract tradition, see my book, *Skepticism and Political Participation* (Philadelphia: Temple University Press, 1990), pp. 94–103.
13 For an elaboration of the distinction between "validation" and "vindication," see the article by Herbert Feigl, "Validation and Vindication: An Analysis of the Nature and the Limits of Ethical Arguments," in Wilfrid Sellars and John Hospers, eds., *Readings in Ethical Theory* (New York: Appleton-Century-Crofts, 1952), pp. 667–680.
14 "The indeterminacy in the notion of rationality does not translate itself into legitimate claims that men can impose on one another. The priority of the right prevents this." John Rawls, *A Theory of Justice* (Cambridge: Harvard University Press, 1971), p. 449.
15 Thomas Nagel, "Review of John Rawls, *A Theory of Justice*," *Philosophical Review*, Volume 82 (1973), pp. 220–234.
16 See the discussion of the meaning of the symbol of "Leviathan" in Carl Schmitt, *The Leviathan in the State Theory of Thomas Hobbes: Meaning and Failure of a Political Symbol*. Trans. George Schwab and Erna Hilfstein. (Westport: Greenwood Press, 1996), pp. 5–15, especially p. 9. I present a critique of Schmitt's reading of Hobbes in my article, "Shakespeare in Advance of Hobbes: Pathways to the Modernization of the European Psyche as Charted in *The Merchant of Venice*," *Telos*, Number 153 (Winter 2010), pp. 132–159, especially at pp. 138–143.
17 Emmanuel Levinas, *The Levinas Reader*. Ed. Sean Hand. (Oxford: Basil Blackwell, 1989), p. 203.

4 Theory and ideology in Levinas

Religion/secularism and theory/ideology from within the context of Levinas' thought

If one of the major conundrums posed by modernity is to come up with alternatives to it that are not themselves modernistically inspired or generated, then we must be able to think through modernity in such a way that we can reconceptualize its dichotomies and redraw its mappings of continuities and discontinuities. A dichotomy that is central to the consciousness of modernity is that between the religious or sacred and the secular, and a discontinuity that is pivotal to its critical self-awareness is that between theory and ideology. I propose to use a re-envisioning of the relationship between theory and ideology as a means of reconfiguring the relationship between the sacred and the secular. By confining the term "theory" to what I take to be integral to Platonic teaching and to negative theology, I shall try and trace a sustained moment of continuity – or what might better be called a "persisting stationary moment" – that lingers from ancient thought straight through to postmodernity. By striving to get our bearings with respect to this persisting stationary moment, we might stand our best chance of grappling with the dilemma of being *in* modernity but not *of* it – and seeing our way clear to a perch beyond it.

The sociological theorist Edward Shils has cleared a path for us to trace the continuity between the secular and the sacred in the manner in which he envisions how the idea of the sacred suffuses the whole notion of theorizing. This is how Shils conceives of the relationship between theory and the sacred:

> In every society, however, there are some persons with an unusual sensitivity to the sacred, an uncommon reflectiveness about the nature of their universe and the rules which govern their society. There is in every society a minority of persons who, more than the ordinary run of their fellow men, are inquiring, and desirous of being in frequent communion with symbols which are more general than the immediate concrete situations of everyday life and remote in their reference in both time and space. In this minority, there is a need to externalize this quest in oral and written discourse, in

poetic or plastic expression, in historical reminiscence or writing, in ritual performance and acts of worship. This interior need to penetrate beyond the screen of immediate experience marks the existence of the intellectuals in every society.[1]

According to Shils, the theorist approximates to the perspective of the sacred in his pursuit of interconnections.[2] God – the epitome of the sacred – manifests the pursuit of interconnections in two ways: The first is that we come to postulate the idea of God as the Creator and Governor of the universe through the pursuit of interconnections. Shils' theorist is highly self-conscious, but most of us wittingly and unwittingly are embarked upon an explanatory quest trying to arrive at the most primary explanation we can attain of the phenomena that puzzle us. In searching for explanations, we confront an immediate paradox. Most of the factors that we invoke to explain something are not self-evidently true, but instead need to be explained in turn. Whatever explanation momentarily satisfies us will also in short order provoke us to pierce beyond it to what is responsible for *it*. As long as we remain in a finite domain, the search for explanations is irresistible and unending. We invoke God as the final explanation because, inasmuch as He is an infinite entity subsisting in an infinite dimension, we cannot by definition probe beyond Him in making sense of any phenomenon. So, in the first instance, we arrive at the sacred through the pursuit of interconnections by striving for ever more comprehensive and inclusive explanations. In the second instance, God, who is postulated as subsisting above space and time as humanly defined and perceived, is also affirmed as encapsulating within Himself all spatial and temporal phases and moments. God personifies interconnections par excellence. All connections are concentrated in Him.

The pursuit of interconnections that the theorist is preoccupied with also manifests itself on a dual level. In terms of the formal protocols of argument that he mobilizes to investigate his subject matter, he pushes them as far as they can go. Whether the pattern of argument is deductive or inductive – or some kind of combination of the two – he probes it as far as it will take him. Doing this makes him aware that, at some point, he needs to presuppose at least part of what he is trying to prove because every first premise that he provisionally adopts cries out for further anchorage. The cutoff point for justification in the grounding of premises is mostly arbitrary because the search for backup premises remains incomplete – no matter where it is artificially terminated.

The substantive picture that emerges once the theoretical argument generated in this manner has been formulated also evokes the pursuit of interconnections. A theoretical argument also harbors a subliminal (or subtextual) trace of its incompleteness. Its inability to fully ground itself carries a skeptical import that affects all areas of human thought outside of itself. No matter what sort of argument we are motivated to make, we are not able to follow through on the theoretical-justificatory project. Our arguments gesture toward a direction that they are not able to consummate. The skepticism that theory insinuates on both a formal and substantive level cannot be sustained in its pure form because skepticism is an inconsistent philosophical thesis. In order to be consistent, the skeptic would have to be skeptical of his own skepticism, which means that his position evolves into a generalized agnosticism rather than getting codified as extreme skepticism. Given the radical incompleteness of the justificatory quest (i.e. the way that it is set up guarantees that it cannot go the full distance in cashing in on the promise of its search), we can say that uncertainty affects the whole map of knowledge. By default, theory ends up validating itself because it has no place else to turn. The pursuit of interconnections turns out to be interminable – with the end(s) of argument remaining permanently elusive.

Shils' "sacred" and the secular – God and the theoretical pursuit of any subject matter – rest upon similarly insecure foundations. The dichotomy between the sacred and the secular presages a barely articulable unity.

I shall begin this chapter with a sketch of this persisting stationary moment that links theory and the sacred together, and then move on to consider how a case for restricting the scope of theory and expanding the purview of ideology can be made on analytical grounds. Throughout the remainder of this chapter, I focus on the theoretical and historical ramifications of the theory vs. ideology distinction in Levinas. In Chapter 6, I have something to say about the mental attitudes and approaches that are engendered by a preoccupation with theory and ideology, respectively – that is to say, something about the ethics of theory and the ethics of ideology. From there, I go on in Chapter 8 to examine Plato's early dialogue, the *Hippias Major*, and juxtapose to it some classical Rabbinic formulations. I then consider Plato's arguments in the *Cratylus* and the *Theaetetus* to further illustrate Plato's conception of theory and its relationship to Levinas' thought.

Monotheism and skepticism

Western monotheism, when interpreted from a classical negative-theological perspective, is skeptical. Skepticism and monotheism confront common dilemmas of consistency and of self-referentialism. In order to emerge as properly consistent, skeptical doctrine must encompass a reflexive maneuver whereby skeptical critical canons are turned against the tenets of skepticism themselves – forcing them into a movement of recoil and thereby inhibiting their adequate formulation. Analogously, the utter conceptual removal of the monotheistic God, which renders him totally unlike anything human (posited by the negative-theological reading of monotheism), requires some kind of grammatical subject concerning whom the continual divestiture of predicates can take place. Skepticism is a doctrine of radical critique that both presupposes and denies a stable subject (in a grammatical sense): tenets of skepticism. Monotheism is also a doctrine of radical critique that simultaneously presupposes and denies a stable grammatical subject, namely, God.

Theory and ideology in Levinas 41

The converse of this thesis is, I believe, equally true: Western skepticism and its most prominent institutionalized expression as liberalism are, in a significant sense, religious. The self-referentialist dilemmas that stand poised to dismantle both skepticism and monotheism suggest that the most coherent readings of both doctrines take the form of a generalized agnosticism. A generalized agnosticism highlights the continuing vitality of the questions it is unable to resolve – which in a crucial sense is what monotheism is about. It constitutes (in Jacques Derrida's famous phrase) "a community of the question."[3] If skepticism must accommodate a moment of self-questioning of its own doctrine, then the most defensible version of skepticism emerges as the one that includes skepticism within its own ambit of skeptical interrogation – i.e., a generalized agnosticism. Analogously, if, under the impact of negative theology, monotheism can no longer literally affirm its utterly transcendent version of God, then, in order to remain properly consistent, it has to acknowledge that it cannot conclusively deny God's existence either. Negative theology is restricted to the more limited claim that monotheistic argument cannot work to establish the veracity of God's existence. Its writ does not extend to proving God's non-existence. For example, negative theology in its extreme rationalism might be construed as clearing a path for more mystical approaches to God that defy easy translation into a rationalist or linguistic register.

The parallel structure between skeptical and monotheistic argument suggests that, on a strictly rationally graspable level, vertical transcendence is best reconfigured as horizontal transcendence – a conception of human time that stretches endlessly forward to infinity. From a generalized-agnostic perspective, vertical transcendence is not rejected. However, it cannot be affirmed either. On procedural grounds, the future is needed as a continuing balancing and compensatory mechanism to augment our knowledge of any given human present. Horizontal transcendence is a continuous placeholder for an endlessly evolving and endlessly deferrable human present.

Maimonides and horizontal transcendence

A transformation of vertical transcendence into horizontal transcendence occurs in the thought of Maimonides, who is both the premier medieval spokesman for negative theology and a theorist of an iconoclastic vision of the messianic age. Maimonides envisages the messianic age as being part of integral human history with no visible disruptions of typical human life cycles and vicissitudes[4] – rather than as being strictly post-historical.

A vision of horizontal transcendence also lurks behind Maimonides' construal of a puzzling verse in Deuteronomy, the basic grammatical structure of which can be interpreted in conflicting ways. I will first cite the verse with Rashi and Maimonides' construction of the conclusion of the first sentence as a question:

> When thou shalt besiege a city a long time, in making war against it to take it, thou shalt not destroy the trees thereof by wielding an axe against

them; for thou mayest eat of them, but thou shalt not cut them down; for is the tree of the field a man, that it should be besieged of thee? Only the trees of which thou knowest that they are not trees for food, them thou mayest destroy and cut down, that thou mayest build bulwarks against the city that maketh war with thee, until it fall.[5]

In his *Code*, Maimonides extrapolates from and generalizes the prohibition encapsulated in this verse as follows:

One may not cut down fruit-bearing trees outside the (besieged) city (for purposes of war) nor divert from them the water conduit, so as to make them wither, as it is stated: "thou shalt not destroy the trees thereof." Whoever cuts them down is liable for the penalty of lashes. But this does not apply merely to the case of a siege, but in all cases. Whoever cuts down a fruit-bearing tree, in a destructive manner, is liable to lashes. But it may be cut down, if it damages other trees or causes harm to neighboring fields or because it fetches a high price. The Torah only forbad willful destruction. This is the case not only with trees. But whoever breaks utensils, tears garments, demolishes a building, stops up a well and willfully destroys food violates the prohibition of "thou shalt not destroy". ... .[6]

Maimonides interprets the verse as issuing forth in a blanket deontological prohibition against willful destruction. It is incumbent upon us as human beings to be faithful trustees for all the transient and fragile givens of our world – including ourselves. The enactment of this trustee relationship appears to be conceptually linked with Maimonides' negative theology, where, because we cannot penetrate to the ultimate numinous source of being, our task as human beings becomes instrumentalized to transmit intact (and possibly enriched) whatever we inherit to the next generation. If we are not able to penetrate to a solution to the riddle of human existence, we must at least preserve the physical infrastructure required for sustaining the question.

The medieval Biblical exegete Abraham Ibn Ezra (1089–1164)[7] (who is followed by the King James version of the Bible) adopts a contrasting utilitarian approach to the verses in Deuteronomy. He reads the puzzling (in Hebrew) last phrase of the first verse cited above in a declarative rather than in an interrogatory manner:

For thou mayest eat of them and thou shalt not cut them down for the tree is man's life.

The last three words of verse 19 – literally, "to come before you in a siege" – Ibn Ezra brackets with the previous phrase, "and thou shalt not cut them down." According to Ibn Ezra's reading, when we engage in a siege we need to sustain ourselves. The Torah is telling us that, during the time of a siege, we are allowed to remove the fruit of our enemies' trees in order to keep ourselves alive. By blocking an interrogatory construction of the concluding phrase of verse 19 (by inhibiting the formulation of a rhetorical question at the end of the verse), Ibn Ezra aborts the deontological route pursued by Maimonides in deriving from the verse the norm of human trusteeship for the whole natural order.

Emmanuel Levinas' thought helps us to see how Western skepticism and its institutionalized expression as liberalism are religious. Given Levinas' adherence in the corpus of his writings to both negative theology[8] and skepticism, his affirmation of the Other cannot be sustained in its own terms; rather, its philosophical force devolves onto the scope and efficacy residing in his distinction between totality and infinity. The harbinger – the conduit – for affirming the trace of God in the human world is the concept of infinity – in resistance to, or rejection of, totality. The trace of God that Levinas has in mind has to be a trace of a trace of a trace (and so forth), that is to say, horizontal rather than vertical transcendence.

The relationship between the Other and Others in Maimonides and Levinas

The formal strategy pursued by Levinas of having the search for the ultimate, supreme Other (namely, God) devolve onto reconfigured modes of ethical relationships to human Others is presaged by Maimonides. In *The Guide of the Perplexed*,[9] in the section discussing the *Akeidah* (the Binding of Isaac), Maimonides says that the command to slay Isaac comes to Abraham "in a dream and in a vision,"which, "in the opinion of the prophet" (namely, Abraham), is "a vision of prophecy." Abraham has to take ultimate responsibility for classifying the experience that he is having as a prophetic vision and for the interpretation that he places upon it. Negative theology debars us (even the most exceptional among us who harbor prophetic capacities) from explicitly affirming that the message we are receiving comes directly from God. From a negative-theological perspective, God cannot speak in a humanly intelligible sense even to His prophets. Before the prophet's audience can consent to receive his teaching as a prophetic message, the prophet must consent to regard his vision as prophetic. Since, in accordance with the tenets of negative theology, God does not speak the way human beings speak, it is only the acquiescence of the receiver of the message (and of those whom he can persuade) to invest it with Divine authority that gives it such authority. The gap between Divine address and human response cannot be closed any less ambiguously than this.

With this premise in place, we are better able to appreciate the second great lesson that Maimonides derives from the *Akeidah*. Maimonides formulates it as follows: We are "being informed of the limit of the *love* for God, may He be exalted, and *fear* of him – that is, up to what limit they must reach."[10] Maimonides states this teaching first and the teaching concerning the nature of prophecy second. When considered in the order in which he draws his inferences – i.e. the teaching concerning the extent to which we need to exhibit the love and fear of God being stated first – Maimonides' elucidation of the *Akeidah* seems to conform to the Muslim interpretation of it[11] (although applied to Yishmael, rather than to Isaac), requiring us to set aside all forms of competitive love, such as the love of one's family, for the sake of focusing exclusively upon the love of God. However, the second inference that he draws from the *Akeidah*, which relates to the centrality of the prophet in interpreting and taking responsibility for his own prophetic message, forces us to reconfigure the impact of the first teaching Maimonides derives from the *Akeidah*.

Monotheistic teaching generally confronts the believer with a stark contrast between two routes that can be followed in order to actualize its content. On the one hand, given the augustness and incomparability of God, it can be viewed as imposing upon its adherents a regimen that requires them to decathect from all of their human attachments for the sake of totally immersing themselves in contemplation of and communion with God. On the other hand, though, given God's unbridgeable transcendence – which we can never engage despite all of our exercises of mystical contemplation – we might say that it is only the way we work out our organization of the human spheres that can possibly be expressive of our relationship with God. To state the dilemma that Abraham confronts in the *Akeidah* more succinctly: What is the role of human Others in relation to the primal Other connoted by God? Does God nudge out of place all Others aside from Himself, or is it mainly in relation to human Others that traces of the Supreme Other (in some never-fully-redeemed metaphorical sense) can be experienced? Maimonides' emphasis on "the opinion of the prophet" in the second half of his analysis suggests that the *Akeidah* is a drama centering on the limits of the prophetic vision and vocation, given the fact that "the opinion of the prophet" cannot be circumvented. Is there one final burst of deliverance available to him by cradling himself completely in the vision of Divine embrace or are the limits affecting his vocation as prophet that are signaled by the necessity of his "opinion" or affirmation of the message received symptomatic of broader limits residing in the content and mode of transmission of those messages mandating the accommodation of the Others before there can be negotiation of the Other? We might say that from Maimonides' perspective, the *Akeidah* registers Abraham's wrestling with the limits of the monotheistic prophetic vision, and that its story records Abraham's resistance to the allurements of Divine deliverance for the sake of affirming an expanded domain of human freedom and responsibility that is itself supremely Divinely grounded in the ethos of negative theology.[12]

Notes

1. Edward Shils, *The Intellectuals and the Powers and Other Essays* (Chicago: University of Chicago Press, 1972), p. 3.
2. This conception of the theorist is also developed by Sheldon Wolin in two highly influential essays: "Paradigms and Political Theories," in Preston King and

B. C. Parekh, eds., *Politics and Experience: Essays Presented to Professor Michael Oakeshott on the Occasion of his Retirement* (Cambridge: Cambridge University Press, 1968), pp. 125–152 and "Political Theory as a Vocation," in Martin Fleisher, ed., *Machiavelli and the Nature of Political Thought* (New York: Atheneum, 1972), pp. 23–75.
3 Jacques Derrida, *Writing and Difference*, p. 80.
4 Maimonides, *The Code*, Book 14: The Book of Judges, Laws Concerning Kings and Their Wars, Chapter 11, Paragraphs 1, 3, 4 and Chapter 12, Paragraphs 1–4. See my discussion of these paragraphs in *Skepticism, Belief, and the Modern*, pp. 166–170.
5 Deuteronomy 20:19–20.
6 Maimonides, *The Code,* Book 14: The Book of Judges, Laws Concerning Kings and Their Wars, Chapter 6, Paragraphs 8 and 10. The translation comes from Nehama Leibowitz, *Studies in Devarim (Deuteronomy)*. Trans. Aryeh Newman. (Jerusalem: World Zionist Organization, 1980), pp. 197–198.
7 In his commentary on Deuteronomy 20:19.
8 In *Totality and Infinity*, Levinas defines religion in general in negative-theological terms: "For the relation between the being here below and the transcendent being that results in no community of concept or totality – a relation without relation – we reserve the term religion." Levinas, *Totality and Infinity*, p. 80.
9 Maimonides, *The Guide of the Perplexed*, III:24:500–502. Citations in the notes refer to part, chapter and page(s) in the Pines translation of this work (See Chapter 2, note 3).
10 Ibid., 3:24:500; italics in original.
11 Shaikh Abd Al-Qadir Al-Jilani, *The Sublime Revelation: A Collection of Sixty-Two Discourses.* Trans. Muhtar Holland. (Houston: Al-Baz Publishing, 1992), Forty-Sixth Discourse, p. 294. Compare Shaikh Abd Al-Qadir Al-Jilani, *The Removal of Cares: A Collection of Forty-Five Discourses.* Trans. Muhtar Holland. (Fort Lauderdale: Al-Baz Publishing, 1997), Forty-First Discourse, p. 242, FN 303. I am indebted to Imam Abdur-Razzaq Miller for pointing out these sources to me.
12 See my article, "Political Abuse of a Biblical Paradigm: The Case of the Akeidah," *Telos*, Number 124 (Summer 2002), pp. 7–54.

5 Levinas and his contemporaries

Buber and Levinas

Levinas acknowledges that the work of Martin Buber represents a *locus classicus* in 20th-century philosophical thought for an attempt to reorient philosophy in the direction of assigning primacy to ethics and validating the Other as a precondition for the exertions (including the intellectual exertions) of the self. His critique of Buber is not unlike my critique of Levinas himself alluded to earlier – namely, that one cannot address the Other without some kind of prior conceptualization that delineates the Other as the Other. Once the priority of conceptualization or theorizing over relationship comes into play, one notices that, despite all the rhetorical flourishes with which one endows the vocabulary of the Other, the problem of skepticism has been camouflaged and deferred without being resolved.

At the outset, I would like to quote from Levinas' neutral characterization of Buber's method and state some of my own objections to it as a prelude to considering Levinas' criticisms of Buber at the conclusion of his essay:

> Let us note the phenomenological character of Buber's descriptions. They are set within the world of *perception*, the perspectives of which have no need of being justified by any intellectual authority. The non-theoretical modes of existence are "meaning-giving" and the ontological structures are never separable from them.[1]

One could argue that it is precisely "the phenomenological character of Buber's descriptions" that renders them vulnerable. This vulnerability is manifested on four levels. The first level has to do with the fact that the phenomenological description presupposes an analytical and descriptive (conceptual) vocabulary already in place from which the current phenomenological description is wrought. If the whole phenomenological description is theorized as a function of the confrontation with the present phenomenon, the words chosen would lack the resonances and associative reverberations to function as descriptions. However, from Buber's perspective, "having an idea of something" prior to the direct address and confrontation of the "something" "belongs to the realm of the I-It" and therefore subverts the primacy of the I-Thou relationship.[2]

A second level of vulnerability inherent in "the phenomenological character of Buber's descriptions" relates to the prospect of an infinite regress opening up in the face of the primacy being assigned to phenomenology. According to Levinas' interpretation of Buber, if you remain faithful to the phenomenological strictures confining your analysis to exact, immediate descriptions of what is in front of you, you will validate the priority of the I-Thou over the I-It relationship. Since it is only a phenomenological approach that is capable of generating and sustaining this priority, the analyst must remain especially vigilant not to overstep the bounds of phenomenology. However, in order for one to have the appropriate phenomenological description of what is in front of oneself, one needs to implicitly or explicitly invoke as frames of reference situations that are comparable to or different from the current one in order to select and affirm the narrative sequence that is uniquely appropriate to the situation at hand. This is to say that, unless one takes the conceptual detour that allows one to compare one situation with another (unless one has already enshrined the primacy of the I-It relationship), one is debarred from access to the I-Thou relationship. In trying to negotiate the I-Thou relationship through pristine phenomenological description, one confronts an infinite regress – the multiple descriptions that we might invoke to phenomenologically capture a particular state of affairs might be seen as regressing infinitely in their attempt to capture the true or experienced situation or state of affairs but failing to phenomenologically illuminate it outside of a setting of decontextualization and recontextualization that relates the current situation to others. This becomes possible only through the subsumption of common features of the various situations under generalized concepts that already presuppose and affirm the world of I-It.

A third level of vulnerability to explore in interpreting Levinas' critique of Buber involves substituting the metaphor of circularity for the metaphor of infinite regress. Given what I have just been saying about the inevitability of generalized terms and concepts in order to render articulate the most acutely specific description of the situation one is confronting – and also given the likelihood that more than one set of general terms and concepts might be adequate, or could even be required, to render the specificity of the situation before oneself – how is the gap between the particular and the general to be closed? Once one acknowledges the need for ascent and contextualization in order to be in contact with the specific, then one is perforce also acknowledging how the particular pattern of ascent and contextualization that one incorporates into one's specific phenomenological description is a function of moves and choices made by the describer, rather than being something intrinsic to the situation one is describing. One sees what one sees and one describes what one describes only because one is antecedently committed to certain modes of perception and description.

A fourth level of vulnerability present in Levinas' elucidation of "the phenomenological character of Buber's descriptions" is that Levinas writes as if there is only one phenomenologically correct way to describe an event or state of affairs. Levinas fails to take into account the relativized nature of phenomenological descriptions. For example, what is perceived and experienced by one party to a relationship as an act of selfless giving might be understood by the second party to the relationship as an act of overweening or subtle egoism. The enactment and reception of a particular moment of a relationship – or of a particular action or state of affairs – are dependent upon the interpretive frameworks (i.e., the general terms and concepts) that suffuse one's actions and perceptions. The conceptual detour to the world of I-It (en route to the world of I-Thou) seems irredeemably primary and unavoidable.

In his critique of Buber, Levinas zeroes in on the untenability of the crucial concept of the *Zwischen* (the "between-the-two") in Buber's thought. Levinas says that "Buber forcefully asserts the radical difference between the soul's silent dialogue with itself and the real dialogue with the other."[3] He theorizes this difference by stating that "the 'between-the-two,' the interval between the I and the *Thou*, the *Zwischen*, is the locus in which the very work of being takes place."[4] Buber believes that "the *Zwischen* is recreated afresh in each meeting, and is ever new, as are the instants of the Bergsonian *duree*."[5] Levinas counterposes to this analysis the question: "But is it not in consciousness, after all, that the *Zwischen* manifests its structures?"[6] Buber is concerned with assigning ontological primacy to the Thou as facilitating the emergence of the I. In order to accomplish this, he invokes the notion of the *Zwischen* as sheer un-narrated event so that consciousness can be circumvented and the primacy of the Thou preserved. It is precisely to this interrelated set of maneuvers that Levinas objects. He states the following very baldly at the conclusion of his essay:

> Man is not just the category of distance and meeting, he is also a separate being. He accomplishes that isolation in a process of subjectification that is not just the recoil from the word *Thou*. Buber does not give expression to the movement, distinct from distancing and the relation, in which the *I* emerges from the self. It is impossible for man to forget his metamorphosis of subjectivity.[7]

One might say that Levinas accuses Buber of failing to pass a test of reflexivity: Theorizing the *Zwischen* is not itself a function of the *Zwischen*. It is only man as self-conscious language-user who is able to theorize the *Zwischen*. Applying Levinas' hermeneutics for making sense of Buber to Levinas himself, we might say analogously to Levinas: "Theorizing the primacy of the Other is not itself a function of the primacy of the Other." Complex layers of consciousness mediate between this philosophical awareness and its verbal formulation. Once the roles of consciousness and self-consciousness are noted in the formulation of even the most self-abnegating philosophical categories, issues of the underdetermination of our verbalizations by facts, which are constitutive of the problem of skepticism, rear their head. Since, as we have seen, skepticism is most coherently sustainable as a generalized agnosticism, the path from self-consciousness to the unalloyed, literal Other remains aborted, and we are left to ponder the ways in which the totality vs. infinity distinction might serve as a functional correlative for the Other.

According to Levinas, the goal toward which assigning centrality to the *Zwischen* is tending is to conceive of man as a process-being: "The interval in which the game of being is played out, and which human existence both creates and bridges, implies the abandoning of the notion of a content being, a realized being, a narrated being – an abandonment that characterizes the entire ontology of our time."[8] If what Levinas summarizes is the motive force behind the importance accorded the *Zwischen* in Buber's thought, then envisioning man as a process-being is precisely what the totality vs. infinity distinction highlights – so that this distinction can function as an effective surrogate for Levinas' Other as well as for Buber's Thou.

One of the major incidental benefits of theorizing a pivotal role for consciousness is that it enables Levinas to move beyond what he calls "Buber's religious liberalism."[9] Levinas says that Buber's "religiosity ... stands opposed to religion, and leads him, in reacting against the fixed, rigid forms of a spiritual dogmatism, to place contact above its content, and the pure, unqualifiable presence of God above all dogma and rule."[10] In other words, "Buber's religious liberalism" consists totally of "mystery" without "commandment."[11] It constitutes a religious formalism in which event succeeds event without ever producing a "content." In his correspondence with Buber on the occasion of the latter's eighty-fifth birthday, Levinas very poignantly indicates what he means by "content":

> I also think that when Rabbi Johanan said in *Sanhedrin*, "*gedolah legimah*," he was not just making a plea for the philanthropic idea of public soup kitchens for the poor. I also think that giving is not the same thing as *giving oneself*, as the *hahamim* perceived when they said that *"bekol meodehah"* means *money* and that money is sometimes more (and in any case different) than giving one's soul and one's life.[12]

Once you allow consciousness to enter into the philosophical picture, the stage is set for assigning a large role to ethical content such as clothing the poor and feeding the hungry. Firstly, consciousness is an instrumentality for registering your awareness of the destitute and for considering what can be done about them. Secondly, since (as we have seen) the philosophical affirmation of consciousness is linked with an acknowledgment of the pervasiveness of skepticism and its dilemmas, philosophical space is cleared for enacting and obeying all of those intermediate ordinances that sustain the life of the individual in the context of the life of the community and that provide meaningful parameters for catering to the needs of Others as well as for accommodating the needs of the self.

Derrida and Levinas

In his essay, "Jacques Derrida: Wholly Otherwise,"[13] Levinas redeploys the critical methodology he mobilized against Buber. In his critique of Buber, Levinas points to the focal role of consciousness in facilitating the delineation of self and Other (an I and a Thou), the relationship of which is encompassed as a series of events, that is, of fugitive ignitings of the *Zwischen*: he underscores the gap between the mode of analysis facilitating the theoretical formulation and the content of the theoretical formulation itself. Likewise, in his discussion of Derrida, Levinas highlights the distance between the critical content of Derrida's thought and what Derrida goes through conceptually in order to formulate it:

> What remains constructed after deconstruction is, to be sure, the stern architecture of the discourse that deconstructs and uses the verb "to be" in the present tense in predicative statements. A discourse in the course of which, amidst the quaking of truth's underpinnings and in opposition to the self-evidence of the lived presence, which seems to offer presence a last refuge, Derrida still has the strength to utter: "Is this certain?" As if anything could be certain at that point, and as if certainty or uncertainty should still matter.[14]

"What remains constructed after deconstruction": Levinas is raising the issue of reflexivity in Derrida. The principles of deconstructive readings of texts and phenomena and their applications have to remain in some sense undeconstructed in order for deconstruction to work. Levinas states the dilemma of reflexivity succinctly on the following page of the same essay: "Nothing can be seen without thematization, or without the oblique rays reflected by it, even in the case of the non-thematizable."[15] Derrida is driven by the dynamic of his argument to affirm the principles of deconstruction in all cases except where he states those principles themselves or works out their applications. Levinas graphically elaborates upon Derrida's dilemma a little later on in the same essay:

> In order to avoid the return of the metaphysics of presence ... Derrida would have the reader seek, for the operative concept of the sign of a failed presence, a reference other than the failure of that presence, and a place [lieu] other than the Said of language (oral or written) – a place other than a language, which, completely at the disposal of the speaker, itself feigns synchrony, the preeminent presence of a system of signs that

is already presupposed by any empirical simultaneity. But would not any attempt to express this lack of presence positively be still one more way of returning to presence, with which positivity converges?[16]

Derrida is caught in the dilemma that his practice of criticism is delegitimated by his very practice of that criticism. His position seems to be chafing against the very limits of logic and language as we traditionally conceive them. Levinas starkly registers Derrida's challenge to the Law of the Excluded Middle. He refers to "this doggedly rectilinear thinking [namely, that of Derrida] ... leading us into the strange non-order of the excluded middle, in which the disjunction of the yes and no, the imperious alternative, thanks to which computers decide about the universe, is challenged."[17] The implicit logic of Derrida's practice of deconstruction points in the direction of multivalued logics that map the suspension of the Law of the Excluded Middle and thereby normalizes (renders subsumable under a new logical norm) what otherwise seems contradictory in Derrida's thought. The metaphysical outlook that is most hospitable to the cultivation and reception of multivalued logics is a generalized agnosticism that posits that the returns are not yet fully in concerning what the nature of the world is like. Levinas alludes to Derrida's adherence to a generalized agnosticism earlier in the essay when he refers to Derrida still having "the strength to utter: 'Is this certain?'"[18] in the face of the withering skepticism encapsulated in his theory and practice of deconstruction. In other words, Derrida adopts an agnostic attitude toward deconstruction, which enables the question of certainty to preserve its intelligibility and coherence.

A generalized agnosticism establishes common ground between Derrida and Levinas. Referring to his own thought, Levinas says that "it is as if the correlation of the *Saying* and the *Said* were a diachrony of the unassemblable."[19] Skepticism provides Levinas with the evidence that he needs for conferring plausibility upon the notion of infinity conceived of as horizontal transcendence. Since formulations of skepticism give rise to dilemmas of reflexivity that are best resolved by envisioning logical grids that enable us to dissociate the "saying" of skepticism from the "said" of skepticism – logical grids that offer us an alternative to the binary constraints of the traditional Aristotelian logic, so that contradiction is normalized – indirect support is received for a generalized agnosticism that engenders receptivity to such logics. A generalized agnosticism leaves the door open to an endlessly unfolding future, which might be the most cogent way to construe Levinas' notion of infinity. It is infinity understood in this way that renders possible Levinas' notion of the Other: "The difference between the Same and the Other is the non-indifference for the other of fraternity."[20] In an indefinitely unfolding future, "non-indifference for the other of fraternity" might emerge. The movement in Levinas' thought appears to be from diachrony, which nurtures a generalized agnosticism, to infinity, conceived of as horizontal transcendence to Otherness and to God. When Levinas, in one of his more programmatic statements, says that "our relation with the Metaphysical is an ethical behavior and not a theology, not a thematization,"[21] he needs to be understood in the light of his critiques of Buber and Derrida as charting a negative, indefinitely unfolding course that leaves the door open to all kinds of contingencies and possibilities (including God) – rather than as unambiguously placing the Other within our reach.

Various themes that I have alluded to – Derrida's suspicion of the vocabulary of the Other as an attempt to establish a philosophical parameter outside of the ambit of deconstruction; taking certain critical scruples into account, it is possible to postulate a fair amount of common ground between Derrida and Levinas; the influence of Plato upon both thinkers – are reflected in Derrida's theorizing of friendship.[22] What Fred Dallmayr refers to as the "postclassical incision" in conceptions of friendship that is exemplified in Derrida[23] is very heavily indebted to negative theology. Negative theology that emphasizes the total Otherness of God and, as a consequence, discounts our whole theological vocabulary as being irredeemably metaphorical initiates a process of displacement of that vocabulary, the most natural focus of which now becomes human beings and their activities in the world. The adjectives and attributes that have been deliteralized in relation to God (terms that highlight certain emotional and intellectual capacities) are adjusted in their signification and reference and transferred to human beings. However, to say that human beings cultivating their intellects and refining their abilities to experience compassion and empathy represents the ultimate resting place (the focal point of application) of the litany of Divine attributes would be inconsistent with the tenets of negative theology as well. The distance that negative theology postulates between man and God is so immense and unbridgeable that one is never allowed to declare that the Divine epithets have been unpacked, even in relation to what is other than God. To do this would presuppose that one understood what those adjectives signified and was therefore able to pinpoint their sense and reference in relation to man. But by negative-theological definition, the terms that apply to God remain "unpackable" – and continue their metaphorical "spin" forever.

Hobbes dramatizes how the unknowability of God affirmed by negative theology becomes a metaphor for the unknowability of man. As we have seen, the coherence of negative theology is enhanced if it is read as being predicated upon a generalized agnosticism that debars us from speaking with certainty about any of the features of our world, including the nature of human beings. To the extent that the paradoxes surrounding the One discussed by Plato in the *Parmenides* prefigure the conceptual quandaries of negative theology, the "postclassical incision" is already evident in ancient thought. The impact of this incision is prominent in Hobbes' thought in the primacy that he assigns to the notion of interest – and particularly self-interest. Human beings do not know who they are except to the extent that they observe themselves in action – doing or pursuing certain things – rather than through sheer introspection or reflection. It is only obliquely through the engagement in action and the retrospective discovery of interest and self-interest that we acquire an identity. Of course, adherence to a generalized agnosticism suggests that that identity is subject to continual reinflections and reinterpretations, since there is no secure reference point (conceptual or material) in relation to which it can be permanently fixed. From the historical and theoretical perspective that I am outlining here, the "infinite distance" (to use Maurice Blanchot's term)[24] that characterizes human relationships (and that suffuses Derrida's understanding of friendship) emerges in a straight line from Plato to negative theology to Hobbes; it is mediated by countless others and then finally continues on to Nietzsche, Blanchot and Derrida.

Plato, Derrida and Levinas

Plato is a significant precursor to Derrida in relation to the argument that friends are "basically 'the friends of solitude,' people who 'share what cannot be shared: solitude.'"[25] Plato, in the *Phaedrus*, defends a similar view. He says that "he [the beloved] should not in the first place have yielded to a lover, to a man necessarily out of his mind; a non-lover, a man perfectly in his senses, is what it should have been."[26] Since the categories of "lover" and "beloved" are relational – each party to a relationship is simultaneously the beloved of his/her partner – Plato's formulation amounts to saying that non-lovers ("the friends of solitude" in Derrida's idiom) make the best lovers. Getting Plato's argument into focus helps to render more intelligible (less paradoxical) Derrida's conception of friendship – and also helps to highlight the crucial role played by the concept of infinity in both Plato's and Derrida's arguments.

On the surface, the *Phaedrus* appears to be split down the middle. Socrates' First Speech, which occupies a central place in the dialogue, is concerned with the nature of love; his Second Speech, until the end of the dialogue, addresses the nature of discourse. Does the *Phaedrus* then really consist of two semi-independent halves, the first devoted to the nature of love and the second concerned with the nature of true discourse? Or is there an underlying connection between the two portions of the dialogue? What is the relationship between love and discourse?

The connection between the two halves of the dialogue might be formulated as follows: The only rationally defensible mode of communication, dialectic – which attempts to institutionalize the teachings of tacit knowledge by never allowing us to lose sight of the submerged pole of discourse, so that we constantly attempt to bring to the forefront of consciousness matters relating to such issues as the translation of theory into practice; appropriateness (generally); the hidden premises and assumptions of the statements that we make; and the suppressed implications to which they lead – is also the only mode of communication possible between lovers. In fact, it is only this type of communication that establishes love as a possible form of human relationship. Ordinary discourse in all its forms, written or spoken, descriptive or hortatory, is manipulative and subversive of the possibility of love. Only dialectic is tentative and exploratory, and capable of addressing and accommodating the other person as an end and not merely as a means. In this conception, the Kantian and the Platonic understandings of human beings as ends come together. People cease to manipulate when they are on the path to infinity – endlessly reconstructing what they have to say to accommodate its infinite points of derivation and its infinite possibilities of continuation. The Platonic vision is that the person who communicates with himself/herself dialectically, who is a pursuer of truth and wisdom in the Socratic sense, can broaden the circle of conversation to include another human being without either sacrificing the integrity of the self or the dignity of the Other.

The reversal of roles between lover and non-lover in Socrates' two speeches underscores the relationship between love and discourse. In his First Speech, Socrates equates love with domination: "So the lover will not willingly endure to have his beloved stronger or an equal but will continually strive to make him weaker or inferior."[27] In his Second Speech, Socrates redefines the lover, so that he assumes many of the personality characteristics of the non-lover in the First Speech: "He[the true lover] gazes upward as though he were a bird and cares nothing for what is here below, so that he is accused of being mad. I have shown that this, of all forms of divine possession, is the best and has the highest origin, both for him that has it and for him who shares in it; and that the man who partakes of this madness and loves beauty is called a lover."[28] This true madness can be cultivated only by the philosopher:

> For to be a man one must understand the content of a general term, leaving the field of manifold sense-perceptions and entering that in which the object of knowledge is unique and grasped only by reasoning. This process is a remembering of what our soul once saw as it made its journey with a god, looking down upon what we now assert to be real and gazing upwards at what is Reality itself. This is clearly the reason why it is right for only the philosopher's mind to have wings; for he remains always, so far as he can, through memory in the field of precisely those entities in whose presence, as though he were a god, he is himself divine. And if a man makes a right use of such entities as memoranda, always being perfectly initiated into perfect mysteries, he alone becomes truly perfected. He separates himself from the busy interests of man and approaches the divine. He is rebuked by the vulgar as insane, for they cannot know that he is possessed by divinity.[29]

The true lover in Socrates' Second Speech is the philosopher, hungering for communion with an eternal realm of Ideas. All other forms of madness, including the ordinary state of being in love, are pale copies of this highest form of madness. They are in a sense substitutes for the all-encompassing intellectual experience that we crave. Plato's non-lover of the First Speech, immersed in his own special otherworldly concerns, has now been redescribed as the highest form of lover. It is precisely at this point that the transition is negotiated between the focus on love in the first half of the dialogue and the concentration on discourse in the second. The intellectual protocols infused with an awareness of the tacit dimension of knowledge that facilitate engagement in dialectical discourse also create the possibility of love. Only someone for whom words are as much an instrument of self-awareness as they are of communication with others can achieve a non-manipulative relationship with the Other. The tact and restraint of Plato's philosophically mad lover promote the achievement of true love.

Part of Plato's criticism of the Sophists in the *Phaedrus* is that they elevate what Plato also takes to be the descriptive condition of most discourse as manipulative into a normative status as well, a limit that discourse cannot transcend. This overlooks the possibility of tacit knowing – and of how a reading out of the intimations of this process creates the intellectual infrastructure for dialectical thought and speech. "As in a mirror," Plato says, "in his lover he beholds himself and does not know it."[30] Given the reversal evinced by Socrates' Second Speech, we can say that the mirror image returned to the lover is that of a coordinate center of freedom, confronting its beloved in its aspect of freedom. The shock of recognition comes when it is *two* human beings who are engaged in the perpetual task of taking risks and taking flight that constitute the Socratic art of dialectic.

Thus, from a joint Platonic-Derridaean perspective, non-lovers – "the friends of solitude" – are embarked on the path to infinity, and are therefore least likely to instrumentalize others because of their infinite preoccupation with the "groundless grounding" of the self.

Derrida's notion of Otherness is, in crucial ways, functionally equivalent to Levinas' concept of Otherness. The paradox encapsulated in Dallmayr's rhetorical question – "In the case of Derrida's presentation, one may puzzle, how can noncommunicative remoteness at all be reconciled with the postulated (Levinasian) responsibility or responsiveness to the 'Other'?"[31] – needs to be converted into something resembling a platitude before the proper depth of Derrida's position can be assessed. This paradox only emerges if one conflates the Derridaean Other with the literal Levinasian Other, then "non-communicative remoteness" seems incompatible with "responsiveness to the 'Other.'" For Derrida, however, the Other remains a categorial construction of the Same – a direct expression of "noncommunicative remoteness," rather than being in tension or conflict with it. How then does the Derridaean Other serve as a prod for an ethical extension of the self if it is acknowledged at the outset to be a construction of the Same? One needs to notice how for Derrida a concept of the Other generated out of the theoretical resources of the Same has parallel unnerving or unsettling affects to a concept of the Other affirmed as literally Other. What intuitions or intimations of the Other are fueled by the traditional repertoire of theoretical moves of the Same? At least in *Specters of Marx*,[32] the Derridaean notion of the Other is linked with Walter Benjamin's weak messianism.[33] Extreme skepticism works to generate in a negative sense its own salvation. The underdetermination of theory by fact means that elements of arbitrariness inhere in even our most ingrained and customary ways of designating phenomena and describing what takes place both within and outside of the self. These insurmountable elements of arbitrariness attaching to our most abstractly inflated and most concretely minute verbal formulations constitute internally-generated prototypes of the Other. They are negative traces – reminders – of the radical insufficiency of the self in its surge toward mastery. They are also weakly messianic by negatively pointing beyond themselves toward an Other – and perhaps an ultimate Other – who will redeem them and us out of our condition, in which we have only negative traces of redemption. One needs to recall that, to be reflexively sustainable, the thesis of the underdetermination of theory by fact has to be viewed as itself underdetermined, which means that the door has to be left open to unequivocal redemption in a straightforward religious sense.

One can also say more acutely that for Derrida flashes of redemption accompany every statement that we make. For Derrida, the line separating the descriptive from the normative is tenuous and evanescent, since no string of words can be shown to fit – or correspond to – something beyond words. From this perspective, every descriptive statement becomes a covert normative stipulation. The gap that is registered by the institutionalized dislocation of both everyday and theoretical discourse makes us aware of our general condition as being one of dislocation and helps us to transform our overall existence into an enduring dramatization of absence (an absence without assurance of a complementary presence) that in its honesty and consistency is able to await with the proper composure the possible fulfillment of the future time.

Ricoeur and Levinas

Paul Ricoeur criticizes Levinas along lines analogous to Levinas' own critique of Buber and Derrida. Ricoeur summarizes Levinas' thought in the following way:

> Each face is a Sinai that prohibits murder. And me? It is in me that the movement coming from the other completes its trajectory: the other constitutes me as responsible, that is, as capable of responding. In this way, the word of the other comes to be placed at the origin of my acts. Self-imputation ... is now inscribed within an asymmetrical dialogic structure whose origin lies outside me.[34]

According to Ricoeur, there is a paradox residing at the heart of Levinas' thought. In order to be able to theorize such a central role for the Other in galvanizing the self into the possibilities of ethical relationship, Levinas has to theorize a self that, left to its own resources, is devoid of the possibility of relationship. In rebellion against the "Husserlian ambition of universal constitution and radical self-grounding,"[35] which makes the capacity for representation the key for understanding the self, Levinas needs initially to project the self as stripped of these representational mechanisms – as locked into a condition of separation and isolation that appears irredeemable. It is the self postulated as being outside the ambit of relationship that makes the Levinasian Other possible. In Ricoeur's summary: "Because the Same signifies totalization and separation, the exteriority of the Other can no longer be expressed in the language of relation. The Other absolves itself from relation, in the same movement by which the Infinite draws free from Totality."[36]

Levinas has two contradictory images to capture "the irrelation implied by ... otherness in its movement of absolution,"[37] one worked out in *Totality and Infinity* and the other developed in *Otherwise than Being*. In *Totality and Infinity*, "Elevation – the face of the Other – ... summons me as though from Sinai ... Since the initiative belongs wholly to the Other, it is in the accusative – a mode well named – that the I is met by the injunction and made capable of answering, again in the accusative: 'It's me here!'"[38] The Other in *Totality and Infinity* is the "master of justice" who calls me to responsibility – to show proper concern and compassion for him. In *Otherwise than Being*, the Other has been transmuted into the offender to whom I must provide expiation. In this work, Levinas speaks of "substitution,"[39] and of the ego not as "an entity 'capable' of expiating for the others: it is this original expiation."[40] In terms of his theory of Otherness, Levinas says that "We have to speak here of expiation as uniting identity and alterity."[41]

Ricoeur attributes "the break effect related to this thought of absolute otherness" in Levinas to hyperbole – "one worthy of Cartesian hyperbolic doubt." Ricoeur defines this term as follows:

> By hyperbole, it must be strongly underscored, we are not to understand a figure of style, a literary trope, but the systematic practice of *excess* in philosophical argumentation. Hyperbole appears in this context as the strategy suited to producing the effect of a break with regard to the idea of exteriority in the sense of absolute otherness.[42]

Ricoeur sees hyperbole as extending to both sides of the Levinasian equation: "Hyperbole ... simultaneously reaches both poles, the Same and the Other."[43] The hyperbole manifested in Levinas' analysis of the Same leads to the hyperbole displayed in his conceptualization of the Other. Where is hyperbole evidenced in Levinas' analysis of the Same? Ricoeur traces it to the eliding of a crucial distinction between ego, or "I", and self: "In truth, what the hyperbole of separation renders unthinkable is the distinction between self and I, and the formation of a concept of selfhood defined by its openness and its capacity for discovery."[44] Ricoeur's critique of Levinas is thus similar to Levinas' own critique of Buber. Levinas had said that Buber's theorizing of the I-Thou relationship constituted as a series of non-continuous events generated in the *Zwischen* was reflexively questionable because it circumvented the role of consciousness and self transcending the discrete events of meeting that facilitated the theorizing of the I-Thou relationship itself. Similarly, according to Ricoeur, Levinas' collapse of the self onto the I, or ego, debars him from adequately registering the mediating role of language in the development of human consciousness. Language helps to account both for Levinas' theorizing of the encounter between the "I" and the Other and also simultaneously enriches and diversifies the "I" of Everyman and Everywoman – so that it becomes more than an I as it interacts with the Other: It becomes (already is, to a certain extent) a self. Ricoeur frames this point as a set of rhetorical questions:

> To mediate the opening of the Same onto the Other and the internalization of the voice of the Other in the Same, must not language contribute its resources of communication, hence of reciprocity, as is attested by the exchange of personal pronouns ... , an exchange that reflects a more radical one, that of question and answer in which the roles are continually reversed? In short, is it not necessary that a dialogue superpose a relation on the supposedly absolute distance between the separate I and the teaching Other?[45]

Parfit and Levinas

Ricoeur's critique of Levinas (echoing as it does Levinas' own critique of Buber) seems to be the appropriate forum in which to raise an anterior question about human selfhood, which Levinas' strategy of analysis enables him to skirt. Levinas wants to theorize a self in which the primacy of ethical injunctions emanating from the Face of the Other to the self has priority over all other phases of the projects of self-delineation and self-knowledge. In order to accomplish this goal, Levinas has to conceive of the self in a unidimensional way as a bare ego, or "I", receiving its linguistic or narrative capacity (its ability to acknowledge itself as a self) from an encounter with the Above of the Other. The starting point of Levinas' argument is thus an I and an Other, which Levinas theorizes in such a way so as to secure the primacy of the ethical relation over all others.

This starting point, however, can be called into question from a number of different – if sometimes overlapping – directions. For example, Derek Parfit in a well-known book published in the 1980s, *Reasons and Persons*,[46] questions, on philosophical grounds, the very existence of a coherent, unitary "I." In an early paper on personal identity, the argument of which is elaborated upon in his book, Parfit introduces the notion of a "q-memory." "To sketch a definition," he says, "I am q-remembering an experience if (1) I have a belief about a past experience which seems in itself like a memory belief; (2) someone did have such an experience; and (3) my belief is dependent upon this experience in the same way in which a memory of an experience is dependent upon it."[47] The point of this definition is to enable Parfit to formulate a concept of memory in which the idea that we can only remember our own memories does not emerge as a logical truth. With Parfit's alternative formulation of a q-memory, the concept of memory is severed from the idea of a person. Memory is no longer dependent upon the continuity of the selfsame person.

Parfit's strategy is evocative of Saul Kripke's deployment of a distinction between "plus" and "quus" in his construal of Wittgenstein's position on rules and the possibility of a private language. According to Kripke's interpretation of Wittgenstein, it is always open to a "bizarre skeptic" to question whether the "plus" sign in arithmetic should not be interpreted as "quus." "Quus" could be defined as requiring that, when dealing with integers less than 57, addition should be performed in the normal way, but when dealing with integers greater than 57, addition (using the quus sign) would always yield a result of 5. The possibility of "plus" actually meaning "quus" haunts each of us, since there exist problems in addition both of whose arguments exceed numbers we have previously worked with. The fact that it is always open to the "bizarre skeptic" to question the application of rules in this way shows for Wittgenstein that meaning is never private and that assertability and utility must displace truth as our central criteria for validating statements.[48]

Both Parfit's and Kripke's philosophical moves, in turn, conjure up Hume's critique of causality and induction. Hume argues that there is no intrinsic physical linkage between a cause and its effect, nor is there any totally indubitable worldly connection between previous occurrences of a natural sequence (such as the sun rising in the morning) and present exemplifications of the same phenomenon. For Parfit and Kripke, as well, the concept of a person and the plus sign do not necessarily have to denote built-in regularities in the order of nature in order for us to be able to account for their use.

In order to maximize the coherence of Parfit's fracturing of the self into a plurality of successive selves, one would need to interpret anti-realistically his notion of multiple selves. If the self is a fiction, then, so too are a plurality of successive selves. The encompassing function performed by the concept of the self does not become theoretically more viable when the time frame of its applicability is reduced. The "q-memory argument," which uncouples the engagements of the self from any continuing substratum called "the self," explodes short-term selves as effectively as it does the more conventional, long-term, enduring notion of the self.

The idea of the human self implicit in Parfit's argument seems to be that of a conceptual lever that enables us at different moments in our lives to transcend both the positive characteristics and the negative disownings and disparagements that we have imputed to ourselves. The self from this pragmatic perspective is almost synonymous with what we might call an "anti-self," with the various moves and lurchings that we engage in to wriggle out of the patterns established by our previous exertions of energy and to facilitate the establishment of new patterns. The idea of the self from this perspective is thus coterminous with the prospect of endless distancing, so that being remains irredeemably retrospective in character, a series of nominalistic reconstructions out of continual becomings.

Parfit wants to erode a unitary notion of personal identity in order to call the notion of self-interest into question and to render more plausible and compelling his utilitarian defenses of intergenerational justice. If the self is a plurality, then we are always calculating "intergenerationally," even within the confines of a single human life – so that there is only a difference of degree, but not one in kind, between calculating "intrapsychically" and calculating intergenerationally in the literal sense.

To the extent that Parfit is literally committed to the notion of multiple selves, his argument is also vulnerable to the criticism that Hume levels against his own theory of personal identity in the appendix to his *A Treatise of Human Nature*.[49] Hume in his theorizing of personal identity ends up with a self-referentialist dilemma that he is not able to overcome. If the self is a bundle of perceptions, and all of our perceptions are distinct existences, "and the mind never perceives any real connection among distinct existences,"[50] then what is the status of the self that pronounces this judgment about the utter severability of the components of the self? Hume's theory of personal identity self-referentially collapses because it is not able to account for itself. A theoretical vantage point that notices that the self consists of nothing more than a bundle of perceptions has to itself consist of more than a bundle of perceptions in order to make such an observation. Hume confesses in the appendix to the *Treatise* that he is unable to fill in the gap in his argument. This gap can be overcome by attributing to Hume a generalized-agnostic version of skepticism, which leaves the door open for the possibility that a multivalued logic that maps the suspension of the Law of the Excluded Middle encodes reality more accurately than does traditional Aristotelian logic. In that case, our alternatives are increased beyond A and not-A, and Hume could affirm that the self both does and does not consist of a bundle of perceptions: it does for all purposes except for that of theorizing this very position itself.

From a Derridaean perspective, it is not only Hume's theory of personal identity but his empiricist epistemology more generally that has its level of coherence raised by a generalized-agnostic interpretation. With his famous notion of *difference*, Derrida calls attention to how the play of signifiers is grouped to yield significant meaning only in relation to receding contexts of what is other than itself – so that problems of regress and circularity attend the dualism of signifier/signified: "All positions – be they metaphysical or political – will perforce dismantle themselves as the condition of their being elaborated."[51] Hume's empiricist epistemology unhinges itself in ways that resonate directly with Derrida's concept of *difference* because the linguistic terms that individuate the sensory particulars that are the building blocks of Hume's empiricism get their individuation endlessly deferred by the unceasing play of difference between what is and what is not themselves.[52] Language, therefore, in a Derridaean reading of Humean empiricism continually forestalls our engagement with the world – and leaves the world a perennially open question. Our relationship to it is sealed in a generalized agnosticism.

In contrast to Levinas' attempt to revivify the central Western moral imperative of "Love thy fellow human being as thyself" by pushing the pendulum of moral deliberation to the other extreme through his delineation of the priority of the Other over the Same, Parfit's theorizing of personal identity leads to what Ricoeur calls a "quasi Buddhism."[53] Parfit's quasi Buddhism asks

> that we concern ourselves less with ourselves, with our aging and our death among other things, that we attach less importance to the question of "whether experiences come within the same or different lives"; hence, that we take an interest in the "experiences" themselves rather than in the "person, the subject of experiences"; that we place less emphasis on differences between ourselves at different periods and others who have had experiences similar to our own; that we ignore as much as possible the boundaries between lives by giving less importance to unity of each life; that we make the very unity of our life more a work of art than a claim to independence.[54]

What emerges from our readings of Levinas and Parfit are two ostensibly incommensurable ways of making sense of moral experience that become inter-translatable and form a common frame of reference only in terms of the skeptical components that reside in each approach.

On the basis of our analysis, we might characterize Levinas as a moral phenomenologist and Parfit as a moral epistemologist. The moral epistemologist affirms skepticism in the face of the evidence and the assumptions of everyday experience – and his own location and range of activities in the world. By contrast, the moral phenomenologist (in Jurgen Habermas' summary of P. F. Strawson's argument in his essay, "Freedom and Resentment") "develops a linguistic phenomenology of ethical consciousness whose purpose is maieutically to open the eyes of the empiricist in his role as moral skeptic to his own everyday moral intuitions."[55] Given, as we have now seen from our discussion of Levinas and Parfit, that it is possible to render intelligible the idea and the activities of the self (however suitably redefined in each case) from the perspective of the moral epistemologist as well as from the vantage point of the moral phenomenologist – that the idea of the self is underdetermined by the facts pertaining to the self – it makes sense to say from the moral phenomenologist's perspective as well that the self, too, is a theory. It is a gigantic, evolving and resilient intellectual construct intended to render more intelligible our multifarious encounters with experience and with other people, and the myriad of insights and obstacles that these encounters engender and occasion. But if the self is a species of theory, and under a generalized-agnostic dispensation theory enjoys no privileged or even certifiable contact with the world, then the concatenation of interrelated subcategories that we call a "self" has to already be at one unverifiable remove from experience in order to constitute a self. To attempt to bridge the gap here by positioning further selves – more abstractly and interiorly situated, as it were, than the original self, and therefore capable of grappling with its dilemmas – only reintroduces the problem at a further level of removal from the one upon which it was originally noticed. The idea of a self – of an agent – thus becomes a hastily improvised notion to forestall awareness of an infinite regress that impugns the very possibility of a self.

The moral phenomenologist rests his case upon borrowed claims. Methodologically, his arguments are living off the classic epistemological thesis that historicism (focusing on the realia of the moral philosopher's situation, that is, his empirical location in the world – rather than upon his theories) supersedes and discredits the moral epistemologist's theoretical stance. Historicism – the moral phenomenologist's assigning of primacy to ontology over epistemology (how the moral philosopher lives, rather than how he systematically and self-consciously thinks) – "works" because classic epistemology "works." One sets the stage (furnishes the background assumptions) for the other. The moral phenomenologist cannot simply proceed as if they were antithetical to one another. The validating source for the historicist discrediting and delegitimation of the epistemological tradition is the epistemological tradition. The contextualization of historical data in historicism (in our case, the grounding of the moral epistemologist in his immediate historical situation) is the counterpart to the primacy assigned to impressions and sense data in classical empiricism. In both cases, we have a search for building blocks that are then assembled into broader syntheses. It is therefore extremely ironic that the moral phenomenologist attempts to impugn the project of classical epistemology by a historicization of it that consists in an application of its very principles to another domain.

Levinas presupposes a conventional "I" in theorizing the asymmetrical relation between the Same and the Other as his particular re-envisioning of the fundamental tenet of traditional Western morality – the Golden Rule, showing unlimited solicitude and respect for the Other. Parfit argues in defense of a disjointed self in pursuing his quasi-Buddhist moral vision. We have seen how issues of underdetermination of theory by fact and generalized-agnostic motifs pervade both arguments and also affect how one can configure their relationship with one another. The upshot of both arguments is to underscore how precarious the ethical enterprise is – how it is constituted out of the most fragile and unpromising of materials. Generalizing from these contrasting positions, we might say that they invite a vision of ethics as characterized by absence, a negative ethics constantly focusing on the inadequacy of justification. What we share with others – what forms the basis for what we might call negative community – is our common need to acclimate to an epistemological and ethical vacuum, a pathos of undecidability.

Ethics and a generalized agnosticism

If displacement is what chiefly characterizes the intellectual life (the centrality attaching to a generalized agnosticism in the fashioning and interpretation of arguments) and the nature of the human person (the Levinasian infinite distance separating the Other from the Same; the Parfitian conception of personal identity suitably agnostically reinterpreted), then we are bereft of any set of feasible materials to provide foundations for ethics. Ethical deliberation, therefore, always needs to be pitched to an anterior level of discussion, whether ethics itself is sustainable as a persuasive mode of human self-reflection and self-actualization. An ethical community is primordially characterized by its sense of what is absent. This negative approach is most appropriately captured in the image of prayer – so that an ethical community is identified by its prayerful waiting for the moment when it itself might more fully come into being.

Ethics as an autonomously established field of discourse and inquiry yields neither justification before the fact of engagement in action nor validation afterward. In keeping with the generalized agnosticism I have been advocating, we need to cultivate an instrumentalized conception of the field of ethics as currently articulated. Ethical and meta-ethical formulations form an orientating guide and handle on the field of action. Ethics facilitates the making of certain moves and revisions in the field of action. The whole activity of theory formation and articulation in ethics constitutes a gigantic smokescreen – a series of unending tautologies – a colossal series of "elsewheres" which enables the process of revision and adjustment to circumstances and to afterthoughts and to reconsideration of particular ethical and political positions to take place. The concepts of justification and validation themselves provide ethical deliberation with such a "smokescreen" which enables it to perform this role of revision and adjustment.

The gap between thinking and reality registered by my generalized agnosticism is compatible with our making (and revising) the sorts of judgments in diverse spheres that on a common sense level we are driven to make. The fact that the returns are not in concerning what the world is like in no way debars us from making the judgments that we are customarily motivated to make. The lack of secure reference points in terms of which to formulate moral judgments does not inhibit our ability to make interim judgments – interim both in terms of fixing what the world is like and what our appropriate response(s) should be. Our incomplete knowledge of objective reality coupled with the implications of protocols of consistency, of self-referentialism, render meta-theoretically plausible the conception of ethical formulation as action facilitating further action. Ethical theorizing is metaphysically subordinate and instrumental to doing. Ethics is a series of moves that we make in an action game. The doing (the engagement in action) is, in the metaphysically most satisfying sense, the theory, as the official, literal theorizing leaves trails of uncompleted and uncompletable argument harboring traces of the issue of consistency, or reflexivity, that get reabsorbed and re-encoded in the doing.

The following is a brief sketch of what a politics and an ethics grounded in a generalized agnosticism might look like:

Theory of truth and its relationship to politics

A generalized agnosticism is suggestive of a continually emerging truth. The only truth that politics institutionalizes (and it institutionalizes it only because it may be true – it does not refuse to countenance the possibility that it might not be true) is the "truth" of openness. Openness has "lexical priority" over any particular political program that is submitted under an agenda favoring openness because of the continuing relevance of the agnostic question that perhaps this (formulated in relation to any specific policy proposal) is not so.

Justice

Justice is just what one is trying to do now, the kind of program or vision one is trying to enact at the present moment. It is not just, as the later work of John Rawls, Michael Walzer and the communitarians would have it, the reading out of the intimations of your own tradition, but also consists in attempts to reconstitute that tradition in light of particular visions concerning how it might be improved or transformed. Justice, however, is not constituted by the shadow structures of blueprints of change or canons of judgment through which current arrangements are condemned or criticized, but by the efforts at change themselves. It is the doing that bespeaks the impulse to achieve justice. The rationalizations and reifications all have to be construed in light of the agnostic imperative that questions both their accuracy as abridgements of concrete political experience and their comprehensiveness as codifications of the ideal. Justice is engagement in a certain activity – a form of doing – and theorizing inevitably distorts and artificially delimits the nature of that doing.

Rights

Current limits on state action are as permanent and enduring as our willingness to mobilize state action in defense of those limits. What we cannot do boils down to what we are unwilling to do at any given moment in historical time. At the base of a constitutional regime lies the tautologous, circular argument – we cannot do it because we cannot do it. We need to emphasize the agnostic seedbed of rights. It is not that we know certain things to be the case, but rather that we are searching on a rhetorical plane for the appropriate institutional translation of openness. The vocabulary of rights that requires negative, adversarial opinion to be heard signifies continual openness to all possibilities – including our questioning of the validity of openness itself.

There is, however, only a rhetorical affinity between a generalized agnosticism and a political system that emphasizes the centrality of rights. The *Grundnorm* of a liberal political system is a metaphysically arbitrary attempt to structure political institutions in the light of the theoretical image of a generalized agnosticism (which does not itself decree that only a liberal ordering of institutions is just).

Political obligation

According to the approach I am developing in this book, political obligation becomes a function of one's obligating oneself in a series of successive presents. The circular statement – one is obligated to obey because one is obligating oneself to obey – becomes the only relevant comment to make with regard to the question of political obligation. This approach circumvents Ronald Dworkin's objection against contractarian, hypothetical obligation in that in being hypothetical, it does not obligate in the present.[56] "Political obligation," like "justice," becomes a concept that is open to the future. It is a notion formulated in the present, summarizing the expected content of future actions.

Parfit, Freud and Levinas

A special heightened prefiguration of Parfit's conception of the self as fugitive and fragmented occurs in Sigmund Freud with his notion of the transference. This is the way Freud defines the phenomenon:

> The most remarkable thing is this. The patient is not satisfied with regarding the analyst in the light of reality as a helper and adviser who, moreover, is remunerated for the trouble he takes and who would himself be content with some such role as that of a guide on a difficult mountain climb. On the contrary, the patient sees in him the return, the reincarnation, of some important figure out of his childhood or past, and consequently transfers on to him feelings and reactions which undoubtedly applied to this prototype.[57]

I think that it is fair to say that for Freud the transference is not only a central feature of the analytic relationship affecting the analyst and her patient, but that its place in analysis is a microcosmic reflection of the pervasive role it plays in everyday life. For Freud, with the primal importance he assigns to one's location within an original network of family relationships – and how even one's reactions and interactions within this original network are shaped by a seething and impenetrable surplus of id-emotions that are coextensive with birth and perhaps even precede it – there are no pristine enactments at any stage or in any context of one's life, but only reenactments. The picture of self-formation and self-nurturance that emerges from Freud is one of temporary selves that get crystallized in relation to transient Others both within and outside the self. The family resemblances that emerge and get reinforced between these multiple selves constitute what we more as a wager than as a confident description of fact call "the self." In our search for an essence and a moment that is irrecoverable and perhaps non-existent, we commandeer persons and situations as occasions for persistent reenactment of a plot line that becomes simultaneously more familiar and more mysterious the more frequently we reenact it. A community of Freudian "selves" of this sort conjures up an image of Otherness bouncing off Otherness – without genuine and unambiguous and unequivocal meeting. A significant metaphysical backdrop to Freud's conception of the transference seems to be his reading of Nietzsche's theorizing of power as the impulse driving human activity in such a formalistic and monotonous way that the urge to make sense of our multiple and unceasing power-assertions – to interpret them – becomes just one more power-assertion or series of power-assertions. In Freud, as well, the larger unit we call "the self" looms as artificial and as opaque as the uninterrupted flow of transferences that it "houses."

Given that Levinas in this book serves as our guide in demarcating between theory and ideology and in delineating the liberal conception of the good, we might, in light of our juxtaposition of him to Nietzsche, Freud, Buber, Derrida, Ricoeur, Parfit and Hume, summarize our reconstructed version of his central teaching as follows: Since Levinas' argument concerning totality vs. infinity is to a certain extent the result of responding to the dilemmas attendant to the formulation of a consistent version of skepticism (this requires the dissociation of the *saying* of skepticism from the *said* of skepticism), and skepticism itself only emerges as an issue in philosophy because of the factor of underdetermination (one can make sense of the relationship between words and the world both on the basis of realism and in relation to skeptical idealism), the idea of the Other, which for Levinas is supposed to be the harbinger of infinity, should not be construed as having a firmer identity than the metaphysical issues that nurture our consideration of the Other. A metaphorical extension of the Talmudic methodological principle of *Dayo L'Bah Min HaDin Lihiyot K'Nadun* (broadly speaking – a solution has to work within the parameters set by the problem, without importing extraneous premises) should be in place here. What sets the stage for a reception of the concept of Otherness is the factor of skepticism as denoted by the underdetermination of language by reality (of theory by fact). This is what enables the skeptic, on skeptical grounds, to entertain the idea of the Other. The most consistent and coherent way to proceed from this premise would appear to be to acknowledge the underdetermination at work in the conceptualization of the Other as well – the concept can be theorized in relation to a whole range of approaches extending from a literal affirmation of the Other to the Freudian transference. We need to remind ourselves that the Other should be construed infinitely in all of its ramifications – rather than totalistically. The Other should be articulated as a category in relation to all of its divergent possibilities which continue to reverberate within it without getting finally resolved. From this perspective, the ethical import of the Other derives from underdetermination itself. The ethics of underdetermination might be described as inducing an endless patience for and preoccupation with process – an infinite caring for actualized and unactualized possibilities that is coextensive with an infinite respect for life itself. This more openly skeptical approach to Levinasian teaching – which converges upon the content of his teaching from a more avowedly skeptical direction than the one that he explicitly pursues – itself illustrates the workings of the principle of underdetermination.

Epistemology, ethics, circularity and a generalized agnosticism

The whole structure of epistemological argument is predicated upon an antecedent circularity. The same is true for ethical argument. Epistemology derives its motive force from a gap between "can" and "ought." Because we can make sense of our conceptual and theoretical vocabularies both by presupposing that they are directly determined by factual states of affairs and by maintaining that we perceive and delineate what is present in the world in relation to the conceptual and theoretical frameworks we affirm, the epistemological enterprise is set in motion. This enterprise is a normative one which seeks to orient us with regard to the uncertainty that attaches itself to the basic framework of human understanding of the world. The basic framework can be described as being constituted by a set of givens or as an assemblage of postulates and categories in terms of which we make sense of our world and identify its "givens." Epistemology deals both with second-order questions of validation of inferences deriving from basic frameworks and vindication of basic frameworks themselves. There is ontological space for epistemology to operate because the skeptic can legitimately reconfigure the bases of our knowledge claims. It is the skeptic's circular intervention that makes epistemology possible.

Ethics by contrast revolves around the gap between "ought" and "can" – between generalized ethical imperatives and the exigencies of daily behavior. An "ought" dimension – and a hiatus between it and what might be – are equally prevalent in epistemology and in ethics. It is only circular argument, which presupposes what it is trying to prove or to prescribe, that closes the gap in either case.

The pervasiveness of circularity is best understood from the perspective of a generalized agnosticism. "Circularity" can be viewed as proceeding on the premises of the incompleteness, and therefore also the at least partially unknown character, of objective reality. Since reality is incomplete and hence also partially unknown, "circularity" – building the salient point(s) of one's conclusion into one's premise(s) – constitutes an artful philosophical strategy for producing a symmetrically designed piece of argument that will provisionally fill in our objective-knowledge gap. If there is no firm external check against a premise or an argument as a whole (as there is not, according to a generalized agnosticism), then "circularity" becomes a fact of (logical) life.[58] In a generalized-agnostic universe, circular argument yields a thought construct that serves as a surrogate for a reality that is not otherwise conceptually containable or referable. The circular argument confers durability and weight upon its components when reality provides neither.

The logical ideal of consistency, which lies in the background to my assigning prominence to circularity in argument, needs to be construed negatively. In order to conform to it, one needs to show that statements are not inconsistent. Consistency in a more positive sense is unrealizable by us because it would presuppose that we have a complete grasp of the sense and reference of the statements that we make. However, if our organizing perspective is constituted by a generalized agnosticism – if our approach to knowledge is shaped by the understanding that the returns are not yet fully in from any domain of human inquiry (scientific, moral or political) – then we, as formulators of statements in all of the domains that have piqued our interest and curiosity, must acknowledge that they remain incomplete both in terms of what they signify and what they refer to. Because of this incompleteness, we cannot apply a test of consistency to them in a positive sense. All we can try to show in a more limited, negative sense is that a particular statement or set of statements are not inconsistent with them.

In accordance with what I have just stated, the case for my meta-theoretical argument concerning the ontological status of ethics and epistemology can be made in terms of the formal ideal or criterion of consistency. If consistency translates into a negative notion of showing that a particular statement or position is not inconsistent with some other statement or position that we hold, then the meta-theory of the underdetermination of theory by fact can uphold the factual structure of the universe just as equitably as postulating a direct correspondence between theory and fact. Since we cannot do better than a negative translation of the ideal of consistency, then my identification of the ontological status of epistemology and ethics as being circular in character receives some formal sanction from the procedural notion of consistency construed in this negative way.

Skepticism, even of a formal, procedural sort, leads to the overtaking of epistemology by ethics – to a recognition that our everyday statements are not only implicitly circular,[59] but implicitly normative. The whole descriptive world becomes normatively suffused. Its normativity is intimately bound up with its circularity. We make sense of it in terms that we supply. From a generalized-agnostic perspective, every descriptive statement is simultaneously a normative statement. Given that the returns are not fully in from any field or domain of inquiry, the gap between "is" and "ought" is closed because we are not dealing here with two types of statement but rather with one: Every descriptive statement is simultaneously a normative statement oriented toward prescribing how we make sense of the world.

At this point, one might raise the objection against my own argument that, applying to it the test of reflexivity, I am responsible for my own epistemological dilemmas by outlining a skepticism that issues forth in an unbreachable gap between words and things. There appears to be a tension between what looks like my advocacy of a pragmatism that assigns priority to doing and making above knowing and my embrace of a meta-epistemological theory that highlights the word-theory gap as the very justification for that pragmatism. As a pragmatist, I could presumably come up with a different meta-theory that would enable me to fashion a different theoretical world. In developing my response to this Wittgensteinian fascination with a beginning that antedates the beginning,[60] I take my cue from Plato's Third Man Argument in the *Parmenides*. What I take Plato to be saying there (which I shall elaborate upon more fully in Chapter 8) is that the search for more encompassing and secure foundations for our foundations cannot be reasonably arrested or foreclosed, and yields a return of both words and things to an ever receding common linguistic plane which institutionalizes their unbridgeable distance forever. The generalized agnosticism that constitutes a reflexive turn in my own argument leaves the door open for precisely the possibility that the potential objector to my argument mentions – namely, that the gap between words and things is a function of my own epistemological handiwork and does not reflect elements of necessity either in the structure of the universe or in the structure of rational argument. It is exactly the case with skepticism as it is with God: We can neither validate these notions, nor can we invalidate them.

A generalized agnosticism, Sellars and McDowell

A generalized agnosticism affords us an appropriate context in terms of which to make sense of Wilfrid Sellars' attack on traditional empiricist epistemology and John McDowell's attempt to fashion an acceptable alternative to it. In attempting to theorize a viable epistemology in the face of Sellars' classic attack on the Myth of the Given,[61] John McDowell does not transcend, but rather presupposes the principle of the underdetermination of theory by fact: "The idea of the Given is the idea that the space of reasons, the space of justifications or warrants, extends more widely than the conceptual sphere."[62] Expanding upon Sellars' argument, McDowell seeks to expose the idea of the Given as mythical by arguing that even if the space of reasons were wider than the conceptual sphere, all that would accomplish would be to give us a basis for "exculpation"[63] were we to make the wrong judgments. However, there is still a tremendous ontological distance between exculpation and justification. In order to close this gap, the tendency has developed "to oscillate between embracing the Myth of the Given and denying that experience has a rational bearing on thought."[64]

In order to counter this oscillation, McDowell proposes that "in experience, spontaneity is inextricably implicated in deliverances of receptivity. We must not suppose that receptivity makes an even notionally separable contribution to its co-operation with spontaneity."[65] To close the gap between exculpation and justification – and to foreclose the oscillation between affirming the Myth of the Given and severing the connection between experience and thought – McDowell proposes that we view thought in quasi-Gadamerian terms as "a repository of tradition, a store of historically accumulated wisdom about what is a reason for what."[66] Here, McDowell is theorizing thought as being coextensive with language, the multiple layers of signification of which encode not only rational bases for judgment, but also the criteria of rationality themselves that enable particular reasons to pass muster as reasons. A semblance of humanly-usable objectivity is restored in the face of the critique encapsulated in the Myth of the Given by historicizing and traditionalizing mind – i.e., "linguistifying" it, so that the space of reasons is both broader (in the sense that its content is not fixed; that it historically evolves) and not broader (since one cannot meaningfully point to anything outside it) than the conceptual sphere. In this circuitous way, McDowell strives to close the gap between exculpation and justification. The world and language in a certain sense are viewed as one.

It is important to note contradictory elements present in the way McDowell interprets the Myth of the Given and formulates his response to it. One can only point to a gap between exculpation and justification if one can envisage on some level of reasoning what it would be like for us to justify our knowledge statements and claims, as well as what it would be like for us to merely let ourselves off the hook by offering a plausible account of how we came to stray in making the wrong judgment. In developing his attack on the Myth of the Given, McDowell needs to invest conceptual coherence in the idea of justification, even as he denies that it is taking place by counterposing to it the contrasting notion of exculpation. Analogously, McDowell, in evolving an alternative position to the impasse encapsulated in the notion of the Myth of the Given, is both withholding the legitimating label of reality from anything that is independent of mind-embedded language and conferring this legitimating label upon such entities in order for the critical force of his alternative to the Myth of the Given to become manifest. He needs to say, after all, that language is the functional equivalent of reality. McDowell thus has to both affirm and deny a reality beyond language in order to mount his argument against, and to delineate an alternative to, the Myth of the Given.

The coherence of both McDowell's critique and his alternative position would be augmented by invoking a generalized agnosticism that stipulates that the returns are not yet fully in concerning the nature of reality. Reality might yet turn out to exhibit a structure most faithfully captured by multivalued logics that encode the suspension of the Law of the Excluded Middle. In this way, the contradictions highlighted in both the Myth of the Given and

McDowell's account of knowledge are normalized as conforming to an alternative logical grid opposed to the traditional Aristotelian one.

From the perspective of a generalized agnosticism, the Myth of the Given circumscribed within the limits connoted by the exculpation vs. justification distinction might be more tenable than McDowell's alternative epistemology. In a generalized-agnostic universe, "exculpation" might be the furthest we can travel on the road to justification. Exculpation, after all, is a negative phenomenon – it points to how and why we went wrong in our judgments. Justification, by contrast, is a positive phenomenon – indicating why a particular judgment is valid. From a generalized-agnostic perspective, all of the exculpatory statements in the world surrounding a particular judgment are not translatable into a justificatory statement. Summing together all the accounts of why a particular judgment went off do not yield a full-scale account of what a justification of the particular judgment in question would look like. From a generalized-agnostic point of view, we cannot be sure that we have fully grasped the complete range of meanings and reference points of our original formulations, so that justification of them looms as an ideal posit rather than as a genuinely accessible goal. The most we can attain are exculpations when we go astray, rather than positive justifications of our original statements. While both the logically circumscribed Myth of the Given and McDowell's epistemological strategies harbor contradictory elements that would be ameliorated from the direction of a generalized agnosticism, the logically circumscribed Myth of the Given already subliminally acknowledges the centrality of a generalized agnosticism by the pivotal role that the implied distinction between justification and exculpation plays in its formulation.

Theory and ideology

To extrapolate from what I have been saying so far to rough definitions of theory and ideology, we might say the following: Whatever evokes and confirms the prospect of circularity (circularity as a function of a generalized agnosticism) is theory. Whatever circumvents or denies it is ideology. From this perspective, theory has to be conceived of negatively as registering a lack or absence. Ideology needs to be delineated as affirming a positive content that from its own cognitive perspective is privileged and transcends circularity.

An additional complementary way to distinguish between theory and ideology is to say that theory applies to itself a test of reflexivity to check whether its preferred critical canon applies to it as well – whereas ideology, generally speaking, directs its critical canon outward, but not inward. Once a test of reflexivity is applied against its own preferred critical canon, the scope and reach of an ethical or political program are usually scaled down, so that they are transformed into particular versions of a generalized agnosticism. A generalized agnosticism (as we have seen) also represents the continuing element between Western religion and Western skepticism.

There is an ethical dimension to the notion of reflexivity: Reflexivity betokens a concern for the impact of one's thoughts and actions upon the self nurturing the thoughts and engaging in the actions. The ethics of theory consists in a deliberate courting of the issue of reflexivity. The ethics of ideology consists in a deliberate jettisoning of the issue of reflexivity.

There is a vast literature that correlates different personality types and their susceptibility to the appeals of totalitarianism.[67] In many respects, totalitarian ideologies constitute the most heightened expression of ideological political thought. In their drive toward certainty, finality and closure, totalitarian ideologies, as the 20th century experienced them, carried the tendencies of ideological thought as I have analyzed them in this essay to their ultimate conclusion. "Ideology" represents an attempt at totalization: A human subject's urge to achieve full-scale assimilation of his/her object of inquiry or study. An ideological disposition seeks to de-temporalize human existence. It wants to banish or at least radically reduce human contingency. It strives to make human experience utterly compliant with and transparent to its manipulative and interventionist urges. By reifying and objectifying the human subject and his relationship to the world, it ends up legitimating a reified and objectified politics that purges human existence of its ambiguous dross and gives it a finished, redeemed veneer.

There is a sense in which descent to ideological mappings of the self and its environment is indispensable even from the larger meta-theoretical perspective that I am developing in this book. In the absence of metaphysical certainty, we must at least generate pragmatic conviction in order to get on with the business of living, and also to produce those interim reports on knowledge in diverse fields of inquiry that are then ontologically consigned to continuing suspended animation by my negative-theologically-inspired conception of theory. In order to organize the multiple worlds of our interaction and inquiry, we need orientating ideologies to give us cues and to chart the most fruitful paths to pursue. Also, from the skeptical perspective that I have been exploring throughout this book, the very open-endedness of human thought means that whatever intellectual constructions we come up with will have by default an ideological cast and hue.

Nonetheless, cultivating a theoretical sensibility of the sort developed and explored in this book constitutes one of our best hedges against being swept up by rabidly ideological political appeals. From the skeptical perspective I have been elaborating, the languages that we deploy (including the languages that give us access to the self) remain irredeemably metaphorical. If our words are underdetermined by any kind of reality outside of themselves, then what they conjure up is to some extent other words and their imagistic and conceptual potential. If there are no secure real-world references for our verbal formulations, then to a certain degree at least the inspiration for our verbal constructions comes from other words, so that language generally on an ongoing basis and with regard to nearly all objects betrays the classic features of metaphor: "a stratification of meaning, in which an incongruity of sense on one level produces an influx of significance on another."[68] The reflexive residues present in some of our most abstract verbal formulations constitute another inlet into the ways in which smooth transit between words and things gets aborted and also indirectly point to the role of metaphor in picking up the slack created by these reflexive blockages. A self imbued with the theoretical self-understandings of the sort that I am sketching is intellectually and existentially poised to delegitimize and discount the totalistic appeals of the most dramatically propagated political ideologies. In the generalized-agnostic version of skepticism that I am proposing, epistemology is already ethics. If knowledge is not unequivocally about the world, then the conception that displaces it is of a "knowledge" of how to act in the face of our uncertainty (considerations of goodness already overshadow issues of truth).

Theory and its limits

The theme of theory and its limits is brought into sharp focus by a collection of essays edited by Alan Sica called, *What is Social Theory? The Philosophical Debates*.[69] The book engages the question of theory at two levels – what we might call the level of grand theory that presents a synoptic view of human nature and society, and the level of testable theory that consists of much more humbly stated propositions that are subjected to empirical testing. Assorted (but related) dilemmas confront theorizing at both levels, and these in many ways constitute the center of gravity of the book.

The dilemmas that beset grand theory are evident in Robert J. Antonio's treatment of what he calls "epistemological perspectivism."[70] For example, he says that "moderate perspectivists" adhere to "conditional ideas of 'objectivity'" and "argue that 'facts' are culturally constituted ... They reject exaggerated claims about the certainty and sweeping scope of knowledge."[71] In a footnote, Antonio adds: "Because of the lack of a readily identifiable alternative, I employ 'epistemology' with reservations. In this context, the term is contradictory, because it has been entwined with the West's representational theory of knowledge (i.e., 'philosophy of the subject' or 'spectator theory') stressing the subject-object dichotomy, primacy of theory, external truth, and knowledge producers as disembodied, neutral eyes."[72] Antonio here touches upon a raw nerve of postmodernist theory, which he deals with in altogether too peremptory a way. Is postmodernism post-theoretical (however one chooses to construe this statement) – or is it a recognizable continuation of the Western theoretical tradition or series of traditions?

The dilemma encapsulated in this broad question can be very distinctly localized and rendered familiar. It harks back to dilemmas surrounding formulations of skepticism from the time of the ancients onward. The "conditional ideas of objectivity" that animate even moderate postmodernists evoke the specter of a world that is largely humanly collectively constructed and sustained. The conceptual markers through which we identify and interact with the physical and social universes in which we have our being are largely a function of human management and assertiveness socially tested and transmitted. Moderate perspectivism as a predominantly skeptical thesis raises a serious issue of reflexivity – of consistency. The moderate perspectivist views perspectivally all claims to knowledge except his own moderate perspectivism. This he implicitly claims to know unconditionally because it serves as a basis for deflating the claims of all other pretenders to knowledge. Antonio recognizes the problem because in the footnote I have quoted he expresses his reservations about using the term "epistemology" altogether to define the position of the moderate perspectivist. However, this seems like too short and question-begging a way to deal with an extremely dense and complicated issue. The skeptic who inconsistently refuses to question his own skepticism can still be accommodated under the rubrics of sets of moves that occupy appropriate niches in the history of logic. Multivalued logics have come to the foreground in the late 19th and 20th centuries as a means for encoding the suspension of the Law of the Excluded Middle, so that logical nomenclature would exist for configuring what look like contradictory statements in ways that given the new notational rubrics sidestep the issue of contradiction. Multivalued logics dissolve the issue of contradiction by normalizing it – designing new sets of conceptual and logical moves and protocols that enshrine these possibilities instead of rejecting them.

A world that is perceived and analyzed under the prism of multivalued logics thus involves a jettisoning not only of Aristotle's Law of the Excluded Middle, but of his Law of Non-Contradiction as well. It is a world that seems in many ways exotically different from the world we currently inhabit. What would make it less strange would be our cultivation of a generalized agnosticism that stipulated that the returns were not yet fully in concerning what the world was like – so that we remained open to the possibility that multivalued logics might capture more accurately what the structure of the world is like than the traditional Aristotelian logic. In this alternative narrative, postmodernism is continuous with the Western past – a kind of philosophical and cultural analogue to developments in modern theoretical physics (which have also stimulated multivalued logical construals of their findings), rather than constituting a rupture with that past.

Postmodernism, at least in the form made famous by Jean-Francois Lyotard in *The Postmodern Condition: A Report on Knowledge*,[73] rebels against the duplicating effects of vocabularies of justification. In its suspicion of meta-narrativity, it seeks to redraw the theoretical landscape so that a statement's legitimacy is established independently of the theoretical umbrella under which it might be subsumed. Where I differ from Lyotard is in my attempt to formally approximate to a postmodernist position utilizing modernist logical justificatory tools. If we deem postmodernism persuasive in its delegitimation of the justificatory enterprise, we can then make the central point that moderate perspectivists want to make about the prevalence of skepticism without having to be concerned about the impact that the denial of knowledge has on our knowledge about the lack of knowledge (the consistency issue). From a postmodernist perspective, we can dissociate the individual points that the skeptic is making from their background assumptions and implications, and thus denial is severable from our inability to fix the (conceptual) object of denial.

Recourse to multivalued logics coupled with a generalized agnosticism enables me to achieve equivalence with the postmodernist argument about severability without having to accept the grandiose meta-theoretical claims of postmodernism concerning the dispensability of justification. With regard to these claims, I believe that the most telling counterargument is the one that emphasizes that the very formulation of (rational) arguments against modernism attests to the endurance of issues of consistency, of self-referentialism. These issues haunt and undermine some of the most melodramatic and flamboyant of the postmodernist critiques of modernism. I would characterize my modernism as formal and procedural. It consists in arguing in defense of multivalued logics and a generalized agnosticism as the most appropriate and revealing argumentative structures for capturing our "foundationless" argumentative plight. From a modernist perspective that invokes a generalized agnosticism and multivalued logics, we can make the same case that postmodernists make (and proclaim as their great breakthrough) about the severability of our assertions from their presuppositions and implications. We can logically legitimate the skeptic being skeptical about everything but his own skepticism. The choice of the postmodernist label, therefore, seems purely honorific, that is, a matter of one's linguistic and stylistic preferences.

Alternatively, I can even make my argument without referring to non-standard or multivalued logics. Since the proponents of moderate epistemological perspectivism are not able to absorb the application of this critical canon in relation to their own position, they are willy-nilly thrust into a generalized-agnostic stance. Since as we have seen the formulation of even moderate epistemological perspectivism is predicated upon a non-perspectival position (the advocates of this position want to claim that it is non-perspectivally true), their mobilization of this position against positions other than their own cancels itself out and yields a generalized agnosticism.

Thomas Nagel, in *The Last Word*, where he defends varieties of realism across a whole spectrum of subfields in philosophy, strategically notes that the target of his attacks is subjectivism rather than skepticism: "In general, I'll use the term 'subjectivism' rather than 'skepticism,' to avoid confusion with the kind of epistemological skepticism that actually relies on the objectivity of reason, rather than challenging it."[74] In the light of this formulation, it is not surprising that Nagel later embraces a version of a generalized agnosticism that is not out of step with the argument of this book: "The aim of universal validity is compatible with the willingness always to consider alternatives and counterarguments – *but they must be considered as candidates for objectively valid alternatives and arguments*. It is possible to accept a form of rationalism without committing oneself to a closed set of self-evident foundational truths."⁷⁵

Antonio identifies radical epistemological perspectivism with "a pure textualism that withholds epistemological privilege from all narratives, suspending completely all judgments based on representational grounds or on the relative truth or falsity of depictions of 'realities' beyond the text. Rather, they focus on 'language games' or 'discursive practices.'"⁷⁶ Many feminists are concerned about the conservative political implications of radical epistemological perspectivism: "Scholars pronounce the death of the subject and of authoritative knowledge just at the point where women, minorities, the oppressed and the previously unspoken and unauthored begin to theorize and speak authoritatively and *knowledgably*, from experience and in various communities, about their silence and oppression."⁷⁷

Again, the political dilemmas surrounding textualism result from not taking sufficiently seriously issues of reflexivity surrounding formulations of skepticism. Taking those issues seriously leads to a recoil from a full expression of skepticism and thereby also liberates and sanctions those political practices that proponents of political radicalism would argue are conducive to the achievement of greater justice and equality. Since textualism as a variety of extreme skepticism is not able to absorb the application of its own critical tenets in relation to itself, it devolves into a species of a generalized agnosticism that creates space for radical political action.

The metaphysical and political dilemmas attendant to textualism are most acutely present in the writings of Michel Foucault. In order to make his case for the pervasiveness of power, Foucault relies on the textualist thesis that meaning is underdetermined by text and that, therefore, in order to account for which interpretations of particular texts historically manage to gain prominence, we must have recourse to a power hypothesis. For Foucault, the order of sexuality and schemes of punishment are texts, and he traces the role of power and the suppression of the other in even these most minimal and characteristic orderings of personality and social relations. To the extent that Foucault adheres to the thesis of textuality – that meaning is underdetermined by text and that, therefore, the interpretation of all texts is literally endless – he is debarred from crossing the boundary from the texts of sexuality and punishment (one that allows for the continuing play of signifiers) to an external reading (one that shifts the burden of interpretation and explanation to worldly configurations of power that shape and distort the constructions that we make). The two halves of the textualist thesis are in sharp tension with each other. If texts are permanently unfinished – they can always go on being interpreted if there is nothing in the text itself that allows for or certifies to closure of interpretation – then a power hypothesis has nothing to latch on to. If a fixed and determinate text can never be authoritatively secured, there is nothing for a power hypothesis to be *about*. If the resources of internal interpretive play can never be (theoretically) exhausted, then it would appear that an external approach that connects interpretation with certain configurations of power in the world can be endlessly deferred. The intellectual space for it will have been denied as long as internalist readings that make only minimal and indirect reference to the world can go on being played out forever.

Foucault's procedure of analysis presupposes some version of positivism – that particular readings of texts are allowed to remain as they are and are not susceptible to more imaginative readings – in order to create theoretical space for his thesis concerning the ubiquity of power to work. The controversy between Foucault and Derrida concerning how to interpret the *cogito* passage in Descartes[78] – with Foucault arguing for complicity between Descartes and medical-juridical structures in excluding those that have been denominated as mad from reflective consideration concerning how human beings think, and Derrida pursuing a purely internalist reading that Descartes wants to call our most characteristic rationalistic processes into question on the basis of the universal experience of the dream state – can be translated and extended into Foucault's philosophy as a whole. It seems that one needs to choose between Foucault and Derrida. One cannot be a disciple of both.[79]

The problematic of textuality and power is far less disturbing in relation to Nietzsche than it is in relation to Foucault because Nietzsche's analyses of power are much less riveted in social analyses and social structuring. In Nietzsche, power is most often attendant upon the normal and traditional operations of the self, and the role of social and political institutions as engines of distortion is much less prominent in Nietzsche than it is in Foucault. It is Foucault's special grafting of Marx onto Nietzsche in his search for social analogues and manifestations of expressions and distortions of power that gives rise to the special tension that is evident in Foucault's writings.

Thomas Kuhn's philosophy of science,[80] which has had such widespread influence upon the humanities and social sciences, can also be understood as incorporating a textualist thesis. According to Kuhn, the will to truth manifested in the master paradigms of extraordinary science is generally undermined in the course of the traditional cyclical patterns of development of normal science, which was fashioned to institutionalize and refine the inspiring paradigms. Puzzles leading to anomalies impede the progressive extension and application of the original paradigms and eventually generate a crisis atmosphere that serves as the occasion for a new institutionalization of the will to truth. In Kuhn's depiction of how the enterprise of science works, efforts at theoretical totalization have their arbitrary character exposed by periodic "returns of the repressed," which unmask the aspirations to truth of the great theoretical innovators as potentially reducible to colossal assertions of power. This explication of the structure and development of science can be read as answering the questions that ask why no theories ever hold up completely and why none of them can be considered to be objectively representing the truth. To a certain extent, theories are textual artifacts and, as such, are always at one remove from the world. The project of interpreting them only fortuitously coincides with the project of finding out the truth about the world.

Turning to phenomenology as a model for doing social theory does not alleviate any of the paradoxes we have been considering. Phenomenology emphasizes "an *experiential turn* that focuses theoretical attention on the wherewithal and presuppositions of human experiencing. In the social sciences that shift shows up in renewed engagement with those qualitative methods where narrators' experiences command center stage."[81] In the words of Maurice Natanson: "Phenomenology turns with great patience to the detailed and the minute and seeks to illuminate the specificity and the uniqueness of what gives us a world. The result is a liberation of detail, an epiphany of the familiar."[82] A feminist philosopher of science such as Evelyn Fox Keller seeks to study the relationship between a scientific investigator and her subject matter in phenomenological terms – to theorize what the scientist is doing as she goes about her daily work and to have that serve as the appropriate focus for philosophical analysis.[83]

What is problematic in this approach is that while experience is intimate, personal and unmistakable, the vocabulary for describing it is not. The language that we use to describe even the most personally affecting experience is underdetermined by that experience. There are multiple conceptual frameworks to capture even the most poignant and urgent experiences. It is misguided to think that immediacy yields certainty. Furthermore, a phenomenologist such as Natanson, in *theorizing* immediacy, has already derogated from the immediacy and certainty that his theory seeks.

Steven Fuller's social epistemology is also bedeviled by certain issues of skepticism that it is not able to tame. Fuller describes social epistemology as "a normative sociology of knowledge."[84] By this, he means an attempt to recapture "the conditions to which those texts [that one is seeking to understand] might be construed as a reasonable response."[85] Adapting R. G. Collingwood's approach in *The Idea of History*,[86] Fuller seeks to recover those questions "that form the 'absolute presuppositions' of his [a theorist's] inquiry."[87] Fuller illustrates his approach by showing the diverse ways in which Friedrich Nietzsche, Leo Strauss and Alvin Gouldner reconstruct Plato. These theorists are less concerned with the content of Plato's thought than with its context – the questions that it was implicitly trying to answer, rather than with the substantive content of the answers provided. Their point of intersection with Plato was in their diverse appreciation of the questions he was implicitly trying to answer, rather than with the presumably intrinsically recoverable content of his answers per se.

There are two methodological concerns that this approach evokes. The first is that it invites a social epistemological approach to itself that would involve a displacement of its content by its context, and the resulting evisceration of its methodological content would leave us little to go by in applying its "method." The second concern has to do with the unbounded character of the questions to which a philosopher's text can be construed as a response. As Hans-Georg Gadamer has emphasized in his philosophy of hermeneutics,[88] in many respects it makes sense to view texts as dialogical exercises – partnered acts – that require the active interrogation of subsequent generations of readers in order to even transiently complete their trajectories. The underdetermination of meaning by text (how possibilities of contextualization and recontextualization remain continually open to us) delegitimates our privileging Plato's or any other theorist's questions ("generated" by their texts) in relation to our own.

Stephen Turner's "Making Normative Soup from Non-Normative Bones"[89] focuses upon Robert Brandom's book, *Making it Explicit*,[90] in trying to account for the phenomenon of normativity: "Brandom asks what justifies explicit normative assertions, such as statements about the correctness or incorrectness of actions and claims, and says that the best explanation is this: ultimately justification rests on implicit norms or 'practices,' meaning, for him, regularities of action which are normative."[91] There are two largely Wittgensteinian arguments that Brandom offers in favor of this conception. The first argument attempts to shut off an infinite regress. Since rules are not self-applying, one cannot point to a rule as a source of obligation in bringing the justificatory quest to an end. In applying a rule, one still needs to invoke implicit rules in deciding upon questions of application. The implicit rules, in turn, presuppose prior rules. The search for justification, therefore, can only stop "at the point of implicit norms or practices."[92] In the end, the social efficacy of practices has to be translated in a normative, non-tautologous way as the statement that "you do it because you do it." The practice itself becomes the norm, without any further elaboration being necessary or possible.

The second argument, which is inspired by Kripke's work on Wittgenstein, centers on what Brandom calls the "gerrymandering problem." Brandom utilizes Kripke and Wittgenstein's example: "Although we 'naturally' continue the series 2,4,6,8 with the rest of the even numbers, there is, and can be, no mathematical reason for doing so."[93] Since there is "such a large array of possible rules or possible sequences" that "are theoretically consistent with the claim that they continue the series 2,4,6,8," the sealing off of these theoretical possibilities so as to ensure the gerrymandered result that 10 becomes the next number in the series has to be seen as resulting from the implicit normativity of the social practice governing the construction of the series.

Turner (following Brandom) seems to have been captivated by the optical illusion spun by Wittgenstein and some of his most vocal followers to the effect that skepticism can be sidestepped and certainty achieved by acknowledging the centrality of "language games" for grappling with philosophical issues. The deceptive tolerance that pervades the surface of Wittgenstein's argument in the *Philosophical Investigations*[94] leads one to think that, epistemologically speaking, "anything goes." But, epistemologically speaking, "anything goes" only because metaphysically – ontologically – speaking, nothing matters. Whether the topic is the laws of logic or the foundations of mathematics, religion or esthetics, the moves that we make in these disparate regions of discourse are ultimately grounded in "the linguistic practices which embody them" – and nothing else.[95]

The most fruitful way to conceptualize the pattern of unity linking the *Tractatus Logico-Philosophicus*[96] with the intervening works of the 1930s and the *Philosophical Investigations* is in terms of a broadening and deepening skepticism. The doctrine of logical atomism that is integral to Wittgenstein's argument in the *Tractatus* leads to the exclusion of certain regions of experience (the ethical, the esthetic, the religious and the philosophical) as falling outside the scope of rational resolution within language. These areas of experience have been completely "privatized," being confined to inner states of feeling and having no objective translation in the shared resources of language. One might say that the *Investigations* completes the project begun in the *Tractatus*. In the *Tractatus*, a good deal of ordinary language can still be salvaged as a vehicle of knowledge and truth. In the *Investigations*, ordinary discourse itself emerges as problematic in character. There are no external points of reference by which to verify even our typical, everyday assertions, so that with regard to the "brute" facts of any given situation, the agent's "institutional" description enjoys no logical priority over that of any other observer.[97] The "privatization" of our experience begun in the *Tractatus* is extended in the *Investigations* from the more specialized realms of esthetics, religion, ethics and philosophy to encompass our everyday transactions with the world, staked out and captured by ordinary language.

From nearly all of the angles explored in *What is Social Theory?*, macro theory emerges as exceedingly vulnerable. It is most often the case that this theory is either a disguised or displaced form of skepticism as in Wittgenstein or Foucault, or, at best, that its critical canon cannot be reflexively sustained. When macro theory is a disguised or displaced form of skepticism, it is only sustainable under the aegis of multivalued logics coupled with a generalized agnosticism – or as a generalized agnosticism taken by itself. When macro theory's critical canon cannot be reflexively sustained, it ends up willy-nilly espousing a generalized-agnostic position since its critical canon cancels itself out.

What is Social Theory? illustrates for us that micro theory fares no better, from a meta-theoretical perspective, than does macro theory. In his essay, "Theoretical Models: Sociology's Missing Links," John Skvoretz expresses his preference for theoretical models above methodological models in doing sociological work. According to Skvoretz, "theoretical models have a number of advantages as links between theory and data [over methodological models] because they more clearly state and more accurately represent a theory's claims."[98] Methodological models, by contrast, "summarize data by general-effect parameters which have no specific referent to theoretical constructs. On the other hand, estimates of parameters in theoretical models have direct interpretation in terms of key theoretical constructs."[99] Theoretical models are thus favored over methodological models for sociological research because of their avowedly more circular character: They exhibit a reciprocal and mutually supportive relationship with the data they purport to explain and interpret. Because of their more content-rich nature in contrast to methodological models, they constitute more fruitful frameworks for sociological generalization.

On a deeper level than that upon which Skvoretz's analysis explicitly elaborates, the explanatory pretensions of sociological theory (and its problematic seems to be symptomatic of social science theory more generally) seem impaled upon the horns of a dilemma. Skvoretz condemns methodological models for surreptitiously and illegitimately bridging the theory-data gulf because in them "theory becomes a matter of informal guesswork about which variables affect which others and in what directions."[100] In other words, the vacuousness and regressive character of methodological models (which depend upon their theoretical presuppositions in order to be a source of explanation at all) signify that when connections are drawn between explanatory variables and empirical outcomes they are supplied by the researcher rather than being disinterestedly generated by his official investigative apparatus. Whatever content thus emerges from the application of methodological models to sociological phenomena can therefore be classified as circular. The situation does not improve by substituting theoretical models for methodological models in sociological research. Now there is content to our theories – but it has been pre-supplied by the orientation of our theories. Since the identifying categories for making sense of our data come from our theories, the data in our theory-data relationship are already being configured to conform to the understandings encapsulated in our theories – rather than being neutrally observed and assessed. The upshot of my analysis is that we end up with circularity either way. In methodological models, the emptiness is expressive of circularity. In theoretical models, it is the content that is expressive of circularity.

If circularity seems to be our destiny on the level of micro theory, then it is worth noting that a generalized agnosticism (as we have seen) contributes to normalizing our condition of enduring circularity. From a generalized-agnostic perspective, the returns are never fully in with regard to any phenomenon that we are concerned to explicate. In order to proceed to a level of even provisional closure and to be able to theorize and explain a "particular phenomenon," we must nurture the illusion that the returns are in – that the speculative questions hovering over the conceptual penumbra of the categories constituting our domains of theory and fact and demarcating between them have already been resolved. Their lack of resolution – and perhaps their irresolvability – yield the yardstick in terms of which we can measure the extent to which we will have assumed what our scientific projects were designed to prove.

Theorizing, as I practice it in the writing of this book, is largely negative in character. It consists in the exposing of limitations – rather than in the clinching of positive points. To forestall the redescription of the negative character of theorizing as a positive achievement, I have adopted a generalized agnosticism, which means that I acknowledge at the outset the possibility of the supersession of my own position. If what is taken for the most part to be theory in *What is Social Theory?* is not real theory, then one ends up with a ratification or reification or re-legitimization of the status quo. Theory (as Michael Oakeshott repeatedly reminds his readers) conjures up the possibilities out of which facts are generated.[101] In my idiom, theory focuses upon the ways in which our classifications of fact remain underdetermined – how there is generally more than one way to make sense of groupings of fact. Where there is no viable theory in the critically self-aware way that I am defining here, all one is left with is fact – i.e. a reflection of the status quo. From this perspective, sociology and the other social sciences conceived in its image or following in its footsteps emerge as new forms of domination – as power grabs – by continually evolving constellations of power-knowledge.

Instrumentalist conceptions of self-knowledge and scientific knowledge can be viewed as the heirs of the skeptical critiques of knowledge discussed here. The negative character of theorizing that is captured by Steven Rytina in his essay in *What is Social Theory?* by such formulations as "Even the most comprehensive deductive reconstruction must somewhere come to ultimate premises and these, for better and for worse, stand on nothing" and "The largest questions are only askable, not answerable"[102] perhaps achieves its most effective translation as a philosophy of instrumentalism. If theory is largely negative in the ways I have described, then its most useful role is as a prodder and a prier to keep us sufficiently loose and flexible to maximize practical and theoretical opportunities at every stage and every moment of our lives.

For example, the choice in our theories of knowledge between literalism and realism, on the one hand, and constructivism, on the other, can be construed as largely an instrumentalist one. Since underdetermination suffuses the relationship between theories and words and things, even terms like "realism" exceed the warrant of their own reference pool. The term (category) "realism" is itself a constructivist label. I have argued elsewhere how the nominalism associated with negative theology, as well as negative theology itself, are morally salutary because, by enhancing our awareness of human freedom, they correspondingly increase our responsibility and our sense of accountability for the worlds that we construct and inhabit.[103] However, there are occasions when we experience our freedom as a blockage. Being free to structure and orient our lives in directions we find meaningful, we yearn for elements of necessity that take us beyond ourselves and provide us with clear, secure markings concerning where we are, where we should be going and how to get there. The instrumentalized ontological space that realism occupies according to my conception means that we are free to invoke "realist" factors to provide us with a sense of orientation and direction in our theoretical and practical quests. From a generalized-agnostic perspective, realism is on no more – and no less – a secure footing than constructivism or skepticism. Therefore, an instrumentalized usage of both realism and its theoretical antagonists makes sense. If realism gives us a more confident sense than skepticism in navigating our own lives, then there is no philosophical barrier to our temporarily adopting it. Our instrumentalist approach to the conduct of our own lives engenders in us an awareness of and commitment to its process-character: How the various substantive packages that go to constitute our intellectual understandings and moral beliefs and values are ontologically situated as instrumentalist probes and levers to enable us to move from where we are to where we inchoately want (and are able) to go.

Our philosophy of science needs to encapsulate the relationship between self and world that I have just summarized. Facts are low-level theories – and theories are underdetermined by facts. Their relationship is largely instrumental. There are theoretically alternative ways for conceiving of both the nature and content of theories and the facts that they help to situate and identify. In the end, whatever constellations of theory-fact exist for us have a largely instrumentalist status in enabling us to move about our worlds with the fluency and grace we desire. Just as in the individual's relationship to the notions he considers realist and to those he regards as constructed, so too, in the fabric of science conceived of as a whole, the overriding factor governing stability and change is the nurturance of movement – of process – itself. In a direct challenge to and inversion of common sense approaches to science, we need to see its substantive content as subordinate to the most economical and masterful maintenance of process – of unencumbered, agile movement. The dilemmas that beset the philosophy of science – whether there is theoretical progress and how it might best be registered; how to meta-theoretically configure the relationship between theories and data or facts, so that the explanations that result from their juxtaposition are non-circular; how to address issues of self-referentialism in philosophical, scientific and everyday formulations, so that dilemmas surrounding discourse do not end up mystifying our grasp of the possibilities of scientific formulation – are all most fruitfully addressed from the organizing perspective I am advancing here.

God, the world, and the self share a common precariousness when viewed from a generalized-agnostic perspective. We can never be sure that our conceptualizations and the apparent advances and refinements that occur between them could not have been other than what they were and thus yielded alternative (equally satisfying – or even enhanced) mappings and identifications of reality. We lack the final assurance that the world is what our theories say it is because of the nagging and irremovable doubt that different conceptual nets would have captured different aspects of "reality" that would have insinuated alternative conceptions of manageability and advance. We do not have access to a sufficiently conceptually unadorned reality to be able to test which set of conceptualizations more accurately reflects the nature of reality. The assessment of theories is done in relation to a theoretically tainted reality that allows for retail judgments (validations) in the face of a range of wholesale pre-commitments. If we were to suspend those pre-commitments, we would not have a "reality" available to interrogate for purposes of our experiments. The linkage between the world and our theories is too mutually supportive to sustain the claim of neutral knowledge of the world as it is.

From a negative-theological perspective, we are equally debarred from making the claim that we know what God is like in and for Himself. God, as the most fundamental explanatory factor in the creation and governance of the world, has to be so totally conceptually distanced from the phenomena He is invoked to explain that further probing becomes logically impossible and the explanatory quest can be satisfactorily halted. The price we pay for attaining closure by affirming unbridgeable infinite distance is that we can never be sure that our descriptions of Divine attributes and behavior are ever more than metaphors answerable to various human needs and purposes, but do not transparently disclose to us the nature of God.

The dilemma that we face in searching for the most ultimate explanatory factor gets replicated on an immediate human level as soon as we embark upon any circumscribed explanatory quest. When we seek to explain a phenomenon, we pose to it a question or set of questions that configure it to generate responses or clues that address our questions. We have no way of reliably determining whether these match the authentic, enduring content of the phenomenon in question. Our scientific descriptions end up harboring a metaphorical taint that is a function of the human needs and purposes that spawned them, rather than opening an unequivocal window onto nature. Just as with God, the search for local explanations themselves goes a long way toward ensuring that the subject of explanation (the factor or factors doing the explaining) will be placed permanently, metaphorically beyond reach.

Human nature is as opaque as God and the world. We have access to ourselves only through internal and external dialogue by questioning ourselves or others questioning us and thereby bringing aspects of our character and behavior into bold relief. It is the interrogation and exploration that brings forth a self, so that the self that emerges is skewed in the directions highlighted by the questions and probings. In this sense, therefore, the languages of the self are also metaphorically tainted, and we are left wondering about the status and character of the self abstracted from internal and external dialogical settings.

Notes

1 Emmanuel Levinas, *Proper Names*. Trans. Michael B. Smith. (Stanford: Stanford University Press, 1996), p. 23; emphasis in original.
2 Ibid., p. 22.
3 Ibid., p. 33.
4 Ibid., p. 23; italics in original.
5 Ibid., p. 24.
6 Ibid., p. 33.
7 Ibid., p. 35.
8 Ibid., p. 24.

9 Ibid., p. 29.
10 Ibid.
11 This set of contrasting terms comes from Leo Baeck, *Judaism and Christianity: Five Essays* (Philadelphia: Jewish Publication Society, 1958), pp. 171–185.
12 Levinas, *Proper Names*, p. 38.
13 Ibid., pp. 55–62.
14 Ibid., p. 58.
15 Ibid., p. 59.
16 Ibid., p. 60.
17 Ibid.
18 Ibid., p. 58.
19 Ibid., p. 59; emphasis in original.
20 Ibid., p. 61
21 Levinas, *Totality and Infinity*, p.78; cited in Robert Bernasconi and Simon Critchley, eds., *Re-Reading Levinas* (Bloomington: Indiana University Press, 1991), p. 150.
22 Jacques Derrida, "The Politics of Friendship," *Journal of Philosophy*, Volume 85, Number 11 (November 1988); Jacques Derrida, *Politics of Friendship*. Trans. George Collins. (London: Verso, 1997).
23 Fred R. Dallmayr, *Achieving Our World: Toward a Global and Plural Democracy* (Lanham: Rowman & Littlefield, 2001), p. 150.
24 See Levinas' essay on Blanchot ("The Servant and her Master") in *Proper Names*, pp. 140–149.
25 Dallmayr, *Achieving Our World*, p. 162.
26 Plato, *Phaedrus*. Trans. W. C. Helmbold and W. G. Rabinowitz. (Indianapolis: Library of Liberal Arts, 1956), 241b–241c (p. 21).
27 Ibid., 238e-239a (p. 18).
28 Ibid., 249d-249e (p. 33).
29 Ibid., 249b-249d (p. 32).
30 Ibid., 255d (p. 40).
31 Dallmayr, *Achieving Our World*, p. 164.
32 Jacques Derrida, *Specters of Marx: The State of the Debt, the Work of Mourning, and the New International*. Trans. Peggy Kamuf. (London: Routledge, 1994), p. 55.
33 Walter Benjamin, *Illuminations*. Ed. Hannah Arendt; trans. Harry Zohn. (New York: Schocken Books, 1968), p. 254.
34 Paul Ricoeur, *Oneself as Another*. Trans. Kathleen Blamey. (Chicago: University of Chicago Press, 1992), p. 336.
35 Ibid., p. 335.
36 Ibid., p. 336.
37 Ibid., p. 337.
38 Ibid., pp. 337–338.
39 Levinas, *Otherwise than Being*, pp. 113–118.
40 Ibid., p. 118.
41 Ibid.; cited in Ricoeur, *Oneself as Another*, p. 338.
42 Ibid., p. 337; italics in original.
43 Ibid.
44 Ibid., p. 339.
45 Ibid.
46 Derek Parfit, *Reasons and Persons* (Oxford: Clarendon Press, 1984).
47 Derek Parfit, "Personal Identity," in John Perry, ed., *Personal Identity* (Berkeley: University of California Press, 1975), p. 209.
48 Saul Kripke, *Wittgenstein on Rules and Private Language: An Elementary Exposition* (Oxford: Basil Blackwell, 1982), pp. 7–8; 68–69; 73.

49 David Hume, *A Treatise of Human Nature*. Second Edition. Ed. L. A. Selby-Bigge and P. H. Nidditch. (Oxford: Clarendon Press, 1978), pp. 633–636.
50 Ibid., p. 636.
51 Matthew H. Kramer, *Legal Theory, Political Theory, and Deconstruction: Against Rhadamanthus* (Bloomington: Indiana University Press, 1991), p. 148.
52 Ibid., p. 203.
53 Ricoeur, *Oneself as Another*, p. 138.
54 Ibid. The intra-quote citations come from Parfit, *Reasons and Persons*, p. 341.
55 Jurgen Habermas, *Moral Consciousness and Communicative Action*. Trans. Christian Lenhardt and Shierry Weber Nicholsen. (Cambridge: MIT Press, 1990), p. 45. Habermas is paraphrasing P. F. Strawson's argument in *Freedom and Resentment, and Other Essays* (London: Methuen, 1974).
56 Ronald Dworkin, *Taking Rights Seriously* (Cambridge: Harvard University Press, 1977), p. 152.
57 Sigmund Freud, *An Outline of Psychoanalysis*. Trans. James Strachey. (New York: W. W. Norton, 1969), p. 31.
58 This formulation presupposes the validity of W. V. Quine's argument in "Two Dogmas of Empiricism" (W. V. Quine, *From a Logical Point of View*, pp. 20–46) that it is the totality of the statements that we take to be true that is hauled before the bar of experience in the face of any given adverse experience; and that therefore the line demarcating between analytic and synthetic statements is shifting and pragmatic – ultimately (but not immediately) rectifiable in the light of experience.
59 Wilfrid Sellars, in his classic essay, "Empiricism and the Philosophy of Mind" (in Herbert Feigl and Michael Scriven, eds., *The Foundations of Science and the Concepts of Psychology and Psychoanalysis. Minnesota Studies in the Philosophy of Science Volume I.* [Minneapolis: University of Minnesota Press, 1956], pp. 253–329) underscores the virtue of circularity: "For empirical knowledge, like its sophisticated extension, science, is rational, not because it has a *foundation* but because it is a self-correcting enterprise which can put *any* claim in jeopardy, though not *all* at once." (p. 300; emphases in original).
60 "It is so difficult to find the *beginning*. Or, better: it is difficult to begin at the beginning. And not try to go further back." Ludwig Wittgenstein, *On Certainty*. Eds. G. E. M. Anscombe and G. H. von Wright; trans. Denis Paul and G. E. M. Anscombe. (New York: Harper & Row, 1972), Aphorism Number 471, p. 62e.
61 Sellars, in Feigl and Scriven, pp. 293–300.
62 John McDowell, *Mind and World* (Cambridge: Harvard University Press, 1996), p. 7.
63 Ibid., p. 8.
64 Ibid., p. 40.
65 Ibid., pp. 40–41.
66 Ibid., p. 126.
67 Among the most prominent and influential contributions to this genre are the following: T. W. Adorno *et al.*, *The Authoritarian Personality* (New York: W. W. Norton, 1969); Karl R. Popper, *The Open Society and its Enemies. Volume 1: Plato. Volume 2: Hegel and Marx* (London: Routledge & Kegan Paul, 1945); Karl R. Popper, *The Poverty of Historicism* (New York: Harper & Row, 1964); Michael Oakeshott, "The Masses in Representative Democracy," in Michael Oakeshott, *Rationalism in Politics and Other Essays*. New and Expanded Edition. (Indianapolis: Liberty Press, 1991), pp. 363–383.
68 Clifford Geertz, *The Interpretation of Cultures* (New York: Basic Books, 1973), p. 210.
69 Alan Sica, ed., *What is Social Theory? The Philosophical Debates* (Oxford: Blackwell, 1998).

70 Ibid., p. 31.
71 Ibid.
72 Ibid., FN 15.
73 Jean-Francois Lyotard, *The Postmodern Condition: A Report on Knowledge*. Trans. Geoff Bennington and Brian Massumi. (Minneapolis: University of Minnesota Press, 1984).
74 Thomas Nagel, *The Last Word* (Oxford: Oxford University Press, 1997), p. 4n.
75 Ibid., p. 69; emphasis in original.
76 Sica, *What is Social Theory?*, p. 33.
77 Jennifer L. Croissant, "Criteria for a Theory of Knowledge," in Sica, *What is Social Theory?*, p. 150; emphasis in original.
78 Descartes' original statement was "Je pense donc je suis," which appeared in his *Discourse on Method* in 1637. Descartes used the Latin "Cogito ergo sum" in his later *Principles of Philosophy* (1644), Part 1, Article 7.
79 See the article by Robert D'Amico, "Text and Context: Derrida and Foucault on Descartes," in John Fekete, ed., *The Structural Allegory: Reconstructive Encounters with the New French Thought* (Minneapolis: University of Minnesota Press, 1984), pp. 164–182.
80 Thomas S. Kuhn, *The Structure of Scientific Revolutions*. Second Edition. (Chicago: University of Chicago Press, 1970).
81 Mary F. Rogers, "A Thesaurus of Experience: Maurice Natanson, Phenomenology, and Social Theory," in Sica, *What is Social Theory?*, p. 76; emphasis in original.
82 Cited in ibid., p. 80.
83 Ibid., p. 86.
84 Ibid., p. 95.
85 Ibid., p. 96.
86 R. G. Collingwood, *The Idea of History* (Oxford: Oxford University Press, 1946).
87 Sica, *What is Social Theory?*, p. 96.
88 *Truth and Method* (1960), which has been reprinted in numerous editions in German and in English.
89 Sica, *What is Social Theory?*, pp. 118–144.
90 Robert B. Brandom, *Making it Explicit: Reasoning, Representing, and Discursive Commitment* (Cambridge: Harvard University Press, 1994).
91 Sica, *What is Social Theory?*, p. 119.
92 Ibid., p. 120.
93 Ibid.
94 Ludwig Wittgenstein, *Philosophical Investigations*. Third Edition. Trans. G. E. M. Anscombe (New York: Macmillan, 1969).
95 David Pears, *Ludwig Wittgenstein* (New York: Viking Press, 1970), p. 179.
96 Ludwig Wittgenstein, *Tractatus Logico-Philosophicus*. Trans. D. F. Pears and B. F. McGuinness. (London: Routledge and Kegan Paul, 1961).
97 See the classic paper by G. E. M. Anscombe, "On Brute Facts," *Analysis* Volume 18 (1958): pp. 69–72.
98 Sica, *What is Social Theory?*, p. 248.
99 Ibid.
100 Ibid., p. 251.
101 "There can be no absolute distinction between 'fact' and 'theorem.' A fact has no finality and no authority over further adventures in understanding: it is a first and conditionally acceptable understanding of a 'going-on.'" Michael Oakeshott, *On Human Conduct* (Oxford: Clarendon Press, 1975), p. 2.
102 Ibid., pp. 197; 217.
103 See my book, *Skepticism, Belief, and the Modern*, pp. 36; 104–108; 78–79; 118–119; 160–161.

6 An ethics of theory vs. an ethics of ideology

Aristotle's ethics as an exemplar of an ethics of theory

Returning to the distinction that I drew earlier between an ethics of ideology and an ethics of theory, I would argue that Aristotle's ethics represents a prime example of an ethics of theory. The major regulative principle of Aristotle's ethics is the Theory of the Mean. This theory, however, illustrates how philosophical statements that are officially neutral with regard to issues of skepticism eventuate in a position of extreme skepticism. Let us take as an example of the application of this theory what Aristotle has to say about anger:

> Mildness is the mean concerned with anger ... The person who is angry at the right things and towards the right people, and also in the right way, at the right time and for the right length of time, is praised. This, then, will be the mild person, since it is his mildness that is praised; for being a mild person means being undisturbed, not led by feeling, but irritated at whatever reason prescribes and for the length of time it prescribes. And he seems to err more in the direction of deficiency, since the mild person is ready to pardon, not eager to exact a penalty.
>
> The deficiency – a sort of inirascibility or whatever it is – is blamed, since people who are not angered by the right things, or in the right way, or at the right time, or towards the right people, all seem to be foolish. For such a person seems to be insensible and to feel no pain. Since he is not angered, he does not seem to be the sort to defend himself; and such willingness to accept insults to oneself and to overlook insults to one's family and friends is slavish.[1]

Aristotle delineates anger at strategically appropriate moments ("mildness") as a mean between two vices – a vice of excess, which is a proneness to anger, and a vice of deficiency, which is an "inirascible" or phlegmatic disposition. How about the Theory of the Mean? What is its status? Is the selection of the Theory of the Mean as the chief regulative principle of ethics itself a function of the mean? On the basis of what higher-order decision-making principle is

An ethics of theory vs. an ethics of ideology 89

the Theory of the Mean selected? With regard to the behavior options available to a moral agent, the Theory of the Mean decrees that one should choose the midpoint between two extremes. But on a higher level of decision-making – the Theory of the Mean vs. other competing moral principles – the contrasting elements are not extremes of behavior, but other guiding principles for moral action. Hence, the Theory of the Mean itself cannot be vindicated in terms of the mean, but only in terms of other unacknowledged decision-making principles. The application of a test of reflexivity (asking whether the Theory of the Mean can account for itself, that is, whether it can make sense of itself in terms of its own priority) dissolves the skeptically neutral character of the Theory of the Mean and discloses it as exemplifying a form of extreme skepticism. The validational (the intermediate justificatory) component of the Theory of the Mean is subsumed under its officially articulated content, but to tease out the vindicationist (the more ultimate justificatory) component requires one to ascend to higher levels of generality and abstraction to discover the theoretical alternatives and antagonists to the Theory of the Mean. At these higher levels of generality and abstraction, the alternatives to the Theory of the Mean (and the theory itself) continue to harbor validational as well as vindicationist elements that are partially resolved and partially deferred when the argument moves to a higher level of generality and abstraction, and so on indefinitely. The vindicationist procedure remains theoretically uncompletable, and serves to highlight the extent to which the initiating moves in argument are nominalistically supplied. From the perspective of this analysis, the floodgates have been opened to extreme skepticism – which one might argue is only sustainable as a generalized agnosticism.

Aristotle's theorizing of friendship – his affirmation of it as a moral ideal to which human beings should strive – is bound up with his larger Theory of the Mean. We might say that Aristotelian friendship constitutes the mean between love and hatred. The friend (in contrast to the lover or enemy) is coherently and rationally accessed and related to, rather than being primarily emotionally engaged. From this perspective, Aristotle's theorizing of friendship is directly continuous with and builds upon Plato's discussion of love in the *Phaedrus* (discussed in Chapter 5). The Otherness connoted by Aristotle's Theory of Friendship remains sustainable in the same way (and precisely to the same extent) that his overall Theory of the Mean is sustainable. The stability and autonomy of the Other is in many ways dependent upon the conceptualization and specification of the Same (in order to enable the Other to emerge as an independent entity and not just to constitute a fervent projection of the Same) – just as the stability and independence of the mean is dependent upon one's prior identification of the relevant extremes of moral action.

There are two striking ways in which Aristotle communicates to us in his discussion of the virtue of mildness itself his sense of the circular and generalized-agnostic character of his whole ethical argument. At 1126a5,[2]

Aristotle refers to the mean as "nameless" and he adds: "The extremes are practically nameless too." Apparently, both the mean and the extremes are nameless because the range of actions coming under each of these categories displays such a penumbra of vagueness that outside of the circular and partially retrospective specification of which actions one should emulate and which actions one should seek to avoid the Theory of the Mean would only insinuate a set of attitudes and predispositions and not harbor a precise content. This reading receives support from the way Aristotle concludes his discussion of the virtue of mildness:

> It is hard to define how, against whom, about what, and how long we should be angry, and up to what point someone is acting correctly or in error.
>
> For someone who deviates a little towards either excess or deficiency is not blamed. For sometimes we praise deficient people and say they are mild; and sometimes we say that people who get involved are manly because we think they are capable of ruling others.
>
> How far, then, and in what way must someone deviate to be open to blame? It is not easy to answer in a [general] account, since these are particular cases, and the judgment depends on perception.[3]

A second way in which Aristotle communicates to us in his discussion of mildness his sense of the insurmountably circular character of ethical argument is through his framing of the conceptual target of his ethical inquiry negatively: "How far, then, and in what way must someone deviate to be open to blame?" The crucial issues for moral deliberation and judgment are formulated negatively in terms of blame and deviation, rather than positively in terms of praise and appropriate action. From a circular, generalized-agnostic perspective, it is easier and clearer to pinpoint what one is ruling out than to indicate what one is embracing.

The repertoire of virtues that Aristotle identifies as conforming to the "nameless mean" – additional examples include courage poised between cowardice and rashness; generosity situated between niggardliness and prodigality; and temperance located between total abstinence and constant self-indulgence – conjures up an image of a human self continually emptying itself in readiness for the perpetual challenges thrown up by life. In advising us to opt for the middle course in each of the situations that he depicts, Aristotle appears motivated to nudge the self into an awareness of its powers and capacities, but at the same time also to deflect it away from any kind of overcommitment to particular strategies and patterns for actualizing them. Aristotle wants to nurture selves that are self-aware and versatile but not overfilled with content concerning who they are and what they can do. Moral virtue is associated by Aristotle with an endless process of de-rigidification. The extremes of behavior that Aristotle rejects involve either passivity, such as cowardice and inirascibility, which means that one is doing nothing in the face of the challenges and provocations of life, or a hyper-activated mode of response such as that epitomized by rashness and anger, which suggests that one is developing an activist correlative to passivity: One is bringing one's energies to a high pitch in responding to an immediate situation, but because the responses are mechanical and along the same track as they have always been, it is as if the rest of the self had gone to sleep (had remained dormant) in diagnosing and deliberating upon the immediate situation. Opting for the middle course appears to be Aristotle's philosophical therapy applied to the self in order to keep it loose and flexible – being open and subtle enough to discern nuances of novelty in evolving situations, so that the self will be enabled to respond freshly and to deflect circumstances in its favor. The Theory of the Mean is a proposal for continual self-emptying and loosening-up appropriate to a generalized-agnostic self situated in a circular dimension that needs to constantly adjust its background postulates and principles as well as its more immediate perceptions and judgments in relation to each other.

The mishnah in *Avot* 4:4 and the Theory of the Mean

There is a well-known mishnah[4] in *Avot* 4:4 that on the surface appears to contravene Aristotle's Theory of the Mean and that Maimonides in his commentary on *Avot* reinterprets as being in conformity with it. The mishnah reads as follows:

> Rabbi Levitas of Yavneh said: Be exceedingly lowly in spirit, for the anticipated end of mortal man is worms.[5]

The Hebrew phrase for which the words "be exceedingly" constitute the translation are *Me'od, Me'od*. In Hebrew, *Me'od* literally means "much" – so that a strictly literal rendition of the Hebrew would read "much, much." Being guided by the literal language of the Mishnaic text, one would then be prone to interpret its content as rejecting moderation and imploring us to go to the extremes of self-abnegation in terms of how we nurture our self-image and conduct our relationships with other people. This, indeed, is the way that Rabbeinu Yonah (died 1263; one of the classic medieval Rabbinic commentators on *Avot*) construes this mishnah. He says that "Even though veering toward the middle in all of the attributes is to be preferred, with regard to the attribute of haughtiness ('Gasut Haruach') one needs to distance oneself from it by going to the other extreme, since there is no attribute more severe [in its consequences] than this one and most of the transgressions of the Torah are dependent on it [are an outgrowth of it]."[6] Rabbeinu Yonah thus understands this mishnah to be saying that because *Gaavah* (haughtiness; an inflated sense of self) is so prevalent, tempting and pernicious, one needs to suspend adherence to the Golden Mean and pursue the other extreme of *Shiflut Haruach* ("lowliness of spirit") in order to avoid being ensnared by *Gaavah*.

The classic Mishnaic commentator Rabbeinu Ovadiah MiBartenura (1445–1515) echoes Rabbeinu Yonah in his approach to this mishnah: "Even though with regard to the other attributes the middle way is to be preferred, with regard to the attribute of Gaavah this is not so but one needs to veer to the opposite extreme of lowliness of spirit."[7]

Maimonides, in contrast to Rabbeinu Yonah and Rabbeinu Ovadiah MiBartenura, maps a reading of this text that subverts its literal import. He says: "We have already explained and mentioned in earlier chapters that humility ('Anavah') is among the most praiseworthy of the attributes and it is situated in the middle between 'Gaavah' and 'Shiflut Haruach' – and it has no other name but 'Anavah.'"[8] There are two things to notice about Maimonides' formulation: The first is how it contradicts the literal language of Rabbi Levitas' mishnah. Rabbi Levitas urges us to become *Shiflei Ruach* (lowly in spirit) – and Maimonides rejects this goal as the epitome of an extreme that a proper ethics shuns. According to Maimonides, Rabbi Levitas of Yavneh is referring to a prefatory stage that facilitates one's attaining the ethically maximal standard of behavior – and not to the ethically maximal standard itself. Maimonides suggests that sometimes one has to move to the opposite extreme from which one is prone to go in order to facilitate a movement to the middle which represents the *summum bonum*. *Gaavah* is such an overwhelming human temptation that the best way to come to *Anavah*, which embodies the mean, is by first surrendering oneself to the extreme that is the opposite of *Gaavah* (namely, *Shiflut Haruach*) as a means of gradually gravitating toward the ethical medium of *Anavah*.

The second thing to notice about Maimonides' formulation is that he says that the midpoint between *Gaavah* and *Shiflut Haruach* "has no other name but 'Anavah.'" Maimonides' wording suggests that, in the end, *Anavah* is just that – a name – in relation to which a corresponding reality has to be continually replotted and reinvented.

Rashi in his commentary on this mishnah much more tersely and economically appears to overlap with Maimonides. He says: "Much ("Meod") prepare yourself to be lowly in spirit (a "Sh'fal Ruach") since the anticipated end of mortal man is worms therefore what are you doing next to 'Gaavah.'"[9] I would suggest that the exegetical focus of Rashi's gloss is concentrated in his reduction of Rabbi Levitas' two *Meods* to one *Meod*. This reduction is suggestive of his construing the mishnah in a parallel way to that of Maimonides. The point of exerting oneself extremely to become a *Sh'fal Ruach* (what is conjured up by the *Meod, Meod*) is to end up at the equilibrium point between two equally unpalatable extremes, *Gaavah* and *Shiflut Haruach*. Orienting oneself toward the *Meod*-point rather than cultivating the *Meod Meod*-point for its own sake means using *Shiflut Haruach* in order to fashion and attain a less intense form of *Shiflut Haruach*, to which Maimonides wants to confine the term *Anavah*, and which Rashi suggests is the goal of the *Meod Meod* strivings.

What is driving the conflicting approaches to the Mishnaic text displayed by these key commentators? According to the GR"A (1720 – 1797)[10] and

An ethics of theory vs. an ethics of ideology 93

Rabbeinu Yonah himself in his commentary on this mishnah, how one makes sense of Rabbi Levitas' statement is a function of how one pieces together the disparate approaches to and understandings of *Gaavah* laid out in the Talmudic *Sugyah* ("discussion") addressing this topic in the tractate *Sotah* (4b–5b). The following are some key formulations found in this *Sugyah*:

> Rav Alexandri said: Every man in whom there is haughtiness of spirit even the slightest wind will disturb; as it is said, "But the wicked are like the troubled sea."(Isaiah 57:20) If the sea which contains so many quarters of a log [a liquid measure, equal to the content of six eggs] is ruffled by the slightest wind, how much more so a human being who contains but one quarter of a log [this was considered the minimum quantity of blood in the body essential for life]. Rav Hiyya b. Ashi said in the name of Rab: A disciple of the Sages [*Talmid Chochom*] should possess an eighth [of pride]. Rav Huna the son of Rav Joshua said: [This small amount of pride] crowns him like the awn of the grain. Raba said: [A disciple of the Sages] who possesses [haughtiness of spirit] deserves excommunication, and if he does not possess it he deserves excommunication. Rav Nahman b. Isaac said: He should not possess it or a part of it; is it a trifling matter concerning which it is written, "Everyone that is proud in heart is an abomination to the Lord!" (Proverbs 16:5).[11]

It would seem that the conflicting approaches to the mishnah in *Avot* of Rabbeinu Yonah and Rabbeinu Ovadiah MiBartenura, on the one hand, and Maimonides and Rashi, on the other, are motivated by which views they take to be binding in the controversies concerning *Gasut Haruach* or *Gaavah* recorded in *Sotah* 5a. Rabbeinu Yonah and Rabbeinu Ovadiah MiBartenura appear to accept the view of Rav Nahman b. Isaac that *Gaavah* is to be rejected under all circumstances, and Maimonides and Rashi, who opt for a middle position with regard to this question, seem to embrace the views of Rav Hiyya b. Ashi, Rav Huna the son of Rav Joshua and Raba that there are mitigating factors that sanction, in however limited a degree, the display of pride. How could one conceptualize these mitigating factors? One clue is contained in the statement of Rav Alexandri cited above. Rav Alexandri diagnoses as the flaw of *Gasut Haruach* that "even the slightest wind will disturb" a person filled with such a spirit. In other words, the most damning thing to be said against *Gaavah* is that it disables one's sense of reality. A person nursing an overly inflated sense of his self-worth is likely to become deeply upset by even minor setbacks, disappointments, slights or things generally not proceeding in accordance with the way he envisaged them. *Gaavah* induces a rigidity of expectation and outlook that debars one from mobilizing the requisite flexibility to adapt to the not-fully-controllable rhythms and contingencies of daily living.

In explicating Maimonides' position, we can say that he notices that even ostensible critics of *Gaavah* like Rav Alexandri condemn it on instrumental grounds, saying that it interferes with one's ability to successfully negotiate reality because of the excessive rigidification of self that it triggers and reinforces. But how about an affirmation of one's sense of self-worth that nurtures greater adaptability? That would seem to escape Rav Alexandri's strictures and appears to form part of the background to Rav Hiyya b. Ashi's statement that "a disciple of the Sages should possess an eighth [of pride]." One misses opportunities in life and adapts less well to life's challenges and exigencies than one is capable of doing both because one expects too much of oneself and others (which is symptomatic of pride) – and because one expects too little (which is indicative of dejection and an overly-deflated sense of self). The disciple of the Sages – the *Talmid Chochom* – for Rav Hiyya b. Ashi and Rav Huna the son of Rav Joshua looms as the paradigmatic human being who encapsulates in his personality the proper balance between opposing forces which the rest of us should strive to emulate. In order to miss as little as possible by way of insight and opportunity in terms of what confronts us in the course of our lives, we need to be as vigilant as possible not to become captives of anyone of our personality traits or predispositions – neither those that make us feel good about ourselves nor those that are demoralizing and dispiriting. Recognizing the impermanence and contingency of all of our self-identifying categories (so that excessive pride and lowliness of spirit are both always premature) keeps us enmeshed forever in the task of getting where we want to go, and of learning from the experience of arrival whether we want to be there at all.

This reconstruction of how Maimonides' subversion of the literal language of Rav Levitas' mishnah is grounded in his reading of the Talmudic passages in *Sotah* receives additional support from two statements found at the conclusion of our *Sugyah* in *Sotah* 5b:

> Rav Joshua b. Levi said: Come and see how great are the lowly of spirit ["*Nemuchei Haruach*," a synonym for "*Shiflei Haruach*"] in the esteem of the Holy One, blessed be He, since when the Temple stood, a man brought a burnt-offering and received the reward of a burnt-offering, a meal-offering and received the reward of a meal-offering; but as for him whose mind is lowly ("*Mi Sh'Daato Shefelah*"), Scripture ascribes it to him as though he had offered every one of the sacrifices; as it is said, "The sacrifices of God are a broken spirit" (Psalms 51:19). More than that, his prayer is not despised; as it continues, "A broken and contrite heart, O God, thou wilt not despise."
>
> Rav Joshua b. Levi further said: He who calculates his ways in this world will be worthy to behold the salvation of the Holy One, blessed be He; as it is said, "To him that ordereth his way will I show the salvation of God" (Psalms 50:23) – read not "*we-sam* [that ordereth]" but "*we-sham* [who calculates]" his way.[12]

In his first statement, Rav Joshua b. Levi ostensibly extols the virtues of those who display *Shiflut Ha'Daat* ("lowliness of mind") over those who manifest

Nemichut or *Shiflut Haruach* ("lowliness of spirit"). It is apparently only the former (but not the latter) who receive a reward far in excess of their original actions and investments. What exactly is *Shiflut Ha'Daat*? Rav Joshua b. Levi's second statement juxtaposed to the first helps to illuminate what this term might mean. The key word in the second statement is *Sham* ("calculate"). A person who persistently takes nothing for granted concerning his own worth or the worth of others, but endlessly calculates, making allowances for what can go wrong in his estimation of self as well as in his evaluation of others, receives Divine salvation. In Talmudic parlance, *Shuma* (the noun form of the verb) connotes reaching a decision (usually informed by compromise) in a climate of uncertainty. For example, in the Babylonian Talmudic tractate *Baba Bathra* a case is cited in which three expert assessors go down, at the behest of a judicial tribunal, to the estate of male orphans to estimate its value. The object of the assessment is to sell the property for the maintenance of the dead owner's widow or his orphan daughters. If the three assessors come up with three different assessments, one view cited in *Baba Bathra* 107a–107b is that the difference between the lowest valuation and the highest is calculated and divided by three – and this quotient is added to the lowest valuation (*Osim Shuma Beineihem U'meshalshin*).[13] Utilizing the connotations of the term *Shuma* in this technical legal context as our model, we can say that for a person to be *Sham Orchosov* ("to calculate his ways"), one must be understood as being involved in a comparable climate of uncertainty, where neither knowledge of the relevant ethical norms, self-knowledge nor knowledge of the Other can be viewed as totally reliable and unshakeable, and where, therefore, one steers toward the middle, toward compromise, affirming ethical norms that are doable and not overly perfectionist in character and perceiving oneself and Others as being "middling creatures," who are neither saints nor sinners and whose behavior is eminently malleable in response to the right menu of incentives and sanctions.

Rashi's elucidation of the phrase *Hasham Orchosov* ("he who calculates his ways") can also be linked with the skeptical perspective developed here. Rashi connects the calculation alluded to in the phrase *Hasham Orchosov* with a previous mishnah in *Avot* 2:1, which states that we should "consider the loss incurred in doing a Mitzvah in relation to its reward and the reward received for engaging in a transgression in relation to the loss [simultaneously] incurred."[14] Doing *Mitzvot* involves certain costs in terms of financial outlay, pleasures renounced and time expenditures diverted away from other activities. Correspondingly, engaging in transgressions often carry their own monetary, sensual or other types of rewards. What Rabbi Judah the Prince (the author of mishnah *Avot* 2:1) advises us to do is to formulate some kind of ledger where we can keep track of the costs and the benefits attached to the performance of *Mitzvot* on an ongoing basis and ponder how the overall picture shapes up. What is theologically significant in Rabbi Judah's formulation is that he is not telling us to perform *Mitzvot* because they are the commands of God and to avoid *Aveirot* ("transgressions") because they are the prohibitions of God. Apparently, Rabbi Judah subscribes to a negative-theological understanding of monotheistic teaching, so that the unbridgeable ontological distance separating us from God incapacitates us from imputing a literal content to the notions that "God commands" and "God prohibits," just like it disempowers us from literally construing all of the other verbs and adjectives ascribed to God. Engaging in a life of *Mitzvot* has to be a function of our calculating which menus of behavior are likely to enhance the coherence of our lives as we periodically reassess where the point of equilibrium between self-expression and self-renunciation falls. Doing *Mitzvot* is not a matter of correspondence – directly conforming to the literally declared and grasped Word of God. Rabbi Judah's understanding of calculation, upon which Rashi relies to fix the meaning of the phrase *Hasham Orchosov*, is not that different from the way calculation is conceived of in *Baba Bathra* 107a–107b.

The higher status accorded to *Shiflut Ha'Daat* ("lowliness of mind") over *Shiflut Haruach* ("lowliness of spirit") in Rav Joshua b. Levi's statements might have served as one legitimating source for Maimonides' substitution of *Anavah* for *Shiflut Haruach* in Rav Levitas' mishnah. In the light of Rav Joshua b. Levi's invidious comparison between *Shiflut Haruach* and *Shiflut Ha'Daat*, Maimonides interprets *Shiflut Haruach* to refer to dejection and he identifies *Shiflut Ha'Daat* with *Anavah* – with humility. From this perspective, *Shiflut Haruach* represents an extreme just like *Gaavah* does. *Shiflut Haruach* as dejection denotes something taken to be natural and given, and constitutes the counterpart term to *Gaavah* ("haughtiness"), which is also taken to refer to sources of superiority that are regarded as natural and given, and therefore also, in a certain sense, immutable. *Shiflut Ha'Daat* ("lowliness of mind") and its synonym *Anavah* ("humility"), by contrast, represent the *Derech Ha'Memutzeh* ("the middle way") between *Gaavah* and *Shiflut Haruach*. In contrast to the latter two terms, *Shiflut Ha'Daat* and *Anavah* represent something artificial – a groping, clarifying mechanism wrought by mind to wend its way around its suspicions, anxieties and safe assumptions.

The upshot of my analysis is that both Rav Alexandri and Rav Joshua b. Levi in *Sotah* 5a–5b provide Maimonides with the hermeneutical keys for interpreting the role of humility in Jewish ethics in the manner that he does.

Hillel and the moral ontology of the Rabbis

This reading of how humility shapes up in the moral ontology of the Rabbis receives further corroboration from a famous story concerning Hillel recounted in the Babylonian Talmudic tractate *Shabbath* (30b–31a):

> Our Rabbis taught: A man should always be gentle like Hillel, and not impatient like Shammai. It once happened that two men made a wager with each other, saying, He who goes and makes Hillel angry shall receive four hundred zuz. Said one, "I will go and incense him." That day

was the Sabbath eve, and Hillel was washing his head. He went, passed by the door of his house, and called out, "Is Hillel here, is Hillel here?" Thereupon he robed and went out to him saying, "My son, what do you require?" "I have a question to ask," said he. "Ask, my son," he prompted. Thereupon he asked: "Why are the heads of the Babylonians round?" [Hillel was a Babylonian]. "My son, you have asked a great question," replied he: "because they have no skillful midwives." He departed, tarried a while, returned, and called out, "Is Hillel here; is Hillel here?" He robed and went out to him, saying, "My son, what do you require?" "I have a question to ask," said he. "Ask, my son," he prompted. Thereupon he asked: "Why are the eyes of the Palmyreans bleared?" "My son, you have asked a great question," replied he: "because they live in sandy places." He departed, tarried a while, returned, and called out, "Is Hillel here; is Hillel here?" He robed and went out to him, saying, "My son, what do you require?" "I have a question to ask," said he. "Ask, my son," he prompted. He asked, "Why are the feet of the Africans wide?" "My son, you have asked a great question," said he; "because they live in watery marshes." "I have many questions to ask," said he, "but fear that you may become angry." Thereupon he robed, sat before him and said, "Ask all the questions you have to ask." "Are you the Hillel who is called the Nasi [patriarch; the religious head of the people] of Israel?" "Yes," he replied. "If that is you," he retorted, "may there not be many like you in Israel." "Why, my son?" queried he. "Because I have lost four hundred zuz through you," complained he. "Be careful of your moods," he answered. "Hillel is worth that you should lose four hundred zuz and yet another four hundred zuz through him, yet Hillel shall not lose his temper."[15]

This conversation between Hillel and the person who sets out to test the limits of his patience and endurance suggests that the route to evenness of disposition – to equanimity of temper – is self-respect. This Talmudic passage highlights how one both should (and can) individuate and differentiate himself from the psychological mess that might be troubling the people around him. The individual person should not be contaminated, or affected, by other people's need to be mean and nasty. Each of us should have the courage to classify other people's hostile behavior by its rightful name and to situate ourselves on the other side. As Rabbinically envisioned, egoism properly asserted paradoxically leads to the practice of humility properly conceived.

Or, stated more strongly, we can say that given the way in which the virtue of humility militates against its own realization (to notice that one is humble and to glory in it is already to have subverted the virtue of humility), the only way that it becomes humanly accessible, albeit in an impure and ostensibly secondary form, is through the manifestation of egoistic pride. Hillel's pride in being able to sustain an even-tempered, inner-directed and inner-controlled disposition nurtures his humble stance in relation to his menacing, gratuitously intrusive provocateur. Humility is a willfully fabricated external mask engendered by a self that is endlessly devoted to continuing calculations and manipulations that will exalt it in its own eyes. Humility forms a limit and a boundary for a self driven toward its self-cultivation and self-transcendence (which turns out to be one further stage in its self-cultivation).[16]

Rabbinic and Maimonidean ethics contrasted with Levinasian ethics

One central thing to notice about the Talmud and Maimonides is that they both situate ethics very differently from the way it is positioned in Levinas' thought. It is extremely striking to see where the dominant emphasis falls in Jewish ethics. *Gaavah* is the primal transgression. It is imputing independent reality (a sense of superiority; a sense of dejection in the case of *Shiflut Haruach*, a mirror image in reverse of *Gaavah*) to what, in the end, is only instrumentally constructed that is the root cause of moral failure. *Gaavah* consists in a failure of the Same – a self that is not able to extricate itself in skeptical terms from the paradoxes and limitations of skepticism. The primary ethical sin for Rabbinic Judaism is not failure to show *Chesed* ("kindness") toward the Other – but a failure to cultivate *Anavah* within the self. The legitimate lowliness of mind encapsulated in the term *Anavah* that recognizes at least part of its lowliness to consist in its skeptically-delineated inability to either affirm or deny the independent status of the objects and categories that it contemplates or confronts – this lowliness that defines itself as the middle between the two always prematurely reified extremes of affirmation and denial – must learn to conceive of itself as a middle that has to be endlessly recalculated, re-appropriated and redefined precisely because the ends with which the middle is contrasted also do not have a perdurable identity. In a properly Rabbinically-conceived genealogy of Jewish ethics, *Chesed* must somehow be traced as emerging out of the quandaries of the specification of the middle confronted by the Same. The Other is just one more category predicated upon the pragmatic wagering and limitless responsibility that characterize the condition of the Same.

We have now examined the Talmudic background to Maimonides' reading of Rabbi Levitas' mishnah. What, however, are the internal dynamics of deconstruction and reconstruction of that text itself? What are the opening wedges in Rabbi Levitas' mishnah that allow Maimonides to pour into it the content he might have imbibed from the Talmudic discussion in *Sotah*?

The redundancy of the *Meod, Meod* in Rabbi Levitas' mishnah might harbor the secret about how Maimonides proceeds to subvert the literal reading of this mishnah. It might disclose to us what his textual starting point is for this subversion. There is an intertwined set of epistemological and ethical dilemmas attached to the apparent virtue of *Shiflut Haruach* (insinuated to us by the repetition of the *Meod* at the beginning of the mishnah), which Maimonides resolves by shifting the center of pedagogical gravity of this mishnah away from *Shiflut Haruach* toward what he defines as *Anavah*.

The epistemological dilemma has to do with how when we self-consciously cultivate humility, every time we feel that we are exemplifying it, we experience a twinge of pride (and hence of non-humility) at its achievement. Working toward becoming more humble involves a performative contradiction. As we work toward it (and succeed), our pride in attaining it mocks the very goal of humility that we are overtly striving for. This dilemma is alluded to by the Tanna in his repetition of the word *Meod*. One *Meod* is never enough when one is seeking humility because of the paradoxical nature of the task itself. But by the same token that one *Meod* with regard to humility is never enough, neither will a million or an infinite number of *Meods* suffice. Every attempt to overcome the dilemma just reinstates it in the very act of trying to overcome it.

The epistemological problematic attached to humility gets duplicated in a psychological sphere that gives rise to what looks like an insuperable ethical dilemma. If one notices how the search for and cultivation of humility can itself nurture pride and one responds by continually deepening his sense of humility, then he risks veering toward extreme self-depreciation and depression. But if one actually plummets to the level of depression, then the epistemological paradox surrounding humility stands poised to reemerge as an acute ethical dilemma. A radically deflated sense of self (as we have seen) looms as a mirror image in reverse of the sin of pride. A person suffering from acute depression is blocking out reality no less dramatically than a person exuding an overly-inflated sense of his self-worth. Both the haughty person and the depressed person are acting as if nothing matters except what they think of themselves. The depressed person no less than the haughty person is unable to relinquish his excessive preoccupation with how he values himself. It is as if part of the subtext of depression is that one is not able to be fully, coherently depressed because some twisted version of the sin of pride gets in the way. The ethical challenge then becomes how one can theorize humility as an ethical virtue while escaping the epistemological paradox summarized by the term "performative contradiction" and avoiding the ethical paradox that the deepest cultivations of humility, such as those reflected in semi-depressed and depressed states of being, bespeak the inextirpability of pride.

Maimonides' resolution of this double-barreled dilemma is his invocation of the middling virtue "that has no other name but '*Anavah*' [humility]." How can *Anavah* be in the middle, between two extremes, when we have just seen that one of the extremes, *Shiflut Haruach* – lowliness of spirit – mires one in a dual epistemological and psychological (ethical) dilemma of extremes? If *Shiflut Haruach* is an unstable extreme, how can one stand in the middle in relation to it? I believe that the answer resides with the artificial, residually arbitrary character of the notion of the middle itself as deployed by Aristotle and Maimonides. When one makes the mistake of identifying lowliness of spirit with some "conceptually unadorned" natural attribute or predisposition of character, there is no middle – only an inexorable devolution to extremes of epistemological and psychological paradox.

The moment of rescue comes when one realizes that there is no natural correlative to the middle. The notion of the middle can be annexed to extremes of behavior that are so despicable that they taint the middle with their odiousness. For example, between a principle of action that sanctions the wanton killing of one hundred people and a principle of action that restricts it to ten people, one opts for the mean between ten and one hundred. This ethically lugubrious example is only meant to highlight how the idea of the mean is a formally neutral term, which can be invested with ethical content only on the basis of premises and assumptions that take us beyond the formal properties and content of the concept of the mean itself. The Aristotelian and Maimonidean category of the mean in ethics is already a reflection of a fallen metaphysical state where underdetermination of words by things has been acknowledged. The epistemologically and psychologically therapeutic powers of the term *Anavah* reside in the fact that it is a frankly and self-consciously proclaimed artificial term created to fill in the blank of the periodically invented and reinvented ethical category of the middle, which is itself a response to our subsisting in a world in which there is a surplus of words over things. The term *Anavah* avoids the realist pitfalls of the phrase *Shiflut Haruach*, but its artificiality encapsulates the idea that it is the very process of fixing again and again in the face of evolving circumstances the extremes to which *Anavah* is opposed that serves as the source of *Anavah* being classified as an ethical virtue.

In a skeptical universe, it is the fact that *Anavah* occupies an artificial middle that is ethically decisive. Any attempt to tinker with our location and identification of the middle and to substitute different concepts aside from *Anavah* in that middle will net us dilemmas that are as fully intractable as our efforts to supply a content for and properly validate *Anavah*. The notion of the middle (of moderation; of avoidance of extremes) has obvious and compelling rhetorical ethical appeal. The philosophical point of the search for the ever-elusive ethical middle is to have the unending preoccupation with skepticism and its limits serve as our orientating marker for ethical deliberation and reflection. In being skeptical and then acknowledging that skepticism itself has to recoil into a generalized agnosticism lest it be vulnerable to the paradoxes affecting humility on an epistemological and psychological level, we learn that the makeshift, provisional exercises in elucidation and translation attendant to the ethics of the mean is itself constitutive of an ethical stance as we acclimate ourselves to stave off certainty, even the certainty accruing from our own persistent uncertainty.

The sheerly stylized, instrumentalized relationship between how one comes to classify the extremes associated with humility and how one delineates the ethical midpoint of humility itself is beautifully invoked by Maimonides in a further citation from the Talmud in *Sotah*:

> Leprosy is a punishment visited upon the haughty. They said: "For a rising and for a scab," (Leviticus 14:56), and *Se'eth* ["rising"] means

nothing else than elevation, as it is said, "Upon all the high mountains, and upon all the hills that are *Nisaot* [lifted up]" (Isaiah 2:14). It is as if the verse said that to the haughty person will befall the fate of becoming a *Sapahath* ["scab"].[17]

The Talmud in *Sotah* 5b states more elaborately that *Sapahath* ["scab"] means nothing else than attachment [making oneself secondary to something else]; as it is said, "Attach me, I pray thee, unto one of the priests' offices, that I may eat a morsel of bread" (I Samuel 2:36).

Apparently, from the Talmud and Maimonides' perspectives, there is a dialectical relationship between *Anavah*, keeping oneself low, and attaining *Gadlut* – becoming *Nisah* – that is, reaching great heights. One has to use (because one has no alternative) the "elsewhere" (the Other) of what one wants in order to get to where (or what) one wants. Given how the words that we use mock and undermine the reality of that which they seek to represent – how the overly-inflated sense of self of the *Baal Gaavah* (the haughty person) renders what he is haughty about more precarious than ever, and how the excessively self-lacerating self-image of the *Shfal Ruach* (the overly meek person) still carries a tinge of the *Gaavah* that he everlastingly seeks to repress – the only way to move about the world of persons and things is to continually use the Other of what one is seeking as a platform for attaining that which one most strongly craves. To live a properly fulfilled and creative human life means that one is always either one step ahead or one step behind oneself – that the names, words and categories that one uses to refer to various ostensible realities are unglued even before they are glued, that they are conceptually overflowing at the very moment of palpable containment, exchanging identities with one or another of their Others to stand a fighting chance of being able to come into their own.

Citing additional Talmudic and Midrashic passages in praise of *Anavah* in his commentary on Rabbi Levitas' mishnah, Maimonides quotes the famous verse in Psalms 111:10 that *Reishit Chochmoh Yirat HaShem* ("The beginning of wisdom is the fear of God"), which he interprets as showing that "the fear of God is greater than wisdom and is the root cause of its existence."[18] In Hebrew, *Chochmoh* connotes wisdom, knowledge and insight – the stock of ideas and repertoire of modes of analysis that impart to us and undergird our sense of mastery over ourselves and the multiple microcosmic and macrocosmic worlds that we strive to inhabit. The fear of God signifies an awareness of limits to which our *Chochmoh* in a collective sense (in all of its ramifications) constitutes a response. Since from the perspective of Maimonidean negative theology the "fear of God" cannot have a literal object to latch on to, what it must be referring to and summarizing is our inability to pierce certain rational limits – such as the infinite regress that emerges when we seek ultimate explanations and the issues of reflexivity that bedevil us when we try to transform our very inability to attain secure knowledge into a theory of knowledge in its own right (namely, skepticism). *Chochmoh* – including ethical *Chochmoh* of the sort encapsulated in the Theory of the Mean – begins in a registering and integrating of the limits to reason. The theological paradigm for this is paradoxically God's creation of the world itself, which is expressive of a gigantic burst of self-limitation to make room for what is other than God. The inextricable link between creation and creativity and the acknowledgment of limits is vouchsafed to monotheists by the opening images of the Biblical narrative itself, which can be read as conjuring up an image of Divine withdrawal as the source of Divine creativity.

The verse in the Psalms that Maimonides is explicating continues by saying, "good understanding to all their practitioners." Human *Chochmoh*, which is grounded in *Yirat Hashem* – an institutionalization of limits – leads to a deliberately designed and cherished conflation of the rational and voluntaristic faculties in human beings registered in the subordinate clause of this sentence. "Understanding" and "practice" are continuous activities. Given the incompleteness of human understanding, it remains relatively arbitrary whether we classify our efforts at understanding as forms of knowing or forms of doing. From this perspective, the Aristotelian and Maimonidean ethical middle are just special applications of a broader metaphysical middle in which the modalities of human rationality and human interaction with the world are more broadly set.

In his commentary on Rabbi Levitas' mishnah, Maimonides also cites, with resounding approval, the following statement made by Rav Yochanan found in *Sotah* 4b:

> Rav Yochanan said in the name of Rav Simeon b. Yohai: Every man in whom is haughtiness of spirit is as though he worships idols; it is written here, "Everyone that is proud in heart is an abomination to the Lord" (Proverbs 16:5), and it is written elsewhere, "Thou shalt not bring an abomination into thine house" (Deuteronomy 7:26). Rav Yochanan himself said, "He is as though he had denied the fundamental principle [the existence of God]; as it is said, 'Thine heart be lifted up and thou forget the Lord thy God'" (Deuteronomy 8: 14).[19]

The verses cited by Rav Yochanan in the name of Rav Simeon b. Yohai and in his own name are suggestive of an indissoluble conceptual linkage between negative theology, skepticism and humility. Affirmation of the monotheistic God can only be nurtured in an ethical context that assigns primacy to a not-fully-appropriable and exhaustively definable middle structured after the model of the broader metaphysical middle staked out by negative theology. The person whose "heart is lifted up" (who exhibits *Gaavah*) is just by virtue of harboring this personality trait already marked as a non-believer. The object of monotheistic belief is irretrievably literally behind us or infinitely in front of us – but in no case can we lay claim to possessing Him. He speaks to us, as it were, out of the context of our own actions, which need to display boundless patience and a limitless ability to accommodate deferral in order for them to evoke a Godly human self. One can lay hold of the principles of monotheism by either examining the tenets of negative theology (cosmic level), exploring the presuppositions and implications of philosophical skepticism (worldly level) or investigating the psychological and ethical rudiments of humility (personal level). Maimonides citing Rav Yochanan as his legitimating Talmudic source reminds us that no matter how we proceed we are focusing upon a common phenomenon from diverse but complementary angles of vision.

In consonance with my argument concerning the Aristotelian and Maimonidean middle, we might also argue that to engage in ideological political thought rests upon a primitive analytical mistake. It is to confuse the single unified picture that one confronts in his/her domain of study with a single, unified account of how the picture comes to be what it is. By contrast, when one does theory, one notices that there is generally more than one way to account for what is. The advantage in self-consciously cultivating a theoretical stance to political phenomena is that doing so is already a self-empowering act for both students of politics and average citizens. Prodding ourselves to think theoretically – to conceive of more than one way to make sense of phenomena – by itself already provides a platform for moving toward effective transformation of those phenomena.

Alasdair MacIntyre and the project of devising an alternative to modernity

From the perspective of our analysis, we can discern something fraudulent – or at least what Derrida, following Marx, would call "spooky"[20] – about Alasdair MacIntyre's whole project of devising an alternative to modernity.[21] MacIntyre begins by denouncing the moral chaos of modernity and ends up endorsing a traditions-based conception of morality which only gives us a somewhat more organized version of the chaos, the chaos classified and codified, as it were. To diminish the chaos, he might have been better off searching for the ways in which the official liberal public value of neutrality translates into some notion with cognitive and political bite. One promising candidate would be that neutrality which summarizes the official liberal subordination of the public realm to the private realm, the priority of the right over the good and the endless deferral of a concerted stand on issues of justice and truth signifies that liberalism is committed to a certain conception of the good, which (borrowing from Levinas' vocabulary, without his preferred set of connotations) we might paraphrase as infinity – or horizontal transcendence. The ultimate task of every human collective present is to render possible the emergence of successor presents. This notion is not devoid of content, as we are witnessing the resurgence around the world of fundamentalist religious movements – in the Christian right in the United States, in Muslim fundamentalist movements in the Middle East, Asia and Africa, and in the Jewish right in the United States and in the State of Israel. These movements represent (to utilize the Talmudic idiom) "a hastening of the end."[22] They insinuate a gross impatience with lived historical time. A negative but not vacuous construal of the supreme moral value of liberalism gives us a significant moral resource for combating some of the most deleterious political movements of our time.

It is also important to note that science cannot be taken to simply canonically inform us about what belongs to the realm of theory and what needs to be consigned to the domain of ideology. From the perspective that I am developing in this book, the activity of being a scientist merges with the activity of being a philosopher of science. Both the scientist and the philosopher of science are trying to get the fit between words and things to work better. Neither of them has access to a domain of pure fact. In Nietzsche's idiom in *Beyond Good and Evil*, the concept of immediate knowledge constitutes a *contradictio in adjecto*.[23] If something is immediate, it cannot constitute knowledge. If we label it "knowledge," then it already subsists on a plane beyond the immediate. For example, the evidence adduced by sociobiologists, evolutionary biologists and psychologists cannot straightforwardly be invoked as a factual resolution of philosophical quandaries revolving around the nature and status of morality. This is like Thrasymachus in Plato's *Republic* trying to bring a philosophical inquiry into justice to an end by citing comparative sociological evidence about the class correlations of the term in existing societies.[24] To think that without complex mediating stages of argument one could make moves of this sort is to be guilty of what Gilbert Ryle called "a category mistake" and of what Aristotle much earlier called "heterotypical predication."[25] A philosophical dispute remains a philosophical dispute and one cannot simply bring it to a close by citing evidence from the sciences which themselves are not able to cross the bridge to a factually pristine reality.

Plato's *Greater Hippias*, the relationship between theory and ideology, and Levinas

Plato in one of his forgotten Socratic dialogues, *Greater Hippias*, indirectly clues us in to a conception of the relationship between theory and ideology that supports the argument of this book. The dialogue addresses the question of the nature of the beautiful. The structure of the dialogue is complex. It is written in a compressed and circuitous way. The only position in the dialogue that is left unassailed is that which identifies "the beautiful" with "the fitting."[26] This formulation, one might argue, meets the test of reflexivity: It is fitting to invoke the fitting as the criterion for assessing the beautiful. Coherence, unlike correspondence, recursively embraces itself in its standard of acceptability. "Correspondence" does not correspond to anything outside of itself. It is intended to capture a relationship outside of itself without validating itself as the criterion to apply to that relationship. "Coherence," precisely because it refers to a purely internal standard, can be taken to encompass itself alongside whatever else it is overtly mobilized to refer to. I shall examine some of the more striking formulations and features of the dialogue in light of this organizing perspective of "the beautiful as the fitting."

Defining the beautiful as the fitting ties in with the Third Man Argument in the *Parmenides* and the way that it impinges upon the Theory of Ideas. When Plato in the *Republic* presents his Theory of Ideas or Forms, it looks like he is making a straightforward argument that is partly logical and partly metaphysical. The following two passages from Betrand Russell clarify the argument:

> Language cannot get on without general words such as cat, and such words are evidently not meaningless. But if the word cat means anything, it means something which is not this or that cat, but some kind of universal cattyness. This is not born when a particular cat is born, and does not die when it dies. In fact, it has no position in space or time; it is eternal. This is the logical part of the doctrine.[27]
>
> According to the metaphysical part of the doctrine [which is elaborated most fully in the last book of the *Republic*] ... the various particular beds are unreal, being only copies of the "idea," which is the one real bed, and is made by God. Of this one bed, made by God, there can be knowledge, but in respect of the many beds made by carpenters there can be only opinion. The philosopher, as such, will be interested only in the one ideal bed, not in the many beds found in the sensible world.[28]

The Third Man Argument in the *Parmenides*[29] forces us to reconceive what is at stake in Plato's Theory of Ideas or Forms. Since a major impetus behind the Theory of Ideas is to facilitate the subsumption of the many by the One – as Socrates formulates the point in the *Republic*: "We have regularly assumed a Form for all the manys to which we apply the same name, one Form for each many"[30] – there is no way to legitimately arrest the search for Forms at the level of the first Form that encompasses all of the particulars that fall below it; but one must ground that Form itself in some still higher Form that grounds it, and so on indefinitely. The paradox emerges that the Theory of Ideas, which seems designed to foreclose the possibility of infinite regress by connecting empirical instantiations of an Idea with some transcendent original, itself renders such a regress inevitable by its very design. Once we provide grounding for the words we use in their rootedness in some higher reality, there is no way to rationally foreclose a search for higher and higher realities to achieve ever more secure groundings.

From the perspective of Plato's Third Man Argument, the search for justification undercuts itself and compels us to redefine the critical edge of Plato's Theory of Ideas. Instead of the theory being about the positive identification of the logical and metaphysical sources of our ideas, the Third Man Argument becomes the critical apparatus that transforms the theory into a skeptical delimitation of the appropriate ways to construe both abstract theoretical notions and their empirical exemplifications. The Third Man Argument affects both the logical and metaphysical commitments of the Theory of Ideas. They both become unmoored (lack adequate sense and reference) as a result of this argument. The prospect of an infinite regress in the search for more ultimate Ideas makes a mockery of the task of finding or establishing an appropriate metaphysical grounding for the terms that we use, but it also undermines the project of definitively tracing (in a non-arbitrary, non-circular way) the conceptual and logical boundaries of the words that we employ in our daily interactions with the world.

The skeptical delimitation of the Theory of Ideas can be read as proceeding on two levels: the level of theory and the level of fact. On the one hand, when Plato in the *Republic* argues that Ideas are more real than their empirical instantiations, he needs to be read in the light of the Third Man Argument as embracing the notion that theories are underdetermined by facts. That facts are theory-dependent makes theories more "real" than facts, but does not redeem facts or theories from a common ontological plane of arbitrariness. Conceptual realism leads to an infinite regress that can be warded off by acknowledging the philosophical non-negotiability of any conceptual territory more durable than language. From the organizing perspective of the Theory of Ideas as skeptical delimitation rather than positive identification, an implicit equivalence is posited by the content of this theory: the groundlessness of fact is read back into the status of theory, so that the Theory of Ideas, which on a formal, explicit level looks like the delineation of a hierarchy, turns out on a submerged, implicit level (in the light of the Third Man critique) to have deflected its argument into the elaboration of an equivalence between theory and fact, so that each remains as uncertain as the other.

It is important to note that one can interpret the skepticism that I have just described as standing guard over a higher unity.[31] Skepticism highlights the not-fully-consummated-or-realized unity in the statements or arguments that one is examining to better preserve the untarnished vision of unity in the realm of the ideal. A strong impetus behind skepticism is to prevent the ideal from being diminished by its not being fully realized in the actual or real. Paradoxically, one important effect of focusing on the skeptical limitations of our sentences and arguments is to enlarge the distance between the actual and ideal, thereby augmenting the integrity and sanctity of the latter. For example, by highlighting dimensions of inconsistency in some of our more innocuous-sounding arguments, the ideal of consistency is indirectly reaffirmed and its status as a unifying conception of mind is reinforced. The distancing of the ideal nurtured by the application of skepticism keeps it intact as a model of unity.

Juxtaposing Plato's argument in the *Greater Hippias* to the *Cratylus* and the *Theaetetus* (which we shall soon discuss) suggests the confluence between epistemological and esthetic ideals. If the emergence of paradox and contradiction leads us to assign primacy to language in our search for what is ultimately real, then the way we map how we move about amongst words is illuminatingly captured by the notion of "the fitting." In order to determine what the most acceptable ordering patterns for words are, we need to think in terms of fit – of coherence. Identifying "the beautiful" with "the fitting" in the *Greater Hippias* can be read as implicitly assigning priority to esthetics over epistemology – or at least pointing in the direction of their coeval nature.

Socrates' definition of the beautiful as "the useful and the powerful for doing something good"[32] is rejected on grounds that dovetail with my reading of how Plato theorizes the relationship between esthetics and epistemology:

soc.: But all humans do many more bad things than good, starting from childhood, and they make mistakes involuntarily.
hip.: This is so.
soc.: What then? Shall we assert that this power and whichever useful things are useful for producing something bad are beautiful, or far from it?
hip.: Far from it, it seems to me at least, Socrates.
soc.: Then for us, Hippias, the powerful and the useful, as seems likely, are not the beautiful.
hip.: Unless, Socrates, they have power to produce good things and are useful for such things.
soc.: Then this much at any rate is gone, namely that the powerful and useful, simply, are beautiful.[33]

In this passage, Plato seems to be pointing to how there is an endless burden of recontextualization in human thinking, which makes a mockery of all of our efforts at stabilization. All tokens of stability in human affairs – from words to concepts to categories to abstract ideas generally – are artificial orientating markers to help us deepen and extend the process of contextualization. To register the pervasiveness of this artificiality of conceptual orientating markers, we assign priority in our ontologies to language above the world.

Plato seems to be vexed throughout the dialogue by the dilemmas associated with being able to distinguish the reality of the beautiful from its appearances. The following is one juncture where this vexation is expressed:

soc.: But we must try to say what that is which makes them [things taken to be beautiful] be beautiful, as I said just now, whether they appear so or not. For this is what we are seeking, if in fact we are seeking the beautiful.[34]

Plato is in search of the reality of the beautiful – in contrast to its appearances. Upon further reflection, the irony turns out to be that the reality (however designated) is just one more instrumentalized appearance geared to generate further appearances.

At 287d–e, Socrates says that "he [the imaginary Other lodged in Socrates] is asking you not what is beautiful but what is the beautiful." The dialogue, to some extent, revolves around the question of whether it is possible to get from "what is beautiful" to "what is the beautiful." The first is largely a matter of context – of making mutual adjustments between concepts, categories and full-scale statements for the sake of maximizing coherence. The second represents a condensation of these mutual adjustments onto some enduring conceptual-material substratum.

A little later on in the dialogue, Socrates impugns the possibility of such a condensation. He says: "Such he [referring to the imaginary interlocutor] is, Hippias, not elegant but vulgar, taking thought for nothing else but the truth."[35] Socrates apparently conceives of truth as a critical tool poised toward deferring truth – rather than capturing it or containing it. The impetus of thought is most keenly felt in the transformation of substance into process – the deconstruction of stable units of ideas into the energies that fostered them.

To ensure the primacy of process over substance, Plato's Socrates engages in dialogue. Dialogue is theorized by Plato from two directions: In terms of what it accomplishes for its interlocutors and in terms of what it accomplishes for the speaker engaging in it. (In dialogue, of course, all participants play a dual role: They are both speakers – advancing their own positions – and interlocutors or interrogators of other people's positions, if only by virtue of espousing an alternative position.) For the interlocutors, dialogue exposes the weakness of their positions: "For I am rather experienced in objections," Socrates says, "so if it makes no difference to you, I wish to raise objections in order that I may learn more firmly."[36] At another juncture in the dialogue, Plato highlights the importance of the role of the interlocutor. Socrates beseeches Hippias: "Be attentive to me and apply your mind completely so I won't babble."[37] Apparently, in order for the speaker to articulate his thoughts effectively and coherently, he must have reflected back to him how he appears on the horizon of the Other. The threshold between babble and talk is crossed when the self catches a glimpse of itself from the perspective of the Other.

Lest we should be tempted to regard the presence of the literal, physical Other as indispensable, we need to notice how even dialogue's effect in exposing the shortcomings of its participants' arguments is mediated for Plato through its role in enabling the speaker of the objection himself to "learn more firmly."[38] The stance of Otherness looms as more significant for Plato than the literal, concrete Other. This point is driven home especially forcefully in the *Greater Hippias* in that the third participant in the dialogue is Socrates' internal other whose questions and musings are reported to Hippias by the physical Socrates. The dialogue projects Hippias, the Sophist author of big, beautiful speeches, as being without the fully developed apparatus of a bifurcated, interrogatory self characteristic of Socrates, who is associated with the more fragmentary assaults and refinements linked with "little speeches."[39]

An ethics of theory vs. an ethics of ideology 109

Dialogue exhibits and enhances Platonic skepticism from a dual direction. On the one hand, the point of Platonic skepticism is to be able to show that the role of thought in the economy of the human psyche is to generate ongoing contexts for what is being thought about – to continually restore the supremacy of context over text. By way of dramatizing for us the priority of context over text, Plato enacts thinking as a partnered activity – as if to encode that context is given as part of every text, that a contextually pared-down, ur-text is an illusion. To succumb to the illusion of genuine, unproblematic Otherness, on the other hand, defeats the very skepticism that was supposed to be communicated by the choice of the dialogue form to expound and develop ideas. Given the larger principle of the underdetermination of theory by fact, the category of the Other is as underdetermined as the rest of our categories. In the *Greater Hippias*, Plato seems to be responding to the challenge of reflexivity lodged in the choice of the dialogue form to communicate his philosophy – that Otherness flags the priority of context over text but only at the cost of validating the Other which itself transgresses skepticism – by embracing a vision of the Other as extending to what is internal and metaphorical, rather than being restricted to what is taken as external and real. By locating Socrates' principal Other in the *Greater Hippias* as being internal to himself, Plato seems to be suggesting that infinity (of interpretation; of dialogical interrogation and riposte) represents the functional correlative or equivalent to the Other. The devolution of Otherness into a distinction between totality (the totality of real-world Others) and infinity (the infinity of internal interrogation and riposte) is thus presaged by Plato as what we might call a corrective before the fact of Levinas' invocation of this distinction to support the priority of this-worldly Others.

The Rabbis and the internalized, metaphorical Other

There are two famous Aggadic[40] statements in the Talmud that also suggest that the Rabbis envisage some key instances of Otherness in internal, metaphorical terms. In *Sukkah* 52a, the Talmud says: "The greater the man, the greater his Evil Inclination (*Yetzer Harah*)."[41] Apparently, the Rabbis conceive of human greatness as a function of process and struggle, rather than as something that placidly follows from innate traits and native endowments. Human greatness is a function of overcoming and perhaps even of overreaching – a function of determining an agenda of goals as well as of following through on them. The Rabbis look upon human beings after the manner of the monotheistic God – as creatures with an impenetrable essence that are defined by their energies of will. To create on a massive scale, which, for the Rabbis, constitutes our actualization of our Divine-like role (our being created in the "image of God"), means that we continually have to fashion structures of necessity that goad us on along our paths. The Evil Inclination is one such structure – one such internally-situated platform or "elsewhere" that enables us to periodically regroup and refocus in order to more effectively negotiate our ends.

The second Aggadic statement occurs on the same page in the Talmud:

> In the time to come the Holy One, blessed be He, will bring the Evil Inclination and slay it in the presence of the righteous and the wicked. To the righteous it will have the appearance of a towering hill, and to the wicked it will have the appearance of a hair thread. Both the former and the latter will weep; the righteous will weep saying, "How were we able to overcome such a towering hill!" The wicked also will weep saying, "How is it that we were unable to conquer this hair thread!" And the Holy One, blessed be He, will also marvel together with them, as it is said, "Thus saith the Lord of Hosts, If it be marvelous in the eyes of the remnant of this people in those days, it shall also be marvelous in My eyes" (Zechariah 8:6).[42]

The mystery surrounding the Evil Inclination does not cease in "the time to come." During the future time, the mystery attendant to the phenomenon of the Evil Inclination is not resolved, but confirmed. Even God is a party to the confirmation of the mystery. In the redemptive moments of human history, the realistic pretensions of the Evil Inclination (that he is a self-subsistent, autonomous entity) are unmasked for one and all. Both the righteous and the wicked come to recognize his relativized, projected, transient role. When the dust has settled somewhat on frenzied human activity, the righteous and the wicked notice how the Evil Inclination is a construction of the self serving as an internalized or introjected Other, or "elsewhere" or platform for the self – either enabling it to expand and transform itself or disabling it from meeting its challenges. The crucial factor in determining whether one succeeded or failed in taming his Evil Inclination has to do with one's ability to live with the theoretical irresolvability of the human condition. The righteous played the game despite all of its ambiguities. They treated the Evil Inclination as an instrumentalized fulcrum for fashioning their projects and realizing their goals. The "take" on the Evil Inclination that is vouchsafed to them in the phase of redemption just validates those limitations that debarred them from the outset to secure a more objective, stable grasp of the Evil Inclination. The "mountain" that they wrestled with to become who they were is affirmed as "a mountain." No reductionist path is carved out for them to solve the riddle. The *Yetzer Harah* as a mountain was what enabled them to become who they were. His being invested with reality was what facilitated their achieving whatever degree of greatnesss they managed to attain. What the wicked learn in the period of redemption is precisely that their largest failing consisted in not being able to live with the limitations and impermeabilities that characterize the human condition. They did not engage sufficiently in those intermediate, transient projections of "Othernesses" and "elsewheres" that would have enabled them to surmount the hurdles of diurnal existence. The greatest rebuke that the Talmud can offer them is that in the time of redemption they realize that the Evil Inclination was thread-like in character – there to be fashioned, shaped and utilized while in the heat of their lives they hankered after certainty, and not being able to achieve it, prematurely dismissed the *Yetzer Harah*.

Rabbi Akiva and the totality vs. infinity distinction

The devolution of Otherness into a totality vs. infinity distinction is in line with normative Rabbinic thought in other ways as well. The Talmudic Sage Rabbi Akiva, who is one of the major theoretical architects of Rabbinic Judaism,[43] engages in two astounding exegeses of Biblical verses that on the surface have little to do with each other, but in which one can discern an underlying pattern of continuity that links up with the Platonic thematics we have been discussing:

> Simeon Imsoni – others state, Nehemiah Imsoni – interpreted every *eth* [the sign of the accusative in Hebrew, followed by a direct object] in the Torah; [but] as soon as he came to *Thou shalt fear* [eth] *the Lord thy God* (Deuteronomy 6, 13), he desisted. Said his disciples to him, "Master, what is to happen with all the *ethin* which you have interpreted?" "Just as I received reward for interpreting them," he replied, "so will I receive reward for refraining [from interpreting them]."[44] Subsequently R. Akiva came and taught: *Thou shalt fear* [eth] *the Lord thy God* is to include scholars.[45]

The division of opinion between Simeon Imsoni and Rabbi Akiva seems to revolve around the ambiguity surrounding the appropriate political response to monotheism – whether a voluntarism culminating in an accentuation of the value of participation in a rarefied and specialized community or a voluntarism giving rise to counter-structures of organization and hierarchy. Simeon Imsoni's position seems to be predicated upon the notion that, given God's majestic Otherness, all our human vocabularies pale into meaninglessness in relation to Him and that the most fitting response to God is one of mystical solitariness and contemplation. There is absolutely nothing to be conjoined to the monotheistic conception of God – not even a hierarchy of expositors and interpreters of the Divine will. The religiously-driven individual can only contemplate in abject humility and aloneness the unfathomable Otherness of God. The *Talmid Chochom* (the scholar) for all his intellectual development and spiritual sensitivity is from the perspective of Divinity projected by Simeon Imsoni no better off in this regard than anyone else. He has just more sophisticated ways for registering his ignorance, but he is metaphysically debarred by the conceptual constraints of monotheism from developing a successful strategy for overcoming it. Given this situation, Simeon Imsoni feels he has no choice but to say: "Just as I received reward for interpreting the *ethin* so will I receive reward for refraining from interpreting them." To strive for authenticity, boundlessness and non-transferability (sometimes with a dim awareness that there exists a small elite community of such mystical strivers) seems to be the appropriate ethical and theological implication to be drawn from the metaphysical content of negative theology. A community of such intensely participatory believers could only be described as a community of the saints.

Rabbi Akiva, by contrast, sees the voluntarism implicit in negative theology as a basis for not only creating spontaneous individual order through the attainment of insight and possible spontaneous interaction with other similarly motivated individuals, but he also extends the voluntarism to include a collectively-ordered response to God's presence through the introduction of systems of authority and hierarchy. The idea of negative theology, with its unconquerable, unbridgeable distance separating God from man, legitimates for Rabbi Akiva the idea of Rabbinic authority.

Rabbi Akiva's gloss on "Thou shalt fear [*eth*] the Lord thy God" provides us with an exegetical key for unraveling a curious juxtaposition in Exodus. The structure of the Jethro story in Exodus is extremely puzzling. The conclusion of the story contains the great revelation at Sinai and the promulgation of the Ten Commandments. The beginning of this section of the Torah, however, is devoted to the comparatively much more mundane topic of appointing local and more remote magistrates. While Rashi in effect tells us in his analysis of these chapters that *Ein Mukdam U'Meuchar B'Torah* (the Torah's narrative does not follow strict chronological sequence and therefore Jethro's advice and its implementation need to be understood as following rather than preceding the revelation at Sinai)[46] the literary structuring of events, in contrast to their actual historical sequence, nevertheless invites independent elucidation. It seems to me based upon Rabbi Akiva's gloss on "Thou shalt fear [*eth*] the Lord thy God" that the passages detailing the routinization of charisma at the beginning of this section of the Torah precede the account of the most charismatically charged moment in Jewish tradition – the revelation at Sinai – as a way of instructing us how to assimilate and respond to the Sinaitic events. Revelation needs to be mediated and channeled through a series of authority structures that dilute its content suitably to the exigencies of daily life. There is a beginning before the beginning in Jewish life, which consists in a recognition of authority as a precondition for and facilitator of religious truth – what conformity to religious edicts requires of the community of believers.

In the Babylonian Talmudic tractate *Baba Metzia* (62a), a famous hypothetical case is recounted that Rabbi Akiva resolves:

> If two are traveling on a journey [far from civilization], and one has a pitcher of water, if both drink, they will [both] die, but if one only drinks, he can reach civilization – The Son of Patura taught: It is better that both should drink and die, rather than that one should behold his companion's death. Until Rabbi Akiva came and taught: "That thy brother may live with thee" (Leviticus 25, 36): thy life takes precedence over his life.[47]

An ethics of theory vs. an ethics of ideology 113

There is a parallel structure to Rabbi Akiva's exegesis of the two verses, "Thou shalt fear [*eth*] the Lord thy God" and "That thy brother may live with Thee." Just as in the first verse, "God" gets displaced onto a cadre of human Rabbinic interpreters, so too, in the second verse, "thy brother" gets displaced onto "thee." The motive force behind the two interpretive approaches seems to be the same. Negative theology which stipulates that we need to discount on a literal level all ascriptions of attributes to God confronts the dilemma that if the only point of access to God is the point of denial (one reaches God only at the cost of denying the literalness of what one is reaching toward), what is one denying? Multivalued and nonstandard logics generally that encode the suspension of the Law of the Excluded Middle are able to accommodate the contradictoriness of negative theology by transforming its anomalous logical status into a new norm reflective of the dissolution of the dichotomy between A and not-A, so that intermediate possibilities exist (become chartable). A generalized agnosticism which declares that the returns are not yet fully in concerning the nature of the world serves as a background metaphysical postulate nurturing the emergence and reception of multivalued logics. The background postulate is a generalized agnosticism rather than simply agnosticism because it is invoked as a response to a general feature of language (that in its Aristotelian-inspired-and-legitimated grids, it is not able to sustain a statement and its opposite – in our case, "denial of attributes to God" and "God"), rather than something specific to religious terminology per se.

Rabbi Akiva implicitly transfers this generalized agnosticism from God to the Other when he assigns primacy to the self over the Other in his second exegetical exercise. The Other is at least partially rejected because his categorial autonomy cannot be sustained from a generalized-agnostic perspective. The sense and reference of the Other are still regarded as being in a state of fluidity. For the sake of consistency, we must acknowledge that the self to which Rabbi Akiva assigns primacy is also in the throes of a constant struggle of self-definition. The self to which Rabbi Akiva yields priority needs to be construed in a negative hermeneutical manner as blocking embrace of the Other – not as literally affirming itself.[48] The self as a generalized-agnostic posit awaiting further confirmation and specification is sufficient according to Rabbi Akiva on negative, pragmatic grounds (the Other cannot do better than the self in validating its claims, and the life-or-death exigencies of the moment need to be resolved in the absence of a clear claim of moral superiority issuing forth from the Other) to justify one's placing one's life ahead of one's neighbor in the circumstances described.

Another famous dictum of Rabbi Akiva's, cited in the Jerusalemite Talmudic tractate *Nedarim* (Chapter 9, Halakha 4), seems to contradict his ruling in the case of the two people and the one pitcher of water in the desert:

> It was stated in a Baraita:[49] Rabbi Akiva said: "Love thy fellow human being as thyself" (Leviticus 19:18) – this is a great principle of Torah. Ben

Azzai says, "This is the book of the generations of Adam" (Genesis 5:1) is an even greater principle than that.⁵⁰

In the case of the one pitcher of water, Rabbi Akiva rules that the life of the person owning the pitcher has priority over that of his neighbor, and with regard to the verse of loving one's fellow human being as oneself, Rabbi Akiva affirms it as a great principle of Torah. How do we reconcile Rabbi Akiva's two rulings?

Baruch Halevi Epstein (1860 – 1941), in his commentary on Torah known as *Torah Temimah*, raises this objection and responds to it by invoking a famous formulation of the Rabbinic Sage Hillel, which he claims serves as a precursor-text for Rabbi Akiva's statement, and casts it in a new light. In the Babylonian Talmudic tractate *Shabbath* (31a), the following story is told:

> It happened that a certain heathen came before Shammai and said to him, "Make me a proselyte on condition that you teach me the whole Torah while I stand on one foot." Thereupon he repulsed him with the builder's cubit which was in his hand. When he went before Hillel, he said to him, "What is hateful to you, do not to your neighbor; that is the whole Torah, while the rest is the commentary thereof; go and learn it."⁵¹

According to the *Torah Temimah*,⁵² Rabbi Akiva's phrase, "This is a great principle of Torah," echoes Hillel's phrase, "That is the whole Torah" (in Hebrew, the continuity in the phrasing is even more striking), and Rabbi Akiva needs to be understood as endorsing Hillel's negative reading of the Biblical verse. Both Hillel and Rabbi Akiva therefore interpret the Biblical verse imploring us to love our fellow human being as ourselves to signify that we refrain from doing things that are hateful to us to other people. There is an infinite range of possible translations of this negatively-construed dictum into a set of positive precepts concerning how we should act. Because the verse is interpreted in negative, minimalist terms, rather than in positive, maximalist terms, – how we should not act, rather than how we should act – the contradiction between Rabbi Akiva's reading of this verse and his ruling in the case of the one pitcher of water in the desert is resolved. Assigning priority to my own life in a context where there are insufficient resources to save my own life, as well as that of my friend, is something that is not hateful to me. (I could even possibly accept my friend doing the same thing to me had his role been exchanged with mine.) Therefore, I am allowed – and perhaps even enjoined – to rescue myself in a context of scarcity as depicted in the Talmudic narrative.

Ben Azzai says that "This is the Book of the generations of Adam" (Genesis 5:1) is an even greater principle than "Love thy fellow human being as thyself" (Leviticus 19:18). The *Torah Temimah* interprets Ben Azzai as tacitly referring to the conclusion of the verse he cites from Genesis – "In the day that God created man, in the likeness of God made He him."⁵³ Ben Azzai, apparently, is disturbed by the relativist implications residing in Rabbi Akiva's negative construal of the commandment to love one's fellow human being as oneself. From Rabbi Akiva's perspective, all that is required is that one not do unto others what is hateful to oneself. What if one is a masochist and enjoys inflicting pain upon himself? According to Rabbi Akiva's negative reading of the Biblical verse, the masochist would be allowed to inflict pain upon others because for him pain is experienced as a source of pleasure. In order to ward off this possibility, Ben Azzai says that the verse which emphasizes that man was created in God's likeness insinuates an even greater principle than the one that Rabbi Akiva cites. Relativized possibilities that are sanctioned by Rabbi Akiva's negative reading of "Love your fellow human being as yourself" are blocked by Ben Azzai's embrace of the principle of the Divine-human likeness, which renders human beings inviolate even in relation to their own preferences and values.

An alternative reading of Ben Azzai would be that he shares the negative-theological tenets of Rabbi Akiva (the metaphysical distance between God and man is, indeed, unbridgeable), but Ben Azzai believes that "distance" itself remains indeterminate. It is compatible both with the picture of radical human isolation favored by Rabbi Akiva and with an image of human beings as trustees for an inheritance that includes their own bodies and psyches which, on a metaphorical level that can never be successfully unpacked, they receive from God. Rabbi Akiva's implicitly preferred metaphor of ownership (of our minds and bodies) and Ben Azzai's favored metaphor of trusteeship are each compatible with the principles of negative theology. The idea of a trustee does not commit one to a literalized Entruster.

Rabbi Akiva, as we have seen, would resist a literal translation of the notion that man was created in God's likeness. When he interprets the "*eth*" in "Thou shalt fear [*eth*] the Lord thy God" to include scholars, he is underscoring for us that there is no unmediated contact with the monotheistic God. There are Rabbinic intermediaries and verbal symbols and metaphors, but whatever it is that they represent has no immediate cash value, but only generates further metaphors. The constraints upon the masochist, therefore, derive from a set of pragmatic considerations having to do with the most economical set of terms for purchasing civic peace, rather than with natural law prohibitions that universally restrict what human beings can do. Given the postulates of negative theology and the ways in which they eventuate in a generalized agnosticism, Rabbi Akiva would challenge the moral objectivist to do better than he in providing a foundation for moral judgment. The closest approximation to objectivity for Rabbi Akiva is the negative argument that no one can do better than the skeptic in supporting philosophical arguments and judgments. Even though his rhetoric is more realist in character, Ben Azzai (as we have seen) can also be read in non-natural-law terms.

If we follow the *Torah Temimah's* interpretation of Hillel's construal of the injunction of "Love your fellow human being as yourself," which is adopted by Rabbi Akiva, then both Hillel and Rabbi Akiva confront an implicit issue

116 *Emmanuel Levinas and the Limits to Ethics*

of reflexivity. To be consistently relativistic requires one to be relativistic about relativism as well as doctrines that compete with it. How can one coherently formulate a relativist position? One possible strategy again is to invoke a generalized agnosticism, which leaves the door open to multivalued logics that map the suspension of the Law of the Excluded Middle. Thereby, the contradiction attendant to relativism – that the relativist is relative about everything but relativism – is normalized by being fitted into a more expansive and accommodating logical grid.

If the text in the Jerusalemite Talmud interpreted in this manner represents the theological view of Rabbi Akiva, then it is no wonder that Rabbi Akiva subscribes to the view that the "crowns" that Jewish law mandates that a scribe place on the letters of a Torah scroll are available for interpretation. Since there is no Realistic Entity posting limits to the activity of interpretation (or establishing the outward parameters in terms of which reliable communication can take place), interpretation looms as an omnipresent and all-pervasive activity.

Rabbi Akiva not only has a negative-theological conception of the nature of God, but (as we have seen) he is also a skeptic in the more conventional sense of doubting the reality, and the consequent moral parity, of other minds and other persons. What is the conceptual linkage between his negative theology and his skepticism? One way of delineating the relationship between the two allegiances is to notice how negative theology (the formulation of its tenets) eventuates in a contradiction and, following Karl Popper (as we have seen), how once contradiction is allowed, no possibility can be logically ruled out, so that one willy-nilly finds oneself in a skeptical position. Negative theology, which says that our only way of conceiving of God is to consistently disown the literalisitc import of any attributes that we are tempted to ascribe to Him, commits us simultaneously to perpetually disowning attributes *while* retaining some recognizable substantive entity called "God," whose attributes are being unceasingly swept away on a literal level. According to negative theology, we have God only for the sake of continually disowning Him on a literal level. Sustaining allegiance to God in a negative-theological context thereby presupposes the normalizing of contradiction. Once contradiction is affirmed, no possibility can be ruled out, and we are therefore ensconced in a skeptical position that is bereft of the resources for defending other minds and all the other traditional elements of the common, everyday world.

Rabbi Akiva's series of statements in the third chapter of *Pirkei Avot*

Rabbi Akiva's cumulative series of statements in *Avot* 3:18 confirms the theological understandings we have been discussing as governing his metaphysics and hermeneutics. As many commentators in the past have noticed and attempted to theorize,[54] there appears to be a systematic theological principle at work in the way that Rabbi Akiva's exegesis of Biblical verses differs from Rabbi Yishmael's – his persistent adversary in many legal settings throughout the Talmud. Rabbi Yishmael is famous for his authorship of the Thirteen *Middot* ("rules") through which the Torah is elucidated. These rules, to a certain extent at least, establish a quasi-rationalistic framework to be uniformly applied in terms of what ways one can make sense of the text of the Torah. These rules include *a fortiori* argument and the role of context in helping to fix the meaning of verses in the Torah. Rabbi Yishmael's approach presupposes that a common framework of rational analysis links together the Mind of God (as the Author of the Torah) with that of the human interpreter, enabling him to penetrate the significations of particular verses by the application of a common set of rules that, as it were, are binding upon Him as well as upon us. From Rabbi Yishmael's perspective, God appears to be bound by something more overarching than Himself, namely, a set of rational interpretive canons that limit Him as well as us in the communication of meaning.

Rabbi Akiva, by contrast, destroys any kind of rationalistic bridge between us and God. Every aspect and component of Torah is wildly, anarchistically available for exegesis without any limiting framework to rationalize the process. Rabbi Akiva would invest with interpretation not only all of the accusatives (*Ethin*) found in the Torah, but also all of the crowns placed by scribes on the letters of the Torah when writing a Torah Scroll in accordance with its Jewish legal [Halakhic] specifications. Apparently, from Rabbi Akiva's perspective, the metaphysical distances separating us from God are unbridgeable by us, so that there is a kind of open season prevailing with regard to opportunities for deconstructing and reconstructing the text of the Torah.

Rabbi Akiva's theological position receives classic expression in the mishnah in *Avot*:

> He [Rabbi Akiva] used to say: Beloved is man, for he was created in God's image; it is indicative of a greater love that it was made known to him that he was created in God's image, as it is said: "For in the image of God He made man" (Genesis 9:6). Beloved are the people Israel, for they are described as children of the Omnipresent; it is indicative of a greater love that it was made known to them that they are described as the children of the Omnipresent, as it is said: "You are children [literally sons] to Hashem [literally, the Name] your God" (Deuteronomy 14:1). Beloved are the people Israel, for a cherished utensil was given to them; it is indicative of a greater love that it was made known to them that they were given a cherished utensil, as it is said: "For I have given you a good teaching; do not forsake my Torah" (Proverbs 4:2).[55]

In crucial respects, this mishnah is about the insurmountability of naming (how things get called in texts) for fixing the identity of both God and the communities of both Jewish and non-Jewish believers. The mishnah begins innocently by citing the famous verse in Genesis that states that man was created in God's image. It then moves on in its second clause to situating the Jews (in contrast to humanity as a whole) as being concentrically closer to Divinity because, instead of being merely made in the image of God, they are called the "sons of God." After the first two clauses take us breathlessly close to the center of Divinity, the third (and final) clause of the mishnah then deconstructs the center itself. This is a moment of high frisson because it redirects the momentum of the mishnah downward (or backward) instead of forward (or upward). The mishnah tells us in the third clause that the people of Israel are beloved because they were given a "cherished utensil." The "cherished utensil" turns out to be the Torah, which is cherished in accordance with the well-known Midrashic formulation that Rabbi Akiva appears to be trading upon because it formed the blueprint that enabled God to create the world.[56] The third clause of Rabbi Akiva's mishnah thus emphasizes that it was a textual source (in fact, the same textual source, the Torah, that is cited in the first two clauses) that had "made known" to God that He was the Creator of the world (that gave Him the linguistic resources to fashion it), just like it was a textual source that had "made known" to humanity at large that they were created in the image of God and to Jews that they were the "sons of God."

This mishnah pretty dramatically communicates to us a negative-theological reading of the nature of God and of our relationship to Him. We cannot approach God in any direct, literal way – nor can any text that is intelligible to us literally name Him or describe Him. Since for us the language pertaining to God is irredeemably metaphorical, even the God-talk that relates to God's own actions (such as Creation) independently of His immediate relationship to us can only be grasped by us on a metaphorical level. Given the unrelievedly metaphorical nature of the Divine vocabulary, which presupposes that there is nothing literal to compare it with in any sense or on any level, there is nothing blasphemous in reversing the pathway of metaphor (because no matter which direction it travels, there is no literalistic exit or translation): Instead of God's actions becoming a metaphor for us (disclosing our potential; highlighting in which directions we should go), our actions become a metaphor for Him (giving us a radically tenuous,metaphorical grip on actions, such as Creation, that are attributed to Him). Once we travel this route, we notice how we inhabit a world fashioned from start to finish by human acts of naming – from the abstract universal, God, to the concrete universal, humanity, to the particular people, Israel. A common universal thread relating to naming links all three.

Hillel as a theological precursor of Rabbi Akiva

Hillel, who is one of Rabbi Akiva's major precursors in the chain of Rabbinic tradition, has a position similar to his with regard to the conceptual and existential inaccessibility of the monotheistic God. The following story is recounted in the Babylonian Talmudic tractate *Shabbath* (31a):

> Our rabbis taught: A certain heathen once came before Shammai and asked him, "How many Toroth have you?" "Two," he replied: "the Written Torah and the Oral Torah." "I believe you with respect to the Written, but not with respect to the Oral Torah; make me a proselyte on condition that you teach me the Written Torah [only]." [But] he scolded and repulsed him in anger. When he went before Hillel, he accepted him as a proselyte. On the first day he taught him *Aleph, Beth, Gimmel, Daleth*; the following day he reversed [them] to him. "But yesterday you did not teach them to me thus," he protested. "Must you then not rely upon me? Then rely upon me with respect to the Oral [Torah] too."[57]

Hillel in effect told his interlocutor that in Judaism one cannot pierce through a structure of authority-relations to some primary level of revelation. The Written Torah and the Oral Torah subsist on the same ontological plane. They are both mediated to us through a scheme of authority-relations to which we agree to be bound – and through no other means. From this perspective, observance of Jewish law (*Halakha*) – including even the engagement in prayer – becomes an end unto itself (or an interminable set of means) – since the invocation of more traditional ends such as achieving a greater communion with God has been foreclosed by the structure of negative theology.

The contemporary Jewish philosopher Yeshayahu Leibowitz taking his cues partially from Hillel and Rabbi Akiva very forthrightly emphasizes the interminableness of the means in Judaism:

> Performance of the Mitzvoth [Divine commandments] is man's path to God, an infinite path, the end of which is never attained and is, in effect, unattainable. A man is bound to know that this path never terminates. One follows it without advancing beyond the point of departure.
>
> "Every day they will appear to you as new," for after each act the position of man remains as it was before. The aim of proximity to God is unattainable. It is infinitely distant, "for God is in heaven and you on the earth" (Ecclessiastes 5:1).[58]

Given Hillel's allegiances to negative theology and a generalized agnosticism that I have tried to reconstruct from his statements in the tractate *Shabbath*, we are able to appreciate more deeply his justly celebrated formulation in *Pirkei Avot* about how transient selves require transient Others in order to form and stabilize their identities:

> He [Hillel] used to say: If I am not for myself, who will be for me? And if I am for myself, what am I? And if not now, when?[59]

Hillel appears to be saying that the self gets formed through its relationship with the Other. He emphasizes, on the one hand, that if there is no realistic awareness of the pervasiveness and centrality of one's embodied self for the organization of daily life, then one is bereft of an appropriate starting point for developing oneself and cultivating those projects that become characteristic of one's life. However, if one remains wedded to the level of the self, one is still very far from becoming a recognizable human self. A self that shuts out the Other is not a proper self – is not yet in realistic contact with its limits and resources. We become who we are through the reflections that are sent back to us in the course of our interactions with Others.

The problem with my exposition of Hillel's statement as I have presented it so far is that it appears to contradict the skepticism and relativism we have discerned in his earlier cited teachings. The self gets formed through the crucible of its interaction with Others. But then there *is* a self – and there *are* Others. How might it be possible to reconcile the Hillel we are currently confronting with his more skeptical statements cited earlier?

One promising route to follow is to notice how Hillel's formulation in *Pirkei Avot* parallels the structure of – and serves as an intertextual gloss upon – that verse in the Torah which we have seen him earlier describe as encapsulating a great principle, namely, "Love thy fellow human being as thyself." The Biblical verse posits the self as the appropriate frame of reference for loving one's fellow human beings – and Hillel seems to be expanding upon this formulation in elaborating upon the dialectic between self and Other that I summarized in the previous paragraph. If this reading is correct, then the third constituent phrase of Hillel's larger statement – "And if not now, when?" – must correspond to the last (and so far unrecorded) phrase of the Biblical verse, namely, "I am God." If we can unravel how "If not now, when?" serves as a hermeneutical gloss on "I am God," then perhaps we will be able to render Hillel's teaching in *Pirkei Avot* consistent with his other previously cited statements.

Given the generalized agnosticism that we have seen generally pervades Hillel's conceptualizations of both God and the Other, he is driven to find a categorial correlative for the phrase, "I am God." The alternative that he opts for is evocative of Maimonides' gloss on one of the names of God found in Exodus, namely, "I am that I am."[60] In his discussion of this Divine name that was revealed to Moses in his first encounter with Revelation, Maimonides says:

> The whole secret consists in the repetition in a predicative position of the very word indicative of existence. For the word *that* [in the phrase "I am that I am"] requires the mention of an attribute immediately connected with it. For it is a deficient word requiring a connection with something else ... Accordingly, the first word is *I am* considered as a term to which a predicate is attached; the second word that is predicated of the first is also *I am*, that is, identical with the first. Accordingly, Scripture makes, as it were, a clear statement that the subject is identical with the predicate.[61]

Taken literally, what Maimonides appears to be saying is that God is existence. However, in accordance with the premises of negative theology, no attributes can be literally applied to God, not even the attribute or quality or character or state of existence. God is without humanly comprehensible predicates. What does it mean, therefore, to say that "God is existence"? This world – our world – constitutes the trace (or series of traces) of a perennially uncompletable metaphor. The world generates the descriptive epithets that we seek to apply to God. But under the impulsion of negative-theological theorizing, God recedes further and further into the background, so that these attributes can only be compared with one another and with other worldly phenomena, but can never be literally asserted of God. The circuit of metaphorical comparison ("this is like that") remains permanently incomplete, since we never penetrate the screen of what exists beyond worldly phenomena. For all practical purposes, therefore, God is the continuously evolving world, which is the scene of all those efforts to match up actions and the descriptive epithets formulated about them with an enduring subject responsible for the actions and the epithets.

"And if not now, when?" can be read as Hillel's hermeneutical deconstruction and reconstruction of "I am God." From Hillel's generalized-agnostic perspective, what is accessible to us (what is amenable to human translation) in the idea of infinity is the notion of horizontal transcendence – of one present succeeding another present – in other words, the passage of time. It is in this context that we need to make sense of Hillel's dialectical understanding of the process of self-formation presented in the first two-thirds of his teaching. For Hillel, it is acknowledging our living in time that both stimulates and facilitates the articulation of the self as a series of interactions with Others. The dialectic between self and Other is not a once-and-for-all enactment. It proceeds throughout our lives. We never manage to appropriate ourselves (indeed it would be ruinous to ourselves and to the significant Others of our lives if we should even aspire to do so) in a complete way. The dialectic between self and Other is constitutive of each moment of our lives. We are the selves who we are during the multiple moments of our lives because of the self-disclosures that have achieved clarity and urgency through our interactions with Others. The Other releases and sanctions the self to become a self – which is an ongoing process and project that never ceases as long as there are selves and Others in mutual interaction. The incomplete – and uncompletable – posits of self and Other mutually sustain each other in a permanent state of suspended animation and not-fully-consummated realization. A self that is not fully known or realized and an Other that is not fully known or realized sustain each other in their not-fully-realized state, without either the self or the Other becoming fully achieved. The opacity and the relatedness become two sides of the same coin.

There are three additional glosses upon the verse, "Love thy fellow human being as thyself, I am God" that take off from the skeptical set of understandings we have been considering. Rav Shneur Zalman of Ladi (the "Baal

Hatanya" and founder of the Lubavitch Chassidic movement) says that the Biblical injunction to love God monotheistically displaces onto the commandment to love your fellow human being as yourself.[62] It is as if the Torah provides an intratextual gloss upon what it means when it says that we should love God by paraphrasing the requirement as a love for human beings. Since negative theology precludes conceptual negotiation of God, we are given what look like conceptually more available targets to work toward – namely, our fellow human beings. Since (as we have seen) the generalized agnosticism that serves as a background postulate to negative theology also inhibits a straightforward negotiation of our fellow human beings, what results is the process of suspended animation I just discussed.

A second gloss on the verse focuses upon the fact that the operative preposition in the verse is registered in Hebrew by a *Lamed* ("L"), rather than by an *Eth*. The Hebrew word for fellow human being is preceded by an L rather than by an *Eth*. *Eth* suggests something finite and appropriable. The L, by contrast, conjures up something more transitional and prospective. The force of the preposition L, in contradistinction to the accusative *Eth*, is to underscore that our relationship to the Other has to be predicated upon an ongoing movement toward, rather than upon the prospect of a complete appropriation.

A third gloss on this verse would account for the juxtaposition of "I am God" with the preceding phrase of "Love thy fellow human being as yourself" by noting that what often thwarts the expression of love between human beings is an analysis of the motives, character or personality of the Other that reads him or her as an unfit subject for the love and affection that we are channeling toward him. Also, we often invest mentally and emotionally in a huge way in calculations (e.g., Is the other person doing enough for me to warrant what I am doing for him?) that undermine and defeat the imperative to love our fellow human beings. To these anxieties, the verse responds by emphasizing, "I am God." The inner self is transparent only to God and is, indeed, fashioned in the image of God, which is to say that it shares God's irredeemable opacity. We postulate the monotheistic God in such a way that human beings are fully transparent only to Him. From a strictly human perspective, there is a premium placed on doing – on acting in accordance with the maxim of "Love thy fellow human being" – as harboring the largest prospect, in a context of imperfect knowledge of self and Other, of transforming one's overall situation to bring about the largest prospect for good for oneself and for Others.

Notes

1 Aristotle, *Nicomachean Ethics*. Trans. Terence Irwin. (Indianapolis: Hackett Publishing Company, 1985), 1126a5; pp. 105–106.
2 P. 105 in the Irwin translation.
3 Aristotle, *Nicomachean Ethics*, 1126b10; p. 107.

An ethics of theory vs. an ethics of ideology   123

4 The Mishnah is the first major redaction of the Oral Law of Judaism and was undertaken by Rabbi Judah haNasi in 220 C.E. It is the first major work of Rabbinic Judaism.
5 *Pirkei Avos: Ethics of the Fathers.* Trans. Nosson Scherman. (Brooklyn: Mesorah Publications, 1984), p. 35. The translation in the text includes one emendation on my part.
6 Rabbeinu Yonah as found in standard editions of the Mishnah; my translation.
7 Rabbeinu Ovadiah MiBartenura as found in standard editions of the Mishnah; my translation.
8 Maimonides' commentary on *Avot* found in the standard editions; my translation.
9 My translation of Rashi's commentary found in the standard editions of *Avot*.
10 An acronym for the "Gaon Rav Eliyahu" (the Aleph in Hebrew is sometimes appropriately transliterated into English by an "E") of Vilna – whose marginalia are printed in the standard editions of the Mishnah.
11 Babylonian Talmud, *Sotah.* Trans. A. Cohen. (London: Soncino Press, 1985), p. 5a.
12 Ibid., p. 5b.
13 My translation.
14 My translation.
15 *Hebrew-English Edition of the Babylonian Talmud: Shabbath.* Trans. H. Freedman. (London: Soncino Press, 1987).
16 See my review of Michael L. Morgan, *Discovering Levinas* (Cambridge: Cambridge University Press, 2007), in *AJS Review*, Volume 33, Number 2 (November 2009), pp. 419–424, especially pp. 422–423.
17 This is my translation of part of Maimonides' commentary on *Avot* 4:4.
18 My translation.
19 The translation comes from the Soncino Press edition of the Babylonian Talmud.
20 In his preoccupation with spooks, Derrida is inspired by Marx. The pervasiveness of spooks in Marx is captured in the very title of Derrida's book, *Specters of Marx*. Trans. Peggy Kamuf (London: Routledge, 1994).
21 Alasdair MacIntyre, *After Virtue: A Study in Moral Theory.* Second Edition. (Notre Dame: University of Notre Dame Press, 1984).
22 "Rabbi Samuel b. [the son of] Nahmani said in the name of Rabbi Jonathan: Blasted be the bones of those who calculate the end." Babylonian Talmud, *Sanhedrin* 97b.
23 Friedrich Nietzsche, *Beyond Good and Evil.* Trans. Walter Kaufmann. (New York: Vintage Books, 1966), p. 224.
24 Plato, *The Republic.* Trans. F. M. Cornford. (London: Oxford University Press, 1945), I. 338 (p. 18).
25 The Aristotelian view forms the basis for Ryle's notion. See Gilbert Ryle, *The Concept of Mind* (New York: Barnes and Noble, 1949).
26 Thomas L. Pangle, ed., *The Roots of Political Philosophy: Ten Forgotten Socratic Dialogues* (Ithaca: Cornell University Press, 1987), 293e (p. 324). Compare the comments by the translator of the dialogue, David R. Sweet, on p. 350.
27 Bertrand Russell, *A History of Western Philosophy* (New York: Simon and Schuster, 1945), p. 121.
28 Ibid., p. 122.
29 Plato, *Parmenides*, 130b–132b.
30 Plato, The *Republic*, 596a. See the discussion of this and related passages in Antony Flew, *An Introduction to Western Philosophy: Ideas and Argument from Plato to Sartre* (Indianapolis: Bobbs-Merrill, 1971), p. 50.
31 Compare the following quote from Holderlin: "Believe me, the skeptic finds contradiction and imperfection in all that is thought, because he knows the harmony of perfect beauty, which is never thought. The dry bread that human reason well-meaningly offers him, he disdains only because he is secretly feasting

at the table of the gods." Cited as an epigraph to Robert Bernasconi's article, "Skepticism in the Face of Philosophy," in Robert Bernasconi and Simon Critchley, eds., *Re-Reading Levinas* (Bloomington: Indiana University Press, 1996), p. 149.
32 Plato, *Greater Hippias* 296d (Pangle, p. 328).
33 Ibid., 296c-d (Pangle, p. 328).
34 Ibid., 294c (Pangle, p. 325).
35 Ibid., 288d (Pangle, p. 317).
36 Ibid., 287a (Pangle, p. 315).
37 Ibid., 295c (Pangle, p. 327).
38 Ibid., 287a (Pangle, p. 315).
39 Ibid., 295a (Pangle, p. 326), FN 36.
40 *Aggadah* refers to the homiletic and non-legalistic exegetical texts in the Talmud and Midrash.
41 *Hebrew-English Translation of the Babylonian Talmud: Sukkah*. Trans. Israel W. Slotki. (London: Soncino Press, 1984).
42 Ibid., p. 52a.
43 "And all [of the primary collections of early Rabbinic teachings] are taught according to the views of Rabbi Akiva." Babylonian Talmud, *Sanhedrin* 86a.
44 If Simeon Imsoni's exegetical strategy breaks down in one textual site, it cannot be applied to other textual locations.
45 *Hebrew-English Translation of the Babylonian Talmud: Pesahim*. Trans. H. Freedman. (London: Soncino Press, 1967), 22b. I have amended the English translation.
46 See Rashi's commentary on Exodus 18:13.
47 *Hebrew-English Translation of the Babylonian Talmud: Baba Mezia*. Trans. H. Freedman. (London: Soncino Press, 1986).
48 I theorize the notion of a "negative hermeneutics" and apply it to Maimonidean negative theology in my book, *Skepticism, Belief, and the Modern*, pp. 72–83.
49 *Braita* (an Aramaic word meaning literally "on the outside") refers to uncodified Tannaitic (early Rabbinic) source material.
50 Jerusalem Talmud, *Nedarim*, Chapter 9, Halacha 4; my translation. This text is cited and commented upon in Baruch Halevi Epstein, *Chumash Torah Temimah: One* (Tel Aviv: Am Olam, 1972), p. 72.
51 *Hebrew-English Translation of the Babylonian Talmud: Shabbath*. Trans. H. Freedman. (London: Soncino Press, 1987).
52 The Rabbinic texts analyzed by the author of the *Torah Temimah* all relate to Genesis 5:1–and are discussed by him on p. 72 of volume one of his work cited above.
53 *The Holy Scriptures*. English translation edited by Alexander Harkavy. (New York: Hebrew Publishing Company, 1936), p. 6.
54 For a systematic discussion of how to theologically situate the different views of Rabbi Yishmael and Rabbi Akiva with regard to a whole host of topics in Jewish law and thought, see the trilogy by Abraham Joshua Heschel, *Torah Min H'Shamayim B'Aspaklaria shel ha Dorot* (Theology of Ancient Judaism) Volume 1, *Darkei Machshavah B'Tekufat ha-Tana'im* (Pathways of Thought in the Age of the Tana'im); Volume 2, *Torah M'Sinai V'Torah Min ha-Shamayim* (Torah from Sinai and Torah from Heaven) (London: Soncino Press, 1962; 1965); A third volume of this work appeared posthumously, subtitled *Elu V'Elu Divrei Elokim Chaim* (Both These Words and Those are the Words of the Living God) (New York: Jewish Theological Seminary of America, 1990). An English translation of this trilogy has appeared, *Heavenly Torah as Refracted through the Generations*. Ed. and trans. Gordon Tucker with Leonard Levin. (New York: Continuum, 2006). My reading in the text of how Rabbi Akiva's systematic interpretive stance

of Biblical passages differs from Rabbi Yishmael's approach is in certain key ways in dramatic contrast to Heschel's.
55 *Pirkei Avos*, III:18; p. 31.
56 "When the Holy One resolved to create the world, He guided Himself by the Torah as by a plan ... For the Torah preceded the creation of the world by two thousand years; and so, when He resolved to create the world He looked into the Torah, into its every creative word, and fashioned the world correspondingly; for all the words and all the actions of all the worlds are contained in the Torah. Therefore did the Holy One, blessed be He, look into it and create the world." *The Zohar, Volume IV.* Trans. Maurice Simon and Dr. Paul P. Levertoff. Second Edition. (London: Soncino Press, 1984), 161a, pp. 56–57. This passage in *The Zohar* can be construed as an intertextual gloss on the much earlier Rabbinic text, *Midrash Rabbah: Genesis*, which says that "the Torah ... preceded the creation of the world by two thousand years" and that "the Torah knows what was before the creation of the world." *Midrash Rabbah: Genesis, Volume One.* Trans. H. Freedman. Third Edition. (London: Soncino Press, 1983), 8:2, p. 56. See the theological discussion of *The Zohar's* and the *Midrash Rabbah's* exegeses in the classic work of Chaim Volozhiner, *Nefesh HaChaim*. Ed. Issachar Dov Rubin. (Bnei Brak, 1989), Shaar 4, Chapter 10, pp. 221–225.
57 Soncino Press translation.
58 Yeshayahu Leibowitz, *Judaism, Human Values, and the Jewish State*. Ed. Eliezer Goldman. (Cambridge: Harvard University Press, 1992), pp. 15–16.
59 *Pirkei Avos*, I:14; p. 13.
60 Exodus 3:14.
61 Maimonides, *Guide*, I:63:154–155.
62 Cited in Chaim Yaakov Zuckerman, *Sefer Otzar Chaim: Vayikrah* (Tel Aviv, n.d.), p. 130.

7 Nietzsche and Levinas

Nietzsche, the Rabbis and Levinas

Conceptions of the Other that one can derive from Nietzsche resonate with Rabbinic thought. Given the centrality that Nietzsche assigns to the concept of power – where nearly all human activities from naming and classifying to producing historical accounts of past events are theorized in terms of the exertion of power – the most fruitful route to the Other in Nietzsche is the negative one of not harboring ressentiment, rather than literally affirming the Otherness of the Other. Experiencing ressentiment in Nietzsche is a function of misdirected power – power masochistically turned inward against the self rather than flowing outward toward the world. The kind of power that Nietzsche talks about would be spoiled for the powerful if the weak continued to play the power game in accordance with the old rules. Power for the strong is something spiritual. Tremendous reserves of inner strength are released for the strong when they follow Nietzsche's precepts concerning power. The power that Nietzsche envisages is not a zero-sum game, but rather a sum-sum game. Nietzsche spurns the manifestations of power associated with zero-sum games as a sign of the weakness of the weak. Power conceived in these terms is bound up with the envy and ressentiment of the weak that Nietzsche loathes. The kind of power desired by the weak is corrupted from within by a conception that sharing signifies losing and diminishing. By contrast, the power of the strong does not give rise to envy and ressentiment because it is conceived from the outset as a sum-sum game. The more people who participate in the project of cultivating their inner strength, the stronger the strong feel. Not having to begrudge Others the strength they are able to cultivate from within is a source of one's own strength.

Nietzsche's theorizing of power as a phenomenon whose presence to a large extent depends upon how it is conceptualized is itself a response to one of the imperatives of power conceived of in a traditional Machiavellian sense. According to Machiavelli, the less one depends on Others and the more one depends on oneself for the attainment of one's objectives, the more powerful one becomes. To eliminate the Other as a threat, as it were, by scorning to begrudge the Other his accomplishments thus constitutes a supreme Machiavellian move on the path toward empowerment.

Nietzsche's route toward Otherness is thus through the totality vs. infinity distinction as a surrogate for a skeptically unavailable direct engagement of the Other. Totalistic conceptions of power evoke the specter of ressentiment – of the prospect of "the excluded" corrupting the power aspirations and exertions of "the included." It is only "infinitizing" expressions of power which remain open to an indefinitely unfolding future of potential inclusiveness that avoid engendering ressentiment on the part of the power-wielders as well as the power-excluded. The totality vs. infinity distinction runs like a leitmotif throughout Nietzsche's thought and is best understood as his own critical gloss upon the concept of power. The following are some illustrations:

1. The idea of "the subject" from Nietzsche's perspective constitutes an effort at totalization, summing and positing a self on the basis of its actions – as if they have finite bounds and finite implications. Nietzsche's emphasis on "deeds" in contrast to a "doer" suggests that actions open upon each other in infinite ways, so as to preclude the prospect of ever declaring and designating a specific "subject."[1] The nature, identity and boundaries of the subject get endlessly deferred as we ponder without limit the significance of the deeds. The collapsibility and reconstructibility of the subject get infinitely regressed onto the collapsibility and reconstructibility of the deeds. In *The Gay Science*, Nietzsche says explicitly: "Rather has the world become 'infinite' for us all over again, inasmuch as we cannot reject the possibility that *it may include infinite interpretations.*"[2]

2. Nietzsche's rejection of totality and affirmation of infinity also influences in ways beyond those I have already explored his discussion of ressentiment. The experience and manifestation of ressentiment are a function of a totalizing disposition and an impatience with infinity. One feels and displays ressentiment when he thinks that his perception of and judgment about a situation in the present constitute the last word. Someone else is more successful than I am so I become jealous and resentful without pausing to think that the situation might be quite ephemeral, or that the sacrifices that rendered it possible might not be worth the costs that the "success" exacted. Or, my station in life and the satisfactions it offers might from some more ultimate vantage point (a "view from nowhere") be more rewarding than the satisfactions attendant to someone else's enjoying a "more successful" station in life. The satisfactions of the two stations might not be fully commensurable or mutually translatable, so that one cannot say conclusively that another person's life is "better" than his own. Paying heed to the ethic implicit in the notion of infinity serves as a hedge against experiencing ressentiment.

"Infinity" is also the metaphysical-cum-psychological mechanism that enables regret, apology and repentance to take place. If "totality" predominated, we would be frozen into a pattern of action dictated by our past. Under the aegis of infinity, we become empowered to continually redefine, reconstruct and reconstitute our lives.

3. Nietzsche's animus against those who manifest ressentiment and transform their begrudging of the strength of Others into the phenomenon of the "bad conscience" (aggressive instincts directed inward, quarantining strength, rather than learning how to emulate it) associated with Christian morality is another classic instance of human beings succumbing to totalization instead of acknowledging the possibility of infinity.[3] Adherents of Christian morality erroneously totalize the available fund of strength or power, viewing it as a zero-sum game: something which someone else unconditionally has and they don't have. They miss the sense in which power is a function of "the moment" – something infinitely exchanged and generated, assuming infinite expressions and embodiments.

4. Nietzsche's generalized-agnostic conception of the human person endorses investing with only provisional credence every commitment, enthusiasm and achievement of the self:

> Not to remain stuck to a person – not even the most loved – every person is a prison, also a nook. Not to remain stuck to a fatherland – not even if it suffers most and needs help most – it is less difficult to sever one's heart from a victorious fatherland. Not to remain stuck to some pity – not even for higher men into whose rare torture and helplessness some accident allowed us to look. Not to remain stuck to a science – even if it should lure us with the most precious finds that seem to have been saved up precisely for us. Not to remain stuck to one's own detachment, to that voluptuous remoteness and strangeness of the bird who flees ever higher to see ever more below him – the danger of the flier. Not to remain stuck to our own virtues and become as a whole the victim of some detail in us, such as our hospitality, which is the danger of dangers for superior and rich souls who spend themselves lavishly, almost indifferently, and exaggerate the virtue of generosity into a vice. One must know how *to conserve oneself*: the hardest test of independence.[4]

The contingency of human becoming – the rejection of being – the denial of any final, quintessential human end is also underscored in *Twilight of the Idols*:

> The fatality of his [man's] essence is not to be disentangled from the fatality of all that has been and will be. Man is not the effect of some special purpose, of a will, and end; nor is he the object of an attempt to attain an "ideal of humanity" nor an "ideal of happiness" or an "ideal of morality." It is absurd to wish to devolve one's essence on some end or other. We have invented the concept of "end": in reality there is no end.[5]

Nietzsche's formulations articulate a point of equilibrium for the self, which runs strikingly parallel to that envisioned by Hobbes in *Leviathan* for society as a whole. Virtually unlimited openness for Hobbes (the subordination of the public to the private sphere) is the conceptual and institutional guarantee of societal stability. In Nietzsche, as well, not becoming "stuck to ourselves" – remaining perpetually open to the instrumentalized, mask-like function of every aspect and pose of the self we have cultivated and assumed (acknowledging the possibility of an infinity of interpretations residing in all of our actions) – is our only route toward conserving ourselves and maintaining ourselves on an even keel.

5. In Section 281 of *Beyond Good and Evil*, Nietzsche refers to "an unconquerable mistrust of the *possibility* of self-knowledge which went so far that even in the concept of 'immediate knowledge,' which theoreticians permit themselves, I sensed a *contradictio in adjecto*."[6] As we saw earlier, if access or exposure to some sector of experience is immediate, it cannot be codified as knowledge. The ascent from "immediate" to "knowledge" destroys the immediacy of the subject matter and therefore renders vulnerable from a strictly objective standpoint the claim to knowledge. Here, again, with regard to our knowledge statements and claims, Nietzsche rejects the view that our theories or names totally correlate with and exhaust the content of reality – and suggests instead that there are infinite possibilities for our theories and names to make sense of and refer to reality. Skeptical idealism militates against totality – and underwrites infinity. Consistent with Nietzsche's skeptical idealism itself, we could say that in the end it is an ethical consideration that guides his choice of this epistemology. There is an implicit emphasis on self-extrication from the quandaries, dilemmas and setbacks that confront us in the course of our lives, which skeptical idealism in its denial of a one-to-one correlation between words and things facilitates and indirectly validates.

Nietzsche's skeptical idealism is also manifested in his genealogical deconstruction of texts, events and phenomena – which in order to be efficacious at all presuppose that theories are underdetermined by facts. The "facts" of Christian morality, for example, can be made to square both with the tenets of Christian morality and with the phenomenon of the "bad conscience" (of aggression directed inward against the self). It is this very surplus of interpretation over fact that yields Nietzsche the space in which to engage in his genealogical deconstructions.

Arthur Danto also attributes an idealist position to Nietzsche. He says: "It doubtless seems strange to couple Berkeley and Nietzsche in this manner, or to think of Nietzsche as holding to a version of idealism. If it is idealism at all, it is *dynamic* idealism to which he was committed."[7] Nietzsche's "dynamic idealism" consists in his believing that "wills act upon wills, and the mode of their so doing is imposing a form, giving a shape which, in the highest level of life, consists in giving or imposing an interpretation."[8]

6. Nietzsche's skeptical idealism is at work even as he envisages the emergence of new orders of being that involve the total transcendence of issues of skepticism and of truth. The freedom to reclassify what were previously identified as epistemological issues as ontological ones (so that we can define and fashion ways of life that sidestep issues of truth and skepticism) suggests that our theories are underdetermined by facts, so that we have a certain amount of leeway in choosing between various possible theoretical descriptions of our situation. The very opting for an ontologically-inspired description of our argumentative condition is a function of the excess of theoretical possibilities over facts, which allows a common set of facts to be subsumed under alternative – and even conflicting – rubrics. Nietzsche (and, in an important sense, also Levinas) are only able to move beyond epistemology (each in his own way) by exploiting the resources made available by one particular epistemological position – namely, skeptical idealism.

The Nietzschean ontologizing of epistemology – his relativizing of the whole quest and his attempt to jettison the distinction between "truth" and "falsehood," which serves as a model for Levinas in trying to collapse epistemology in favor of ethics[9] – can also be understood as his way of theoretically encoding the ultimate circularity of all epistemological arguments. Since the phenomenon of circularity achieves its maximum coherence within the theoretical ambit of a generalized agnosticism (under the auspices of a generalized agnosticism, we cannot hope to transcend circularity because there are no indubitable sets of premises in terms of which our arguments can take off), Nietzsche can be understood as at least implicitly embracing a generalized agnosticism. It is only in relation to a restricted agenda of inquiry that epistemological concerns arise. When we are motivated to validate and justify our knowledge statements and claims, then epistemological arguments get formed and have their being. But validation is only one among many diverse stances that we can assume in relation to our beliefs and knowledge claims. We can, for example, posit certain premises as being true without caring whether they can be appropriately validated or not, but only concerned to test what results such a theoretically nonchalant embrace of premises might engender. We might also be attracted to certain premises as esthetic artifacts – "theoretical playthings" – that we relish in their own right and not for the impeccability of their validational credentials or the argumentative utilities that they yield. The validational bias of epistemology already stakes out a certain set of categories, argumentative moves and conclusions as privileged. In this sense, the epistemological enterprise is circular – moving within the charmed circle of its own theoretical accents and priorities. The answers are correlated with – and made to fit – the questions. The questions are formulated with a certain set of (possible) answers in view. Nietzsche's apparently theoretical lurch beyond epistemology can therefore be most compellingly conceptualized as a series of moves within epistemology itself, highlighting its infinite, in contrast to its totalistic, character.[10]

Nietzsche's classic dichotomy in *The Birth of Tragedy* between Apollonianism, with Socrates as its chief apostle, and Dionysianism can also be interpreted from a "totality vs. infinity" perspective.[11] Socrates is fiercely condemned because of his pursuit of the project of total rationalization – his attempt to make all aspects of human personal and social life transparent to the light of reason and subject to its priorities of analytical dissection and theoretical categorization.

Nietzsche's image of Socrates assigns priority to Socrates the implacable questioner and jettisons the Socrates of the *Theaetetus* who is an equally indefatigable self-questioner, acknowledging his inability to come up with satisfactory positive alternatives to the positions he impugns. Such a Socrates is on the verge of becoming the herald of the mythological status of reason: a reason unresponsive to its own limits is itself a form of intoxication – a madness – that shields from view the larger madness (a more enhanced role for the irrational) that the integration of those limits implies. For the Socrates of the *Theaetetus*, Dionysus himself can be said to become the implicit tutelary deity for a self-critical conception of reason that in effect sees it as the ultimate passion, utterly passive and helpless in the face of its limits as diagnosed by the skeptic.

Dionysus, in contrast to Apollo, symbolizes for Nietzsche in *The Birth of Tragedy* the mysteriousness and unfathomableness of human life – the sense in which each engagement in interpretation and understanding serves as a platform for further engagements in interpretation and understanding. In Nietzsche's imagery, the Apollonian Socrates incarnates the aspiration toward totalistic understanding, whereas Dionysus captures the sense in which the objects of our understanding endlessly recede before us. The Nietzschean Apollonian Socrates is identified with denatured reasons and explanations, while Dionysus personifies myth – what remains irreducible to reasons and explanations:

> Without myth every culture loses the healthy natural power of its creativity: only a horizon defined by myths completes and unifies a whole cultural movement ... The images of the myth have to be the unnoticed omnipresent demonic guardians, under whose care the young soul grows to maturity and whose signs help the man to interpret his life and struggles ... By way of comparison let us now picture the abstract man, untutored by myth; abstract education; abstract morality; abstract law; the abstract state; let us imagine the lawless roving of the artistic imagination, unchecked by any native myth; let us think of a culture that has no fixed and sacred primordial site but is doomed to exhaust all possibilities and to nourish itself wretchedly on all other cultures – there we have the present age, the result of that Socratism which is bent on the destruction of myth.[12]

Negative theology erodes the myth of the literal, palpable God – but it does so only at the cost of keeping that God perpetually alive as the object of a series of infinite disownings. It thus coheres with a Dionysian positioning toward infinity, rather than being what Nietzsche condemns as a Socratic totalization that annuls a search for anything beyond its own grasp. Negative theology consists, as it were, in the creation of a "negative myth."

8. Nietzsche's philosophy of science can also be fruitfully explicated from the perspective of the "totality" vs. "infinity" distinction. In *On the Genealogy of Morals*, Nietzsche says that:

> Strictly speaking, there is no such thing as science "without any presuppositions"; this thought does not bear thinking through, it is paralogical: a philosophy, a "faith," must always be there first of all, so that science can acquire from it a direction, a meaning, a limit, a method, a *right* to exist. (Whoever has the opposite notion, whoever tries, for example, to place philosophy "on a strictly scientific basis," first needs to stand not only philosophy but truth itself *on its head* – the grossest violation of decency possible in relation to two such venerable females!).[13]

In science, the organizing set of assumptions, dominant understandings and reigning methodologies determine the nature of the problems addressed and therefore also indirectly the content of the solutions reached. Truth in science is not able to transcend the taint transmitted to it by the numerous limitations built into its starting points. Science cannot consist in a cumulative approach to truth because each phase of its work is marked by adherence to presuppositions that resist further probing without erupting into an infinite regress. By assigning primacy to the paradigms and theoretical commitments informing scientific inquiry over the concrete findings and results achieved through such inquiry, Nietzsche calls into question a progressive, totalizing conception of science as putting us in indubitable contact with the relevant "facts" of particular scientific domains. He contrasts to this image of science a vision of it as always generating truths from particular points of view, which enables us to remain open to infinite prospects of reconceptualization spawning new mappings of facts (at least partially based on the inventiveness of our theoretical formulations) concerning what the furniture of the world is like.

9. Nietzsche's genealogy of German historicism – his critique of its "general renunciation of all interpretation (of forcing, adjusting, abbreviating, omitting, padding, inventing, falsifying, and whatever else is of the *essence* of interpreting)" as constituting "broadly speaking, as much ascetic virtue as any denial of sensuality (it is at bottom only a particular mode of this denial)"[14] – can also be construed as a rejection of "totality" in favor of "infinity." Nietzsche counterposes to the objectivist, fact-centered bias of historicism the need for a protective mist – of mystery – of the possibility of infinite interpretations that nurture and sustain life: "Every living thing needs to be surrounded by an atmosphere, a mysterious circle of mist: if one robs it of this

veil, if one condemns a religion, an art, a genius to orbit as a star without an atmosphere: then one should not wonder about its rapidly becoming withered, hard and barren."[15]

10. "Power" in Nietzsche functions in some contexts in a conventional sense as a deflationary, reductionist, totalizing category that assigns the proper weight to the factors truly responsible for shaping a situation and determining its outcome. A subtle dialectic is at work in Nietzsche. On the basis of the application of power in its reductionist, totalizing sense, the individual is enabled to act resourcefully and creatively in ways that manifest power that is oriented toward infinity. A prefiguration of this relationship of "power" as a totalizing category nurturing "power" as an infinitizing category is found in Thomas Paine's *Common Sense*.[16] Paine, invoking power in the first sense, shows how from a geopolitical perspective America's victory in the War of Independence against England is assured. America's isolation and insulation guaranteed by the Atlantic Ocean – and the inherent expansionist dynamic associated with its continental size – ensure the prospect of American victory. The only thing remaining to be done is the actual engagement in battle to achieve victory. "Power" in the first sense works to neutralize the feelings of guilt and anxiety attendant to the engagement in action, in the seizing of power and authority away from the colonizing power, the "mother country," and thus facilitates a mobilization of power in the second sense, which in its strategic and interpretive reaches stretches forward to infinity.[17]

11. Nietzsche partially uses "power" instrumentally as a conceptual tool to abolish interiority with regard to the self, history and science. There is no stable substratum undergirding and supporting our individual actions, partially because power invoked in a reductionist, totalistic sense gets us to collapse the ideational content of the self onto a series of power moldings and interventions by ourselves and Others that make a mockery of whatever *concept* of self we might have developed. Analogously, with regard to historical events, power in a reductionist, totalistic sense works to call into question any set of officially-delineated descriptions of events by juxtaposing to them fluid and dynamic power moves and relations. The partiality of the premises and paradigms informing any given scientific formulation are to some extent exposed by a totalistic power analysis that highlights who the beneficiaries and losers are in any particular scientific "take" on the world.

Power invoked in this reductionist, totalistic way brings to the foreground certain affinities between Nietzsche and Marx. However, Nietzsche's usage of power as the most adequate, most basic, most self-sufficient mode of explanation gets immediately transformed (in fact, the division between the two halves is for heuristic purposes only) into power as opening up onto infinity – with infinite possibilities residing for making sense of the actions undertaken in "fashioning a self," establishing a "hardcore factual account of an historical event or text" and evolving a particular scientific paradigm or set of premises. Once everything is reconceived as an assertion of power, as an action (including our "acts of interpretation"), then they await redemption in further assertions of power – further actions – to pin down and apply what was present in our original assertions. We might say that one major point of Nietzsche's vocabulary of power is as an individuating device to help highlight how each aspect – each moment – of our emotional, imaginative and ratiocinative lives constitutes discrete assertions of power that form an interdependent network that opens out onto infinity. "Power" in Nietzsche both reflects a striving for and a registering of the futility of "totality" and its transmutation into a device for gauging and effecting the transformation of "totality" into "infinity."

Another more logical-conceptual route for getting at the same point is the following: Part of the attraction of the concept of power for Nietzsche is that it enables him not only to state his original position, but also to grapple with logical dilemmas attendant to its formulation. If "power is everything" (the underlying source of explanation of phenomena), then Nietzsche's formulation of this thesis itself needs to be seen (consistent with its own premise) as nothing more than an assertion of power. In what sense can it privilege itself as a uniquely revealing insight into the human condition? We might say that Nietzsche requires or presupposes at this point a multivalued or nonstandard logic that enables him to map the suspension of the Law of the Excluded Middle. Under these circumstances, Nietzsche's options are expanded beyond A and not-A, so that he can hold the thesis of the pervasiveness of power in all cases (i.e., in all cases of application), except where this thesis itself is being formulated which is predicated upon the non-pervasiveness of power. The supposition of a multivalued logic makes sense in the context of a generalized agnosticism that posits that the returns are not yet fully in concerning the nature of reality – so that as the structure of reality gets more finely and fully revealed (if it does get revealed), perhaps a multivalued logic comes closer to capturing that structure than the traditional Aristotelian two-place logic does. In the context of a generalized agnosticism, all of our theoretical and practical musings and interventions from a negative standpoint (since no firmer category or set of categories seem available) get reclassified as assertions of power. They get reclassified this way because nothing more positive can with finality be attributed to them. At this stage of conceptual clarification with a generalized-agnostic backdrop, the notion of power has shed its totalistic reductionism and beckons toward infinity.

Theory and practice in Rabbinic Judaism

The theory of Rabbinic Judaism that can be distilled from the sources we have been examining so far in this book is largely shaped by negative theology and spells out the ways in which God is beyond the semantic, conceptual and existential pale. The philosophical content of the religion elaborates upon these rational limitations – and its practical content structures and organizes the lives of a community of Jewish religious believers to preserve their cohesiveness and identity in faithful relation to these limitations. The relationship between the philosophy and the practice of Judaism is one of rhetorical affinity – not logical entailment.[18] The conceptual and existential unapproachability of the monotheistic God creates space for the practical precepts to take root and have their being as a means of nurturing collective identity and continuity in the period of prolonged waiting. Monotheistic theory does not in any logically constraining way determine the content of religious practice. The set of understandings defining a Jew's relationship to God is theory. The protocols stipulating how individual and collective Jewish life should be organized constitute a set of precepts governing practice, and they are a function of tradition and ongoing interpretation.

There is a remarkable Midrashic formulation that encapsulates how skeptical idealism might be envisioned as the key to the theological system propounded by Judaism. The Midrash says that "the Torah was not given except to those that ate manna."[19] The Midrash appears to be drawing an implicit analogy between the Jews who ate manna (the special food designed and delivered by God) in the desert and the Jews who considered their study of and compliance with Torah in its manifold aspects as the repository of both the Written and the Oral Law as being the chief sources of their connectedness with God. From these Jews' perspective, both manna and the Torah occupy an equally anomalous, if not outright contradictory, position. Manna is food only in terms of the function that it serves of satiating Jews' appetites without having either the texture or the appearance of food.[20] Manna is food when you consider the nourishment that it provides, but it is not food when you focus on the conditions and manner of its appearance (every morning with the dew), as well as the configuration of the manna itself (resembling hoarfrost). Similarly, the Torah is supposed to contain the sacred word of God, but it is available to all beholders who open it and study it. From the point of view of Jewish tradition, the Torah both is and is not God, just as manna both is and is not food. The Midrash is telling us that those who experienced the miracle of manna would more likely be receptive to the miracle of the Torah. The minds of the manna-eaters would have been trained to notice that the line separating the abstract from the concrete gets pushed endlessly in the direction of the abstract. The more one attempts to pin down the concreteness of an object of thought, the more one has to have recourse to the abstracting resources of language to delineate the shape and texture of the concrete. The "concrete" itself is one more term in the lexicon of the abstract.

Analogously, mobilizing all of one's intellectual resources to study Torah (the Written and Oral Law) – pushing reason to its limits – highlights for us the possibility of God. Reason, which is predicated upon the cultivation of verbal language or some other system of symbolization, positions us to search for foundation after foundation, which then propels us to consider the possibility of the infinite God as the final explanation or first cause. As we struggle to break out of our network of conceptual tools (a continually evolving causal-explanatory chain), we stumble upon (or we are situated to theorize about) the post-conceptual, where a word has to substitute for an argument that we cannot develop.

The Midrash underscores for us that the mundane is fully in the image of the sacred. Inventorying its furniture is as much an exercise in charting the unreality of the real (because of the underdetermination of theory by fact, and the infinitely regressive character of explanation) as elaborating a theological discourse about God (where logical conundrums prevent us from literally validating the existence of God). The common denominator between manna and the Torah is that absence becomes the only mode of presence. God is the paradigm of the real.

One finds an almost fervent embrace of the dichotomy between theory and practice, which subsists as a mystical, barely articulable unity in the practical, everyday life of the Jew in the Talmud itself. In *Gittin* 59b, the following dictum is found as part of a conversation between the two Amoraic luminaries,[21] Abaye and Rav Joseph: "But the whole of the Torah is also for the purpose of promoting peace, as it is written, 'Her ways are ways of pleasantness and all her paths are peace' (Proverbs 3:17)."[22] Apparently, from the perspective of these two conversation partners, there is a background, overriding purpose to the commandments and prohibitions of the Torah, which renders largely instrumental the substantive purposes listed alongside many commandments. Jewish religion wants to foster the creation of a community that will remain faithful to its underlying theoretical insights. Since those theoretical insights are bound up with an awareness of rational limitation and incompleteness, the positive incentives and sanctions that might sometimes legitimate for individuals and nations their behaving in hostile, aggressive ways are deflated from the outset in Judaism. In this negative sense, the theoretical emptiness that resides at the core of Judaism can be summarized by the term "peace."

However, a common appreciation of the truth of certain insights will not necessarily foster community by itself. For this, one needs intermediate mechanisms that will fashion and sustain foci of loyalty and dynamics of allegiance within the broad community. Law and its appurtenances of ritual and symbol become the more immediate factors motivating obedience and loyalty to particular traditions of Jewish belief and practice, which are valued by their most sophisticated adherents as repositories of those theoretical insights for the sake of whose safeguarding the community was formed.

Without a traditional diffusion and condensation of the theoretical insights of the religion, they would not survive. Their survival and flourishing depend on the fashioning of a whole way of life devoted to their primacy. But the ideology that nurtures survival is not theory, and the theory is not ideology. The rivalries, resentments and rancor that have historically poisoned relations between proponents of conflicting ideological translations and embodiments of Judaism as theory need to be ameliorated in light of the recognition that, given the content of the theory, all of our traditional strivings and efforts at communion with God remain incomplete. "Shalom," meaning "peace," is one of the names of God.[23] The negative-theological God is preeminently the God of peace in the negative sense that He does not offer any permanent succor or reassurance to any one of His ideological proponents. By nurturing an ethic of peace in their relations with each other, even as they try to persuade each other of the "rightness" of their respective interpretations of Jewish tradition and Jewish law, the diverse sects of Judaism display their fidelity to the utterly transcendent Biblical God, whose intrareligious and interreligious correlative (in relation to other monotheistic religions) can only be peace.

Given the theological positions of Hillel and Rabbi Akiva that we have examined in this book, we can say that Judaism's ideological categories and practices are designed to be largely protective of its theory. They carve out a distinctive way of life whose "center" is animated by deferral and withdrawal. Perhaps this constitutes the enduring attractiveness of Jewish religion: that it connects to a moment of theoretical reticence and withdrawal.

An alternative and perhaps more satisfying way to look at the question of the relationship between monotheistic theory and monotheistic practice (at least from the perspective of particular monotheistic faiths and sects) is to say that given the contradictory status of the theory that paradoxically legitimates the entry of further, unlimited contradictions into the body of statements that we take to be true, the practices sanctioned and/or required by any particular monotheistic religion or sect might be reasonably classifiable as unqualified, unconditional truth – and therefore escape the taint of being regarded as ideologies. Since monotheistic theory requires us to persistently disown the literal applicability of any set of attributes to God in order to sustain His transcendent Oneness, it engenders the contradiction that it presupposes a substantive cognitive stratum to be present in the notion of the monotheistic God in order for the process of divestiture of literal attributes to preserve its intelligibility; at the same time, since these acts of divestiture are postulated as being our only mode of cognitive access to God, we cannot pinpoint who or what we are divesting of literal attributes. As a result, the whole notion of the monotheistic God (construed in the negative-theological terms which I have just summarized) becomes contradictory. However, once we admit this contradiction, we have deprived ourselves of any mechanism for censoring or filtering out further contradictions, so that the idea of the monotheistic God accompanied by the sets of rituals and practices ordained and/or required by any of the three monotheistic religions or any of their sects can be accorded the status of logically invulnerable truth. The admission of one contradiction has the liberating effect of removing "contradiction" as a criterion for determining the truth value of any of our statements – including those pertaining to the epistemological status of religious practices. If one opts to go this route in delineating the relationship between theory and practice in monotheistic religion, then the promotion of peace emerges as a pragmatic imperative in order to enable the various monotheistic faiths and sects to persevere in a condition of radical indeterminacy vis-a-vis each other.

Notes

1. Friedrich Nietzsche, *On the Genealogy of Morals and Ecce Homo*. Ed. and trans. Walter Kaufmann. (New York: Vintage, 1967), p. 45.
2. Friedrich Nietzsche, *The Gay Science*. Trans. Walter Kaufmann. (New York: Vintage, 1974), p. 336; italics in original.
3. Nietzsche, *Genealogy and Ecce Homo*, pp. 84–85.
4. Nietzsche, *Beyond Good and Evil*, p. 52; italics in original.
5. Friedrich Nietzsche, *Twilight of the Idols*, in *The Portable Nietzsche*. Ed. and trans. Walter Kaufmann. (New York: Viking, 1954), p. 500.
6. Nietzsche, *Beyond Good and Evil*, p. 224; italics in original.
7. Arthur C. Danto, *Nietzsche as Philosopher* (New York: Macmillan, 1965), p. 232; italics in original.
8. Ibid.
9. The classic formulation of this Nietzschean position is in "On Truth and Lie in an Extra-Moral Sense": "What, then, is truth? A mobile army of metaphors, metonyms, and anthropomorphisms – in short, a sum of human relations, which have been enhanced, transposed, and embellished poetically and rhetorically, and which after long use seem firm, canonical, and obligatory to a people: truths are illusions about which one has forgotten that this is what they are; metaphors which are worn out and without sensuous power; coins which have lost their pictures and now matter only as metal, no longer as coins." *The Portable Nietzsche*, pp. 42–47, on pp. 46–47.
10. Compare my discussion of Michael Oakeshott vs. Martin Heidegger on this issue of whether Nietzsche can most cogently be construed as attempting to supersede epistemology or whether his arguments still deploy the received repertoire of tools of epistemology itself in my book, *Michael Oakeshott's Skepticism*, pp. 158–164.
11. Friedrich Nietzsche, *The Birth of Tragedy and The Case of Wagner*. Ed. and trans. Walter Kaufmann. (New York: Vintage, 1967).
12. Ibid., pp. 135–136.
13. Nietzsche, *Genealogy and Ecce Homo*, pp. 151–152; italics in original.
14. Ibid., p. 151; italics in original.
15. Friedrich Nietzsche, *On the Advantage and Disadvantage of History for Life*. Trans. Peter Preuss. (Indianapolis: Hackett, 1980), p. 40.
16. Thomas Paine, *Common Sense Addressed to the Inhabitants of America*, in Merrill Jensen, ed., *Tracts of the American Revolution 1763–1776* (Indianapolis: Bobbs-Merrill, 1967), pp. 401–446.
17. Ibid., pp. 419–428.
18. For Maimonides' discussion of the relationship between the "generalities" and "particulars" of commandments, see *Guide*, III:26:508–509. For an exploration of diverse strategies of reconciliation of Maimonides' philosophical work with his codification of Jewish law, see my *Skepticism, Belief, and the Modern*, pp. 157–163. Also see my article, "Skeptical Motifs Linking Together Maimonides' *Guide* and his *Mishneh Torah*," in Georges Tamer, ed., *The Trias of Maimonides: Jewish, Arabic, and Ancient Culture of Knowledge* (Berlin: Walter de Gruyter, 2005), pp. 151–174.
19. *Mechilta, Beshalach, Parsah* 17; *Tanchuma, Beshlach, Ot* 20. A variant reading of this midrash states that the Torah was only given to those who interpret the

eating of the manna. Compare the discussion of this midrash in Eliyahu Eliezer Dessler, *Michtav M'Eliyahu*, Volume 1 (Bnei Brak, 1973), pp. 185, 205. Rav Dessler interprets the midrash to mean that the concept of Torah is antithetical to the idea of "nature." Only when daily occurrences were subsumed under the category of "miracle" (when the boundary demarcating between "nature" and "miracle" had been effaced) did the Jews become ready to receive the Torah. Reb Chaim Wolozhoner construes this midrash to mean that Torah, in its most optimal sense, was only given to a Jewish population that could manage to shed its preoccupation with matters of daily sustenance and shift its gaze totally to God, who rewarded such complete trust with Divine nurturance of the community. Chaim Wolozhoner, *Nefesh HaChaim*, p. 31. I offer an alternative reading of this midrash in my book, *Skepticism, Belief, and the Modern*, pp. 35–36.
20 This is the Biblical account of the Jews' encounter with manna" (Exodus 16:13–15): "And in the morning there was a layer of dew round about the camp. And when the layer of dew was gone up, behold, upon the face of the desert there lay a small peeled thing, as small as the hoarfrost on earth. And when the children of Israel saw it, they said one to another, What is it? [This is the literal meaning of the Hebrew word *Mun* (translated into English as "manna.")]: for they knew not what it was. And Moses said unto them, 'This is the bread which the Eternal hath given you for food.' *Exodus*, Rosenbaum-Silbermann edition, pp. 83–84.
21 The Amoraim were renowned Jewish scholars who transmitted and expounded upon the teachings of the Oral Law of Judaism from 200 to 500 CE in Babylonia and the Land of Israel. Abaye, who died in 339 CE, was a disciple of Rav Joseph, who died in 323 CE. Both Rav Joseph and Abaye were heads of the prominent Babylonian yeshiva at Pumbedita.
22 *Hebrew-English Edition of the Babylonian Talmud: Gittin*. Trans. Maurice Simon. (London: Soncino Press, 1963).
23 Babylonian Talmud, *Shabbath* 10b; *Vayikra Rabbah*, 9:9; *Masechet Derech Eretz Zutah*, Chapter 11.

8 Plato and Levinas

Monotheistic religion and Plato

We have found in Plato an analogous vision of the relationship between theory and ideology. Theory consists in a generalized-agnostic disarming of one's own preferred formulation in light of the critical canon, enshrined in the theory itself, which one cherishes. Ideology, by contrast, renounces this last stage of self-correction insinuated by the protocols of consistency. Thus, in the *Greater Hippias*, the virtue of a theory of beauty that identifies beauty with "the fitting" is that it can reflexively encompass itself. The theory of beauty as the fitting is itself a function (an expression) of an impulse to maximize the fit between our various intuitions concerning beauty and the objects and occasions in the world – and their linguistic correlatives – when an esthetic vocabulary is fittingly invoked. Plato's theorizing of beauty in the *Greater Hippias* thus indirectly discloses to us his conception of theory in contrast to ideology. The rational projection of beauty without the reflexive gesture is ideology. The inclusion of the reflexive gesture, which cuts Plato's own theorizing down to the same level as the objects of his theorizing, is theory. Theory situates itself on the same ontological plane as its targets. It self-consciously affirms its circular character.

This theme concerning the relationship between theory and ideology in Plato is corroborated by a reading of the *Republic*. How does one reconcile the numerous components of Plato's argument – the presuppositions of the dialogue form, which evoke the foundationless character of starting points; Socrates' reenactment of his traditional role as exposing the limitations of other people's arguments instead of advancing a satisfactory positive alternative of his own, which is characteristic of the early sections of the *Republic*; Plato's Theory of Ideas and its compressed allusion to the notion of the underdetermination of theory by fact; the pivotal role played by the Sophist, the skeptical Thrasymachus, in the dialogue; etc. – that resonate with skepticism and liberal democracy with Plato's apparent flaunting of an authoritarian, and even totalitarian, society as epitomizing his vision of a just ordering of human beings? A persuasive strategy of resolution that suggests itself is that we need to read the *Republic* as a self-referentialist text dramatizing for us how little is the positive illumination cast (how small is the positive guidance yielded) by theory. The presuppositions of the dialogue form, which converge on the notion of the circularity of all argument and the idea of the underdetermination of theory by fact implicit in the Theory of Ideas, which also highlights the concept of circularity, push to center stage a vision of theory as being largely negative and critical in character. It delineates most clearly what reason cannot accomplish and does not justify what reason strives to do. From one angle of vision, the ostensibly incoherent fit between the theory and the actual modes for organizing practice (the ideology) advocated in the *Republic* just redound to the deeper coherence of the theory itself. The skeptical theory of the *Republic* just reflects endlessly back upon itself confirming its circular character, without offering the possibility of establishing any theoretically grounded bridges between itself and worldly affairs of any sort. On one level of interpretation, we can simply say that the incoherent fit between theory and practice in the *Republic* is itself the most enduring testimonial to the theoretical coherence of the work. Theory can never point unequivocally, with certainty, beyond itself.

Or, alternatively, we might say that as a self-referentialist theoretical text, the *Republic* dramatizes for us what happens when the limits to reason posted by theory are transgressed – how ideological truculence can promote a social ordering subversive of human freedom as symptomatic of supreme virtue. If we are not sufficiently vigilant, aggressive ideological declamation such as that evident in Plato's putatively positive projection of a well-ordered, just society fills in the space created by the built-in reticence of theory.

Plato's *Cratylus* and *Theaetetus*, skepticism and totality and infinity

The theme of skepticism and strategies for relating to it (the content of theory in contrast to ideology) are amply reflected in two of Plato's dialogues, the *Cratylus* and the *Theaetetus*. The project of the *Cratylus* (in its own words) is "to explain in what respect the primary names have been properly imposed."[1] Socrates is ostensibly in search of mechanisms of correspondence that show how words relate to things. However, he offers an immediate corrective to this reading of his intention by invoking the term "method." He says that "the painter who wants to depict anything sometimes uses purple only, or any other color, and sometimes mixes up several colors, as his method is when he has to paint flesh color or anything of that kind."[2] Apparently, there is no simple correlation between words and their constituent components and things and their constituent elements outside the context of a preexisting "method" that establishes certain conventions of representation differently for painters than for writers – and presumably establishes enough leeway for both painters and writers to choose and mix between conventions in order to be able to leave their own imprint on the visual and verbal artifacts that they are fashioning. In the same passage, Socrates equates the "namer" with the "rhetorician"³ thereby again underscoring the futility of the search for an intrinsic, essentialist connection between words and things.

Socrates throughout the dialogue dramatizes a kind of *reductio ad absurdum* pertaining to linguistic behaviorism. For example, he says that "in all of these sorts of movements" represented by such words as "trembling," "rugged," "strike," "crush," "bruise," "break" and "whirl," the "imposer of names" "generally finds an expression in the letter R because ... he had observed that the tongue was most agitated and least at rest in the pronunciation of this letter, which he therefore used in order to express motion."⁴ This sort of analysis begs the important question of how we move from the physiological constraints governing the utterance of the letter "R" to the rest of the letters of the particular words in question – from "R" to "trembling," from "R" to "rugged," from "R" to "strike," etc. Socrates' causal-physiological account of the formation of these particular words explains only a limited percentage of each of the words in question. Unless this account already presupposed what it was designed to make sense of – namely, the existence of these particular words – it would not be an account at all. There appears to be a tacit premise of circularity built into Socrates' analysis of the origins of the words in question.

At some point a little later on in the dialogue, Socrates frames the issue even more sharply:

SOC.: But if the name is to be like the thing, the letters out of which the first names are composed must also have a natural resemblance to things. Returning to the image of the picture, I would ask, How could any one ever compose a picture which would be like anything at all, if there were not pigments in nature which resembled the things imitated by portraiture, and out of which the picture is composed?
CRAT.: Impossible.
SOC.: No more could names ever resemble any actually existing thing, unless the elements of which they are compounded bore, from the first, some degree of resemblance to the objects of which the names are the imitation: And the original elements are letters?
CRAT.: Yes.⁵

Plato in this passage is utilizing pictorial representation as a foil for language. The circuit between artwork and reality is closed by the fact that there are "pigments in nature which resemble the things imitated by portraiture." But in linguistic construction, the counterpart to pigments are letters. Socrates sets up a foil to his own earlier position. "Letters," as it were, carry their connection to events and phenomena in the world much more precariously and equivocally than do pigments. It is now as if Socrates were laying the groundwork for raising a question against his former position: How could letters be expressions of certain emotions if there was no antecedent vocabulary to register these emotions which in all likelihood contained those very letters whose evocation of these emotions presumably made them the ideal candidates on a primitive level to represent them? Thus, in a crucial sense the words had to be available from the outset in order for the letters to be able to register the guttural-physiological realities that supposedly render the words in a causal sense representational.

The character Cratylus himself in the dialogue bearing his name defends a resolutely anti-pictorial, anti-representational conception of the relationship between words and things. He says: "I suggest that may be true, Socrates, in the case of pictures; they may be wrongly assigned; but not in the case of names – they must necessarily be always right."[6] A little bit earlier on in the dialogue, Cratylus affirms this position with an even more slightly aggressive edge:

SOC.: Nor is one name, I suppose, in your opinion, more properly imposed than another?
CRAT.: Certainly not.
SOC.: Then all names are rightly imposed?
CRAT.: Yes, if they are names at all.[7]

Cratylus apparently adopts this position (that naming, logico-linguistic fiat, is the key factor responsible for the words that we use) because of certain dilemmas of reflexivity, of consistency. He says: "Why, Socrates, how can a man say that which is not? – say something and yet say nothing? For is not falsehood saying the thing which is not?"[8] According to Cratylus, the idea of uttering or formulating a falsehood gives rise to a daunting issue of reflexivity. A statement that one designates or acknowledges to be false is both a statement and a non-statement. In order to identify that which one is ruling out as being false one needs to utter a string of words – which one then goes on to declare or show to be unsustainable (as formulated). The sentence(s) has (have) to be both viable for identification purposes – and unsustainable for argumentative or truth-affirming purposes. It would appear that if a sentence lacks an adequate truth-content, it also lacks that degree of intelligibility and coherence to be able to expose itself as a sentence that lacks an adequate truth-content. The idea of a false statement or sentence appears to be inconsistent, trying to have it both ways: The statement has sufficient logical coherence and autonomy *to be able to be identified* as a statement that is not true.

Cratylus' resolution of this dilemma of reflexivity is to invoke nominalism. Everything beyond bare, discrete particulars (however ultimately defined) is a function of a human naming process. For Cratylus, the "bare particular" is an ideal limit to the generalizing, abstracting capacities of thought. In order to speak about "generalizing" and "abstracting," one needs to have an effective contrasting vocabulary centering on such notions as "discrete particulars." While the postulation of an "ideal limit" to generalizing might be true in the rough – synoptically, when one surveys the scene as a whole – on a piecemeal, case-by-case basis, it is nearly always possible to theorize underdetermination – how the concrete particulars of a case could have been theoretically subsumed under alternative sets of conceptual frameworks, how theory in the particular case was underdetermined by fact. Socrates, rather than Cratylus, underscores this point in the dialogue: "Thus the names which in these instances we find to have the worst sense will turn out to be framed on the same principle as those which have the best. And anyone I believe who would take the trouble might find many other examples in which the giver of names indicates, not that things are in motion or progress, but that they are at rest; which is the opposite of motion."[9] Socrates in this passage admits that his causal-physiological account of the origins and development of language is flawed because the oral trajectory of letters (in the Greek language) that can be theorized as symbolizing motion can just as easily be conceived of as symbolizing rest. What configurations the sounds evoke is not a function of the sounds themselves but of the imaginative theoretical frameworks that pick up and capitalize upon a particular set of intimations gleaned from the sounds. Socrates laments how this systematic ambiguity affects the term "knowledge" itself: "Observe how ambiguous this word is, seeming rather to signify stopping the soul at things than going round with them."[10] In terms of how the word "knowledge" is spelled in the Greek language, the dominant cases of linguistic usage of this term are compatible with a neurophysiological analysis of the articulation of its key letters that emphasizes how they biologically encode and link up with perpetual movement – as well as how they encode and connect with rest. The contrasting theoretical frameworks that lie in the background of the letters used to compose the word "knowledge" yield different visions of reality – so that "reality" (realistic factors) cannot be used as a basis for validating a particular conceptual framework.

Nominalism construed and practiced in the fashion evoked by Cratylus offers us a strategy for coping with issues of reflexivity by conjuring up the prospect of multiple and severed theoretical frameworks that would enable different stages of our arguments – and different components of our sentences – to work on different levels. This would be an example of Lyotard's "suspicion of metanarrativity"[11] enacted on a micro logico-linguistic level. Nominalism blocks recourse to a unified, stable reality as the appropriate frame of reference for our use of language and deployment of theory. Reality becomes what the structure of our linguistic formulations yields – rather than something that independently constrains our linguistic formulations. If stating that a theory is false is in some sense inconsistent or self-contradictory, then the different components or strata of the statement that give rise to the self-contradiction have to be regressed onto different theoretical backgrounds. Utilizing the Levinasian vocabulary, we need to dissociate the "saying" from the "said" of negation. The *attribution* of falseness (which is the upshot of our sentence) has to be assigned to one theoretical background and its *declaration* (the actual formulation in words of what we take to be false) has to be relegated to another theoretical background. Given the absence of a commitment to a unified, overarching reality, the fragmented, occluded versions of reality carried in the train of our nominalistic commitments become the operative vision of reality for us.

Circularity enters the argument at two points: in terms of what it officially acknowledges and also in terms of what it presupposes. If reality does not exert an immediate constraint upon our theoretical formulations, but instead is to be understood as what those theoretical formulations themselves yield (and if many of our key sentences of whatever metaphysical stripe are logically imperfect and need to be broken up into constituent units understood along the lines that I have sketched), then what stabilizes a particular theoretical formulation so that *its* language and presuppositions, rather than those of theoretically possible alternatives, become constitutive of reality for us? Socrates' answer at one point toward the conclusion of the *Cratylus* is convention. He attributes to Hermogenes (a character in the dialogue) and to "many others" the view that "names are conventional, and have a meaning to those who have agreed about them, and who have previous knowledge of the things intended by them, and that it is convention which makes a name right; and whether you abide by our present convention, or make a new and opposite one, according to which you call small great and great small – that, they would say, makes no difference, if you are only agreed."[12] According to this view, convention becomes a kind of institutionalized circularity. What usurps the space created by the denial of contact between our theoretical formulations and an independently certified reality is agreement between the members of particular communities and subcommunities to regard certain theoretical categories and understandings as binding. In the end, the process of belief and affirmation becomes a circular one. We believe because we believe.

Circularity is also presupposed by Plato's nominalistic resolution of the dilemmas of reflexivity. If dilemmas of reflexivity can be warded off by assigning priority to the theoretical formulations that we employ over the reality that they ostensibly conjure up, then what about the reality conjured up by nominalistic doctrine itself? Is this not just one more version of reality that we can appropriately relate to on a take-it-or-leave-it basis? On what grounds can it privilege itself as an ordering vision of how thought relates to reality? One possible approach at this point is to move the argument in the direction of a generalized agnosticism. This stand posits that our knowledge of objective reality remains incomplete and remains hospitable to the idea that multivalued logics – those that map the suspension of the Law of the Excluded Middle – might encode reality more accurately than traditional Aristotelian logic does. Our alternatives are thereby increased beyond A and not-A, and we are able to circumvent the Law of the Excluded Middle and refer to nominalism in all cases without either affirming or denying its predication upon non-nominalism. To remap the argument concerning the relationship between language and reality in terms of a generalized agnosticism and multivalued and nonstandard logics again reinforces the role of circularity. Multivalued and nonstandard logics can only be defended vis-à-vis the more traditional logic in relation to their conceptual payoffs – and not because of their intrinsic rational superiority. If one can maximize the coherence of Plato's argument by invoking these background factors, it only strengthens the presence of circularity in his argument.

The *Theaetetus* intensifies and systematizes Plato's argument concerning circularity, which is developed to one extent or another not only in the *Greater Hippias* and the *Cratylus*, but also in the *Sophist, Protagoras, Meno, Parmenides* and *Phaedrus*. The three poles of the *Theaetetus*' argument encompass some of the major theoretical connections I have been pursuing in this book. In the *Theaetetus*, Plato sets up an ideal typology between two diametrically opposed starting points for Greek philosophy and shows how they both terminate in incoherence. Heraclitus and Protagoras had assigned centrality to constant flux and motion, and therefore also to immediate perception as the source of knowledge. Parmenides had shifted the emphasis to theoretical frameworks (with their extreme heightening in the notion of the One) as enjoying primacy in the generation of knowledge. Plato shows from numerous perspectives how we cannot move from either starting point to the familiar epistemological judgments that we make without already presupposing what we are trying to prove. The *Theaetetus* is also one of the most unabashedly biographical (or autobiographical) of the Platonic dialogues – where Socrates speaks in an intensely personal vein in analyzing the mainsprings of his intellectual career. He identifies that career (by way of further extension of the model provided by his mother) with metaphorical "midwifery" – attending to the germination of ideas that his carefully selected interlocutors are struggling with. The overwhelming emphasis of the Socratic self-analysis and self-delineation falls on "process" – perpetual reengagement with the throes of intellectual creation despite the vulnerability, instability and often unsustainability of most of the ideas produced by human rational inventiveness. Like the midwives of his time, Socrates claims to be barren. Creativity resides in the Other – and turns out to be a function of process, rather than substance. In the *Theaetetus*, we have a classic prefiguration of how certain limits to knowledge and to truth are most in harmony with a continual wrenching away of supremacy from substance and its reallocation to process. I will elaborate on each pole of the argument of the *Theaetetus* in turn.

Socrates establishes a conceptual linkage between the Protagorean notion that man is the measure of all things and the Heraclitean conception that everything is in flux. Translated to the field of perception, the idea that man is the measure of all things signifies that "perception is knowledge." "Whatever the individual judges by means of perception is true for him." "No man can assess another's experience better than he, or can claim authority to examine another man's judgment and see if it be right or wrong." "Only the individual himself can judge of his own world, and what he judges is always true and correct."[13] What lies in the background of the Protagorean position is Heraclitean metaphysics. If everything is constantly changing, then what we perceive at any given moment is our only source of knowledge as to what the world is like. Socrates invokes against the Protagorean-Heraclitean position the issue of reflexivity: "How could it ever be, my friend, that Protagoras was a wise man, so wise as to think himself fit to be the teacher of other men and worth large fees; while we, in comparison with him the ignorant ones, needed to go and sit at his feet – we who are ourselves each the measure of his own wisdom? Can we avoid the conclusion that Protagoras was just playing to the crowd when he said this?"[14] Both Protagoras' and Heraclitus' formulations fail to pass tests of reflexivity. Obviously, Protagoras wants his relativist position to hold against all competitors. But if "man is the measure of all things," then a philosopher's objectivist, anti-relativist position is as much "the measure of things" as Protagoras' own relativist position. On what theoretical, cognitive basis can Protagoras privilege himself in relation to the positions he rejects? Analogously, Heraclitus considers everything to be in flux except his own view that "everything is in flux." How can he close the gap between what his statement officially communicates and his point in making the statement in the first place? Why is his formulation exempt from his own strictures concerning the pervasiveness of flux?

Another casualty of the Protagorean-Heraclitean position is the possibility of genuine disagreement and mutual correction and criticism: "To examine and try to refute each other's appearances and judgments, when each person's are correct – this is surely an extremely tiresome piece of nonsense, if the *Truth* of Protagoras is true, and not merely an oracle speaking in jest from the impenetrable sanctuary of the book."[15] If everything is always in flux, and perception is knowledge, then we are always talking past each other and have no way of acknowledging or stabilizing or building upon common reference points in our interactions with one another.

Socrates points to the absurd, self-destructive consequences of the Protagorean position. The logic of his position requires Protagoras to be committed to the falsity of his own position:

SOC.: Protagoras admits, I presume, that the contrary opinion about his own opinion (namely, that it is false) must be true, seeing he agrees that all men judge what is.
THEOD.: Undoubtedly.
SOC.: And in considering the truth of the opinion of those who think him wrong, he is really admitting the falsity of his own opinion?
THEOD.: Yes, inevitably.
SOC.: But for their part the others do not admit that they are wrong?
THEOD: No.
SOC.: But Protagoras again admits this judgment to be true, according to his written doctrine?
THEOD.: So it appears.
SOC.: It will be disputed, then, by everyone, beginning with Protagoras – or rather it will be admitted by him, when he grants to the person who

contradicts him that he judges truly – when he does that, even Protagoras himself will be granting that neither a dog nor the "man in the street" is the measure of anything at all which he has not learned. Isn't that so?

THEOD.: It is so.

SOC.: Then since it is disputed by everyone, the truth of Protagoras is not true for anyone at all, not even for himself.

THEOD.: Socrates, we are running my friend too hard.

SOC.: But it is not at all clear, my dear Theodorus, that we are running off the right track. Hence it is likely that Protagoras, being older than we are, really is wiser as well; and if he were to stick up his head from below as far as the neck just here where we are, he would in all likelihood convict me twenty times over of talking nonsense, and show you up too for agreeing with me, before he ducked down to rush off again. But we have got to take ourselves as we are, I suppose, and go on saying things which seem to us to be. At the moment, mustn't we maintain that any man would admit at least this, that some men are wiser than their fellows and others more ignorant?

THEOD.: So it seems to me, at any rate.[16]

Plato shows how with very slight logical nudging Protagoras' position metamorphoses itself into its opposite. The phrase "man is the measure of all things" connotes rampant equality. Fleshed out more fully, it is as if the sentence read "Each man is the measure of all things." However, given his own premise, Protagoras must admit the truth of those who dispute this judgment even when they affirm that they are right and Protagoras is wrong. (Given his premise, Protagoras, of course, has to affirm that he may be wrong and his antagonists right.) But if Protagoras' statement can be so easily turned on its head, then what he is saying really amounts to the opposite of what he appears to be saying, namely, that "man is not the measure of all things." The undermining of the original Protagorean premise is suggestive of inequality – that some men and women enjoy a privileged insight into the nature of things.

Conjoining the premise that "knowledge is perception" with the key premise of its background theory that "everything is in motion" only deepens the paradoxes of reflexivity:

SOC.: Is it possible to give any name to a color which will properly apply to it?

THEOD.: I don't see how one could, Socrates; nor yet surely to anything else of that kind, if, being in flux, it is always quietly slipping away as you speak?

SOC.: And what about any particular kind of perception; for example, seeing or hearing? Does it ever abide, and remain seeing or hearing?

THEOD.: It ought not to, certainly, if all things are in motion.

SOC.: Then we may not call anything seeing rather than not-seeing; nor indeed may we call it any other perception rather than not – if it be admitted that all things are in motion in every way?

THEOD.: No, we may not.
SOC.: Yet Theaetetus and I said knowledge was perception?
THEOD.: You did.
SOC.: And so our answer to the question, "What is knowledge?" gave something which is no more knowledge than not.
THEOD.: It seems as if it did.
SOC.: A fine way this turns out to be of making our answer right. We were most anxious to prove that all things are in motion, in order to make that answer come out correct; but what has really emerged is that if all things are in motion, every answer on whatever subject, is equally correct, both "it is thus" and "it is not thus" – or if you like "becomes," as we don't want to use any expressions which would bring our friends to a standstill.
THEOD.: You are quite right.
SOC.: Well, yes, Theodorus except that I said "thus" and "not thus." One must not even use the word "thus"; for this "thus" would no longer be in motion; nor yet "not thus" for here again there is no motion. The exponents of this theory need to establish some other language; as it is, they have no words that are consistent with their hypothesis – unless it would perhaps suit them best to use "not at all thus" in a quite indefinite sense.
THEOD.: That would at least be an idiom most appropriate to them.[17]

The key background postulate to the Protagorean position that "perception is knowledge" – the Heraclitean notion that "everything is in flux" – both supports and undercuts the Protagorean theory of knowledge. If "everything is in flux," then all we have to go by in validating and constructing an external world are our perceptions from moment to moment. By the same token, however, there is no perception (or series of perceptions) stable enough to be able to sustain the weight of an external world. The Heraclitean metaphysics both directs us to assign credence to the notion of "perception" and deprives that concept of any philosophical usefulness.

We are now in a position to more deeply appreciate how the two parts of the *Theaetetus* relate to one another. On the surface, there appears to be an abrupt transition in the dialogue between a discussion of Protagoras and Heraclitus in the first part and a consideration of Parmenides in the second. What underlying currents of thought link the two parts of the dialogue to one another? One possibility is that after confronting the dead ends that conferring primacy upon perception yields, Plato turns to Parmenides as a theorist of mind-ordained categories potentially facilitating a release from the conundrums surrounding philosophical concentration on perception:

> But I was almost forgetting, Theodorus, that there are other thinkers who have announced the opposite view; who tell us that "unmoved is the universe" and other similar statements which we hear from a Melissus or a Parmenides as against the whole party of Heracliteans. These

philosophers insist that all things are One, and that this One stands still, itself within itself, having no place in which to move.[18]

"This One stands still, itself within itself" can be understood as a metaphorical expression of the idea that Parmenides is in search of organizing categories in terms of which to make sense of "reality" – and that these categories enjoy ontological primacy over the "reality" that they group together and organize. The One constitutes the most abstract and encompassing category of all that brings to a satisfactory halt the search for reasons and causes. In fact, we might say that the Shadow of the One is the human maker, artificer, nominalistic coiner of words, phrases and concepts. The densely abstract Parmenidean formulation devolves into the latter set of notions.[19]

What are the reflexive dilemmas that arise from an invocation of mind-ordained categories in contrast to direct perception as the source of knowledge? The focus of the second part of the dialogue (personified by Parmenides) is that "knowledge is to be found not in the experiences but in the process of reasoning about them; it is here, seemingly, not in the experiences, that it is possible to grasp being and truth."[20] Socrates adds that, "We shall not now look for knowledge in sense-perception at all, but in whatever we call that activity of the soul when it is busy by itself about the things which are."[21] Theaetetus adds that this activity is called "judgment" (in contrast to perception).[22]

Socrates then begins developing an issue that was central to the argument of the *Cratylus*, namely, the issue of false judgment, and ends up driving the argument in the same direction as that pursued in the earlier dialogue. The reflexive dilemma surrounding this issue is that "if admitted, it would mean that the same man must, at one and the same time, both know and not know the same objects."[23] If what one knows is a judgment, it could not possibly be false. If it is false, it is not – and could never have been – a judgment. What are the logical mechanics of a judgment that is false? How does a string of words manage to support both identities simultaneously? Socrates buttresses his theory of judgment with an arresting account of what is involved in thinking:

> A talk which the soul has with itself about the objects under its consideration. Of course, I am only telling you my idea in all ignorance; but this is the kind of picture I have of it. It seems to me that the soul when it thinks is simply carrying on a discussion in which it asks itself questions and answers them itself, affirms and denies. And when it arrives at something definite, either by a gradual process or suddenly, when it affirms one thing consistently and without divided counsel, we call this its judgment. So, in my view, to judge is to make a statement, and a judgment is a statement which is not addressed to another person or spoken aloud, but silently addressed to oneself.[24]

En route toward grappling with this dilemma of reflexivity – that we classify something as a "judgment," and yet declare it to be "false" – Plato invokes two themes that are amplified more fully elsewhere in his philosophy: The paradoxes of knowledge in the *Meno* and the role of tacit knowledge in the *Phaedrus*. The following quotation seems to be a recapitulation of Plato's paradoxes in the *Meno*:

> Soc.: Well, then, don't you think it is a shameless thing that we, who don't know what knowledge is, should pronounce what knowing is like? But as a matter of fact, Theaetetus, for some time past our whole method of discussion has been tainted. Time and again we have said "we are acquainted with" and "we are not acquainted with," "we know" and "we do not know," as if we could to some extent understand one another while we are still ignorant of what knowledge is. Or here is another example, if you like: at this very moment, we have again used the words "to be ignorant of," and "to understand," as if these were quite proper expressions for us when we are deprived of knowledge.[25]

The invocation of tacit knowledge occurs in the following passage:

> Soc.: Then using our image of possessing and hunting for the pigeons, we shall say that there are two phases of hunting: one before you have possession, in order to get possession, and another when you already possess in order to catch and have in your hands what you previously acquired. And in this way even with things you learned and got the knowledge of long ago and have known ever since, it is possible to learn them – these same things – all over again. You can take up again and "have" that knowledge of each of them which you acquired long ago but had not ready to hand in your thought, can't you?[26]

In order to grapple with the paradoxes of reflexivity that accrue when one assigns priority to mind-ordained categories over perception in the generation and validation of knowledge (and thereby illuminate the affinities between these paradoxes and the paradox of knowledge of the *Meno* and tacit knowledge), Socrates follows the trajectory of argument of the *Cratylus*: He again invokes nominalism. The precise juncture at which he does this is when he asks Theaetetus to formulate an amplified theory of knowledge in the face of the mounting paradoxes affecting the priority-of-mental-categories epistemological position:

> THEAET.: Oh, yes, Socrates, that is just what I once heard a man say; I had forgotten, but now it's coming back to me. He said that it is true judgment with an account that is knowledge; true judgment without an account falls outside of knowledge. And he said that the things of which there is no account are not knowable (yes, he actually called them that), while those which have an account are knowable.

SOC.: Very good indeed. Now tell me, how did he distinguish these knowables and unknowables? I want to see if you and I have the same version.

THEAET.: I don't know if I can find that out; but I think I could follow if someone explained it.

SOC.: Listen then to a dream in return for a dream. In my dream, too, I thought I was listening to people saying that the primary elements, as it were, of which we and everything else are composed, have no accounts. Each of them, in itself, can only be named; it is not possible to say anything else of it, either that it is or that it is not. That would mean that we were adding being or not-being to it; whereas we must not attach anything, if we are to speak of that thing itself alone. Indeed we ought not to apply to it even such words as "as itself" or "that", "each", "alone," or "this," or any other of the many words of this kind; for these go the round and are applied to all things alike, being other than the things to which they are added, whereas if it were possible to express the element itself and it had its own proprietary account, it would have to be expressed without any other thing. As it is, however, it is impossible that any of the primaries should be expressed in an account; it can only be named, for a name is all that it has. But with the things composed of these, it is another matter. Here, just in the same way as the elements themselves are woven together, so their names may be woven together and become an account of something – an account being essentially a complex of names. Thus the elements are unaccountable and unknowable, but they are perceivable, whereas the complexes are both knowable and expressible and can be the objects of true judgment.

Now when a man gets a true judgment about something without an account, his soul is in a state of truth as regards that thing, but he does not know it; for someone who cannot give and take an account of a thing is ignorant about it but when he has also got an account of it, he is capable of all this and is made perfect in knowledge.[27]

The second, Parmenidean portion of the *Theaetetus* can be read in one of two ways: It can be seen as a broadening of the problem introduced in the first part of the dialogue – pursuing a dialectical plan of philosophical exploration that exhibits how issues of reflexivity emerge just as forcefully when one assigns primacy to mind-ordained categories as when one accords primacy to perception – or it can be viewed as a delineation of a solution to the problem sketched in both the first and second parts of the dialogue predicated upon the intermediate role performed by a particular mind-ordained category – namely, nominalism. While the structure and content of the dialogue as a whole (as we have seen) clearly suggest a broadening of the problem, on a more subterranean level, the dialogue also insinuates enough elements to facilitate the working out of the second approach. Especially when viewed against the backdrop of Plato's argument in the *Cratylus*, it is possible to read the *Theaetetus* (and might even be compelling to do so) as presenting nominalism as a solution to its problem and not just as illustrating how pervasive the problem is.

The second part of the *Theaetetus* can be read as a return to the implicit strategy of the *Cratylus*. Nominalism restores consistency to our otherwise aborted statements by invoking circularity for the smallest possible meaning and reference quotients of sentences, which now cannot fail the test of consistency because nominalism facilitates the establishment of a rigid barrier between one minute meaning and reference quotient and the next. With regard to the paradoxes attendant to the formulation of the notion of a false judgment, the content of falseness has to be nominalistically severed from the articulation of the judgment – with the presuppositions of statement and utterance in each case closely matching (or duplicating) the logical requisites of sentential coherence. By blocking out contact with and reference to an external world, nominalism enables meaning and reference to be distributed across sentences in a thoroughly insular, circular fashion. What we need, by way of background theoretical assumption and presupposition, to make a particular component of a sentence work is nominalistically supplied. If circularity appeared first as a problem – we couldn't get our sentences to work as we read back the fractured results of the requirements of consistency into the presuppositions and theoretical backgrounds of the words and phrases going into the composition of our sentences – then nominalism provides us with a key to transform circularity into a solution for its own problem by insulating the requirements of sentential consistency and coherence from the constraints exerted by the external world and from the other constituent elements in our sentences. We can now apportion "assumptions," "presuppositions" and "implications" governed exclusively by the requirements of reflexivity undisturbed by considerations of what the world is supposed to be like and what the other components of our sentences appear to presume.

Plato's philosophy of tacit knowledge can be understood on one level as a response to his awareness of how nominalism in philosophy facilitates a creative use of circularity. Establishing non-overlapping and non-interfering meaning and reference quotients for the various components of sentences is such a complex and delicate task that for the most part we need to see it as already embedded and submerged in linguistic usage and practice, rather than something that can be (or needs to be) systematically plotted. The *Theaetetus* alerts us to another stratum among the non-fully-rationalizable elements that are subsumed under the term "tacit knowledge": the drastically severed sense and reference of key sentential terms whose uninterrupted flow engenders dilemmas of reflexivity. Tacit knowledge, therefore, in the *Theaetetus* (and the paradoxes of knowledge in the *Meno*, which forms part of the case for tacit knowledge)[28] constitute part of the alchemy whereby circularity as problem gets transmuted into circularity as solution.

There are two tiers left to Plato's argument in the *Theaetetus* that strengthen the argument concerning the pervasiveness of circularity and its transformation from problem into solution through the nominalistic strategies I have outlined. Theaetetus had defined knowledge as "true judgment with an account."[29] According to this approach, "true judgment without an account falls outside of knowledge."[30] Since the "primary elements" in any judgment can only be brutely, nominalistically given, they "have no account" and can only be named, but cannot be known.[31] Socrates goes on to attack what he claims "looks like the subtlest point of all – that the elements are unknowable and the complexes knowable."[32] He points out how arbitrary the whole matter of individuation is; whether something is regarded as single and without parts or composed of many parts is more a matter of nominalistic stipulation than anything else:

SOC.: Now, my friend, a little while ago, if you remember, we were inclined to accept a certain proposition which we thought put the matter very well – I mean the statement that no account can be given of the primaries of which other things are constituted, because each of them is itself incomposite; and that it would be incorrect to apply even the term "being" to it when we spoke of it or the term "this" because these terms signify different and alien things; and that is the reason why a primary is an unaccountable and unknowable thing. Do you remember?
THEAET.: I remember.
SOC.: And is that the reason also why it is single in form and indivisible in parts or is there some other reason for that? I can see no other myself.
THEAET.: No, there really doesn't seem to be any other.
SOC.: And hasn't the complex now fallen into the same class as the primary, seeing it has no parts and is a single form?
THEAET.: Yes, it certainly has.
SOC.: Well now, if the complex is both many elements and a whole, with them as its parts, then both complexes and elements are equally capable of being known and expressed, since all the parts turned out to be the same thing as the whole.
THEAET.: Yes, surely.
SOC.: But if, on the other hand, the complex is single and without parts, then complexes and elements are equally unaccountable and unknowable – both of them for the same reason.[33]

The way to resolve this dilemma is to openly acknowledge and embrace the presence of circularity: Certain elements in verbal-conceptual complexes are designated as primary, while other elements are taken to be complex, even though the classification of the first as single and without parts and the second as multiple and consisting of many parts remains fundamentally arbitrary. Through nominalistic stipulation, we render the division into these two categories immune from any hypothetical real-world constraints – and ensure that whatever constraints might hypothetically exist are predicated upon this division, rather than the other way around. Protocols of tacit knowledge reinforce and transmit these habits of individuation through mechanisms of ordinary speech.

Plato and Levinas 155

In an effort to escape the pervasiveness of circularity, Socrates proposes one last revision in his definition of knowledge. He says that "if a man with correct judgment about any one of the things that are grasps in addition its difference from the rest, he has become a knower of the thing he was a judger of before."[34] Socrates condemns this expanded definition, as well, on grounds of circularity. He says that if under this altered definition "we are required to get to *know* the differentness, not merely judge it, this most splendid of our accounts of knowledge turns out to be a very amusing affair. For getting to know of course is acquiring knowledge, isn't it?"

THEAET.: Yes.
SOC.: So, it seems, the answer to the question what is "knowledge?" will be "correct judgment accompanied by *knowledge* of the differentness" ...
THEAET.: Apparently so.
SOC.: And it is surely just silly to tell us, when we are trying to discover what knowledge is, that it is correct judgment accompanied by *knowledge*, whether of differentness or of anything else? And so, Theaetetus, knowledge is neither perception nor true judgment, nor an account added to true judgment.
THEAET.: It seems not.[35]

The Socratic inquiry terminates with the circular notion that knowledge depends upon knowledge. This can be interpreted either in a minimalist way as suggesting that whether we focus our analysis on immediate perception or shift it to a preoccupation with mind-ordained categories, we cannot avoid circularity. Or, this notion can be understood in a more maximalist way as affirming that circularity deliberately applied via the intermediacy of a nominalist metaphysics resolves dilemmas associated with both reflexivity and circularity by dramatizing as keenly as possible that there is no alternative to circularity, so that circularity can only be regarded as virtuous.

The *Theaetetus* is unusual among Plato's dialogues for its Socratic autobiographical musings. Socrates tries to fix for Theaetetus the nature and limits of his personality. The supreme metaphor that he adopts – the ramifications of which he discusses fully – is that of the midwife:

SOC.: Then do you mean to say you have never heard about my being the son of a good hefty midwife, Phaenarete?
THEAET.: Oh, yes, I've heard that before.
SOC.: And haven't you ever been told that I practice the same art myself?
THEAET.: No, I certainly haven't.
SOC.: But I do, believe me. Only don't give me away to the rest of the world, will you? You see, my friend, it is a secret that I have this art. That is not one of the things you hear people saying about me, because they don't know; but they do say that I am a very odd sort of a person, always causing people to get into difficulties. You must have heard that surely?

THEAET.: Yes, I have.

...

SOC.: I mean that it is the midwives who can tell better than anyone else whether women are pregnant or not.

...

SOC.: There's another thing too. Have you noticed this about them, that they are the cleverest of matchmakers, because they are marvelously knowing about the kind of couples whose marriage will produce the best children?

...

SOC.: So the work of the midwives is a highly important one; but it is not so important as my own performance. And for this reason, that there is not in midwifery the further complication, that the patients are sometimes delivered of phantoms and sometimes of realities and that the two are hard to distinguish. If there were, then the midwife's greatest and noblest function would be to distinguish the true from the false offspring – don't you agree?

THEAET.: Yes, I do.

SOC.: Now my art of midwifery is like theirs in most respects. The difference is that I attend men and not women, and that I watch over the labor of their souls, not of their bodies. And the most important thing about my art is the ability to apply all possible tests to the offspring, to determine whether the young mind is being delivered of a phantom, that is, an error, or a fertile truth. For one thing which I have in common with the ordinary midwives is that I myself am barren of wisdom. The common reproach against me is that I am always asking questions of other people but never express my own views about anything, because there is no wisdom in me; and that is true enough. And the reason of it is this, that God compels me to attend the travail of others, but has forbidden me to procreate. So that I am not in any sense a wise man; I cannot claim as the child of my own soul any discovery worth the name of wisdom. But with those who associate with me it is different. At first some of them may give the impression of being ignorant and stupid; but as time goes on and our association continues, all whom God permits are seen to make progress – a progress which is amazing both to other people and to themselves. And yet it is clear that this is not due to anything they have learnt from me; it is that they discover within themselves a multitude of beautiful things, which they bring forth into the light. But it is I, with God's help, who delivers them of this offspring.

...

SOC.: There is another point also in which those who associate with me are like women in childbirth. They suffer the pains of labor, and are filled day and night with distress; indeed they suffer far more than women. And this pain my art is able to bring on, and also to allay.[36]

I believe that we are presented in the *Theaetetus* with a central connection that is integral to the design and justification of liberal democracy. Philosophical thought beginning at either end – the particular and perceived or the general and imposed – eventuates either in incoherence or in a radical adjustment of our expectations with regard to the rationality of arguments. Whether we start with what we see or with what makes sense to us to invoke as the organizing framework for our perceptions, we are not able to easily bring our analytical apparatus into harmony with our judgmental and decision-making practices. The gap between how we reason on a secondary philosophical level and how we judge on a primary practical level can only be closed by assigning a central role to circularity in reshaping our premises in light of the directions and ends of action we wish to pursue.

Given the limitations of our argumentative condition, the appropriate organization of human life consists in a preoccupation with process. The quintessentially human moments are associated with movement, with fashioning the new, with giving birth. The common thread running through Socrates' self-description and self-presentation is that his powers are largely defined in negative terms. He is not able to attain truth, but he can perform the much more humble task of helping his interlocutors to distinguish between "phantoms" and "reality" – to be able to reject "un" or "non" truth. He can point to logical fallacy and expose the weaknesses of arguments – even if he cannot arrive at truth. Socrates himself is "barren of wisdom." He can only nudge others onto deeper levels of critical awareness and onto more refined and self-aware reformulations of their positions. The progress some of his dialogue partners make "is not due to anything they have learnt from" him. He merely gets them to see more clearly who they are – what is already within them. Intellectual growth is defined negatively in terms of the losses it exacts from those devoted to it – as "labor," rather than in terms of the fulfillment of some positive goal. The cultivation of "midwifery" is a function of the "tongue-tiedness" of thought. The "tongue-tiedness" of thought in turn (as the *Theaetetus* makes clear) is a function of certain logico-linguistic constraints – and is not just a matter of Socrates' verbal aggression against his interlocutors.

After the beginning – the articulation of new possibilities – there are endless deflections, distractions, reconsiderations and reformulations that restore us to some point in the middle (poised for a new beginning) instead of the end glimpsed in the first crystallization of the beginning. Since the return to beginnings is everlasting, the appropriate – the defining – philosophical emotion becomes wonder: "This is where philosophy begins and nowhere else."[37] Wonder is pre-eminently the emotion that defines our attitude toward beginnings. To be in a position to initiate things again and again is a primal source of human wonder.

Polytheism and monotheism; convergent and divergent thought

Umberto Eco has argued that key varieties of fascism are "pagan" and "polytheistic."[38] Contrary to the view of some theorists, that monotheism with its aggrandizing of total power and total knowledge to God serves as an important model for totalitarianism, Eco argues that it is precisely the pluralist, immanentist theologies of polytheism and paganism that are the most significant metaphysical precursors for totalitarianism. Eco's argument is reinforced by Plato's *Theaetetus*. Monotheism grounds human experience and human history in a source so ultimate and so impalpable that human beings are willy-nilly thrust upon their own devices to organize their personal and collective lives (even their religious lives) in order to make sense out of their experience. The causal and explanatory framework is so remote and abstract that it serves as a veritable invitation to members of the religious community to mobilize their own resources to enable the monotheistic texts to speak to them in ways that work to ameliorate their individual and social conditions. A prime model of how abstract frameworks and patterns of analysis produce conundrums of reason that thrust the reasoners back upon their own limited resources and a continuing preoccupation with the engendering of new beginnings (the process-character of human life) is provided by the *Theaetetus*. The Heraclitean and Protagorean categories of "flux" and "perception," as well as the Parmenidean category of "the One," are deconstructed by Plato and shown to be vacuous, circular categories whose meaning and reference are determined by periodic human theoretical and practical investment. It is their very emptiness that sets the stage for a heightened awareness of the process-character of human life.

In terms of the historically most influential negative-theological construal of the tenets of monotheism, Plato's *Parmenides* plays a decisive role because his elucidation of the One that has to be totally distinguished from all human embodiments and contrasts that evoke it serves as a formative analytical model of how the monotheistic God needs to be separated and distinguished from all things human.[39] It is our intellectual and existential drive toward ultimacy that leads us to postulate the indivisible One, who for this very reason has to be totally differentiated from all things human – and therefore restores us back to a reengagement with the human.

Quite paradoxically, therefore (but very much to the historical and theoretical point), polytheism and paganism by fashioning an immanentist universe usurp and undermine the role of the human. Monotheism by unrelentingly emphasizing metaphysical distance confers legitimacy and credibility upon an irredeemably human universe – where all doubts, anxieties and metaphysical yearnings (and their resolutions) have to be consistently re-anchored in the domain of the human.

Plato's argument in the *Theaetetus* also lends support to Stuart Hampshire's contention that "it would be a gain in clarity to discard the old psychology of separate faculties, with its distinction between reason and imagination, and to substitute for it the contrast between convergent and divergent thought."[40] Plato shows how dominant categories and values postulated by reason, such as "perception," "flux" and "the One" (indivisible unity), are really devoid of defensible and sustainable content outside the ambit of circular definition. Communities of language-users engaging in discourse with Protagorean and Heraclitean biases need to reach convergence among themselves concerning the precise content to be invested in such a term as "immediate knowledge." "Circularity as solution" then provides us with a formal mapping tool for reinserting the revised content into the original term. The prominence of "circularity" in Plato's argument challenges us to cultivate a scaled-down conception of reason that is attentive to the ways in which it represents a congealed set of judgment-rendering social practices (convergences), rather than a group of criteria that can be objectively defined, defended and applied.

The fluidity of the boundaries between reason and the imagination gives us an additional gloss to bring to bear on Socrates' emphasis on "process" in the *Theaetetus*. What is being created anew each time through Socrates' application of his art of "midwifery" is not just a particular person's capacity to refine his argument and become more critically self-aware. It is not just individual acts of thinking – it is also thought itself that is being recast through Socratic prodding. "Reason" and "imagination" are porous categories that get continually rearticulated in the light of each application of Socratic negative, critical reason.

Circularity, the political and dialogue in Plato

Circularity is manifested in many subtle, but significant, ways in Plato's *Republic* as well as in his other dialogues. Circularity suggests that philosophical arguments don't eventuate in anything. They reflect back to us what we put into them. How then does the discourse called "philosophy" proceed? What points are being made? And how *can* they be made?

Two dominant characteristics of Plato's philosophical writing can be accounted for in relation to these questions. The first is the proliferation of multiple analogies – multiple "elsewheres" – in Plato's writings. If circularity suggests that what you theoretically initiate first bubbles up with possibilities and then trails off into logical incoherence, then the argumentative thread – the thread of philosophical inquiry – has to be spread across numerous philosophical initiatives, which while they don't build cumulatively upon one another yet subterraneously trade upon each other's insights and associations. Plato is the philosopher of "narrativity" par excellence – rather than a philosopher of facticity. For him, what we conceptually articulate defines the multiple worlds that we inhabit – rather than what exists constraining what can be said. Narratives can be built up through quantum leaps and elisions – through mirror-like reflections on each other's starting points that enable the self-contained mini-narratives, metaphors and analogies to respond, expand upon and revise each other's initiating impulses without composing or yielding an argument.

Let me adduce two examples to illustrate what I have in mind. In many of Plato's dialogues, the gods loom as a significant "elsewhere" – as a revealing analogy for the human subject matter under discussion. The gods, as it were, become a drawing board for a discourse about humanity. In the *Cratylus*, for example, Socrates juxtaposes the relationship between words and things to our understanding of the gods: "Saying by way of preface, as I said before of the Gods, that of the truth about them we know nothing, and do but entertain human notions of them."[41] Even though Plato is writing in a polytheistic cultural setting, his invocation of an abstract theoretical vocabulary to make sense of experience already begins to engender those dilemmas of unbridgeable distancing between words and things (so that they are brought into some kind of workable alignment largely through mechanisms of circularity) which prefigure dilemmas that negative theology was later to highlight in relation to the monotheistic God. In the passage just quoted, Plato projects these dilemmas growing out of his analysis of abstract conceptual frameworks pertaining to the relationship between language and reality onto the Greek polytheistic gods. He thereby initiates a process of transforming our understanding of language as well as of religion away from literalism toward skepticism with its attendant dilemmas.

A second example of circularity engendering a proliferation of "elsewheres" has to do with the "just soul"/"just commonwealth" analogies that are central to the *Republic*. Throughout the *Republic*, Plato works with a conception of politics as an omnipresent human phenomenon, one that is not restricted to what takes place in the public sphere. According to Plato (with his tripartite division of the soul), politics does not arise in a determinate historical and social context as a response to a preexisting situation of conflict between men. Instead, it emerges whenever human beings attain to that degree of self-consciousness that allows them to perceive that acting in recognizably human ways nearly always involves the subordination of certain aspects of the self to others. Since the very activity of structuring, divorced from historical or social setting, is regarded as a manifestation of the political, of the exertion of power, politics emerges as a kind of primary datum in human experience.

It is possible to decode the relationship between the Theory of Ideas, the Just Soul and the Just Commonwealth as a series of conceptual circles reflecting off each other in a state of permanent disequilibrium. From this perspective, the line separating "metaphor" from "reality" becomes shadowy and blurred. The political realm itself can be viewed as the institutionalization of a gigantic "elsewhere." Politics is invented partially in order to be able to pin down more readily the nature of the human, the personal and the private. As the largest and most impressive realm of the constructed, it is most revealing of the capacities and inclinations of human beings. Or, conversely, the soul, as a forum for the application of political ordering categories such as "justice," is suggestive of the need for the invention (or the periodic reinvention) of the human, and of how ironic and futile that task is. The theoretical urge to encompass "reality" and the underdetermination of theory by fact which points to an inescapable role for circularity in shaping and delineating the nature of reality suggest that the human will always be a politically chiseled structure despite all of our periodic efforts to rescue it from the political and to arrive at its most pristine elements. The fact that the political straddles both the public and the private spheres in Plato's *Republic*, that each sphere is invoked as a "circular mirror" to reflect the other, can be read as an ironic commentary on the shackling effects of our most overwhelming urges toward liberation. As we notice our powers, we have a tendency to fall more into the grip of the categories that reflect them and that also highlight our inability to move beyond them.

A second dominant characteristic of Plato's philosophical writing that can be accounted for in relation to issues of circularity is his choice of the dialogue form. We might say that for Plato the dialogue form facilitates the emergence of instant "elsewhere"'s. The incursion by interlocutors with diverse points of view into the speaker's presentation of his theories engenders the proliferation of "circular mirrors" even as the speaker unfolds his ideas. The contrasting perspectives in conversation indicate diverse starting-points, and thus illuminate the circular character of each speaker's contribution. In addition, there are a number of other ways in which dialogue functions as an implicit meta-philosophical commentary on the radical incompleteness of the philosophical enterprise:

1. The choice of the dialogue as a form in which to communicate one's philosophical teaching suggests that we can never travel further in philosophy than what is legitimated by our presuppositions and assumptions. Even the most elaborately argued philosophical treatise, therefore, has the character of a conversation or dialogue. There is an implicit interrogation hovering over the edges of every philosophical work which contributes to articulating and explicating the unarticulated and perhaps un-thought out of which the philosophical argument springs.
2. Discourse of whatever sort remains unintelligible without presupposing discourse's relation to its other (or one of its others) – namely, silence. What can be quarried from the silence at any given moment in historical time is, to some extent, a function of our networks of interpersonal relationships or our intrapsychic imagined dialogical interactions. What finds its way into discourse is to some extent released and sanctioned by whom we are relating to. All discourse at some pragmatic level is dialogue.
3. In dialogue – conversation – language approximates to the self-consuming rhythms of silence. Discourse – language – is overwhelmed by silence. The cutting-in by interlocutors of diverse and unpredictable perspectives is suggestive of the impoverishment and defenselessness of language in the face of what has not yet been put into words. The jagged edges of language that human speech has not yet refined (which is a prominent characteristic of language emerging in the course of conversation) evokes an image of language perpetually on the defensive – unable to adequately protect itself against the destabilizing incursions of the awareness of the unsaid and the unsayable. The pouring-forth of interactive speech by

communication partners restores us to a condition that can be characterized as either pre- or post-linguistic, where words serve as the preeminent pointers of what is inadequate about speech. In addition to all of the other perspectives that we bring to bear on it, language has to be interpreted negatively hermeneutically – as highlighting what is not being or cannot be communicated, rather than merely serving as a vehicle of communication.
4. Another way of getting at the same point: Time continually destabilizes discourse. What we have just said (at any given moment in time) stands on the brink of dissolving in the face of the onslaught of new sense impressions and new internally-generated words and images that are a function of the dispersal of our being over an extended and continuing time frame. Dialogue temporalizes discourse. It projects it as being a function of time. By their very diffraction and fragmentation, dialogue and conversation conjure up an image of a beginning that antedates all beginnings – when the convergence of "language" with its world of experience is preserved through the unavailability of language. Issues of reflexivity in philosophy constitute the negative, obdurate traces in the logical spaces of language of this pristine and undifferentiated moment in the history of consciousness. Alternatively, the dialogue form by its very transitory and fragmentary character evokes the specter of a pre-linguistic state where wholeness is metaphysically interchangeable with speechlessness (the absence of language).

Notes

1 Plato, *Cratylus,* in *The Dialogues of Plato Volume III*, trans. Benjamin Jowett. (Oxford: Clarendon Press, 1964), 426a (p. 89).
2 Ibid., 424d–424e (p. 88).
3 Ibid., 425a (p. 88).
4 Ibid., 426d–426e (p. 90).
5 Ibid., 434a–434b (pp. 98–99).
6 Ibid., 430d–430e (p. 94).
7 Ibid., 429b (pp. 92–93).
8 Ibid., 429d (p. 93).
9 Ibid., 437c (p. 102).
10 Ibid., 437a (p. 102).
11 "The grand narrative has lost its credibility, regardless of what mode of unification it uses, regardless of whether it is a speculative narrative or a narrative of emancipation." Lyotard, *The Postmodern Condition,* p. 37.
12 *Cratylus*, 433e (p. 98).
13 Myles Burnyeat, *The Theaetetus of Plato*. Trans. M. J. Levett. (Indianapolis: Hackett, 1990), 161d (p. 285).
14 Ibid., 161d–161e (p. 285).
15 Ibid., 161e–162a (p. 285); italics in original.
16 Ibid., 171a–171d (pp. 298–299).
17 Ibid., 182d–183b (pp. 312–313).
18 Ibid., 180d–180e (p. 310).

19 Compare the discussion of the *Parmenides* in my book, *Postmodernism and Democratic Theory* (Philadelphia: Temple University Press, 1993), pp. 104–106.
20 Plato, *Theaetetus*, 186d (p. 318).
21 Ibid., 187a (p. 318).
22 Ibid.
23 Ibid., 196b–196c (p. 331).
24 Ibid., 189e–190a (p. 323).
25 Ibid., 196d–196e (p. 332).
26 Ibid., 198d (p. 334).
27 Ibid., 201c–202c (pp. 338–339).
28 For a discussion of the *Meno*, see my book, *Skepticism and Political Participation*, pp.70–71.
29 Plato, *Theaetetus*, 201d (p. 338).
30 Ibid.
31 Ibid., 202a–202b (p. 339).
32 Ibid., 202d–202e (p. 340).
33 Ibid., 205c–205e (p. 344).
34 Ibid., 208e (p. 348).
35 Ibid., 209e–210b (p. 350).
36 Ibid., 149a–151a (pp. 268–271).
37 Ibid., 155d (p. 277).
38 Umberto Eco, "Ur-Fascism," in *The New York Review of Books*, Volume XLII, Number 11 (June 22, 1995), pp. 12–15, on p. 14.
39 Compare the discussion in my book, *Skepticism, Belief, and the Modern*, pp. 24–26.
40 Stuart Hampshire, "Review of *Looking at Giacometti* by David Sylvester," in *The New York Review of Books*, Volume XLII, Number 12 (July 13, 1995), pp. 46–48, on p. 48.
41 *Cratylus*, 425c (p. 88).

9 Can there be an ethics that is otherwise than being?

The phenomenological background to *Otherwise than Being*

In *Otherwise than Being*, Levinas pursues much more audaciously and systematically than he does in *Totality and Infinity* the phenomenological mode of philosophizing inaugurated by Husserl and extended by Heidegger. The constitutive categories of this phenomenology – "substitution," "passivity" and "incarnation" – do not even appear in the index to *Totality and Infinity*. While Levinas revises and is critical of the work of his two famous predecessors, there is no mistaking his intent to contribute to the same philosophical genre that Husserl had created and Heidegger had rearticulated with his own preferred set of subcategories. As Leszek Kolakowski has argued,[1] this philosophical project is both metaphysically and logically vulnerable, which makes it subject to criticisms that have been leveled against the work of Husserl and Heidegger.

Husserl invented the phenomenological method of doing philosophy "to restore hope in the return to absolutely primordial insight in cognition and to achieve victory over relativism and skepticism ... The concept of certainty can be regarded as the key to Husserl's thought."[2] The certitude achieved in both deductive and inductive modes of argument was at the price of circularity, which only fueled the epistemological challenges of the skeptic. Deductive modes of argument only rigorously elaborate upon what is already implicit in their premises, and inductive arguments succeed in conferring order and regularity upon our perceptions of how the world works only because they already presuppose the truth of induction. Induction allows the world to fall into place because it already assumes what its argument is designed to prove and to illustrate. Descartes in his attempt to restore the reliability of the everyday world after engaging in the thought experiment encapsulated in the famous *cogito* passage was also guilty of circularity. He "made use of the criterion of evidence in order to prove the existence of God, and then he used God to validate the criterion of evidence."[3] Finally, Ernst Mach and Richard Avenarius, as leading figures in German and French empiricism, respectively, at the end of the 19th century, emphasized the implicit circularity of the whole epistemological enterprise. Our very formulation of questions concerning knowledge insinuates criteria of relevancy and priority in the subject matter to be examined which taints the objectivity of the answers arrived at beyond retrieval. We never get to a world outside of the parameters of our questions. An argument of this sort (as we have seen) had already been made in Plato's *Meno*.

According to Husserl, psychologism as practiced by Mach and Avenarius which assimilates the meaning of a judgment to the act of judging cannot have the last word because saying there is no truth is itself incoherent: "The very concept of truth makes it impossible to say 'there is no truth,' for this would mean 'it is true that nothing is true.'"[4] There are reflexive conundrums attached to skepticism and to relativism that call their sustainability into question. Even if one could manage to come up with more coherent versions of these doctrines, Husserl would be opposed to them because of their devastating impact upon European culture. In order to salvage Reason, we need to sever the implicit tie between logic and psychology that governs much of the empiricist critique of truth. We need to arrive at "the transcendental foundation of certitude."[5]

The factors that I have just sketched "led Husserl from his attacks on psychologism to his program of phenomenology, as a method of describing necessary structures of the world, a method that is free from the impact of psychological constructions. Eventually it led him to the idea of transcendental consciousness, which constitutes these structures as correlates of its own intentional acts – to transcendental idealism."[6] Before proceeding any further in my explication of Husserl, it is arresting to note how his alternative to what he rejects bears an uncanny similarity to that position. In order to salvage truth and contain skepticism and relativism, Husserl counterposes to intermediate psychological processes situated between the human agent and the world a subjectivism that is so complete that the "correlates of intentional acts" become primary reality to the exclusion of selves and world and their patterns of perplexing relationship. Instead of the solipsism that has sometimes accompanied skeptical positions in philosophy, in Husserl you have the advocacy of what we might call a "pre-solipsistic stage of argument" where in order to get rid of what is problematic in the relationship between self and world, we need to reduce not only the relationship but "self" and "world" themselves to the common denominator of "correlates of consciousness' own intentional acts." Skepticism in its denial of rational foundations to knowledge issues forth in a world characterized by extreme arbitrariness. Husserl in outlining a position to contain skepticism does skepticism one better. He dismantles the resources to pronounce even judgments of arbitrariness, as he reduces the theoretical landscape to the bleakly detached units of the "correlates of consciousness' own intentional acts."

In the light of this analysis, it is not surprising that, as Kolakowski says, "Husserl's critics have repeatedly noticed that his attack on psychologism made arbitrary assumptions concerning the ideal units of meaning which were not products of human thought and were independent of human psychology, biology, and history. What reasons do we have to believe in this realm of meaning?"[7] How can we certify to the truthfulness of the "correlates of our own intentional acts"? Recourse to language cannot help us because in order for language to function in this role it would require intersubjectively accessible (if not, in some sense, verifiable) frames of reference, which have been obliterated by Husserl in his campaign against skepticism. The upshot of this is (as Kolakowski says) that "the experience of certitude in Husserl's sense appears as incommunicable as a mystical experience."[8]

We are back in the realm we were in earlier when, in summarizing Husserl's case for the pervasiveness of skepticism, I spoke about how the deductivist and the inductivist were committed to opposing sets of circular arguments (privileging contrasting initial premises), so that in a confrontation between them concerning which type of argument was superior they would be condemned to a state of eternal combat, speaking indefinitely to their own affirmers and always past each other. The same sort of plight haunts the Husserlian transcendental phenomenologist confronting the empiricist. Each side privileges a set of initial premises denied by the other. The empiricist will say that the transcendental phenomenologist privileges a set of ideal meanings that remain empirically untethered. The transcendental phenomenologist will argue that the empiricist unduly privileges worldly experience whose primacy is precisely what is at stake in the debate between himself and the empiricist. The transcendental phenomenologist compels the empiricist to focus on the major casualty of his argument – which is the concept of truth. To assign priority to experience means that our verbal formulations are ultimately unmoored in truth, since experience (the different sectors of it) are compatible with multiple (and even contradictory) conceptual framings. The empiricist forces the transcendental phenomenologist to focus on the major casualty of his argument – which is the proliferation of entities that cannot be empirically, or sometimes even rationally, accounted for.[9]

Latter-day empiricism would argue that the turns of argument that the transcendental phenomenologist employs are excessive because science does not need "truth" in order to preserve its identity as science – i.e., achieving greater knowledge of and mastery over experience.[10] If our theories are underdetermined by facts – if experience can be captured by alternative and even contradictory conceptual frameworks – then we are indeed skeptics, but skepticism can be reformulated as a sustainable philosophical position. If we make the reflexive move of incorporating skepticism of skepticism within the protocols of skepticism, we eventuate in a generalized agnosticism that is compatible with science. Later generations of scientific investigators can continually revise or reject the work of their predecessors based upon piecemeal reconfigurations of the theory-fact relationship without any clear terminus for the respective inquiries being in sight. The intermediate criteria for revision or rejection of theories can be immanent to the work already done in respective fields of inquiry – or they can be based upon inspirations that are extraneous to a particular field, without it being transparently apparent to everyone what is irresolvably wrong in current approaches and what is irrevocably right in the new ones. Science can call its global connection to truth into question at the same time that it achieves local successes both in terms of theoretical elucidation and in terms of technical mastery.

Popper as a skeptical philosopher of science *malgre lui*

Karl Popper was one of the 20th century's most prominent philosophers of science to argue in favor of a conception of science where theories do not enjoy a higher ontological status than "conjectures," and experiments ("successful" experiments that ostensibly confirm a theory) do not enjoy a higher ontological status than (failed) "refutations."[11] Through this negative mode of theorizing science, Popper appears to have effectively dissociated the enterprise of science from the concept of truth. However, there is one lurking inconsistency in Popper, which Kolakowski appropriately criticizes:

> When Popper argues that in the development of science we can, on empirical grounds, eliminate certain hypotheses as contrary to experience, and that such an elimination never establishes the rival hypotheses as true, he should draw the conclusion that we never are (and never will be) able to exclude the possibility that our knowledge of the world is made up entirely of false statements. However, if that is so, it makes no sense to talk about the development of science as a movement closer and closer to the truth. Still, this is precisely how Popper views science.[12]

I would like to amplify and reinforce Kolakowski's critique of Popper. Even in relation to Popper's own broader corpus of argument, there appears to be a central tension – or even contradiction – in his work. On the one hand, as we have seen, Popper says in "What is Dialectic?" that a toleration of contradiction means that no possibility can be ruled out, and therefore science becomes impossible. On the other hand, in "Conjectures and Refutations,"[13] Popper opts for what I am calling a "negative construal" of the structure and dynamics of science. We can make sense of the role of hypotheses and theories in science by classifying them as no more than conjectures, and we can on a meta-theoretical plane theorize the role of experimentation in science as engagement in an adversarial relationship with a hypothesis or theory. As a result, we can categorize every successful experiment that meets a theory's predictions as a failed disproof or refutation.

Popper is implicitly acknowledging that the theory of science is underdetermined by the actual enterprise of science. He appears to be proceeding after the manner of the skeptic. Science can be made sense of in a grandiose, positive way as consisting of theories that stake out a claim to truth and of experiments that either confirm them or fail to confirm them. Or else science can be grasped more humbly and negatively as consisting of conjectures and refutations or failed refutations (the theories and experiments of the old nomenclature). What takes place in science can be accommodated under either meta-theoretical dispensation. One major advantage of Popper's negatively-inspired formulation is that it conforms to a methodological principle of parsimony better than more ambitious, positively-conceived meta-theories concerning the nature of science. It can explain the same phenomena by postulating less rather than more. In any event, the underdetermination of theory (in this case, meta-theory) by fact is both what provides Popper with an opening wedge for inserting his position and yields the analytical framework that indirectly lends support, via the principle of parsimony, to his reading of the nature of science.

The upshot of this analysis of Popper's philosophy of science is that its crucial conceptual and logical hinge is the entertainment of the dual, contradictory possibility that science makes positive claims about truth and that it does not make such claims. Popper's theorizing of the nature of science sustains the underdetermination of theory by fact throughout – and trades upon this underdetermination in order to be able to theorize and render plausible its own position. By being skeptically predicated upon the principle of the underdetermination of theory by fact, Popper's philosophy of science acknowledges the presence of contradiction. According to Popper's argument in "What is Dialectic?", Popper has thereby undermined the prospect of science.

An additional factor that makes Popper vulnerable to the charge that the argument of "Conjectures and Refutations" is in sharp tension with (if it does not openly contradict) that of "What is Dialectic?" has to do with Popper's insistence in the former essay that all of the successful corroborations of a scientific hypothesis in the world do not constitute a confirmation of a theory in a conclusive sense. Apparently, part of the concern is that in the course of time new ways of conceptualizing what is at stake in the hypothesis will have an impact on the design of experiments that can contribute toward corroborating or disproving it. What is captured in a scientific hypothesis is subject to theoretical reconfiguration – and not just to empirical proof or disproof based upon an "enduring" conceptual identity. It is the admixture of the factor of theoretical instability (influenced directly or indirectly by interactions with actual or conceivable empirical translations) – and not just that the experimental process can proceed indefinitely and that the future might not resemble the past – that ensures that all the failed disproofs of hypotheses in the world do not yield a successful confirmation of a hypothesis.

What emerges from this analysis is that the notion of the underdetermination of theory by fact is manifested in two places in Popper's argument. The first place is where it provides support for his understanding of the structure of science as conforming to the model of conjectures and refutations through the instrumentality of a covert principle of parsimony. Since the range of ontological commitments is much more drastically reduced under the negative, Popperian reading of science than under more traditional positivistic readings, a methodological principle of parsimony provides indirect support for Popper's reading. The second place is where it helps to fix the content of Popper's theory – and not just in constituting an additional argument in support of it. Part of the reason why Popper theorizes science as "conjectures and refutations" rather than in more literal, positivistic terms is that reconceptualization of a scientific hypothesis always remains as an unforecloseable possibility, so that an unequivocal reading of the impact of experimentation remains endlessly deferred.

My critique of Popper alerts us to what we might call a general paradox of explanation. Given the principle of the underdetermination of words by things, every explanation can be immediately reclassified as a redescription, which merely restarts the quest for explanation. The failure of the project of explanation is guaranteed by (is encoded in) the giving of an explanation. Or, stated somewhat differently, every description invites (and often requires) an explanation. This is one of the major roles of theories or hypotheses in the sciences. Once an explanation is provided, however, given the principle of "underdetermination," it becomes a new description (a redescription). As a description, it requires an explanation – and so the round continues indefinitely, without offering any possibility of breaking out of it.

In the light of what I have just argued, Wittgenstein was being far too optimistic when he said: "At some point one has to pass from explanation to mere description."[14] Explanation does not only founder on the problem of an infinite regress, namely, that every explanation needs to be explained in turn, so that unless we accept one of our explanations as a pure description, the explanatory process will have not worked at all. It is not just that the linguistic logic of the term "explanation" points to its overlap with the linguistic logic of the term "description." The paradox concerning explanation that I have just outlined suggests beyond these considerations that in terms of what we might call its metaphysical logic, the concept of explanation does not get off the ground at all. When we explain, we have merely redesigned the object that needs to be explained, and have not explained anything. Explanation renders explanation impossible.

The paradox of explanation helps us to see that the whole Kantian epistemological framework which distinguishes between a domain of appearances and irretrievable and barely conceptualizable "things in themselves" is implicit in the Western philosophical and scientific quests themselves with their obsessive concern with explanation. Kant's philosophical work can be read as constituting an intertextual gloss on these quests. The search for explanation on skeptical principles creates its forever elusive shadow structure of "things in themselves." The explanation that emerges *becomes* the thing that needs to be explained in turn, and so on indefinitely – with the thing that one is seeking primordially to explain being necessarily endlessly deferred. In an explanatory setting, what is being described and the explanation always merge, so that the thing (the presumed object of explanation) is always left behind as the "thing in itself."

The paradox surrounding explanation sets the stage for a paradox about God. God cannot both be and have a name. If He has a name, then, since the name is humanly coined and humanly exchanged, it needs to be viewed as subject to the principle of underdetermination, which betokens that He could be more than One. This, of course, conflicts with the constitutive principle of His being as enunciated in Biblical religion. If He is at all, then He remains utterly, overwhelmingly nameless. This might be a major factor motivating Spinoza's pantheism.

Levinas and Jeanne Delhomme

It is interesting to note that in 1967 (in the same year in which he delivered a lecture on "Substitution," which forms the centerpiece of *Otherwise than Being*), Levinas published an essay called "Jeanne Delhomme: Penelope, or Modal Thought,"[15] which implicitly endorses and amplifies upon the line of criticism of transcendental phenomenology sketched out above. Levinas says:

> As for the intentionality of consciousness that finds or invents its object, it would be, in this view, dogmatism itself: even by an object still forming itself within it, intentionality is supported as if the object were completed. Intentionality, the taking over of the conscious act by its object, whether encountered or constituted (which is perhaps the original event of history), would be precisely the modality of thought that subordinates the possible to being, and consequently sacrifices the possible *qua* possible. The thought of being becomes the being of thought. The genitive of intentionality is reversed. Historical continuity resumes, despite the ideality of the intentional object. Every attitude of consciousness changes into consciousness of the attitude, which passes into being, causes much ado, and becomes history.[16]

From Levinas' perspective, transcendental phenomenology succumbs to the same skeptical currents it was designed to overcome. "The intentionality of consciousness that finds or invents its object" is as fertile a breeding ground for the proliferation of underdetermination as the empiricism it sought to supplant. Instead of the relationship between theory and fact and word and thing being underdetermined, it is now the relationship between consciousness and object that is underdetermined. It is this underdetermination that is intrinsic to how consciousness identifies and defines its objects that ensures that "the thought of being becomes the being of thought," with history usurping the role that transcendental phenomenology originally sought to assign to philosophy. Since there is no way to securely ground consciousness' identification of its objects, instead of arriving at a masterful transcendental account of the objects of consciousness we are left with a historical legacy of how different transcendental positionings of consciousness delineated their objects. From Levinas' vantage point, transcendental phenomenology merely reinscribes skepticism – without overcoming it.

The philosophical vision that inspires the founders and classical practitioners of transcendental phenomenology – of creating "an always unheard-of modality of a language that undoes (in the intervals that separate the days) the weaving of ontologies"[17] – remains unfulfilled. Levinas seems to agree with Delhomme that "Modal thought – intelligence opposed to reason which posits and articulates the seamless coherence of being – is philosophy."[18] Where he differs from her apparently is in the tracing of a metaphor and the drawing out of its implications: Whereas Delhomme seems to be groping for what lies "*behind* being," where "one could hear the sarcastic laughter of irresponsibility, for which the freedom within being is not free enough," Levinas is searching for what resides "*beyond* being," which "would extend the goodness of unbounded responsibility, for which that freedom [exercised within being] is not generous enough."[19] The Levinasian philosophical vision consists in wanting to shape "a relation in which the servitudes and encumbrances of history appear in a new modality, that of ethics transcending ontology."[20]

Levinas and his phenomenological predecessors Husserl and Heidegger

A crucial question confronting the interpreter of *Otherwise than Being* is how (in what precise ways) "ethics transcending ontology" constitutes "a new modality" for doing philosophy. On the surface, despite obvious discontinuities, there appear to be significant continuities between Husserl's, Heidegger's and Levinas' arguments concerning how to reform and refocus philosophy. These differences and similarities can be schematized as follows:

Given the unbridledly subjectivist program of Husserl's phenomenology – its circumvention of skepticism consisting in a denial of priority being assigned to experience – it is not surprising that phenomenology in his hands appears as "an eternal program that is never applied."[21] Aside from his emphasis on absolute self-responsibility,[22] Husserl provides very few applications of his own philosophical program. The applications are mainly supplied by Heidegger and Levinas.

There are important differences between Husserl, Heidegger and Levinas, but what legitimates and serves as the backdrop to their divergent theorizing is the (anti-) epistemological model formulated by Husserl. Among the major differeces between Husserl, Heidegger and Levinas are the following:

Husserl's suspension of experience and his preoccupation with the "correlates of our own intentional acts" is matched by his emphasis on "absolute self-responsibilty" in contrast to "the satisfaction of wants of human nature" as epitomizing "the telos of theoretical culture which is determinative of Western spirituality."[23] The political bias of Western epistemology is in favor of a self that cannot get its bearings from the world because the world can be subsumed under relativized and contradictory frameworks. However, since Western epistemology postulates the primacy of experience and reason provides an insufficient basis for organizing experience and making it available for human use, modern Western epistemology has very often been formulated in tandem with a liberal political theory that assigns primacy to the passions and to the interests that they nurture which constitute a species of rationalized passion.[24] Husserl, for whom "the correlates of our intentional acts" usurp the role of the primacy of worldly experience in liberal empiricism, very naturally counterposes "absolute self-responsibility" to the "satisfaction of wants" as the highest moral and cultural ideal.

"Absolute self-responsibility" constitutes the highest moral ideal for a self liberated from the need of locating itself along the skepticism-truth axis. Western philosophy which Husserl rebelled against was not able to overcome skepticism, but by the same token it was still in the grip of a preoccupation and fascination with truth. Skepticism is just a placeholder for an unrealized truth. Husserl, by attempting to transcend skepticism altogether by denying the primacy assigned to worldly experience in earlier philosophy, in effect did not opt for truth that was dialectically bound up with skepticism, but for the displacement of truth by an ethic of "absolute self-responsibility" or by what has come to be called "authenticity."

Heidegger's variation on the theme of authenticity is to require a "leap beyond what is as a whole [Being] into the abysses of death."[25] Only a proper confrontation with our finitude and mortality prepares us for the "absolute self-responsibility" toward which Husserl's diagnosis of our philosophical condition positions us. As I shall shortly be elaborating upon more fully, Levinas identifies what is "Otherwise than Being" with "a relationship with the Good, which is over and beyond Being."[26]

One can argue that "authenticity" is the self-validating principle of phenomenology itself. Since the "correlates of consciousness" by definition cannot receive external corroboration, they can only be confirmed by invoking the principle of authenticity. Authenticity, in turn, can only be affirmed in relation to itself. Authenticity authenticates authenticity. Authenticity, as it were, suspends the need for higher-order principles of justification. The objectifying of the subjective, which authenticity strives for, renders the search for more comprehensive justification inherently (and immediately) redundant.

Heidegger's claim to have superseded skepticism is thus vulnerable to the charge of foundering on a performative contradiction. In elaborating upon his own position by theorizing authenticity, Heidegger exposes and dramatizes the circular character of his own thought. Skepticism can be paraphrased as the philosophical thesis that highlights how the unanchored character of virtually all initiating premises in argument reduces nearly all arguments to a condition of circularity. If Heidegger can only triumph over skepticism by reenacting it, he has not advanced one iota beyond skepticism, despite all of his claims to the contrary.

For both Heidegger and Levinas, the concept of "substitution" is important – but each philosopher gives it a reading in accordance with his own set of philosophical priorities. For Heidegger, "substitution" relates to my temporarily assuming someone else's perspective on Being, which remains completley outside of the context of this substitution. In Heidegger, I need to return from

Can there be an ethics that is otherwise than being? 173

this substitution to assume the singular burden of my own death which, in turn, enables me to assume the singular responsibility for my own life. For Levinas, "substitution" (alterity in its most heightened form) constitutes a necessary disruption of Being that allows it to assume post this disruption the highest level of coherence that it is capable of attaining.[27] It is through placing myself under the ethical imperative of substitution for the Other that my singularity is achieved. A central question in dispute between Heidegger and Levinas is thus whether the sensibility of consciousness is infiltrated primordially by an awareness of mortality or by an awareness of alterity.[28]

Connected with what we have been discussing, another difference between Husserl and Heidegger, on the one hand, and Levinas, on the other, has to do with the role of the Other in the first constitution of universal space. For Husserl and Heidegger, the Other does enter into this constitution. Universal space is constituted by multiple Others. Levinas wants to go further and make my relationship with the Other the precondition for the emergence of "the sensuous expanse and the practical layout itself."[29] The ethical has to come first before the "perceptual or pragmatic" can have their shaping effect upon Being.[30]

Husserl and Levinas also differ concerning where the idea of infinity has its origins. Husserl identifies infinity with "an idealization of spatial sense of horizontal openness" and in "the absolutization of the idea of truth." Levinas, by contrast, emphasizes the ethical inspiration of the idea of infinity. The Other cannot be properly apprehended by us and he is the source (just as a function of his very existence) of impossible demands.[31]

With this context in place of the anti-epistemological genesis of the Husserlian project and of the divergent ways in which Heidegger and Levinas still remain faithful to it, we are in a position to assess Levinas' argument in *Otherwise than Being*. A prime focus of our analysis will be to consider to what extent the vulnerabilities of the original Husserlian position in trying to overcome epistemology still apply to Levinas – and whatever other vulnerabilities emerge in the course of doing philosophy in the reconfigured space delimited by Husserl. I shall approach *Otherwise than Being* from a series of interrelated perspectives reflective of this larger framework.

Levinas in the conclusion to *Otherwise than Being* tries to deflect criticism away from his argument by acknowledging the utopian character of the work. He says: "The openness of space as an openness of self without a world, without a place, utopia, the not being walled in, inspiration to the end, even to expiration, is proximity of the other which is possible only as responsibility for the other, as substitution for him."[32] "Substitution," the key ethical category of Levinas' book, is then "utopian" – literally "without a place" to latch on to. Even as a utopian argument, however, what would render it initially attractive and compelling would be its role, if it could, *per impossible*, be realized, in addressing thorny philosophical issues. Another way of looking at Levinas' argument in *Otherwise than Being* is as a piece of rhetoric to make a world that none of us yet inhabits seem less exotic and more alluring, as a first step toward getting us to move toward the fashioning of such a world.

In what follows, I seek to address Levinas' argument on both levels: The philosophical and the rhetorical. To the extent that Levinas wants to capitalize upon "substitution" as harboring philosophical promise for disentangling thorny philosophical knots associated with skepticism and a maximally coherent organized perspective on ethics, I try to argue that it boomerangs – that it intensifies those knots without resolving them. As a rhetorical vision aiming at eventual transformation of human consciousness, I argue that it partakes more of the character of a dystopia than a utopia, since it presupposes, or is likely to lead to, the explosion of some of our most cherished ethical ideals.

Levinas' ethics as a Christian ethics

Christian imagery suffuses Levinas' ethics in *Otherwise than Being*. Some of the key terms of his ethical vocabulary in this work are "passivity," "incarnation" and "substitution." This sort of vocabulary which communicates manifest certainty is in tension with the skepticism that helps Levinas make his case for the primacy of ethics in the first place. The interrelated character of these three terms – and what they signify – are encapsulated in the following passage which is centrally situated at the beginning of Levinas' argument in *Otherwise than Being*:

> The responsibility for the other can not have begun in my commitment, in my decision. The unlimited responsibility in which I find myself comes from the hither side of my freedom, from a "prior to every memory," an "ulterior to every accomplishment," from the non-present par excellence, the non-original, the an-archical, prior to or beyond essence. The responsibility for the other is the locus in which is situated the null-site of subjectivity, where the privilege of the question "Where?" no longer holds.[33]

The ethical stance originates for Levinas (and is sustained) in a position of total passivity, what he refers to as "the supreme passivity of exposure to another, which is responsibility for the free initiatives of the other."[34] The ethical demand knows no limits: I incarnate the Other, substituting for him; and then ethics can be said to properly begin: "The one is exposed to the other as a skin is exposed to what wounds it, as a cheek is offered to the smiter."[35] Ethics for Levinas involves "a denuding beyond the skin, to the wounds one dies from, denuding to death."[36] He continues:

> This being torn up from oneself in the core of one's unity, this absolute noncoinciding, this diachrony of the instant, signifies in the form of one-penetrated-by-the-other. The pain, this underside of skin, is a nudity

more naked than all destitution. It is sacrificed rather than sacrificing itself, for it is precisely bound to the adversity or suffering of pain. This existence, with suffering imposed on it, is without conditions.[37]

The self "is a self despite itself, in incarnation, where it is the very possibility of offering, suffering and trauma."[38]

In *Otherwise than Being*, Levinas is also very attentive to what he considers to be the problem of "the third party" – how our being dominated by the absolute demands of the Other takes place against the background of the coexistence of multiple Others with their heterogeneous claims upon us and the inadequacy of the psychological and material resources at any individual human being's disposal for appropriately ethically dealing with all of the Others. Levinas acknowledges that "The third party [that is, persons other than any particular one you are engaged with or related to] isn't there by accident. In a sense, all the others are present in the face of the other."[39] The awareness of the presence of the third party for Levinas constitutes the Greek phase of Western moral development,[40] which renders conceptualization, generalization, theorizing and comparative assessment and judgment necessary in all arenas of human deliberation, including the ethical. The "third party" also places moral dilemmas (how to preserve the oneness of the one in the face of the plurality of many ones) at the very heart of the moral enterprise. Morgan rightly says that "these [dilemmas] are not challenges to his [Levinas'] ethical insight but rather part of the process of coping with it and living with our realization of it."[41] "Ultimately, then," according to Morgan's reading, "Levinas hopes for a kind of utopia, the ground for which is a permanent, deep feature of all human existence."[42]

As against Morgan, who in interpreting Levinas speaks of "passivity as a transcendental condition" for ethics,[43] one could argue that passivity merely pushes the question of how to make sense of Levinas one stage back without firmly resolving it. Subordination of one's interests and concerns to those of the Other could just as easily and validly be nurtured by metaphors of distance – as they are by metaphors evocative of overwhelming proximity. If the Other is irredeemably separate and distinct from me, then I also cannot legitimately transform him into a means toward my ends. The affirmation (and even the priority of the Other, barring cogent countervailing considerations on my part) can just as convincingly be predicated upon metaphors of distance as upon metaphors of total closeness and identification. In fact, Morgan concedes as much when he discusses how Levinas conceives of *Ma'asei Mitzvah* (conformity to Divine Commandments) in general and ritual acts in particular in Judaism: "Such ritual acts, which help train Jews to acknowledge otherness and thus to recognize one's responsibility to others, do so by occurring in nature by setting up a 'distance' between the Jew and God as other. Ritual acts, that is, are part of the mythology of theology; they deal with Jews and God, but what they accomplish is a first step in the process of education that leads to the acknowledgment of the face of the other person."[44]

Levinas' skepticism juxtaposed to that of Quine and Reb Chaim of Brisk

The self conceived as being saturated in the Christian imagery that marks Levinas' argument is in tension with the case for the inescapability of skepticism that Levinas also makes in *Otherwise than Being* and that is supposed to clear the ground for receptivity to Levinas' extreme ethical position. In Chapter Two of this work, Levinas argues how a principle of underdetermination governs the relationship between language and reality. Everything that we want to state about the world can be formulated in a noun-accented vocabulary that emphasizes substantialization – and also in a verb-slanted vocabulary that underscores movement and process:

> Language qua said can then be conceived as a system of nouns identifying entities, and then as a system of signs doubling up the beings, designating substances, events and relations by substantives or other parts of speech derived from substantives, designating entities – in sum, *designating*. But also, and with as much right, language can be conceived as the verb in a predicative proposition in which the substances break down into modes of being, modes of temporalization. Here language does not double up the being of entities, but exposes the silent resonance of the essence.[45]

According to Levinas, there is nothing intrinsic to the events or phenomena in the world that we seek to describe that would serve to validate a noun-centered vocabulary (which is in the passive voice) in contrast to a verb-centered one (which is in the active voice). The two vocabularies appear to be inter-translatable on a gross level, but not on a minute one. The displacements and ellipses of the one become the stuff of direct statement by the other. The world exerts no secure constraint upon the task of choosing between these two vocabularies. The systematic ambiguity of language which Levinas theorizes is not further rationally resolvable, and is symptomatic of the underdetermination of theory by fact or language by reality which is constitutive of philosophical skepticism.

There are two instructive analogues to Levinas' skeptical analysis in the passage cited above – one growing out of the tradition of analytical philosophy and represented by the work of Quine and the other growing out of the tradition of Talmudic and Rabbinic interpretation and found in the work of Reb Chaim Soloveitchik of Brisk (1853–1918). In arguing in defense of the thesis of language's indeterminate relationship to reality, Quine famously adduces the hypothetical example of the field linguist who discovers that when a rabbit crosses the native's path, he utters the word "gavagai." Instead of the linguist being able to straightforwardly record that in the native's language the word "gavagai" stands for "rabbit," the native's spontaneous locution gives rise to an irresolvable philosophical quandary:

"Rabbit" is a term of divided reference. As such it cannot be mastered without mastering its principle of individuation: where one rabbit leaves off and another begins. And this cannot be mastered by pure ostension, however persistent. Such is the quandary over "gavagai": where one gavagai leaves off and another begins. The only difference between rabbits, undetached rabbit parts, and rabbit stages is in their individuation. If you take the total scattered portion of the spatiotemporal world that is made up of rabbits, and that which is made up of undetached rabbit parts, and that which is made up of rabbit stages, you come out with the same scattered portion of the world each of the three times. The only difference is how you slice it. And how to slice it is what ostension or simple conditioning, however persistently repeated, cannot teach.[46]

"How to slice it" is precisely what is at stake in the philosophical points that Quine and Levinas are making. There is nothing intrinsic to the object running in front of the native and the field linguist that can resolve the question of whether "gavagai" refers to a whole rabbit, undetached rabbit parts or rabbit stages. Correspondingly, there is nothing implicit to an object or state of affairs in the world that mandates the use of a noun-centered, passive-voice verbal construction or a verb-centered, active-voice verbal construction. Even though (as Quine says about rabbits) it looks like we will be coming up with "the same scattered portion of the world" no matter how we "slice" the sentence (whether in the active voice or in the passive voice), the immediate reference of these two verbal constructions will nevertheless be different. Many of the objects and situations in the world that look from a purely formal, abstract perspective like they yield undivided reference, when language "hooks up" to them end up covertly pointing in the direction of divided reference. They can be "linguistically-captured" in referentially divergent ways without the objects or situations by themselves being able to offer any guidance concerning what the appropriate referential delimitation is/should be. From this perspective, "gavagai" becomes emblematic of the multiple objects in the world that have an implicitly divided reference. They can be referred to in the active voice or in the passive voice – and there is nothing about the objects per se that clues us in as to the appropriateness of the voice.

In the late 1940s, Levinas came under the tutelage of (and formed a strong intellectual and emotional bond with) a remarkable Rabbinic scholar by the name of Mordechai Shoshani.[47] Levinas says that "Shoshasni knew by heart the entire oral tradition to which the Scriptures gave rise. He knew by heart the Talmud and all its commentaries, and the commentaries on the commentaries."[48] In addition, Levinas says that "Alongside this purely exterior knowledge, by memory, M. Shoshani was gifted with an extraordinary dialectical power: the quantity of notions thought together and combined left an impression of savageness, in their unpredictable inventions … Shoshani knew how … to make an always restless dialectic rebound sovereignly."[49] Given

Shoshani's extraordinary combination of textual intimacy with the whole Rabbinic canon and dialectical imagination and inventiveness, it would not be surprising if Levinas received from him some exposure to the methodology and ideas of Reb Chaim Soloveitchik of Brisk, who was the leading luminary of the yeshiva world of the late 19th and early 20th centuries, and whose dominant influence on yeshiva study of the Talmud continues down until the present day. In an age when German historicism and its aftermath had relativized the study of everything from national history to religious texts, Reb Chaim approached the Talmudic text with a set of highly abstract, transhistorical categories (themselves deriving, at least in the first instance, from the Talmud) that enabled Talmudic authors, medieval commentators and Reb Chaim himself to converse upon what looked like common ground.

A major dichotomy that Reb Chaim worked with was between *Cheftzah* ("thing") and *Gavrah* ("person"). In his Talmudic analyses, Reb Chaim often pointed out how incoherencies and discrepancies in Rabbinic and Talmudic formulations could be ironed out by working through the question of whether the particular Rabbinic or Talmudic statements at issue were formulated from a *Cheftzah* or a *Gavrah* perspective. The most revealing paraphrase of this distinction, I believe, is the one cited from Levinas earlier. A statement construed in a *Cheftzah* manner is one in which the passive voice predominates. A statement interpreted in a *Gavrah* manner is one in which the active voice predominates. Multiple perplexities in Jewish law could be clarified utilizing this approach. Reb Chaim strove to show how the pervasiveness of divided reference not only has micro-impact on the different ways to translate the larger word or statement – with the larger word or statement (the macro level) remaining superficially intact – but also how, on occasion, the micro variations in reference yield conflicting configurations on the macro (original word or statement) level itself, which can help account for conflicting readings of the original Talmudic text by classical commentators.

Reb Chaim illustrates, for example, how the scope of the legal requirement that one forfeit one's own life rather than commit murder gets variously circumscribed depending upon whether the Talmud's rationale for this requirement gets interpreted from a *Cheftzah* or a *Gavrah* perspective.[50] To justify this requirement, the Talmud does not invoke a Biblical text, but simply resorts to reasoned argument in the form of a rhetorical question: "Who says that your blood is redder, maybe the blood of the other person is redder still?"[51] Reb Chaim addresses the borderline case where one is being thrown as a passive object to extinguish the life of another human being, in circumstances where his life would be threatened if he did not conform to the request of his coercer. Does allowing oneself to be used in this object-like way come within the purview of the Rabbinic injunction, or does only the active killing of another person fall within the prohibition?

The answer according to Reb Chaim (according to which the conflicting views of Talmudic commentators can be conceptually reconstructed) depends upon whether the Talmudic rationale is paraphrased in an active or a passive way.⁵² On the surface, one would want to argue that interpreting the Rabbinic injunction against killing despite the fact that one's own life was in jeopardy in a passive way – "that someone else should not be killed by me" – encompasses the case where I am being thrown upon someone else for purposes of killing him. However, if one construes the Rabbinic formulation in the active voice – "that I should not kill someone else in order to save myself" – then, in this case, where I am being used as a thrown object, it is not I who is doing the killing, and I should therefore be exempt. I would be allowed to prefer my own life in relation to that of the other person upon whom I am being thrown by a third party. This is the position of the Tosafists⁵³ cited by Reb Chaim.⁵⁴

The fungibility and elasticity of the *Cheftzah-Gavrah* distinction, however, are such that the application of these categories to the situation at hand can be reversed. One could argue that if one translates the Talmud's reasoning actively (in a *Gavrah* mode) – that one should not kill another human being – then any way that a person could be implicated in the murder of another human being (even if the person behaved only passively by allowing himself to be used as a thrown object) is sufficient to render his behavior subsumable under the Talmudic rationale – and is therefore prohibited. However, if one translates the Talmudic rhetorical question passively (in a *Cheftzah* mode), then it would read that another person should not be killed through my actions. In this case, where I am being used as a destructive object, one could argue that since I am not directly *doing* anything, my position is morally equivalent to that of the person whose life is being snuffed out by my being thrown upon him. We are both being passive. Why should he have a claim against my life that is not being matched by my equal claim against his life in a case where both of our lives are mutually at stake? Since we are both not directly doing anything, why should his claim against me be stronger than my claim against him? Translating the Talmudic reasoning passively (that another person should not be killed through my actions) allows me to get off the hook when a third party seeks to compel me (on pain of death) to serve as a passive instrument in the destruction of someone else because this other person is not being killed through *my actions*. Paraphrased in a *Cheftzah* mode, we could argue that it is only when I would directly snuff out the life of the next person that the prohibition against assigning priority to my own life in the case of murder becomes applicable. However, with a *Gavrah* translation of the Talmudic rationale, as long as there is an "I" in there somewhere (in this case, consenting, in however attenuated a sense, to be used in a passive manner to destroy the life of the next person), the Talmudic prohibition against sparing one's life at the expense of one's victim remains in force. This is the position of Maimonides cited by Reb Chaim.⁵⁵

The underdetermination of words by things ("gavagai" and rabbits) and the underdetermination of meaning by text (that someone being thrown upon someone else [being used as a passive object] to snuff out his life can/cannot be considered a murderer) are not only a matter of alternative conceptual frameworks being theoretically possible to make sense of what on the surface looks like a common set of things or texts. The discussion of Quine and Reb Chaim highlights more pointedly that even within what appears to be a common verbal locution (such as the word and sentence cited above) there lurks divided reference that reintroduces and reinforces the factor of underdetermination.

The upshot of my reading of Reb Chaim is that all legal possibilities in the case discussed are conceptually reconstructible under the conflicting categorial auspices of *both Gavrah* and *Cheftzah*. The radical indeterminacy of the textual basis of the law could not be more dramatically exemplified.

The centrality of the *Cheftzah-Gavrah* distinction in Reb Chaim's analysis of Rabbinic texts highlights for us not only the extent to which theory is underdetermined by fact and text, but also the extent to which theory is also underdetermined by the regressive theoretical frameworks in which one wants to embed the theory that helps us make sense of the "facts" or "texts" in the first place. This notion concerning the uncontainability of underdetermination also forms part of the import of Quine's analysis of "gavagai." The underdetermination of theory by the fleeting passage of the "rabbit" in front of the field linguist is not redeemed by further regressions of the theory onto broader, more expansive and more abstract theoretical frameworks.

What does the fate of skepticism in philosophy license Levinas to argue about ethics?

Levinas' blunder is to build upon the principle of the underdetermination of words by things, which is symptomatic of skepticism, a positive ethical theory of the sort set forth in *Otherwise than Being* concerning passivity, incarnation and substitution – rather than being content to stay within the limits of negative theory, arguing that the possibility of such ethical formations cannot be blocked (not that one has clinched the case in support of their existence). Underdetermination of words by things, which is a prime manifestation of skepticism, merely clears philosophical space for the notion that our beholdenness to the Other comes before all philosophical argument. Negative theorizing needs to be content with acknowledging the possibility of the primacy of the ethical claims of the Other over us. As a result of the pervasiveness of skepticism, we are simply bereft of arguments to block the view that the original datum of the human condition that releases and indirectly legitimates (if they are conducted in light of this priority) all other types of human activity – including the activity of philosophizing – is the priority of the Other. On strictly logical grounds, we have no positive case to make in support of this view. Levinas also violates a principle of parsimony by drawing a positive inference (as opposed to a merely negative one) from our overall skeptical argumentative condition.

The Rabbis' practice of a negative hermeneutics that creates space for the realization of some of the most widely-touted but mysterious elements of the

Jewish theological vision is in dramatic contrast to the approach adopted by Levinas in *Otherwise than Being*. A negative hermeneutics is evidenced in the following reading of a Biblical verse by Rabbi Meir:

> It has been taught: R. Meir said: Whence do we know resurrection of the dead from the Torah? From the verse, "Then shall Moses and the children of Israel sing this song unto the Lord" (Exodus 15:1): not "sang" but "shall sing" is written: thus resurrection of the dead is taught in the Torah.[56]

One philosophical route for making sense of this exegetical derivation is to say that the existence of the future is only a skeptically-generated extrapolation out of the past because, as Hume said, "induction is not deduction." The future is not a certainty. Its warrant is logically and in an empirically full-blooded sense uncertain – grounded only in probability. The status of the future as a skeptical posit is most coherently sustainable from a generalized-agnostic perspective, which both requires and presupposes a continually unfolding future to serve as a balancing and corrective mechanism to our judgments in the present. An indefinitely open and unfolding future leaves the door open to all possibilities – including the resurrection of the dead. The "then sang" – the epistemologically problematic future tense – of Moses' Song affords us the trace or space which enables us to speculate concerning resurrection of the dead as a future contingency beyond our current imaginings.

Another central manifestation of skepticism which is also "hijacked" by Levinas for positive uses when it can merely serve negative, clearing functions is the discrepancy that emerges between the "saying" and the "said" of the tenets of skepticism themselves. Levinas seeks to ground the primacy he attaches to passivity, incarnation, substitution and being hostage to the Other – what he labels as the content of what is "Otherwise than Being" – in the career and fate of skepticism in philosophy:

> Skepticism, at the dawn of philosophy, set forth and betrayed the diachrony of this very conveying and betraying. To conceive the *otherwise than being* requires, perhaps, as much audacity as skepticism shows, when it does not hesitate to affirm the impossibility of statement while venturing to *realize* this impossibility by the very statement of this impossibility. If, after the innumerable "irrefutable" refutations which logical thought sets against it, skepticism has the gall to return (and it always returns as philosophy's illegitimate child), it is because in the contradiction which logic sees in it the "at the same time" of the contradictories is missing, because a secret diachrony commands this ambiguous or enigmatic way of speaking, and because in general signification signifies beyond synchrony, beyond essence.[57]

Once skepticism is thematized – formulated discursively – it undercuts itself as statement. To be properly skeptical means that one has to be skeptical of skepticism as well – which undermines the coherence of skepticism as a "said" (fully verbally articulated) statement. What is sustainable in skepticism is the "saying" – the verbal inspiration to articulate it, rather than its fully realized verbal content. Skepticism is only sustainable as a diachronic moment – a "pure event" – rather than as a synchronized content. The following quotation from Jeanne Delhomme (which Levinas cites in his essay upon her work) captures the spirit of the distinction between diachrony and synchrony perfectly. Delhomme theorizes philosophy as a whole – and not just skepticism – as:

> an absolute event that does not take its place or rank in any succession; a rupture, not a filiation, an instant with neither past nor future. It imposes and posits itself without references or antecedent. It enters into no process, and does not constitute the moment – not even the privileged moment – of a progressive, growing evolution, because it is an original concept and a new language. History without materiality, succession without trace, such is the history of the philosophies. Appearance without representation; advent without postulation of reality; present without past – such is a philosophy.[58]

Levinas argues that the ineradicableness of skepticism from philosophy – its "eternal recurrence" after being continually logically discredited – provides us with an important trace of a "secret diachrony" that "commands this ambiguous or enigmatic way of speaking." In other words, the diachronous nature of discourse highlighted in skeptical utterances clues us in to an otherwise impenetrable content that lies "beyond essence" – namely, the passivity, incarnation and substitution that fundamentally reposition us in relation to other human beings and to the world at large. Diachrony (which is the inevitable fate of skeptical statement) in Levinas' thought constitutes a kind of "emanation" of a colossal transvaluation of values that resides "otherwise than being" that (when noticed and taken seriously) harbors the potential of transforming our relationship to ourselves, to others and to our whole mode of being in the world. Immanent to the structure of the anomalous and paradoxical relationship subsisting between words and things encapsulated in skeptical statement are a set of clues concerning what lies "otherwise than being" that is both paradigmatic of, and in some inexplicable way can even be considered a generative force behind, the very disruptions between words and things reflected in skeptical statement itself. Following in the footsteps of his predecessors Husserl and Heidegger, Levinas seeks to formulate a transcendental phenomenology that takes us beyond skepticism by disclosing the secret (and counter-skeptical) conceptual grid that renders skepticism as a pure "saying" without a "said" possible. Levinas as transcendental phenomenologist discloses the secret and mysterious source of "disruption," which he identifies with a set of impossible ethical demands that permanently disrupts the synchronous ways in which we generally organize and structure our lives and our relationships with others.

The trap that Levinas falls into here is exactly the same as the one he falls into when he notices how seemingly unequivocal reference most often serves as a mask or a cover for divided reference – and the positive theoretical implications concerning the existence of a stratum of existence that is "otherwise than being" that he draws from that. Just as the systematic ambiguity that hovers over our sentences in terms of their susceptibility to both noun-centered and verb-centered (passive-voice and active-voice) translations gives rise to contradictory possibilities, so, too, does the dissociation of the "saying" from the "said" of skepticism give rise to mutually antagonistic possibilities. In both cases, we can either move in the direction of positive theory and invoke a claim to certainty (in Levinas' case having to do with the unlimited claims of the Other upon us) to fill in the space created by an irresolvable skepticism, or proceed in the direction of negative theory, which uses skepticism to set limits to the aspirations of human thought and then tries to coherently resituate the world in relation to those limits. If the limits of thought are projected onto the world, then one is guilty of surreptitiously subverting rational limits and converting them into illicit forms of knowledge. In order to remain faithful to the mandate of skepticism, we need to turn in the direction of a generalized agnosticism and be skeptical of our own skepticism. Skepticism thereby clears a path for the acknowledgement of genuinely open possibilities – e.g., a world populated by real Others with strong claims upon us and where God is experienced as a real presence. In no way can skepticism be transformed into a platform for achieving certainty with regard to either of these questions.

Just as in the case of ostensibly unequivocal reference masking divided reference, so, too, with regard to the unstatability of skepticism, Levinas is too extravagant and violates a methodological principle of parsimony by opting for his ethical postulates as the content that lies "otherwise than being," filling in the gaps and insufficiencies discernible in being.

The tension between "diagnosis" and "resolution" in Levinas

Levinas' inconsistency with regard to skepticism – his embracing it in order to create space for his theorizing of the primacy of the ethical and his abandoning it in the particular way that he theorizes the content of the ethical – is heightened by the Christian imagery that suffuses his ethical theorizing. In theorizing the ethical relationship as being bound to the Other to the extent of regarding ourselves as substituting for him, Levinas invokes a distinctly Christian imagery that is suggestive of arriving at a layer of human relationship that is so primordial and fundamental that in effect some kind of circumvention of skepticism is taking place. As we have seen, in theorizing our pre-discursive relationship to the Other, Levinas invokes such terms as "passivity," "incarnation" and "substitution" that suggest that we have hit upon a level of analysis that is so bedrock that it neutralizes the effects of the skepticism that created the space for its recognition and acknowledgment in the first place.

Theologically speaking, there is also a tension between the two halves of Levinas' analysis. The diagnosis is articulated in a Jewish vein – and the resolution to the problematic uncovered by the diagnosis is formulated in a Christian theological idiom. Levinas reads the human condition as haunted by skepticism – with the connection between language and reality remaining enduringly, systematically insecure. Skepticism both feeds into – and derives part of its metaphysical sustenance from – a doctrine of radical human freedom, which is the major metaphysical concomitant or offshoot of the negative theology constitutive of Judaism. If the ontological distance separating us from God is unbridgeable (so that our theological vocabularies remain irredeemably metaphorical), then from a theological perspective we remain continually free to fashion the categories (including the religious ones) and the overall vocabulary that we use to orient ourselves to the world, and to define and justify the moves that we make within it. Skepticism in a sense is an epistemological encoding of the limitlessness of our freedom enshrined in negative theology.

Levinas' ethical response to the radical extent of human freedom consists in an impairment of it through the invocation of Christian theological imagery. Passivity, incarnation of the Other and substitution for the Other conjure up the picture of a renunciation and a sacrifice so complete that one can only make sense of it on the basis of a gnosis that Levinas does not render explicit. "Choosing life," in the Hebrew Scriptural sense,[59] means learning to live in a theoretical and moral climate of unlimited freedom. Ethics for Levinas can only be grounded in a renunciation of life that is so complete that the freedom to prefer the self over the Other has been squelched by a "pre-ontological" positioning of human beings, where passivity, incarnation and substitution define our relationship to other human beings.

In a Nietzschean idiom, we can say that Levinas' ressentiment is philosophically expressed in his identification of the optimal moral stance of human beings with abject powerlessness, passivity and self-sacrifice that carve out ethical space for the claims of the Other by the total abnegation and surrender of freedom and power by the self.

In addition, very paradoxically, but still within the bounds of coherence, Levinas' ethical vocabulary ends up reinforcing skepticism rather than neutralizing it. "Passivity," "incarnation" and "substitution" all have the effect of showing how to render properly ethical judgments from the perspective of one person if that person is thoroughly passive and incarnates within himself his substitution for the myriad Others who go to constitute the universe. This sort of substitution is compatible with skepticism in the sense that the only person who needs to be real on this account of ethics is the person engaging in the substitution. His behavior remains the same whether other minds are real or not.

One set of mitigating circumstances can be taken into account at least by way of rhetorically making sense of Levinas' ethical vocabulary. Levinas was living, after all, in the midst of a Christian civilization – and the rhetoric that would most likely be persuasive with his audience (would carry the most resonance) was a Christian rhetoric emphasizing passivity and sacrifice. Also – for someone like himself who lost some of his closest family members during the Holocaust (*Otherwise than Being* contains a dedication in Hebrew to their memory, as well as a dedication in English to all the other victims of the Nazis), the point of his ethical terminology is to subtly and tacitly remind his Christian readers that during the Nazi era Christians were unfaithful to their own dogmas and theological understandings. The import of some of the key terms of the Christian theological vocabulary according to Levinas is to emphasize the need for total self-abnegation for the sake of displaying and sustaining care, compassion and solicitude for the Other. The burden of Levinas' implicit indictment is that Christians failed by their own standards of what it means to be a Christian: They were untrue to themselves.

Notes

1 Leszek Kolakowski, *Husserl and the Search for Certitude* (New Haven: Yale University Press, 1975; republished South Bend: St. Augustine's Press, 2001).
2 Kolakowski, *Husserl*, pp. 3; 5.
3 Ibid., p. 12.
4 Ibid., p. 19.
5 Ibid., p. 23.
6 Ibid.
7 Ibid., p. 25.
8 Ibid., p. 26.
9 Ibid., p. 29.
10 Ibid., p. 25.
11 Popper, *Conjectures and Refutations*, pp. 3–65.
12 Kolakowski, *Husserl*, p. 28.
13 The essay by this name that appears in the book that has the same title.
14 Ludwig Wittgenstein, *On Certainty*, Aphorism Number 189, p. 26e.
15 Reprinted in Levinas, *Proper Names*, pp. 47–54.
16 Ibid, p. 48.
17 Ibid., p. 47.
18 Ibid., p. 49.
19 Ibid., p. 54; emphases added.
20 Ibid., p. 53.
21 Kolakowski, *Husserl*, p. 3.
22 Alphonso Lingis, Introduction to *Otherwise than Being or Beyond Essence*, p. xi.
23 Ibid. The theme of responsibility is most fully discussed in Edmund Husserl, *The Crisis of European Sciences and Transcendental Phenomenology: An Introduction to Phenomenological Philosophy*. Trans. David Carr. (Evanston: Northwestern University Press, 1970).
24 See Albert O. Hirschman, *The Passions and the Interests: Political Arguments for Capitalism before its Triumph* (Princeton: Princeton University Press, 1977) and my book, *Skepticism, Belief, and the Modern*, Chapter 4.
25 Lingis, Introduction, p. xii.
26 Ibid.
27 Ibid., p. xxiii.

28 Ibid., p. xxvii.
29 Ibid., p. xxix.
30 Ibid.
31 Ibid., p. xxxii.
32 Levinas, *Otherwise than Being*, p. 182.
33 Ibid., p. 10.
34 Ibid., p. 47.
35 Ibid., p. 49.
36 Ibid.
37 Ibid., pp. 49–50.
38 Ibid., p. 50.
39 Jill Robbins, ed., *Is it Righteous to Be? Interviews with Emmanuel Levinas* (Stanford: Stanford University Press, 2001), p. 168; quoted in Michael L. Morgan, *Discovering Levinas* (Cambridge: Cambridge University Press, 2007), p. 24, FN 73.
40 Morgan, *Discovering Levinas*, p. 340.
41 Ibid., p. 418.
42 Ibid., p. 25.
43 Ibid., pp. 158–159.
44 Ibid., p. 378.
45 Levinas, *Otherwise than Being*, p. 40; italics in original.
46 W. V. Quine, *Ontological Relativity and Other Essays* (New York: Columbia University Press, 1969), pp. 31–32. See the parallel discussion in W. V. Quine, *Word and Object* (Cambridge: MIT Press, 1960), Section 12, especially pp. 51–52.
47 See the discussion of Levinas' relationship with Shoshani in Robert Gibbs, *Correlations in Rosenzweig and Levinas* (Princeton: Princeton University Press, 1992), p. 7 and Robbins, *Is It Righteous to Be?*, pp. 73–77.
48 Robbins, *Is it Righteous to Be?*, p. 74.
49 Ibid., p. 75.
50 Chaim Soloveitchik, *Chiddushei Rabbeinu Chaim Halevi* (New York, n.d.), p. 1.
51 Babylonian Talmud, *Sanhedrin* 74a; my translation.
52 Even though Reb Chaim utilizes the *Cheftzah-Gavrah* dichotomy in many of the exegetical discourses contained in his book cited above, he does not explicitly apply it to the topic that I am dealing with in the text. However, I try to show how his analyses of the issues dealt with in the text fit into the *Cheftzah-Gavrah* framework, and achieve an enhanced analytical resonance as a result.
53 The *Tosafot* (whose opening words are "But did not Esther transgress publicly") is found on p. 74b of the tractate *Sanhedrin* in standard editions of the Babylonian Talmud. The Tosafists were medieval rabbis from France and Germany who are among those known in Talmudic scholarship as *Rishonim* (there were *Rishonim* in Spain also) and who created critical and explanatory glosses (questions, notes, interpretations, rulings and sources) on the Talmud. They were called *Tosafot* ("additions") because they were additions to the commentary of Rashi. The Tosafists lived from the 12th century to the middle of the 15th century, and the *Tosafot* are a compilation of the questions, answers and opinions of those rabbis.
54 For a good outline and schematization of Reb Chaim's arguments concerning the division of opinion between the *Tosafot* and Maimonides, see Yonoson Hughes, *Understanding Reb Chaim: Reb Chaim HaLevi Soloveitchik zt"l of Brisk* (Israel, 2010), pp. 32–60.
55 *Chidushei Rabbeinu Chaim Halevi*, p. 1; Maimonides, *Hilchot Yesodei HaTorah*, Chapter 5, Paragraphs 1 and 2.
56 Babylonian Talmud, *Sanhedrin* 91b; cited in Rashi's commentary on Exodus 15:1.

57 Levinas, *Otherwise than Being*, p.7; italics in original.
58 Jeanne Delhomme, *La pensee et le reel. Critique de l'ontologie* (Paris: Presses Universitaires de France, Collection "Epimethee," 1967), pp. 54–55; cited in Emmanuel Levinas, *Proper Names*. p. 51.
59 Deuteronomy 30:19.

10 The tension between Levinas' ethics and his political theory

The tension

In the light of the foregoing analysis, a sharp tension emerges between Levinas' ethics and his political theory. His political theory is liberal – and his ethics is radically Christian. The liberal political theory, with its postulation of a common metaphysical profile encompassing all human beings – with reason being subordinate to the passions and reason functionining as a species of rationalized passion to calculate means to ends – assumes that every Other in the world is a replication of me, with my constant preoccupation with the pursuit of self-interest. In his ethics, Levinas affirms the priority of the Other and his persecuting glance and stance over the self, which only gets formed in relation to an internalization of that positioning of its identity.

Levinas' ethics is grounded in phenomenological descriptions of passivity, incarnation and substitution. His political theory, by contrast, affirms the values of liberal individualism and is heavily mistrustful of an organic communitarianism that would seem to follow as a political translation of the ethical value of substitution.[1] Levinas has not formulated an anthropology and ethical theory to match his political theory. His skeptical metaphysics and epistemology comport with it, but his projection of what it means to be a human being and his ethical postulates do not correspond to it. As with Jean-Jacques Rousseau, there is a totalitarian potential lurking in Levinas' anthropology. If there is one stage in the evolution of the human – or one perspective from which to theorize our humanness – in which total equality, non-competitiveness and even substitution prevail, this would harbor an implicit legitimation for a charismatic political leader concerned with promoting virtue and justice more than political success to unilaterally impose a political ordering to recapture these lost possibilities. In Rousseau's terrible and terrifying phrase, there is no reason why under the tutelage of the properly motivated political innovator we should not be "forced to be free"[2] – or to be properly ethical.

For Levinas (just like for Rousseau), there is something to be known and presumably implemented that transcends the self-centeredness, partiality and fragmentariness of daily life and ordinary politics. The knowledge concerning

The tension between Levinas' ethics and his political theory 189

human social evolution beginning with the utterly uncompetitive earliest phases of the state of nature, or a proper phenomenological unpacking of what the notion of "saying" in contrast to the "said" discloses, arm followers of Rousseau and Levinas with a blueprint and a set of reassurances for transforming human personal and social organization.

What Levinas, and more ambivalently Rousseau, whose overriding commitment is to republican communitarianism rather than to liberalism, are not sufficiently taking into account is that in order to emerge with a maximally coherent liberal political theory the stages that lead to the affirmation of a liberal political state (or – to switch metaphors – the conceptual materials out of which it is constructed) have to match the fully developed liberal state and not be out of sync with it. The beauty and persuasive force of Hobbes' state of nature resides in the fact that it represents an unbridled microcosm of all that is artificially and instrumentally controlled in the full-blown civil state itself. There is no marked discontinuity in Hobbes' account between the motivational apparatus and the limits to knowledge affecting the people who populate the state of nature and the motivational mechanisms and the limits to knowledge characteristic of members of the social-contract society. The major difference between the two phases of individual and social development for Hobbes and for social contract theory generally is the creative transmutation of the limits to goodness registered in the motivational apparatus governing people in the state of nature and the limits to knowledge disclosed in the epistemology and metaphysics accompanying social contract theorizing from its inception in the state of nature to the fully-developed political society – the creative transmutation of these joint limits to goodness and to knowledge into a set of constitutive factors shaping a new political order called "liberalism." The limits to knowledge and to goodness can be mobilized against the limits. If we all share comparable limits, then we have an incentive to cooperate in order to maximize our goals within those limits. Manifesting limited goodness suggests that political order has to be fashioned out of appeals to self-interest. Limited knowledge nurtures the vision of a state committed to procedural rules and safeguards that on a transient and ongoing basis generates different configurations of political substance. The theorist in the end is on a par with the human beings he theorizes about and is the first citizen of the ideal republic to submit to the imperative of equality.[3]

Being gripped by the human Other as the pre-theoretical moment that renders theorizing possible

An additional approach to Levinas' unusual and arresting ethical vocabulary might be to dwell on the tight, if not indissoluble, conceptual bond between God and the Other in his work. Levinas is emphatically committed to negative theology. He says that, "For the relation between the being here below and the transcendent being that results in no community of concept or totality – a relation without relation – we reserve the term religion."[4] Negative theology in many respects is the program of the religious rationalist who seeks to invoke God as the ultimate rational and causal factor responsible for all that is going on in the universe by way of bringing the quest for reasons and causes to a satisfactory halt. In order to accomplish this goal, God has to be postulated as being so totally other that his very difference from things human unravels the search for ever more adequate or comprehensive reasons or causes. Levinas theorizes our relationship to the human Other along the same lines that negative theology conceives of our relationship to the Divine Other. Levinas begins with the skeptical premise that the persons and things of this world click into conceptual focus in relation to the vocabularies that we invoke (the terms that we impose) for organizing and categorizing them. There is always a surplus of words over persons and things, so that in the end we cannot discount the factors of conceptual grouping and naming as contributing at least to some extent to the shaping of the world that we inhabit. The human Other who remains confined to the verbally circumscribed ambit of being is thus an "Other" whose Otherness is in jeopardy because of the excess of words over both persons and objects in the realm of being. Fortunately (from Levinas' perspective) this dilemma is "trumped" by another dilemma whose resolution illuminates the first dilemma.

The second dilemma revolves around the idealist understanding of the relationship between words and things. This understanding tacitly feeds off the contrast with entities that are there (that are in some sense given) in order for idealism to harbor the prospect of offering a coherent explanation of the field of knowledge. However, if the idealist understanding of the relationship between words and what they purport to describe were to be carried all the way back to the most elementary configurations of relationship between self and self, self and Other, and self and world, something resembling an infinite regress would occur, which would defeat the philosophical point and intelligibility of idealism. The contrastive force of idealism would be lost – and idealism would lose its explanatory efficacy.

According to Levinas, it is only when one can locate the originary moment of theorizing in some gripping by the Other that precedes the congealments of consciousness and the coincidings and assimilations established between thought and "reality" that idealism can be sustained. To circumvent the logical dilemma attendant to idealist theorizing, Levinas chooses to theorize our being gripped by the human Other as the "pre-theoretical" theoretical moment that renders theorizing (in the sense practiced by idealists from Plato onward) possible. The terms that Levinas uses to refer to this formative moment – passivity, incarnation, substitution – constitute a significant shift in tense and ontological position from ordinary theorizing. Instead of actively organizing our world through the invocation of what look to us like rational factors (words transparently fitting the things they seek to designate and communicate about) and what under philosophical scrutiny are exposed as harboring elements of arbitrariness, in the originary moment that Levinas

The tension between Levinas' ethics and his political theory 191

theorizes we are commanded by the Other and reduced to a position of total subordination and even substitution. In regular theorizing, what looks like our reason is the logical operator. In the originary moment, by contrast, it is the ethical will ensconced in the Otherness of the Other that is the logical operator. By functioning as a foil to the imperium of rational mastery definitive of being, the commands of the Other – rather than our reason – become the crucial factor conferring strategic coherence upon the activity of theorizing, with its resultant underdetermination.

I do not believe that this defense of Levinas will survive critical scrutiny. The following are some key countervailing considerations:

If Levinas invokes a primordial stage of subordination and obligation to the Other at least partially in response to the need to fashion a conceptual foil for skepticism (since once the category of being clicks into place without this foil being clarified the coincidence between our vocabularies and the world they seek to describe follows suit – and because it is *our* vocabularies that serve as the medium through which this coincidence is being established, the underdetermination of words by things and, consequently, the specter of skepticism can never be fully ruled out), then Levinas is going too far in tracing this foil to the originary moment in the history of consciousness (or its phenomenological reconstruction in individual life) when the emerging self is totally riveted by and substitutes for the Other. The check on an overweening skepticism that undercuts its explanatory power could simply have been the movement of recoil that formulations of skepticism need to reflect in order to emerge as consistent, which can be denominated as the transformation of skepticism into a generalized agnosticism – where skepticism of itself gets interlaced into the official formulation of the doctrine of skepticism. This would obviate the need for delineating a key stage of self-formation as substitution for the Other.

To make an analogous point from a somewhat different direction, Levinas says:

> The latent birth of the subject occurs in an obligation where no commitment was made. It is a fraternity or complicity for nothing, but the more demanding that it constrains without finality and without end. The subject is born in the beginninglessness of an anarchy and in the endlessness of obligation, gloriously augmenting as though infinity came to pass in it. In the absolute assignation of the subject the Infinite is enigmatically heard: before and beyond.[5]

In this passage, Levinas seems to be conflating "substitution" with "infinity" – whereas in fact there appears to be a tension, and possibly even a contradiction, between these two notions as he conceives of them. Levinas says that "the *beyond* has meaning only negatively, by its non-sense."[6] Presumably, therefore, vertical infinity which conjures up a "beyond" is literally nonsensical – and is only inferrable as a possibility from the negative traces (from the things that are not "it") that one encounters in this world. One of the strongest negative reminders of a "beyond," of vertical infinity penetrating to the reaches of the unknown, impalpable and unfathomable, might therefore be horizontal infinity – the succession of human actors interacting with their respective worlds that succeed one another in the course of the unfolding of human time. Someone committed to infinity in the mitigated sense of horizontal transcendence needs to confront the possibility that "substitution" both as concept and as presuppositional postulate of the self might become undone (perceived as incoherent) in the course of time.

Substitution (one self substituting itself for another) is clearly not a widespread empirical reality. If it occurs at all, it is episodic and rare. How does Levinas arrive at the notion of "substitution" – and what status does he assign to it? In his phenomenological analysis and reconstruction of the self under the impetus of locating a foil for being which invests the subject with a potentially unlimited naming capacity that underwrites the skeptical underdetermination of words by things, Levinas comes up with his delineation of the self as substituted Otherness. This understanding emphasizes how I am gripped by and obligated and subordinated to the Other on a plane (in a dimension) that is otherwise than being – anterior to the emergence of "being" with its mechanisms of coincidence between subject and object.

The notion of substitution in Levinas thus constitutes the logically and phenomenologically driven normative stratum in his definition of the self. Its point in the context of Levinas' theorizing is to defuse the challenge posed by the ambiguity of the concept of infinity by accounting for how obligation *enduringly precedes* freedom. In this sense, his linking of substitution with infinity seems contradictory because infinity conjures up the prospect of reshuffling of conceptual boundaries so that both the problem (finding a conceptual foil for "underdetermination") and its solution (identifying "substitution" as subsisting "otherwise than being") might be eroded and superseded in the course of time.

However, if, as I have argued, "substitution" might figure in the normative conceptualization of the self, then theorizing "substitution" does not constitute an exception to the model of theorizing conducted under the auspices of being (where subject and object coincide), but serves rather as a further exemplification of it. Theorizing conducted under the auspices of being suggests that there is a surplus of words and concepts in the repertoire of the subject over the objects that he seeks to elucidate and explain. There is never an intrinsic fit between word and object, but the principles of being ensure that the subject's conceptual fecundity will subsume the objects of his attention in one (contradictory) way or another. Since the description cannot be fully supported by the facts (which are susceptible of other readings), it becomes willy-nilly a normative statement. Levinas' theorizing of the self as substituted Otherness thus does not constitute an exception to the mode of theorizing carried out under the auspices of being, but serves rather as a continuation and perpetuation of it. The infusion or identification of the normative element(s) encapsulated in description is a hallmark of the very skepticism that Levinas seeks to temporarily arrest and render more intelligible by his theorizing of the self as substituted Otherness – and does not constitute an exception to it. The normative elements interlaced in every description (including Levinas' depiction of the self) are symptomatic of the skepticism surrounding all descriptions – of "description's" inability to be an accurate, pristine reflection of objects beyond itself.

Infinity in the sense of horizontal transcendence therefore needs to be invoked to rescue Levinas' theorizing of the self, as it is needed to render coherent all of our other descriptions. If all of them harbor inescapably normative dimensions reflective of the insurmountability of skepticism, then the way to proceed is to make sure that the version of skepticism one is implicitly giving credence to by acknowledging normative strata of meaning in our descriptions is the most intelligible and coherent one can come up with. This suggests that our allegiance should be to a version of skepticism that incorporates skepticism of itself into its own formulation: A generalized agnosticism. A generalized agnosticism, in turn, requires an indefinitely unfolding future to revise and complete (on an ongoing, interim basis) our previous formulations and understandings. Infinity in the sense of horizontal transcendence appropriately complements Levinas' theorizing of the self, as it does all of our other descriptions. The remarkable thing about *Otherwise than Being* is that even though Levinas already has a niche in his argument for horizontal transcendence in the form of his declaration that "the *beyond* has meaning only negatively," he does not connect it as a possible solution to the problem that "being" is inescapably tainted by skepticism – and that skepticism in its baldest, most immediate formulation is incoherent.

The priority and primacy of human freedom

What reinforces a generalized-agnostic approach to the logical dilemma posed by skepticism is that from the moral perspective shared by Rabbinic thought and Western liberalism there is nothing that can precede human freedom. This is the fundamental datum that a Rabbinically-inspired ethics – and a Western liberal ethics – take centrally into account. The following mishnah in the Babylonian Talmudic tractate *Avodah Zarah* hauntingly captures the pivotal role of freedom as a Jewish moral value:

> The elders [Rabban Gamliel, Rabbi Elazar ben Azariah, Rabbi Yehoshua ben Chananiah, and Rabbi Akiva, who visited Rome in 95 C.E.] were asked, "If [your God] has no desire for idolatry, why does he not abolish it?" They replied, "If it was something unnecessary to the world that was worshipped, he would abolish it; but people worship the sun, moon, stars, and planets; should he destroy his universe on account of fools!" They said [to the elders], "If so, he should destroy what is unnecessary for the world and leave what is necessary for the world!" They replied, "[If he did

that], we should merely be strengthening the hands of the worshippers of these [the essential things which God spared], because they would say, 'Be sure that these are deities, for behold they have not been abolished.'"[7]

This mishnah very poignantly dramatizes for us from a Rabbinic perspective the radicalness of human freedom. If God were to destroy the unuseful idolatrous artifacts that people worshipped and preserve the useful, he would be diminishing human freedom because this would only confirm the idolaters' impressions that the objects that they worshipped were divine.[8] The world exists under an impenetrable veil (what Nietzsche, in another context, called "a necessary mist"[9]), so that the absence of givens in the world affords people the opportunity to make the wrong choices, the wrong calculations. This radical freedom is a crucial background postulate for relating to the monotheistic God. If the freedom were diminished or diluted in any way, we would be idolaters. If there were something intrinsic to an object that made it worthy of worship, the practice of worshipping it could not be a monotheistic religious practice. The Biblical-Rabbinic God is utterly transcendent. Our manner of worshipping Him has to be commensurate with our inability to project His content – which is to say that freedom becomes the premier mode of relating to God. Divine emptiness, as it were, in terms of fixed preordained content, has to be matched by human emptiness in terms of the absence of any set of metaphysical, natural or *moral* givens that fixate us on God. In the God-man relationship as conceived by Judaism, there have to be inexpugnible elements of freedom from top to bottom: From an acknowledgment and affirmation of God to the choice of categories in which to delineate our relationship to Him to the outlining of laws and rituals attendant to this particular relationship and the application of them to particular cases. Monotheism gives us the old, unknown inner and outer worlds to work with to create "places" for God, who is Himself (in a way that we cannot conceive or grasp) the "Place" of the world.[10]

Maimonides echoes his Rabbinic predecessors in emphasizing the paramountcy of freedom as a Jewish moral value. In the Laws of Repentance in his *Code*, he addresses the traditional theological conundrum concerning the need to reconcile Divine omniscience with human free will and comes out almost unboundedly in favor of human freedom:

> Perchance you will say, "Does not the Almighty know everything that will be before it happens"? He either knows that this person will be righteous or wicked, or He does not know. If He knows that he will be righteous, it is impossible that he should not be righteous; and if you say that He knows that he will be righteous and yet it is possible for him to be wicked, then He does not know the matter clearly. As to the solution of this problem, understand that "the measure thereof is longer than the earth and wider than the sea" (Job 11:9), and many important principles of the highest sublimity are connected with it. You, however, need only to

know and comprehend what I am about to say ... We lack the capacity to know how God knows all creatures and their activities. Yet we do know beyond doubt that a human being's activities are in his own hands and the Almighty neither draws him on, nor decrees that he should act thus or not act thus.[11]

In the Laws of Repentance, Maimonides also very significantly interprets the concept of repentance in a formal, procedural sense to represent a turning in either direction: From bad to good *or* from good to bad. In Chapter 3, Paragraph 3 of the Laws of Repentance, Maimonides deals with the case of someone who regrets the good deeds that he has performed within the context of "repentance" – as if to underscore the formal, procedural, non-essentialist character of the notion. "Repentance," like the substantive actions or transgressions that it is attached to, has to be a function of unlimited human freedom in order to be monotheistically intelligible.

The moral psychology that Thomas Hobbes bequeaths to modern liberalism envisions reason as being subordinate and instrumental to the passions.[12] Reason (or, more precisely, the notion of reason that Hobbes rejects) is identified by him with what is objective and universal – and the passions are diagnosed as referring to what is subjective and variable. The dominant passions actuating human beings, according to Hobbes, are the pursuit of pleasure and the avoidance of pain. The categories of "pleasure" and "pain" in Hobbes are largely tautologous and vacuous. They receive a content only retrospectively on the basis of human beings' actual, ongoing interaction with other human beings and with their environments. The understanding of reason that Hobbes validates is that of a calculating mechanism that enables human beings on a continuing basis to strategically adjust means to ends. Liberal man as envisioned by Hobbes is thus a creature exercising radical freedom both in his choice of the ends of life and in his delineation of the means for realizing them.[13]

Levinas is problematic because even though in many respects he wishes to align himself with Rabbinic thought and with liberalism, in his thought (in contrast to theirs) our indebtedness to and substitution for the Other precedes freedom. For Levinas, the moral stance as he conceives it comes before freedom. For the Rabbis and Hobbes, by contrast, freedom is the organizing background postulate for both moral judgment and action.

In his essay, "Freedom and Command,"[14] Levinas addresses the question of how it is possible to theorize ethics as being prior to human freedom – but in an unsatisfactory manner. In this essay, Levinas theorizes violence and counterposes to it the concept of freedom. He says that "the supreme violence is in that supreme gentleness [characteristic of true heteronomy]. To have a servile soul is to be incapable of being jarred, incapable of being ordered. The love for the master fills the soul to such an extent that the soul no longer takes its distances. Fear fills the soul to such an extent that one no longer sees it, but sees from its perspective."[15] Levinas' later theorizing of substitution is in tension with his earlier delineation of the nature of violence. "The soul no longer taking its distances" is an acute summary of Levinas' understanding of substitution, where passivity, incarnation and the urge to sacrifice obliterate all distances between the self and the Other. Yet, in his 1953 essay on freedom, the destruction of distances is the epitome of violence!

How is violence to be neutralized and contained? Through the establishment of freedom. How is freedom generated? "Freedom consists in instituting outside of oneself an order of reason, in entrusting the rational to a written text, in resorting to institutions. Freedom, in its fear of tyranny, leads to institutions, to a commitment of freedom in the very name of freedom, to a State."[16] Freedom limits and combats violence through its establishment of institutions whose *raison d'etre* is to manage relationships between individuals and between organizations – and not through any mechanisms of substitution, which in its passivity before the Other circumvents the need for institutions. "The supreme work of freedom," Levinas says, "consists in guaranteeing freedom."[17] Freedom for Levinas is thus a procedural concept – and achievement – and not a substantive one, after the manner of substitution.

Levinas continues to theorize violence by saying that it "is a way of acting on every being and every freedom by approaching it from an indirect angle. Violence is a way of taking hold of a being by surprise, of taking hold of it in its absence, in what is not properly speaking it."[18] From this perspective, substitution is again violence because it takes hold of the Other from "an indirect angle" – before the Other has had a chance to develop his individuality and to juxtapose or counterpose it to mine in the public space of institutions.

In order to be able to break out of the institutional networks constitutive of liberalism and establish a case for the primacy of ethics in the form of substitution for the Other, Levinas points to the problem of an infinite regress in the institutionalization of human freedom: "Is there not already between one will and another a relationship of command without tyranny, which is not yet an obedience to an impersonal law, but is the indispensable condition for the institution of such a law? Or again, does not the institution of a rational law as a condition for freedom already presuppose a possibility of direct understanding between individuals for the institution of that law?"[19] What law and institutions officially create – opportunities to register consent and to be formally obligated – have already to be presupposed in order for law and institutions to emerge and to be efficacious in the first place. Law and institutions work only in accordance with a set of principles that they embody (they have to be presupposed in order to account for how they work in the first place), which seems to render the problem of making sense of their institution outside of the context of an infinite regress well-nigh insuperable.

Levinas searches for a point of certainty outside of human fashioning that can abort the regress. He finds it (as by now we have come to expect) in "the direct relationship with a being ... that is not simply uncovered, but divested of its form, of its categories, a being becoming naked, an unqualified substance breaking through its form and presenting a face."[20] A face, according to Levinas' conceptualization, is an uncategorized "substance, a thing in itself."[21] However, Levinas' own previous argument in this very essay concerning the relationship between violence and freedom – how freedom is the result of institutionalizing and categorizing (it has to begin as a series of acts of naming before it can be actualized, however imperfectly, in the real world) and violence is a function of the "indirect angle" of naked confrontation, which forever eludes us because of the overwhelming fecundity of the human naming capacity – provides us with the compressed argument we need to show that liberalism is predicated upon skepticism, upon the very form of naked disclosure (that outside of a human naming process there is nothing for us to relate to) that Levinas strives so strenuously to refute. The thesis that is central to my critique of Levinas is formulated by Levinas himself as somehow a complementary "shadow" of his more overt and insistent argument concerning the given, substance-like character of the Other personified by the face.

In the vocabulary of his essay "Freedom and Command," what is at stake between Levinas and myself is whether there is a "command prior to institutions"[22] – or whether commands are a function of institutions and are neither empirically nor ontologically prior to them. Levinas says that "the face is the fact that a being affects us not in the indicative, but in the imperative, and is thus outside all categories."[23] What Levinas is apparently not noticing is that the "imperative" is a category (in this case, a grammatical form) like all other categories. Levinas is merely metaphorically registering the distance between the indicative and the imperative by calling the former a category and the latter a non-category. But this surely has to be acknowledged as a metaphorical way of registering a gap – and not as a literal way of distinguishing between what is categorically dependent and what is indubitably, purely substantively there. What Levinas refers to as the "plenitude of meaning prior to any *Sinngebung*"[24] describes our relationship to all things and phenomena in the world – as well as to all persons – and is not a unique feature of our relationship to the Other. Levinas is indeed right that intelligibility precedes us.[25] We always move from the less intelligible and coherent to the more intelligible and coherent – in our relation to people as well as to things. It is never the case that we move from zero to one hundred percent. However, enhanced and deepened intelligibility is a function of our interventions, interactions and involvements in the world. This sort of view is relevant for all of the phenomena – as well as for all of the persons – in the world.

In order to render Levinas' ethics compatible with his theory of a liberal society, there should not be any necessary points of origin just as there should not be any mandated points for arrival or destination for the individual or society. Just as liberalism precludes any necessary destination points in human personal or social development – its pluralism and toleration embrace multiple varieties of human personal and social ends – so, too, does liberalism implicitly delegitimate any preferred points of origin for historically depicting or theoretically envisioning the sequence of human development. Liberalism has historically emphasized from the time of Hobbes onward – with his defense of nominalism and conventionalism – the role of the "made" in "fashioning" the "given," and has been appropriately suspicious of those political theories and ideologies that have sought to reify or sanctify particular versions of the given. To privilege originary moments is already to be implicitly sanctioning a forceful interventionist role by the state in restoring such moments.

An additional problematic feature of Levinas' ethical theorizing is if freedom is nonexistent at the stage (or at the moment) when substitution for the Other occurs, has substitution anything to do with ethics? Ethics was carved out as a mode of human inquiry by creatures who were capable of scaling the heights of human altruism and plummeting to the depths of human selfishness and depravity. It is because we have the freedom to go in either direction – that we are not predetermined in any recognizable sense to go either way – that ethical deliberation has point and relevance. Ethical theorizing generates a whole set of factors to take into account in deciding upon what to do, which, of course, is predicated upon the assumption that our decision matters.

Both Greek and Jewish thought converge in their delineation of this key presuppositional postulate of ethical theorizing. For Aristotle, ethical and political theorizing both have a point because man is a metaphysically middling creature – neither God nor beast. The common feature that links God and beast is that they both operate in a vacuum of freedom. God oversteps the limits that make freedom possible – and beasts have not attained the intellectual and moral threshold that would enable them to exercise freedom. God's omniscience and omnipotence means that He is beyond freedom. He knows too much and is too powerful for freedom to be significant for Him. The gap between deliberating and doing is by definitional fiat closed for Him. Beasts (at the other extreme) are too much a captive of their instincts and too little able to surmount them for ethical deliberation to serve as a transition between impulse and action. It is only human beings who occupy the complex intermediate zone between God and beasts – who have knowledge and power, but only in limited amounts; who are driven by instincts, but are capable of surmounting or restraining or channeling them – for whom ethics becomes a possible mode of inquiry (on a theoretical level) and of deliberation (on a practical level).

The Hebrew Scriptures in the *Psalms* already give classic expression to human beings' occupying a middle position: "When I behold your heavens, the work of your fingers, the moon and the stars that you have set in place: What is man that you should remember him, and the son of mortal man that you should be mindful of him? You have made him but slightly less than Elokim, and crowned him with glory and splendor. You gave him dominion over your handiwork, everything you placed under his feet."[26] Man occupies a niche somewhere between being "slightly less than Elokim" and "what is man that you should remember him." He has the capacity of being both the greatest and the most abject of God's creatures. What defines him is neither the one pole nor the other but the capacity to fluctuate between them, and the freedom to decide on an ongoing basis which one he chooses to cultivate and at least provisionally inhabit.

Similarly, Rabbi Tarfon in *Pirkei Avot* says: "You are not required to complete the task, yet you are not free to withdraw from it."[27] Given the limitations of human knowledge and human powers, the task (the multiple tasks associated with self and world improvement) always exceed our abilities to carry them through completely. Even when we officially succeed, unforeseen eventualities often disrupt or deflect our achievements. As a result, the "task" gets endlessly prolonged. Given the gap between our aspirations and our limitations, we are nearly always in the position of having to choose what to do next. There being a "next" (moment of choice) is a function of the radical irresolvability and incompleteness of the human project. Ethics addresses man in his volatile middling state, helping him to clarify the most beneficial options that will be relevant for carving out the next moment.

Judaism (unlike Christianity) posits no unbridgeable gap between an originary moment (of consummated redemption) and the worldly context of ethical deliberation. In Rabbi Tarfon's idiom, Judaism projects an everlastingly prolonged middle, which confers intelligibility and coherence on further moves and decisions along the same lines that one has undertaken before – and withholds intelligibility and coherence from moves aspiring to a different order of magnitude by either inflating the stakes of human life, so that we aim at total redemption instead of the plurality of partial redemptions that Rabbi Tarfon envisions – or, failing at the project of inflation, turning in the completely opposite direction of collapsing the stakes by letting loose with a torrent (an orgy) of destruction and self-destruction. The Jewish approach encapsulated in Rabbi Tarfon's statement points to a tremendously important role for *Mitzvot* in serving as the vehicles for the achievement of partial redemptions. *Mitzvot* sanctify individual moments and individual activities – trying to raise them to their highest potential without harboring the illusion that it is possible to transform the entire landscape so that the need for engagement in *Mitzvot* itself becomes redundant.

Levinas, by contrast, by positing an unbridgeable gap between an originary moment of substitution and the worldly context of ethical deliberation, fits in much more closely with a Christian theological framework than with a Jewish one. The originary moment personified in Jesus' crucifixion is also about passivity, sacrifice and substitution. Christian theology, of course, creates a climate that is systematically hostile to the performance of *Mitzvot*. If total redemption was achieved once, the goal of human life should be to plug in to that one irreplaceable moment by cultivating and espousing the right set of beliefs and salvational reenactment rituals. The partial redemption of daily moments has been eclipsed and overshadowed by the glory of the originary moment.

In many of his explicitly political writings, Levinas is a proponent of liberalism. Liberalism in crucial senses spurns the Christian model of a total redemptive originary moment and opts for the Jewish projection of human life as consisting in an endless succession of not-fully-redeemed moments. In liberal theorizing, we move from the state of nature characterized by larger or smaller degrees of tension and conflict to the social-contract society that strives to reduce tension and conflict still further (beyond what emerges as the highly tenuous and unstable equilibrium of the state of nature) without fully eliminating them. The social-contract (liberal) society is a society pitched to the attainment of partial redemptions – with the implicit understanding that more totalistic programs would be fatally counterproductive.

There is a tremendous irony in Levinasian ethics in the extent to which the Levinasian self consists of substituted Otherness. Levinas says that "the order that orders me to the other does not show itself to me, save through the trace of its reclusion, as a face of a neighbor. There is a trace of a withdrawal which no actuality had preceded, and which becomes present only in my own voice."[28] The limitless responsibility to the Other becomes evident "only in my own voice." The opposites seem to have merged into each other: Levinas' extreme altruism merges into extreme solipsism. Levinas seems to have shut the trap door upon himself. As I have previously argued, the theorizing of the self as substituted Otherness just prolongs and intensifies Levinas' skeptical plight – and provides no release from it.

The Levinasian self is a self that has totally expelled its selfhood to make room for Otherness – and in the end cannot even survive as a container of Otherness because it is committed to sacrifice. Levinasian ethics, in the name of the moral ideal of Otherness, denudes the world of all the Others who have now been substituted for by the solitary human being gripped by the imperatives of substitution and responsibility. The solitary human being also disappears by way of displaying his allegiance to the ideal of sacrifice. Levinas ends up removing people and restoring a mute earth to its condition of prelapsarian sanctity. The self in a metaphorical sense for Levinas is "expelled from everywhere and from itself."[29] Levinas' liberalism, but *not* his ethical theory of substitution, is sensitive to the fact that what wards off Hitlerism is the willingness, on the part of more and more people to assume the risks of individuality – rather than the assurance of grace enshrined in a privileged salvational moment such as the substitution that resides on the "hither side of being."

Affirmation of the Other and self-affirmation

A major problem that Levinasian ethics confronts is that, as Nietzsche and Freud(among others) have reminded us, the affirmation of the Other is only possible for someone who has achieved self-affirmation. The two processes are correlative. Only someone who has accepted himself can embrace the Other. In circumstances of ultimate substitution – where embrace of the Other substitutes for (or comes before) self-acceptance – what results is a Nietzschean pyrotechnics of ressentiment. The primordial embrace of the Other preceding any kind of cultivation of the self becomes a legitimating conduit – a disguise – through which one is able to display and to enact the most intense manifestations of self-hatred and self-destruction, which translate soon enough into destruction of Others. Theodor Adorno and others have linked this personality type who shuns individuality with the mass-man who in the course of the 20th century has been most receptive to the appeals of fascism.

Because the self is a creation and not a given, part of the unconscious force of Levinas' "substitution" metaphor is to mutilate this conception of the self as self-creation and to insert givenness where creation should be. The propulsion to do this represents a misreading of how genuine and enduring affirmation of the Other comes to be. The self must be able to live with itself before it can live with the Other. Living with itself means constant doing, constant assertion, constant activity – as well as constant interaction with the Other. This is what engenders the sense of self-worth that enables the self to be reconciled with itself. This is the very opposite of the passivity, incarnation and substitution that Levinas extols.

A self that inserts the Other in a position of priority over itself is in the end not able to do justice to either the claims of the Other or of the self. It becomes an incoherent mass of jumbled ressentiment that misses the boat both with regard to the Other and with regard to the self. On phenomenological grounds, therefore (because it misreads what actually takes place in processes of self-formation and affirmation of the Other), I am arguing against Levinas' phenomenological reconstruction of ethics.

Part of the force of the Biblical image of *B'Tzelem Elokim* – that man was created in the image of God[30] – is to communicate to us the notion that to be human means to approximate to the enigmatic individuality of the Divine. Just as God is action, assertiveness, will without a personality that we can penetrate, so, too, is the human self formed and sustained by a commitment to the primacy of action, assertiveness and will, with the retrospective congealments that constitute the normal accoutrements of selfhood such as personality traits, habits and dispositions being regarded more as instrumental and transitory in character, than as bedrock, substantive givens. The essentialist opacity at the core of the self is the source of human creativity – just as it is the source of Divine creativity. Levinas' wanting to pierce this opacity and situate beholdenness to the Other as the primal layer of human identity represents a sophisticated and ostensibly humane gnostic yearning. To see us all as more humane, Levinas wants to insert infinite responsibility to the Other as the foundational layer of human selfhood. As with other versions of gnosticism, the price of an excessive and unwarranted claim to knowledge (even metaphorical and speculative philosophical knowledge) is the counterproductive release and legitimation of human destructive potential often initially exemplified as an excessive vulnerability to charismatic leadership.

Plato and Levinas: words and things

Given the fact that Levinas identifies Plato as a precursor for his own view "that the conclusions of our basic philosophical questions are to be found beyond metaphysics in ethics,"[31] it is remarkable how sharp the metaphysical divergence is between them. Is there a "saying" independent of the "said" – or is the "saying" itself something that has already entered the domain of the "said" in terms of the distinctly verbalized concept of the "saying"? For Plato, there is nothing behind the words that we use. The Third Man Argument of the *Parmenides* points to the infinite regress that emerges if we try to ground our words in something more secure than themselves.[32] In dialogue, we only confront "circular mirrors" implicitly exchanged between the various interlocutors that disclose and highlight the arbitrariness of beginnings (how no conceptual beginning can ever be authenticated as the true beginning). Levinas in *Otherwise than Being* is chafing against the Platonic limits – trying to come up with a beginning that antedates all officially ontologically-locatable beginnings. Taking his cue from the philosophical career of skepticism which surfaces again and again throughout the whole history of philosophy despite all attempts at refutation and containment, Levinas wants to be able to locate such a beginning that precedes all beginnings. As we have seen, he traces it to our being a "hostage" of the Other who "commands" our "incarnation" of him and "substitution" for him. From all of the points of view we have considered, this is far too extravagant and unsustainable a move. Levinas could follow a much more negative, humble and parsimonious path to carve out a niche for the Other. Once skepticism is recognized as being unavoidable in philosophy – and skepticism is understood as a shorthand term for the thesis of the underdetermination of theory by fact (i.e. that alternative and conflicting formulations can make sense of the selfsame body of fact), then we must acknowledge (with Popper) that "if two contradictory statements are admitted, any statement whatever must be admitted; for from a couple of contradictory statements any statement whatever can be validly inferred."[33] This juncture, I submit, becomes the most appropriate place to attest to the possibilities of God and the Other. I would like to spell out in some more detail how contradiction emerges in our conceptualizations of God and the Other:

From the perspective of negative theology, the conventional idea of God is contradictory. God's serving as the ultimate explanatory factor for all the goings-on in the universe is predicated upon His gross dissimilarity from all things human, which allows the search for the most primary explanation to culminate in Him. However, the literal unintelligibility of the God-concept in effect points to its inability to explain anything at all. The notion of God is thus contradictory. On the one hand, its role in the explanatory pyramid suggests ultimacy, but, on the other hand, that very location ensures that it is not able to explain anything. But if the idea of God is contradictory, we need to notice that any single contradiction in the field of statements that we take to be true has the effect of domesticating or naturalizing contradiction, and we are thus bereft of any effective argumentative or logical resource with which to block the possibility of God.

The same pattern of negative argument can be invoked in defense of the possibility of the human Other. Our empirical evidence for the existence of the Other is insecure because our senses might be deceiving us, and the logical inferences that we might draw from the assumptions and generalizations that we make and from the typical structure of our discourse to the existence of the Other would also not indubitably certify to the existence of the Other because these assumptions, generalizations and inferences could be the same even if no Other existed but was merely a projection of the Same or self. In the cases of both God and the human Other, our inability to consummate positive arguments for God and the Other clears negative space through the unavoidability of contradiction to the possibility of their existence. The upshot of this approach is that one does not need to identify a dimension that is otherwise than being; one only needs to cultivate the argumentative resources of a coherent skepticism in order to carve out conceptual niches for God and the Other.

When one gets rid of the mythology and utopianism in *Otherwise than Being*, what one is left with is an articulation of the concept of a "saying" that is logically dissociated from the "said." Either Aristotelian logic (once the infiltration of its premises by contradiction is analyzed in the manner indicated by Popper) or nonstandard logics can accommodate this dissociation. The upshot under either logical dispensation is the same: Nurturance of – or receptivity to – a generalized agnosticism. The proliferation of contradiction after the introduction of even one contradictory premise in Aristotelian logic means that we are living in a generalized-agnostic universe in which intelligibility and order are on the defensive. If the dissociation of the "saying" from the "said" is assigned to the rubric of nonstandard logics, then we need to be committed to a generalized agnosticism in order to keep our theoretical horizons open to the emergence and legitimation of such logics. A principle of charitableness in interpretation as well as a search for the deepest level of coherence in Levinas' argument might both reinforce an implicit convergence between my overt critiques of Levinas in *Otherwise than Being* and the shape and weight of his argument when reformulated in "reflective equilibrium."

From the possibility of the Other one could then move on to philosophically chart and validate the moral claims and even priority of the Other. But, contra Levinas, these claims and priority could only be negotiated pragmatically, rather than primordially or irrevocably. In order to promote human peace and flourishing starting with our own, we need to fashion a social universe that legitimates the interests and claims of the Other. In a generalized-agnostic universe of discourse, the logical-operators are selves that persist with their explorations and inquiries from generation to generation, thereby providing themselves with opportunities to continually readjust the theoretical equilibria (and the specific content of theories) inherited from previous generations. From the generalized-agnostic perspective that I am sketching, the only entity that is not "trumpable" or instrumentally renounceable (as a presupposition for the playing out of pragmatism) is human life itself, for each human being alive during each generation of human time. The persistence of human life provides the infrastructure for the manifestation and operation of a generalized agnosticism that endlessly revises its stock of beliefs and understandings without reaching a final point of resolution.

The advantage of this approach in contrast to approaches that flaunt greater certainty is that it does not muddy our perception with regard to the fragility and vulnerability of human existence. The self as "logical operator" can encounter other selves as "logical operators" hellbent on destroying it – and aside from pointing out to its opponents the benefits of mutual compromise and accommodation, the self is bereft of any resources (except a recognition of its own imperative need to act) to ward off powerful enemies. In order to meet the challenges of those who would assault and undermine human life and human flourishing, it would be preferable to keep the outer, justificatory structure of argument soft and exposed – so that we do not deceive ourselves into believing that there is some impregnable layer of value and justification that stands between us and destruction and self-destruction. It is a recognition of our limitations and vulnerability – and our determination to proceed despite (or because of) them – that offers us our best hope of nurturing and sustaining human life, and contributing toward its ongoing flourishing in individual and collective settings.

One can also construe Levinas' distinction between the "saying" and the "said" as a metaphorical expression of the ways in which spoken and written discourse distort and falsify the inspirations that guided them. All the "saids" of our written and spoken discourse constitute primordially attempts to catch, pin down and institutionalize the fleeting glimpses and insights that prod and motivate us as we are about to speak or write. The initial relationship conjured up by the categories of the "saying" and the "said" is not to anything external but to the internal fragments of consciousness that become viable conceptual units only in the course of being elaborated upon as what Levinas calls "the said." Part of the problematic of Levinas' distinction between the "saying" and the "said" is that the "saying" from a compelling phenomenological perspective is largely a fictive entity generated to make sense of and to goad on the actual formulation of the "said." In order to be able to say what we want to say, we have to generate instantaneous "elsewheres" or "others" that are inchoate and not fully formed – indeterminate starting points that are correlated with indeterminate destinations – that help us fill-in

The tension between Levinas' ethics and his political theory 205

with content what we are trying to say. The "saying" is a necessary fiction that helps the "said" get formed.

One of the greatest stumbling blocks to Levinas' mode of ethical theorizing construed on a strictly literal level is its implicit assumption of the facticity of the self in relation to the fragility of the Other. The ethical vocabulary of "substitution" suggests on some level that a robust and overly self-regarding self needs to learn how to properly subordinate itself to Others. But we need to notice that before the Other is treated as an instrumentalized posit by the self to promote certain satisfactions, the self is also treated as an instrumentalized posit by the self to promote certain satisfactions. The self is not a given or a substance or an end – but rather a series of endless movements, a process, a transition between successive nodal points that are only retrospectively identified and solidified. The self is a series of ongoing constructions and deconstructions that lays claim to secure identity only honorifically and for the sake of reassuring ourselves and others that we are indeed coherent centers of action and discourse.

From this perspective, the problem with Levinas is that despite all of his efforts to get at the most compelling presupposition of being, he is already positioned after the fact. "Substitution," "incarnation" and "passivity" already take for granted a self-formation and self-identity that are much more fugitively and transiently formed (and then often revised and superseded) than Levinas allows. Levinas' ethical theorizing is already situated at a threshold of self-definition and self-formation that the self rarely attains. From the perspective of the psychological dynamics of self-formation as well as from the more purely philosophical perspective considered earlier, it makes more sense to view self-Other as a continuum that never quite completes itself at either end, and that on both psychological and philosophical grounds is most intelligibly addressed by a skeptical analytical apparatus that never for an instant ceases to interrogate both the categories that are being formed as well as the steps that are being mobilized to lead to and solidify those categories.

Rabbinic tradition subverts Levinasian teaching

Situating Levinas in relation to Rabbinic tradition, it is important to note that a central Talmudic passage dealt with in *Nine Talmudic Readings*, and some key Biblical passages cited in the endnotes to *Otherwise than Being*, which Levinas invokes as supporting his ethics of "substitution" actually end up subverting it. I would like to deal with each of these passages in turn:

In its description of the supreme moment of Revelation at Mount Sinai, the Bible says: "And Moses brought forth the people out of the camp towards God; and they placed themselves at the nether part of the mountain."[34] Rashi in his gloss on this verse says: "According to its literal meaning this signifies 'at the foot of the mountain.' But a Midrashic explanation is that the mountain was plucked up from its place and was arched over them as a cask, so that they were standing beneath (under) the mountain itself."[35] One of the interrelated texts in *Shabbath* 88a that Levinas also addresses elaborates upon Exodus 24:7: "And he took the book of the covenant and read in the ears of the people and they said All that the Eternal hath spoken will we do and hearken." The Talmud glosses this verse as follows: "Rabbi Eleazar has said: When the Israelites committed to doing before hearing, a voice from heaven cried out: Who has revealed to my children this secret the angels make use of, for it is written (Psalms 103:20): 'Bless the Lord, Oh, His angels, you mighty ones, who do His word, hearkening to the voice of His word.'"[36]

In commenting upon these interconnected texts, Levinas says that "The priority of knowledge is the temptation of temptation ... It will no longer leave the other in its otherness but will always include it in the whole, approaching it, as they say today, in a historical perspective, at the horizon of the All. From this stems the inability to recognize the other person as other person, as outside all calculation, as neighbor, as first come."[37] In order to affirm the genuine Otherness of the Other and thereby secure the primacy of ethics over all other forms of inquiry and types of knowledge, Levinas reads the "we will do and hearken" and "overturned cask" passages as signifying that what "is at stake here is not simply *praxis* as opposed to theory but a way of *actualizing without beginning with the possible*, of knowing without examining, of placing oneself beyond violence without this being the privilege of a free choice. A pact with good would exist, preceding the alternative of good and evil."[38] In conclusion, Levinas says:

> To be a self is to be responsible beyond what one has oneself done. *Temimut* [uprightness] consists in substituting oneself for others ... The impossibility of escaping from God – which in this at least is not a value among others – is the "mystery of angels," the "We will do and we will hear." It lies in the depths of the ego as ego, which is not only for a being the possibility of death, "the possibility of impossibility," but already the possibility of sacrifice, birth of a meaning in the obtuseness of being, of a subordination of a "being able to die" to a "knowing how to sacrifice oneself."[39]

Though in many respects a skeptic and an adherent of negative theology, Levinas in his interpretation of the two Talmudic passages cited above misses the full import of both doctrines and how they relate to each other. The Hebrew word that is translated above as "hearken" or "hear" is *Nishma*. *Lishmoah*, as in the central credo of the Jew, *Sh'mah Yisroel* (literally translated as "Hear O Israel") means to listen with the inner ear – i.e. to understand. The secret that the angels have grasped that the Jews apparently appropriated at Mount Sinai is how doing precedes knowing. Since our knowledge of any subject matter remains incomplete, it is only through doing that we are able to achieve (relative) mastery of things without being able to attain completion or closure. "The mountain being held over them as an overturned cask" metaphorically duplicates and reencodes the teaching of

"We will do and we will hear." God, as it were, enacts for the Jewish community the doing that precedes the understanding. Given the inapplicability of the verbs and attributes that we ascribe to God (such as holding the mountain over us like an overturned cask) to God, the rebounding of these metaphorical descriptions can only cease by translating them in relation to ourselves, the subjects seeking to make sense of these metaphors in the first place. The metaphor of the cask being turned over upon us is an appropriate gloss on the "We will do and we will hear" passage because it represents an optimal response to the skepticism encapsulated in the negative-theological figuration of God in this same passage. The rational distance between us and God (the distance that we attempt to close through reasoned argument) can never be bridged, so that our doing and our actions need to precede our understanding in order for our understanding to have a viable object (no matter how inchoate our understanding remains in the end) to be about. On the basis of reason, we could go on speculating, inquiring and adducing relevant considerations and counter-considerations forever. It is only by artifically inducing or imposing closure that we can move on in the world. This is what is metaphorically captured for us in the image of the mountain being overturned upon us like a cask. What metaphorically speaking God did to us at the foot of Mount Sinai we have to do to ourselves in a multitude of contexts every day in order to lead optimal human lives. So, contra Levinas, the metaphor of the "overturned cask" is symptomatic and a function of our radical freedom partially related to our skeptical argumentative condition. It does not represent how obligation (in the form of substitution and sacrifice) precedes all assumptions and expressions of freedom – but rather insinuates disguised counsel about how to proceed in the face of our infinite freedom and lack of secure knowledge.

Levinas' interpretation of "The mountain was held over them as an overturned cask" – just like his theorizing of substitution overall (for which his Talmudic reading is supposed to provide some kind of supportive text) – violates negative theology and contravenes skepticism. "The mountain was held over them as an overturned cask" is parallel to "We will do and we will hear." It duplicates its content (which is reflective of a nominalistic, voluntaristic metaphysics) on a metaphorical level.

In Chapter 3 of *Otherwise than Being*, Levinas says that "In proximity the absolutely other, the stranger whom I have 'neither conceived nor given birth to,' I already have on my arms, already bear, according to the Biblical formula, 'in my breast as the nurse bears the nursling.'"[40] Levinas uses the verse in Numbers to strengthen his case that ethics constitutes "primary philosophy," with all other branches of philosophical inquiry grouping themselves and achieving their maximum coherence around this primacy. From a more expansive Rabbinic perspective, this verse actually illustrates how epistemology comes before ethics and contributes toward the conferring of point and relevance upon ethical behavior. Moses relates to the Jewish people as a "nursing father" because epistemologically his claim to knowledge of God in a positive, literalist sense is no better than that of the multitude of ordinary Jews. In a famous statement in the Babylonian Talmudic tractate *Yebamoth*, the Talmud distinguishes between the prophecy of Moses and that of all other prophets. Whereas all other prophets saw "through a glass that was not clear," Moses saw "through a clear glass." Rashi in his commentary on this passage says that "he knew that he did not see Him face to face."[41] Subverting the expected reading of this passage, Rashi says that Moses' clarity consisted in a more clairvoyant demarcation of his ignorance than later prophets were capable of mustering. Whereas they in their moments of prophetic transport might have felt that they perceived some glimpse of Divinity, Moses never fell prey to such an illusion. In moments of potentially supreme intoxication, he sustained his clearheadedness and "knew that he did not see Him." Once one contextualizes the Biblical passage in Numbers and Rashi's commentary upon it in this way, the reading ends up being almost the opposite of what Levinas proposes. Common ignorance – a theological ignorance shared with the broader community – with Moses being more self-conscious about it than the other members of the community can serve as a basis for intense bonding and solicitude. One does not have to postulate a "pre-ontological" lurch toward "substitution" as governing Moses' behavior in order to make sense of the image of the "nursing father."

In support of the view that "in passivity the ego is a self under a persecuting-accusation of a neighbor," Levinas cites Rashi's commentary on Numbers 12:12, "which here follows the ancient tradition of *Siphri*."[42] The Biblical text deals with Aaron's pleading with Moses concerning the plight of their sister Miriam, who had just turned leprous as a result of having falsely accused Moses of "taking a Cushite woman." Aaron beseeches Moses to pray for Miriam's recovery: "Let her not be as one dead, of whom the flesh [literally, his flesh] is half consumed when he cometh out of his mother's womb." Levinas, citing Rashi, draws an inference from the grammatical construction of this verse in support of his ethical philosophy of "substitution." The following is Rashi's gloss:

> It ought to have stated "of our mother's womb" [instead of "his mother's womb"], only that Scripture modified the expression. Similarly, "half of his flesh" – it ought to have said "the half of our flesh is consumed," only that Scripture modified the expression. [Scripture uses these expressions with the suffix of the third person singular instead of the first person plural, because it wishes to avoid an ominous expression referring to Aaron and Moses as being leprous.] – The meaning is: Since she came forth from the womb of our own mother she in her present state is to us as though the half of our flesh were consumed. It is the same idea as is expressed in the words (Genesis 37:27) [with regard to the brothers selling Joseph], "for he is our brother, our own flesh."[43]

Levinas uses Rashi's explication of the verse in Numbers to show the degree of passivity and substitution ("our flesh is being consumed") that human beings are required to exhibit toward their fellow human beings.

I believe that Levinas is wrenching Rashi's reading out of context in order to invoke it in support of his ethical theory. One of the thirteen exegetical principles of Rabbi Yishmael[44] that should govern our interpretation of Torah (presumably not only the legal materials in the text of the Torah, but also the non-legal materials such as the incident with Miriam) is *Davar Halamed M'Inyano* – a matter deduced from its context. Aaron is trying to counter and neutralize Moses' response to Miriam's outburst. How does the Torah describe Moses' response to her accusation? "Now the man Moses was very meek above all the men who were upon the face of the earth."[45] The Torah stresses Moses' humility – his rejection of anger and, indeed, his refusal of any attempt to justify and exonerate himself. Does Moses beseech God to defend him – to directly intervene and show his "familial enemies" who was right and who was wrong? He does nothing of the sort. His patient, self-effacing response becomes a general model of how human beings should respond when they feel they have been erroneously accused of wrongdoing by other human beings in the world. Moses' refusal to treat Miriam's shaming him as a provocation that would justify his lashing out at her becomes from a Rabbinic perspective an enactment of how he would want God to relate to him – to suffer his iniquities and transgressions without seeking immediate retribution.[46]

"God" cannot be literally engaged or negotiated by us. Also, on strictly moral grounds, we cannot claim that we are able to surmount our bias toward ourselves sufficiently to arrive at a neutral, disinterested grasp of a situation in order to justify petitioning Divine intervention on our behalf. It is significant that it is God who describes Moses' unique relationship to Him – that God speaks to him "mouth to mouth"[47] – rather than Moses making such a claim on his own behalf. God, the supreme Biblical metaphor whose "cash value" can never be "unpacked," attests that Moses has traveled the furthest that a human being can go in relating to Him (and the route can be construed, as we have seen, as a negative one of registering distance, rather than as a positive one of overcoming it). God's (the supreme symbol of the limitations of human reason) attesting to this accomplishment suggests that Moses has not achieved the original human aim of totally squelching the distance between God and himself. The final verdict or judgment on Moses' relationship to God is voiced by God – not Moses. God, the impenetrable metaphor, affirms the specialness of Moses' relationship to Him.

Given the theological, epistemological and moral constraints upon Moses' directly beseeching God to vindicate him, he opts for the negative-theological option of imitating God's ways – the attributes we ascribe to Him. Since the postulates of negative theology foreclose applying these attributes directly, literally to God, they instigate a movement of recoil that in the end allows these attributes to find no resting place except in relation to man, where their metaphorical status is not overcome, but merely momentarily unpacked and applied. When one probes behind the front line of metaphors to pin down a referent for the descriptive epithets that we employ in relation to God, what we discover behind it without end are just further strings of metaphors. The rebounding of these metaphors can only be temporarily suspended when we fill out how these metaphors might be relevant for human behavior. The Rabbinic imperative enunciated in relation to the verse *V'Halachtah B'Drachav* – that one should walk in the ways of God – Is it possible for human beings to cleave to God? But what the verse must mean is that just as He is merciful and compassionate, etc., so should we be merciful and compassionate, etc. – is at least partially governed by the logic of negative theology.[48] The displacement of Divine epithets initiated by negative theology can only achieve partial, provisional closure by delineating how these epithets apply to human beings.

This extended application of the principle of *V'Halachtah B'Drachav* is also found in the Babylonian Talmudic tractate *Berakoth* (58a) in a story concerning Rav Shesheth:

> Rav Shesheth was blind. Once all the people went out to see the king, and Rav Shesheth arose and went with them. A certain Sadducee came across him and said to him: The whole pitchers go to the river, but where do the broken ones go to [i.e. what is the use of a blind man going to see the king]? He replied: I will show you that I know more than you. The first troop passed by and a shout arose. Said the Sadducee: The king is coming. He is not coming, replied Rav Shesheth. A second troop passed by and when a shout arose, the Sadducee said: Now the king is coming. Rav Shesheth replied: The king is not coming. A third troop passed by and there was silence. Said Rav Shesheth: Now indeed the king is coming. The Sadducee said to him: How did you know this? – He replied: Because the earthly royalty is like the heavenly (*Malchuta d'arah k'ein malchuta d'rekiah*). For it is written: Go forth and stand upon the mount before the Lord. And behold, the Lord passed by and a great and strong wind rent the mountains, and broke in pieces the rocks before the Lord; but the Lord was not in the wind; and after the wind an earthquake; but the Lord was not in the earthquake; and after the earthquake a fire; but the Lord was not in the fire; and after the fire a still small voice (I Kings 19:11–13).[49]

This dialogue between Rav Shesheth and the Sadducee provides a prooftext for the idea that the principle of *V'Halachtah B'Drachav* is extended and generalized by the Rabbis outside of the sphere of emulation of Divine attributes of mercy and kindness to encompass the multiple ways in which the Divine world and the human world constitute mirror images of each other. Since on one level the Divine vocabulary is all-metaphorical, it most suitably needs to be construed as encoding the ordering principles that govern (relate to) the human world. From one urgent theological perspective, we need to see ourselves in the behavioral moves ascribed to God.

Another illustration of how pervasively the Rabbis apply the principle of *V'Halachtah B'Drachav* comes from the *Amidah* – the central prayer that Jews recite three times a day. This prayer consists of nineteen blessings, one of which focuses on the *Tzaddikim* – the righteous. The prayer beseeches God to bestow "goodly rewards to all who sincerely believe in His name," from "the righteous," "the devout," "the elders," "the remnant of our scholars," "righteous converts," on down to "ourselves." The prayer pleads with God to "put our lot with them [those who sincerely believe in His Name] forever." The prayer continues: "for we trust in you. Blessed are you, Hashem [literally, the Name, referring to God, who for us remains only an undecodable name] Mainstay and Assurance of the righteous."[50]

Bitachon – belief or trust – is what equalizes all of the different levels of Jews referred to in the prayer. We ask God to place "our lot with them [that have proper *Bitachon*] forever." *Bitachon* constitutes an inner state of being that can only be reliably accessed by God. No human being can ever be certain that his trust in God is authentic. The mere search for self-authentication puts authentication beyond reach. To trust in someone or something is to acknowledge in advance that certainty eludes us. To introspect and try and pin down whether your trust is real represents a futile attempt to try and recover on the secondary level what you declare in advance to be absent on the primary level. You can only proceed infinitely regressively to search for trust (i.e., the substitute for certainty) which, if you had it in the first place (or, if it was intelligible for you to initially appropriate it), you would not need the trust. Trust is one of those words in the human vocabulary that displaces itself as a condition of its use.

As if the circumstances I have described were not dire enough, the picture gets further complicated by the fact that the object of trust in the *Amidah* is the monotheistic God, whose attributes we have to immediately and literally discount. We can only indefinitely say what God isn't – but not what He is. Human beings who cannot access and confirm their trust are confronted by a God whose being on sheerly theological grounds can neither be accessed nor confirmed. In prayer, the unknowable trust of a human being comes "face to face" with the God in whom he trusts. The unknowable meets the unknowable. How does the prayerful relation get resolved?

The prayer for the righteous in the *Amidah* has a brilliant answer to this question, which is communicated to us by the juxtaposition of its three central phrases: "Give goodly reward to all who sincerely believe in your Name; put our lot with them forever; and we will not feel ashamed for we trust in you." Since trust is opaque and rationally impenetrable from both a human and a Divine perspective (we cannot literally pin down the nature of God as the object of our trust), the only way that trust can be validated is by the results that it is taken to achieve. If God blesses and rewards us – placing "our lot with them [that trust in Him] forever," then this is the only secure, tangible manifestation that we are trusting. "Put[ting] our lot with them forever" is the only proof possible that "we trust in you." Worldly payoffs and consequences are the only attestations possible for the presence of trust. Just as God, as it were, is only known through *His* actions, we are known (the level and virtuousness of our belief and trust are/become known) through the abundance and quality of the "rewards" that we receive.

What this benediction concerning the righteous in the *Amidah* inscribes, therefore, is the interpretive scope that the Rabbis confer upon the principle of *V'Halachtah B'Drachav*. Given the premises of monotheism which emphasize infinite distance and the infinite character of God, He can only be known and identified through His actions (or what we affirm are His actions), namely, the creation and the governance of the world. God being unknown and unknowable, we only "know" God by what He does, not by what He is, to which we have no access.[51] Correspondingly, the trust that fixes the caliber and character of the relationship that human beings can have with such a God is also unknown and unknowable (or incoherent and untranslatable), but can only be provisionally reconstructed by its fruits, the rewards and the benefits that God bestows upon us. Believers are disclosed as harboring the same limitations and profile as the object of their belief.

Returning now to the Biblical narrative concerning Moses' confrontation with his two older siblings: Moses was responding to the provocations of Miriam and Aaron by emulating one of the Thirteen Divine Attributes of Mercy – that of being *Erech Apaim* ("Slow to Anger").[52] He did not in any way chastise his brother and sister – or even challenge what they said about him. He manifested to the highest human degree possible, the patience and endurance that we project onto God under the rubric of *Erech Apaim*. From the analytical-interpretive perspective that I am developing, Aaron does not plead with Moses to abandon the negative-theological framework (whose key presupposition is unbridgeable distance between God and man) that he is inhabiting, but only to switch attributes within this framework. Another one of the Thirteen Attributes is *Rav Chesed* – which means "Abundant in Kindness." Unlike *Erech Apaim*, which is largely passive and renunciatory (renouncing anger and the desire for revenge) in character, *Rav Chesed* connotes tremendous activism. Aaron pleads with Moses that he not rest content with impassively swallowing his sister's insults – but that he mobilize all of the resources of prayer to intercede actively on her behalf.

In key respects, Rabbi Yishmael's Thirteen Exegetical Principles for Interpreting Torah constitute an intertextual gloss upon the Thirteen Divine Attributes of Mercy. The Hebrew word *Middot*, which literally means "measures," is used in both contexts – to refer to exegetical principles in the first instance and to Divine attributes in the second. Rabbi Yishmael, by selecting for his principles the same mystically-charged number – thirteen – as that assigned to the attributes of God, wants to intimate to us that just as his Thirteen Principles of Biblical Interpretation relate to how human beings interpret the text of the Torah given their location in the world and the moral, social and political (etc.) ends that they pursue, so, too, the Thirteen Divine Attributes of Mercy are interpretations arrived at and generated from a human perspective. Just as in the case of Rabbi Yishmael's Thirteen Exegetical Principles there is no pretense to have exhausted the depths of the Torah but only to have excavated (in terms of Biblical support for Rabbinic legal formulations, etc.), what is momentarily sought – so, too, with regard to the Thirteen Divine Attributes there is (should be) no pretense to have exhausted the depths (or essence) of Divinity but only to have highlighted the features or ascriptions that are eminently humanly relatable or usable, and that promote human flourishing to the utmost extent. The number thirteen is selected in both instances because the *Gematria* (numerical value) of the Hebrew word *Echad*,[53] which means "one," is also thirteen. To preserve the psychic integrity of human beings and the balance in the universe requires us to rigidly circumscribe the limits of possible penetration of the text of the Torah and of the nature of God. We need to position ourselves to relate to the Torah and to God with a set of questions and parameters that reflect our location in the world and our needs, aspirations *and* limits. The Thirteen *Middot* in both cases bring to the foreground what is humanly usable and exploitable in the fathomless text of the Torah and the fathomless concept of the monotheistic God. Staying on this side of the limits staked out by the Thirteen *Middot* in both cases redounds to our ability to sustain the oneness of human existence. By observing the limits encapsulated in the Thirteen *Middot* of Divine Mercy and the Thirteen *Middot* of Biblical Interpretation, we fortify ourselves against the formation of dualisms (such as those characteristic of gnosticism) that stand poised to overwhelm and destroy human existence.

The famous statement in the *Zohar* that *Yisroel, V'Oreitah, V'Kudsha Brich Hu Chad Hu* ("Israel, the Torah, and God are one") can be interpreted along the lines sketched out here. Staying within the precincts of oneness (as delineated above) that guides us in our approaches to the Torah and to God is the secret of the mental and spiritual intactness of the People Israel. We preserve our oneness not through encompassing everything, but through recognizing that our very inability to do so, if not reified into a substantive principle in its own right (so that only the future will tell where the final equilibrium will fall between belief and skepticism), is the greatest source of consolation and succor that human beings can cultivate.

It is important to note that contra Levinas' reading, the negative-theological framework is not suspended but remains in force throughout the whole Biblical narrative of Aaron's interceding with his brother Moses on behalf of their sister Miriam. Striving to imitate attributes that we ascribe to God (which, as I have argued, guides Aaron in his beseeching Moses to intercede on Miriam's behalf) presupposes the whole skeptical dynamic of negative theology. God can only bring the explanatory quest to a halt because He fails to explain anything in any humanly intelligible way. His very ultimacy as an explanatory factor is achieved at the price of vacuousness. The dislodging of an ultimate explanatory force means that we are left with insecurely moored words and concepts to do our explaining. It also insinuates that often divergent and even contradictory strings of words can do the explaining and conceptual-subsuming of phenomena that we seek. We are bereft of objectively sustainable mechanisms of resolution to adjudicate between these potentially contradictory strings of words. There is no room in this picture – in fact, this picture fully militates against – the radical substitution of self for Other that takes place "otherwise than being" under a mysterious veil of knowledge that defies critical scrutiny and interrogation.

Rashi in support of his reading in Numbers 12:12 of the incident with Miriam cites Genesis 37:27, where Judah advises his brothers that they should pull Joseph out of the pit into which they had thrust him and sell him to a caravan of passing Ishmaelites because "he is our brother our flesh." In terms of construing this phrase in a Levinasian sense of substitution, the irony, of course, becomes that Judah utilizes this phrase by way of buttressing his proposal that his brothers sell Joseph into servitude to the Ishmaelites rather than restoring him intact to his father – which is a far cry from the total subordination to the Other which is what Levinas means by "substitution." This idea that a brother is "our flesh" is only taken seriously by Judah and his brothers later on in Genesis, when Joseph, as Pharaoh's prime minister in Egypt sustaining his brothers in a time of famine prior to disclosing his true identity to them, tries to coax them into reenacting the scene of "the selling of Joseph" in relation to their youngest sibling – Benjamin.

Joseph's very puzzling and ostensibly immoral behavior at this juncture has provoked manifold Rabbinic commentaries. Maimonides in his Laws of *Teshuvah* (Repentance) in his *Code* gives us a significant clue for reconciling Joseph's behavior with the tenets of Judaism.[54] Maimonides writes about how optimal *Teshuvah* consists in a duplication of the circumstances of the original transgression, where a person manages to triumph over the temptations that engulfed him the first time.[55] From this perspective, we can view Joseph before reestablishing his bond with his brothers as deliberately trying to engineer a set of circumstances that would tempt his brothers to their former excesses of jealousy and resentment – by way of testing the depth and extent of their repentance. He tries to offer them every justification and inducement in the world to abandon Benjamin (now their father's favorite, as the only surviving son of his preferred wife, Rachel) to his fate in Egypt. It is only at that point (the second time around, as it were) that Judah and the rest of his brothers relate to Benjamin as "their brother, their flesh."

Again, it is important to note, as in the case of the "family romance" of Miriam, Aaron and Moses, the negative-theological backdrop against which the Bible's narrative unfolds. The idea of *Teshuvah* is thoroughly suffused with negative-theological and skeptical understandings. *Teshuvah* in some sense is about wiping the slate clean and starting over. There are two key metaphysical presuppositions that render the phenomenon of *Teshuvah* possible. The first is that human beings are not defined by some preordained essence that limits in advance what we can do. *Teshuvah* assumes that we are defined by our actions. As long as we are capable of altering them, the other apparently more enduring constituents of our personalities such as our beliefs, character traits and emotional patterns will vary accordingly. *Teshuvah* posits that in a crucial sense we are what we do. The hermeneutical key for making sense of human nature encapsulated in the notion of *Teshuvah* is borrowed from the negative-theological construal of God. Just as negative theology denies our access to what God is like in and of Himself, *Teshuvah* denies that it is possible to know human beings in and for themselves. It is the "actions" imputed to God (such as the creation of the world) that make God "knowable." Analogously, it is what human beings do (rather than what we "enduringly are") that makes us intermittently and partially transparent to others and to ourselves.

A second metaphysical presupposition of the concept of *Teshuvah* that confers plausibility upon it is the notion of the incompleteness of human action. Everything that we do can be analyzed on at least two levels: The level of the discharge of neurophysiological energy and the interpretive frameworks that we invoke to make sense of, describe and communicate what we are doing. *Teshuvah* posits that actions are completed only on the first level – but not on the second. As we insert our "neurophysiological discharges" into new interpretive contexts and make sense of them in new ways, they become new actions. Even if the new interpretive context is that of *Teshuvah* itself, where we regret what we have done and seek to transform our modes of behavior, that is sufficient to rearticulate the nature of the action originally undertaken. *Teshuvah* becomes one stratum of orientating meaning for locating and identifying the "original" action itself.

The *Teshuvah* setting where Judah's statement about Joseph that "he is our brother and our flesh" resonates the most is only conceivable in the negative-theological, skeptical framework where both the identities of God and human beings are fugitively and ambiguously disclosed in moments of metaphorical and literal action. From this perspective, there is no self to substitute for another (because there is simply no stable, enduring, intrinsically known self), so the Levinasian ethical vision cannot even get off the ground. The human self is largely impervious to itself, just as the Divine Essence is impenetrable by the humanly-invoked conceptual apparatus of the negative-theological God. In the cases of both God and man, there are only retrospective hints and congealments that get rectified by later retrospective hints and congealments. There is no argumentative space in which to insert an ongoing prospective substitution.

A monotheistic ethics: the mishnah of Ben Zoma (*Avot* 4:1) as a case in point

To most tellingly capture how a profoundly self-centered ethics is the focus of Rabbinic theorizing, I would like to conclude my critique and re-appropriation of Levinas with a discussion of Ben Zoma's famous mishnah in *Avot* 4:1. The grand alchemy of this mishnah – its being able to distill an ethic of human behavior from a steadfast confrontation with human personal and rational limitations – dramatizes for us how a world made safe for Otherness can be achieved and enhanced without leaving the terrain of the self. I shall begin by citing the mishnah and will then proceed to explicate it.

> Ben Zoma says: Who is wise? He who learns from every person, as it is said: 'From all my teachers I grew wise' (Psalms 119:99). Who is strong? He who subdues his personal inclination, as it is said, 'He who is slow to anger is better than the strong man, and a master of his passions is better than a conqueror of a city' (Proverbs 16:32). Who is rich? He who is happy with his lot, as it is said: 'When you eat the labor of your hands, you are praiseworthy and all is well with you'(Psalms 128:2). 'You are praiseworthy' – in this world; 'and all is well with you' – in the World to Come. Who is honored? He who honors others, as it is said: 'For those who honor Me I will honor, and those who scorn Me shall be degraded' (I Samuel 2:30).[56]

Ben Zoma's mishnah is astounding from a number of different but interrelated perspectives. He indirectly addresses four of the most central, vexing questions emerging out of human experience – What is wisdom, knowledge, truth? What is strength, power, courage? What is wealth, exalted status? What is honor, reputation? – and manages to turn the questions on their head and resist answering them. His first move in this strategy of resistance is to transform inquiry into these various qualities and attributes into an investigation of the person claiming or aspiring to possess them. This displacement is momentous. Instead of there being a known, finite, delimited entity to theorize about, there is the amorphous, infinite person trying to get a grip on the category that he (the inquirer, Ben Zoma) is implicitly trying to explicate. The questions surrounding these questions open up upon themselves – interrogate themselves – as Ben Zoma resituates the virtues and achievements alluded to in his mishnah in the menu of activities of the people claiming to exhibit them or striving toward them.

Ben Zoma subverts the attribution of any specific content to any of the virtues that constitute the oblique subject matter of his mishnah. Wisdom is identified with continual learning – strength is linked with perpetual surmounting of temptation – wealth is correlated with contentment – and honor is associated not with what we receive but with what we give to and confer upon other people. The process of preoccupation with these virtues or characteristics trumps any substantive designation of them. Virtue (Ben Zoma appears to be telling us) is a matter of striving – a striving, moreover, that constitutes a seamless web commencing with the possibility and definition of virtue and continuing on to a consideration of the actions that might promote it. To be on the path of intellectual and moral virtue is to be forever traveling on the path to the path – traversing a preliminary terrain that proves to be unexitable and becomes the effective substitute and counterpart of virtue itself.

For Ben Zoma, the pursuit of virtue becomes a series of unending tautologies. To become wise (he tells us), constantly learn from other people – become someone who is wise. To become strong and courageous, always overpower your baser inclinations: Become someone who is strong. To become wealthy, always be content with what you have. Then in one fell swoop you will have achieved what wealth is generally seen as an emblem of – supreme mastery and contentment. To be honored, enact for others what you hope they will display in relation to you: Honor them. More than that you cannot do. Instead of eliciting a content for the virtues that are central to his mishnah, Ben Zoma tells us to become the people who display these virtues. Ben Zoma's teaching conjures up an ethics of endless becoming – where the ethical purification and sublimation of our personalities is manifested as much in the ongoing movements that we engage in as it is where we periodically and transiently end up as a consequence of those movements.

With these general features of Ben Zoma's mishnah in view, let us micro-analyze each of the virtues that he discusses. The *Chochom* – the wise man – the person eager to pursue and cultivate wisdom, knowledge and truth – opens himself up to everyone and learns from all of the people he meets. There is a remarkable alchemy at work in the first section of Ben Zoma's mishnah. Wisdom, knowledge and truth, which seem at first blush to be metaphysical and epistemological categories, have been transformed into ethical ones. *Chochmah* is not a function of what one knows – but of how one acquires knowledge. If one is continually interacting with and learning from other people, then Ben Zoma stamps what is imbibed from them as *Chochmah*. The openness and receptivity with which one approaches others – not the precise content of what is acquired from them – makes one into a *Chochom*. The content of knowledge, wisdom and truth is endlessly controversial and contestable. Closure does not appear to be attainable. Wisdom resides in how one goes about conducting the search – not in specific results that are obtainable from it. If one is able to engage in conversation with others, converting all of one's partners and interlocutors into teachers as well as students, then one is wise. Wisdom consists in learning how to cultivate the resources of process and in learning how to inhabit and to navigate the plane of process, without succumbing to the temptation of trying to dissolve it and move beyond it. Ethics, the domain of the interim (what do I do now?) and the interpersonal, usurps the roles of the metaphysical and the epistemological, the realms of the enduring and the transcendent. The *Chochom* is a person whose life enacts and dramatizes that substitution. The *Chochom*, the mode of being in the world of someone who actively pursues wisdom, displaces *Chochma* – the consummated doctrines expressive of wisdom and of truth – in the worldview of Ben Zoma.

What are the theological antecedents and models of this displacement? The chief ones are the monotheistic conception of God and its implications. The Absolute Singularity and Uniqueness of the Biblical God, which debars us from inserting Him into any comparative human context for the sake of elucidating His essence and attributes, suggests that there is no humanly-graspable discursive truth that we can affirm about Him. We can only follow the large-scale injunction of *V'Halachta B'Drachav* – walking in His ways, which is to say, trying to translate to the extent possible into the fabric of our own lives the necessarily metaphorical descriptions of God (that He is Merciful, Compassionate, etc.) found in the Biblical text. Monotheistic theology immediately supplants knowing with doing, and Ben Zoma follows suit by configuring *Chochma* as a continuous activity, rather than as a finite lore or body of precepts.

In his next clause, Ben Zoma seeks to define and theorize strength. Here, too, as in his delineation of wisdom, strength is not reducible to a finite set of resources or abilities, but is rather an ongoing activity that is only explicable in an interpersonal human context. Strength is identified with subduing one's personal inclination (*Yetzer Harah*) to explode, get angry, behave aggressively, counterproductively, to blow it all for the sake of achieving an intense sense of immediate emotional relief. Since our provocations to anger most often come from our interactions with other human beings, strength (like wisdom) is envisioned by Ben Zoma as a virtue that is cultivated and expressed in an interpersonal setting.

Strength in all of its different dimensions – physical, emotional, psychological, whatever confers upon us the magnitudes of power to which we can lay claim – is not something objectively given or measurable. It is a function of relationship. What it takes to subdue the *Yetzer Harah* will vary with the circumstances and with the nature of the provocation. There are no *a priori* definable and delimitable sets of strategies that are guaranteed to work to contain and defeat the *Yetzer Harah*. Just as with wisdom, that it is the fluency of our movement from one person to the next in being able to discern and absorb what they have to teach that defines the wise person, so, too, with regard to strength, it is the fluency of our movement in warding off provocations attendant to our interactions with one person after another that solidifies our identity as strong. It is not something discursively statable that is at the core of wisdom or strength. It is rather factors pertaining to how we structure and organize our mode of being in the world – how we attempt, as it were, to master our movement through time – that determine the extent and depth of our wisdom and strength.

The Rav (the acronym for Rabbeinu Ovadiah MiBartenura, one of the classical commentators on the Mishnah) has a reading of the prooftext of the second clause of Ben Zoma's mishnah that casts his teaching in the second clause (and its relationship to the first clause) in a new light. This is the way the Rav construes the prooftext to Ben Zoma's second clause:

> This is the meaning of the verse: "He who is slow to anger is better than the strong man, and a master of his passions is better than a conqueror of

The tension between Levinas' ethics and his political theory 219

a city." Being slow to anger is better when it comes from the strength associated with subduing the *Yetzer* – not from softness of nature. And being a master of his passions is good when it comes from a conqueror of the city, from a king who after he captures a city and there come before him the people who rebelled against him, masters his passions and does not kill them.[57]

The Hebrew preposition *Mem* in the verse from Proverbs that Ben Zoma cites as prooftext to his second clause is ambiguous: It can be read as "than" or "from." In the standard reading of the verse, the *Mem* is translated as "than.": The person who is slow to anger is better *than* the strong man, and the master of his passions is better *than* a conqueror of a city. The Rav substitutes "from" for "than." Softness and compassion are best coming *from* someone who is strong.

The Rav's reading of the verse from Proverbs works to recast the meaning of Ben Zoma's second clause – and its relationship to his first clause – by highlighting the dialectical interplay between categorial opposites in the second clause, whose counterparts can now also be discerned in the first clause. From the Rav's perspective, the strength that Ben Zoma values is a function of "strength" going the distance in its drive toward self-realization and engaging in a movement of recoil that leads to its transformation into its dialectical opposite number – namely, compassion, empathy, softness. Strength pursued singlemindedly and monomaniacally often boomerangs and becomes counterproductive – as the strong man instills fear and awe in his enemies, causing them to beef up their strength, and thereby exacting a greater expenditure of strength on his own part (in order to vanquish them) in a never-ending spiral. In order for strength to realize its ends, it needs to transform itself into its opposite – to learn how to become soft and conciliatory – so as to keep the stakes lower, thereby rendering its ends more attainable. The *Yetzer Harah* pushes one to follow the inexorable, internal logic of strength: To go on raising the ante of confrontation with self and Others until both self and Other are destroyed. To follow the dialectically unmodulated dictates of strength is to be in the grip of a death instinct. It is only when strength begins to approximate to the identity of its other – namely, weakness, softness – that the ends endemic to its career in the world stand a chance of being realized. It is this phenomenon of approximation to its dialectical opposite number that Ben Zoma refers to as "subduing one's personal inclination." In doing this, one raids the armory of the opposing camp in one's consciousness and learns how to be giving, "soft" and conciliatory.

A comparable dialectical exchange is evident in the first clause of the mishnah. "Who is wise? Who learns from every person." The internal logic of the activity of pursuing knowledge, truth and wisdom pushes one toward closure. One generally feels that he has attained true knowledge when he understands things completely – when there are no loose ends and everything within his horizon of understanding hangs together. An acute irony and paradox emerges when we realize that the urge toward completeness is the approach most fully guaranteed to expose incompleteness. For example, the skeptic who is obsessed with the possibility of arriving at knowledge of the truth – even if the truth be skeptical (that we cannot know the truth) – is challenged by the self-referentialist dilemmas surrounding skepticism (to be properly skeptical requires one to be skeptical even of skepticism, so that extreme skepticism cannot be coherently formulated) into acknowledging the open-endednes of his quest: If the naturalization of contradiction is where we find ourselves, we need to await the ongoing returns of multiple communities of investigators in diverse fields of knowledge, operating over multiple generations, in order to see whether they corroborate this picture, thereby rendering alternate (non-Aristotelian, nonstandard) logics persuasive, or not. In the pursuit of knowledge, truth and wisdom, closure is transformed into openness as a means for realizing the imperative that closure was supposed to achieve. The dialectical movement that Ben Zoma's mishnah implicitly discerns in epistemology and metaphysics prefigures and overlaps with the dialectical movement that he perceives in ethics.

The background model for these dialectical exchanges to take place with regard to wisdom and strength is how the Rabbis envision the monotheistic God's relationship to the world He has created. If, as the prophet says, God's glory fills the whole world (Isaiah 6:3), how can there be room for anything else in the cosmos aside from God? The very existence of the world (and of human beings within it) constitutes a theological embarrassment – a worldly counter-series of data – to the Absolutely Unique, Singular, All-Powerful, All-Knowing and All-Compassionate monotheistic God. God's Oneness – the monotheistic believer can plausibly argue – not only precludes insertion of any one of His attributes within a comparative human context, it delegitimates and invalidates the possibility of the context. In order to reconcile the monotheistic God with a human world and human beings, a classic metaphor deployed by the Rabbis is to envision God as receding and withdrawing in order to make room for what is other than God – namely, the world and its inhabitants. As the Singular God, God is all-expansion. A world in which God coexists with his creations is a world marked by the withdrawal of God to make room for what is other than Himself.

On logical grounds, this metaphor cannot be about God without being inconsistent with the tenets of monotheism. If we project this *metaphor* concerning a dialectic between expansion and withdrawal onto God, then we are claiming to know that literally these terms carry no meaning in relation to Him. We then know something decisive and momentous about God, which the protocols of monotheism (emphasizing God's singularity and uniqueness) debar us from knowing. If the metaphysical distances separating us from God are yawning and unbridgeable, we not only do not know about Him what we thought we knew, but we also do not know what we do not know. The whole categorial dichotomy between literalism and metaphor gets shattered in relation to God.

The tension between Levinas' ethics and his political theory 221

Our major recourse at this point – endorsed by the Rabbis – is to shift the focus of the metaphor from God to human beings. The metaphor of expansion becoming withdrawal – of presence becoming absence – encapsulates and encodes for us how human beings operate in the world. For us, some of the dominant categories that we deploy to facilitate our mastery of and flourishing in the world – categories such as knowledge, truth, wisdom and strength – recede in favor of their dialectical opposites in order to enable us to wax maximally creative, and to bring means and ends into some kind of harmonious relation. The background dialectical exchange of monotheistic theology enables some of the dominant organizing categories of worldly human existence to click most appropriately and illuminatingly into place.

On the surface, there appears to be a hiatus between the first two clauses of Ben Zoma's mishnah and the final two clauses. The first clause is about the intellectual virtue called *Chochma* ("wisdom") and the second clause is about the moral virtue called *Gevurah* ("strength," "self-control," "courage," "self-mastery"). The gap between the first two clauses is closed (as we have seen) by the ethical reorientation of the first clause. Knowledge and wisdom in Ben Zoma's first clause are conceived as forms of ethical cultivation and mastery, which renders the transition to the second clause, officially dealing with a moral virtue – namely, *Gevurah* – smooth and intelligible. A jarring hiatus looms, however, with regard to the third and fourth clauses. *Osher* ("wealth") and *Kavod* ("honor" or "reputation") are neither intellectual nor moral virtues. The cultivation and attainment of one or the other – or both – appears to have nothing to do with ethics, but forms rather the subject matter of a sociological statement, inference or generalization: So-and-so is wealthy; so-and-so is honored (has a very good reputation within the community). Or, alternatively: The majority of people worldwide are preoccupied with the pursuit of wealth and honor. How do we relate the latter two clauses in Ben Zoma's mishnah to the first two clauses?

A consistent motif of all four clauses is how with regard to the abstract entities that Ben Zoma deals with – wisdom, strength, wealth and honor – the crucial factor in making sense of them is not to focus upon their independently arrived at and ascertainable cognitive content but rather upon what human beings bring to them. Wisdom is not a matter of what we passively receive from others (officially-designated teachers or peers), but of what we actively conjure up through our interactions with all human beings. Similarly, strength is not a function of the cultivation and application of a set of raw precepts as to what constitutes strength and of the best strategies for garnering it, but of how we navigate the challenges of daily life that are partially the result of our improvisations of the moment. In Ben Zoma's moral universe, both the designation of the challenge and the formulation of the response are at least partially innovations in relation to context, which cannot be codified or charted in advance.

Statements concerning people's attainments under the rubrics of wealth and honor, which on the surface have nothing to do with intellectual or moral virtue, can now be seen as straightforwardly continuous with the manner in which Ben Zoma has analyzed those virtues. Ben Zoma utilizes his deconstructions of wisdom and strength as a model for deconstructing two pervasive sociological phenomena that appear to have nothing to do with intellectual and moral virtue – namely, wealth and honor – so that an ethical dimension might be disclosed and highlighted even within them. The worldly phenomena of wealth and honor can be analyzed from the same perspective as the virtues of wisdom and strength, and then a strange alchemy occurs. When we look at wisdom and courage from the perspective of what we bring to them, their character as intellectual and moral virtues, respectively, seems to be jeopardized, and then we need (as we have seen) to conceptualize in novel ways how they retain their character as virtues. When we approach the ostensibly non-moral phenomena of wealth and honor from this perspective, exactly the opposite effect results. We are able to see them, perhaps for the first time, as moral phenomena. If wealth is about the achievement of a certain sense of satiety and serenity, then these concomitances or outcomes of wealth can imaginatively (on moral grounds) be willed into existence, so that one enjoys the functional equivalents of wealth without having to engage in the endless squabbles and scrambles that deplete and undermine one's emotional and moral resources. Wealth can be "moralized" and "humanized" by emphasizing the human factors that we bring to it (its pursuit and accumulation) and hope to get out of it. Once wealth is reconstructed in this way, we are absolved of the need to physically and morally degrade ourselves to the extent necessary to physically acquire it.

The same sort of deconstruction-reconstruction is possible with regard to honor. Honor is cherished by human beings because it affirms and enhances our sense of self-worth. When others see us in the way we would like to be seen, we are more prone to believe that we have the qualities that we like to tell ourselves we have. Ben Zoma theorizes a strategic shortcut to the emotional rewards that typically accrue to a person who is being honored. Our sense of self-worth can be equally reinforced and enhanced – but, in all likelihood, with a greater sense of honesty and self-assurance – if we are able to muster the requisite self-confidence and aplomb to honor Others and heap praises upon them. I must really be good if I don't feel threatened or undermined by placing a favorable spotlight upon someone else. By giving, I accomplish the same emotional and psychological results as receiving – without the accompanying anxieties and self-doubts. Since giving honor to Others is in many key respects functionally equivalent to receiving honor from them and is purchased in moral terms at a much lower price – I do not have to jeopardize my moral standing by doing all of those things, such as accumulating huge sums of money, and all that is often entailed in achieving this result, that catapult people into a position of being honored by Others – then Ben Zoma advocates that we should opt for honoring Others rather than being honored ourselves.

What I have just described is the downward current of movement in Ben Zoma's mishnah: How his deconstructive strategy applied to the intellectual and ethical virtues of wisdom and strength and transferred to the worldly phenomena of wealth and honor works to elevate and "moralize" them. There is also, I believe, an upward current of movement in Ben Zoma's mishnah: The sociological focus on wealth and honor in the second half of the mishnah translates into a sociological vein of analysis applied to intellectual and moral virtue in the first half of the mishnah. Instead of knowledge, truth and wisdom being a function of an indubitably self-evident set of principles rigorously applied to situations and problems emerging in the world, Ben Zoma suggests that both the categories of knowledge and the data that are generated on their basis result from what we learn from other people. Nothing is fixed or given in advance. How to approach and define what we want to know – as well as what we claim to know once the search has been completed to one extent or another – are a function of the cues, signals and overt concepts that we pick up from other people. There are no preordained boundaries separating knowledge from fantasy – products of reason from products of the imagination – and *a fortiori* what comes under these rubrics is not known or validated in advance. The enterprise of knowledge is deceptive. What look like autonomously chartered and authorized modes of inquiry built upon well-established, indigenously (internal to each discipline) developed sets of principles turn out upon further scrutiny to be much more informally and contingently grounded. Inspirations, possibilities and metaphors taken over from our conversations with other people often have a lot more to do with the generation of knowledge than the strict cultivation and perpetuation of previous lines of knowledge. Sociological reports concerning how and what people are learning are often more directly constitutive and revealing of knowledge than more formalistically-structured models that treat the other and others of knowledge as insular domains.

Something analogous appears to be the case with regard to strength. What will work to subdue our inclinations will vary from person to person, circumstance to circumstance, exigency to exigency. There are no *a priori* sets of principles that codify what strength is – or how it is acquired or maintained. It is only sociological reports on our interactions with the others of strength (temptation, weakness, softness) that stand a chance of reflecting back to us and to Others how we are generating strength and by what means we are sustaining it.

Ben Zoma, in all four clauses of his mishnah, projects human beings as radically limited and impoverished creatures. He envisions the pursuit of knowledge, truth and wisdom as being a collective enterprise dependent upon the openness and goodwill of all people. Ben Zoma seems to entertain the image of human beings having to collectively make do (by learning from and buttressing each other) in the absence of authoritative voices of reason and unambiguous and indisputable renderings of tradition. We all need "to get by with the help of our friends." From a countervailing perspective to what

I developed earlier, Ben Zoma's mishnah can be read as implicitly plotting a descent from logically tenuous contact with Others into the deepest recesses of the self. There is a logical conundrum attendant to the first clause of Ben Zoma's mishnah. If wisdom consists in learning from every person, then where does the content that any given person is learning from some other person come from? If we are all always learning from Others, then what do we have to teach to Others? In his equalization of all of our positions as students, he seems to have undermined the capacity of any one of us to teach. If learning is as endlessly regressive as Ben Zoma envisions (with each person learning from all other people), where is there ontological space for the carving-out of the first teaching-content that other people can learn from – and the generation of subsequent teaching-content?

This paradox surrounding Ben Zoma's assigning primacy to learning over teaching is evocative of the paradox surrounding negative theology. Negative theology, by being overwhelmingly preoccupied with delineating what God is not (He does not possess knowledge the way human beings possess knowledge; He is not powerful in the ways that human beings are powerful, etc.), confronts the paradox that unless there is some conceptually accessible core to God's Essence all of negative theology's disownings and discountings of God's attributes seem to lack an object to be about. If God subsists only in the discountings, then there is nothing to discount. Analogously, in the case of Ben Zoma, if intellectual pursuits are all a matter of learning and not of teaching, then one confronts the logical perplexity of being able to pin down and delimit what is being taught. If everything that we know is a matter of learning from Others, then the content of learning has disappeared into thin air.

One way around this paradox is to say that just as negative theology does not put us conceptually in contact with God – not even to intelligibly and coherently inform us what God is not – but only pushes to the forefront of our consciousness the logico-linguistic limitations that put God out of reach for us, so, too, Ben Zoma's reflections on knowledge, truth and wisdom as a learning from Others which is logically undecipherable by us brings to the center of our attention how mysterious and inexplicable – how egoistically mired and tainted – the whole process of learning is. By formulating a theory of knowledge that is unexitable for any given learner (student) in terms of its not being able to account for his receiving access to a finite body of material to learn, Ben Zoma's theory, on a deeper level, seems to be about the mysteriousness of the whole learning phenomenon in relation to a self that cannot be coherently theorized as exiting or migrating from itself sufficiently to imbibe an indubitable content from outside its own ambit. Just as knowledge of Divine things remains inscrutable to us from the perspective of negative theology, knowledge of human things remains impenetrable to us from the perspective of Ben Zoma's statement.

The descent into the self is deepened in the subsequent clauses of Ben Zoma's mishnah. Strength is not a matter of triumph over Others, but rather a function of mastery over the adversarial and fragmenting impulses within the self. The primary data that confront the self in dealing with situations and threats that appear to be external to it are its own motley assortment of images, thoughts, impulses and feelings, out of which both the identification and the specification of the threatening Other – and the response to him – are constructed. Similarly, wealth is at least as much a matter of nurturing and managing an internal environment as it is a function of inhabiting an external social scene. In many respects, the first is the phenomenological correlative of the second. Honor, as well, has its locus in the self mobilizing its energies and seizing the initiative in honoring other people – not in a passive assimilation of encomiums received from unproblematic Others.

In the light of the later clauses of Ben Zoma's mishnah, we can say that knowledge (the ostensible subject matter of his first clause) is for him a matter of the continual and proliferating self-bisections of the self, increasing the points of leverage from which to imagine and project a world beyond the self, with its multitude of Others that can only be improvisatorially and fleetingly accessed by a self-referentially benighted self.

Notes

1 Levinas' 1934 essay, "Quelques reflexions sur la philosophie de l'hitlerisme," *Esprit*, Volume 2, Number 26, pp. 199–208, presents a staunch defense of philosophical and political liberalism. In this essay, Levinas says that "In the world of liberalism, man is not weighed down by History in choosing his destiny. He does not experience the possibilities open to him as a series of restless powers that seethe within him and already push down a determined path. For him, they are only logical possibilities that present themselves to a dispassionate reason that makes choices while forever keeping its distance." (Emmanuel Levinas, "Reflections on the Philosophy of Hitlerism," *Critical Inquiry* Volume 17, Number 1 (Autumn 1990), pp. 63–71, on p. 66. This article constitutes a translation of the original 1934 article.) *Totality and Infinity* has quite a number of passages extolling the virtues of liberal individuality. The following is one example: "Activity does not derive its meaning and its value from an ultimate and unique goal, as though the world formed one system of use-references whose term touches our very existence. The world answers to a set of autonomous finalities which ignore one another. To enjoy without utility, in pure loss, gratuitously, without referring to anything else, in pure expenditure – this is the human." (p. 133).
2 Jean-Jacques Rousseau, *The Social Contract*. Trans. Maurice Cranston. (Baltimore: Penguin Books, 1968), Book I, Chapter 7 (p. 64).
3 This paragraph is taken from my book, *Michael Oakeshott's Skepticism*, pp. 190–191.
4 Levinas, *Totality and Infinity*, p. 80.
5 Levinas, *Otherwise than Being*, p. 140.
6 Ibid., p. 137; italics in original.
7 Babylonian Talmud, *Abodah Zarah*. Folio 35b to the end. Trans. Abraham Cohen. (London: Soncino Press, 1988), p. 54b.
8 See the commentary of the Tosafot Yom Tov (Yom-Tov Lipmann Heller [1578–1654])on this mishnah in the standard printed editions of *Mishnayot: Avodah Zarah*, Chapter 4, mishnah 7.
9 Friedrich Nietzsche, *On the Advantage and Disadvantage of History for Life*, p. 40.

10 "From the verse 'And the Lord said: Behold, there is a place by Me' (Exodus 33:21), we may infer that God is the place of the world, and that His world is not His place." – *Pesikta Rabbati*. Trans. William G. Braude. (New Haven: Yale University Press, 1968), Volume 1; Piska 21; Paragraph 10; p. 431.
11 Maimonides,*The Code,* Book 1: The Book of Knowledge, The Laws of Repentance, Chapter 5, Paragraph 5, p. 87b.
12 "For the thoughts are to the desires as scouts and spies to range abroad and find the way to the things desired." Thomas Hobbes, *Leviathan*. Ed. Michael Oakeshott. (Oxford: Basil Blackwell, 1946), Chapter 8, p. 46.
13 See my discussion of Maimonides and Hobbes on "Reason and the Passions" in *Skepticism, Belief, and the Modern*, pp. 112–122.
14 Emmanuel Levinas, *Collected Philosophical Papers*. Trans. Alphonso Lingis. (Dordrecht: Martinus Nijhoff, 1987), pp. 15–23.
15 Ibid., p. 16.
16 Ibid., p. 17.
17 Ibid.
18 Ibid., p. 19.
19 Ibid., p. 18.
20 Ibid., p. 20.
21 Ibid.
22 Ibid., p. 21.
23 Ibid.
24 Ibid., p. 22.
25 Ibid.
26 Psalms 8:4–6. *The ArtScroll Tehillim*, p. 13; translation amended on my part.
27 *Pirkei Avos* 2:21.
28 Levinas, *Otherwise than Being*, p. 140.
29 Ibid., p. 146.
30 Genesis 1:27.
31 Introduction by John Wild to Levinas, *Totality and Infinity*, p. 17. The understanding in Plato that can be taken to prefigure Levinas is "Plato's well-known statement at *Republic* 509 that the good lies beyond being." (Ibid.).
32 See my argument earlier in this book and also my discussion of Plato's Third Man Argument in my book, *Skepticism, Belief, and the Modern*, pp. 2–4.
33 Popper, *Conjectures and Refutations*, p. 317.
34 Exodus 19:17.
35 *Pentateuch and Rashi's Commentary (Exodus)*, Trans. M. Rosenbaum and A. M. Silbermann, p. 100. The Midrashic text that Rashi cites is also found in the Babylonian Talmudic tractate *Shabbath* (88a). It is the Talmudic discussion in *Shabbath* 88a and 88b that constitutes the focal point of Levinas' chapter on "The Temptation of Temptation" in *Nine Talmudic Readings*. Trans. Annette Aronowicz. (Bloomington: Indiana University Press, 1990), pp. 30–50.
36 Levinas, *Nine Talmudic Readings*, p. 31.
37 Ibid., p. 35.
38 Ibid., p. 43.
39 Ibid., pp. 49–50.
40 Levinas, *Otherwise than Being*, p. 91; citing Numbers 11:12.
41 Babylonian Talmud, *Yebamoth* 49b.
42 Levinas, *Otherwise than Being*, Chapter 3, EN 24 (p. 192).
43 *Pentateuch with Rashi's Commentary: Numbers*. Trans. M. Rosenbaum and A. M. Silbermann. (Jerusalem, 1973), p. 60a.
44 Contained in the opening of the Tannaitic Midrash, *Sifra* – and included in the daily liturgy as the last item for recitation before the official start of the morning prayers.

45 Numbers 12:3.
46 The Babylonian Talmud in *Erubin* 13b raises the question that if as the Talmud itself states the differing positions of the School of Shammai and the School of Hillel in a wide range of halakhic controversies stretching across the whole Babylonian Talmud *both* represent the word of the living God, why were the followers of Hillel deserving of having the law fixed in accordance with their views in all cases? In strictly epistemological, truth-oriented terms, the law could have gone either way. Why were Beth Hillel elevated to their special position of halakhic authority? The Talmud's response in *Erubin* is that they were *Aluvin*, which means humble, willing to overlook slights and even insults to themselves. By way of illustration of this latter point the Talmud says that Beth Hillel studied and transmitted not only their aguments and positions, but those of their halakhic adversaries, Beth Shammai, as well, and always cited Beth Shammai's teachings before their own.
47 Numbers 12:8.
48 Deuteronomy 28:9. The relevant Talmudic and Midrashic sources that elaborate a negative-theological reading of this text are the following: Babylonian Talmud, *Sotah* 14a; *Ketuboth* 111b; *Shabbath* 133b;*Vayikrah Rabbah* 25:3; *Sifre*, Piska 49.
49 *Hebrew-English Edition of the Babylonian Talmud: Berakoth*. Trans. Maurice Simon. (London: Soncino Press, 1984), p. 58a.
50 *ArtScroll Siddur*, p. 107.
51 The coalescence of God's doing with his being remains inscrutable, and it is impenetrable by us.
52 These attributes are delineated in Exodus 34: 6–7.
53 Hebrew letters have numerical value. They are simultaneously numbers.
54 See the discussion in Nehama Leibowitz, *Studies in Bereshit [Genesis]*. Trans. Aryeh Newman. (Jerusalem: World Zionist Organization, 1972), pp. 460–461.
55 Maimonides, *The Code*, Book 1: The Book of Knowledge, The Laws of Repentance, Chapter 2, Paragraph 1.
56 *Pirkei Avos*, p. 35.
57 *Mishnayot Yachin U'Boaz with 51 Additions*, Volume 7. (New York: Pardes, 1953), p. 199; my translation.

Index

Abaye 136
action 7, 11 21, 23, 52, 63–64, 104, 109–10, 116, 127, 180, 201, 215, 218–19; and deferral 102; and ethics 63; God's 118, 212, 215; God is 201; and identity 205; moral 89, 195; original 215; political 76; primacy of 201; principle of 100; and virtue 216; *see also* doing
activity *see* action, doing
Adorno, Theodor 201
Akiva, Rabbi 193; as a theological precursor to Hillel 118–22, 137; on the Golden Rule 113–16; on *Avot* 3:18 116–18; on totality and infinity 111–16
Alexandri, Rav 93–94, 96
alterity 57, 172–73
Anselm, St. 20
Antonio, Robert J. 73, 76
Aristotle 24, 99, 198; on friendship 89; and heterotypical predication 104; and the law of the excluded middle 74; and the theory of the mean 88–91
attaining great heights (Gadlut) 101
authenticity 16, 84, 111–12, 172, 202, 211
authoritarianism 140
Avenarius, Richard 164–65
Avot and Ben Zoma's mishnah at 4:1 215–25; R. Akiva's mishnah at 3:18 116–18; and R. Levitas' mishnah 91–96; and R. Tarfon 199; and the Theory of the Mean 91

bad conscience 128–29
beauty: as the fitting 104–5, 107–8, 114; in Hobbes' state of nature 189; and madness 54; nature of 104, 108

being and becoming 59–60, 197
belief (Bitachon) 4, 102, 136, 145, 199, 211–12
Ben Azzai 114–15
Ben Zoma 215–25
Benjamin, Walter 55–56
between-the-two (Zwischen) 48–50
beyond, the 181, 183
blessing and blessedness 27–29
Brandom, Robert 79
Buber, Martin: and dialogism 13–14; Levinas' critique of 46–50, 52, 56–58
Buddhism 61–62
bundle theory of identity 60

causality and induction 59, 164, 181
Chaim of Brisk, Reb 176–80
charisma 112, 188, 202
Christianity: fundamentalism in the US 103; and the Holocaust 185; imagery 174, 176, 183–84; and Judaism 5, 199; and Levinas 174–75, 188; and liberalism 200; morality 128–29; perfectionist ethics of 2, 7
circular mirrors 161, 202
circularity: of affirmation and belief 145; and Aristotle 89–90; and constitutional regime 64; Derrida 60; and dialogue form 141; and epistemology 67, 130; and generalized agnosticism 67–69, 71, 89–91, 130; and Heidegger 172; and Husserl 164; metaphor of 47; and Nietzsche 130; and nominalism 145; and normativity 68; and Plato 140–41, 145–46, 153–55, 157–61; and political obligation 65; and theory 140
civil matters (*Dinei Mamonot*) 7
Cogito argument 16–17, 19–21, 77, 164

Collingwood, R. G. 78
communitarianism 64, 188–89
community of believers 111–12
compassion 8, 25, 29–31, 52, 57, 185, 210, 218–20
concrete and abstract 56, 118, 132, 135
consistency *see* reflexivity
constructivism 82
content and context 78–79
contractarianism *see* social contract theory
contradiction normalized 51, 71, 116
convergence and divergence 157–59, 162, 203
conversation *see* discourse
courage 90, 216–17, 221–22
creation 8; and givenness 201; in God's image 109, 114–15, 117–18, 122, 201
creativity 101–2, 131, 133, 146, 201, 221

Dallmayr, Fred 13, 52, 55
Danto, Arthur 129
deconstruction: and categories of flux 158; geneological 129; and Hillel 121; internal dynamics of 98; practice of 51; principles of 50–51; and the self 205; and sociology 222–23; and substance and process 108; of texts 50; in the Torah 117–18; and wisdom 223
Delhomme, Jeanne 170–71, 182
democracy 35–36, 140, 157
depression 99
Derrida, Jacques: and a community of the question 41, 50–61; and *difference* 60–61; and Levinas 50–53; and the Other 55–56; on philosophizing 14; and Plato 53–56
Descartes, Rene 164; and the Cogito 16–17, 19–21, 77, 164; and Levinas 19–23; and nominalistic deflation 21; and ontological argument 19–21
diachrony and synchrony 23, 25, 32, 51, 174, 181–82
diagnosis and resolution 183–85
dialogue: as form 13–14, 58, 61–62, 104–5, 108–9, 141, 161–62; internal and external 84, 202; philosophy as 13; soul's silent 48
difference 60–61
discourse 32, 204–5; and Derrida 50; diachronous nature of 182; and dialogue 162; dilemmas surrounding 83; and ethics 63; about humanity 160; grounded in linguistics 79; and love 54–55; nature of 53; oral and written 38, 204; and the Other 24, 31, 161; as philosophy 159; theological 136, 159; theoretical 56; and time 162; *see also* linguistics, dialogue
disruption 41, 173, 182
Divine commandmants (Mitzvot), conformity to 7–8, 29, 95–96, 119, 175, 199
Divine, center of the 118
doing (*Asiya*) 6–8, 28–30, 34, 52–53; and becoming 6; and being 7–8; God and human 28–29; and justice 64; of Mitzvah 7; priority of 69; as theory 63–64; *see also* action
dualism 60, 213

Eco, Umberto 157–58
ego (I) and self 57–58
egoism 5, 15, 48, 97, 224
Eleazar, Rabbi 206
Eliyahu of Vilna, Gaon Rav 92–93
elsewhere(s): evil inclination as 109–10; and indeterminacy 204–5; and philosophy 159–61; in Plato's theory 63; of what one wants 101
empiricism 60–61
endless deferral: and action 102–3; and empiricism 60; and explanation 169; of human present 41; and Judaism 137; and liberalism 35; and ontology 3; and power 33–34, 36, 76–77; and skepticism 46; and the subject 127; of truth 108
epistemological perspectivism 73–76
Epstein, Baruch Halevi 114
equanimity *see* temperance
eternal recurrence 182
ethics: Aristotle's 88–91; Christian 174–76; and circularity 67–69; and epistemology 67–69; and generalized agnosticism 63–69; and ideology 88–91; Levinasasian 98–103, 174–76, 188–89; Maimonidean 98–103; monotheistic 215, 217, 220–21; and otherwise than being 164–67; and political theory 188–89; primacy of 12–15; Rabbinic 98–103; routes to the 11; and the same 27–31; the Talmud on 27–31; and theory 27–31, 88–91; and totality and infinity 11–12
evidence, criterion of 164
evil inclination (Yetzer Harah) 109–11
exceedingly, be (Me'od, me'od) 91–92

230 *Index*

exculpation and justification 69–71
experience and reason 171–72

fascism 157–58
flux, everything is in 146–49, 158
forced to be free 188
Foucault, Michel 76–77
freedom: and Christian imagery 184; and Divine deliverance 44; of God and beasts 198–99; hither side of 174; and ideology 141; and institutions 196; and love 55; and necessity 82; and obligation 192; primacy of 193, 195; radical 184, 194–95, 207; and substitution 198; and violence 195–97; within and beyond being 171
Freud, Sigmund 65–66
friends of solitude 53, 55
friendship 24, 52–53; 89
Fuller, Steven 78

Gadamer, Hans-Georg 70, 78
Gamliel Beribbi, Rav 30
generalized agnosticism 69–71; and circularity 67–69, 71, 89–91, 130; and ethics 63–69; and Hobbes 36, 52–53; and Same/Other 63; and skepticism 3; *see also* negative theology, skepticism
golden mean *see* middle way
golden rule (love thy neighbor as thyself) 61–62, 113–16, 120–22
Goulder, Alvin 78

Hampshire, Stuart 158–59
hastening of the end 104
haughtiness (Gaavah) 91–93, 96, 98, 101–2
haughtiness of spirit (Gasut Haruach) 93
Heidegger, Martin 12–14, 164–65, 171–73, 182
Heraclitus 146–47, 149–50
Hermogenes 145
Hillel: and the golden rule 115; and moral ontology 96–97; as a precursor to Rabbi Akiva 118–21; theological positions of 137; and the whole Torah 114
historicism 62, 132–33
hither side of being 200
Hitlerism 200
Hiyya b. Ashi, Rav 93–94
Hobbes, Thomas: generalized agnosticism 36, 52–53; and liberalism 34–36, 198; and modernity 11; and openness 129; on passion 32–33; on power 12, 32–34; and the social contract 189; and the state of nature 189
Holocaust 185
horizontal transcendence 4–5, 35–36, 41, 51, 192–93
human condition, the 110–11
human nature 73, 84, 171, 215
Hume, David 59–61, 66, 181
humility (Anavah): and fear of God 6; as foundational Rabbinic virtue 5–6, 92, 98; between haughtiness and lowliness of mind 92; and Hillel 96–98; and lowliness of mind 96; Maimonides on 92, 96, 98–103; Moses' 209; and negative theology and skepticism 102–3; and the Otherness of God 111; and pride 99–100
Huna, Rav 93–94
Husserl, Edmund 13–14, 56, 164–66, 171–73, 182
hyperbole 57

Ibn Ezra, Abraham 42
Identity 1, 15, 25, 53, 57, 60, 127, 188, 201, 205, 218; *see also* Same/Other
ideology: in Levinas 38–40, 104; and theory 38–40, 71–73, 104
idolatry 102, 193–94
I-It and I-Thou 46–48, 50, 57–58
implicit norms or practices 79
Imsoni, Simeon 111–12
incarnation 164, 174–75, 180–84, 188, 190, 196, 201–2, 205
individualism 35, 177, 188
institutions 196
instrumentalism 82
intentional acts, correlates of 165–66
interconnections 39
interpretation 116–17
interventionism 198
Isaac (Akeidah), binding of 43–44
Isaac, Rav Nahman b. 93

Jethro 112
Johanan, Rabbi 49
Joseph, Rav 136
Judah, Rabbi 95–96
Judaism 135
justice 60, 64

Kant, Immanuel 35
Keller, Evelyn Fox 78

Kenny, Anthony 19–20
killing 178–79
kindness (Chesed) 5–6, 8–9, 29, 98, 210, 212
kingdom of ends 22
knowledge: of any given human present 41; authoritative 76; and (un)certainty 40, 73; and consistency 74–75; and discourse 55; ethical 90; and justification 70; limitations of 199; McDowell's account of 71; moderate perspectivism 74; and neutrality 73, 84; and power 82; sociology of 80; objective 67–68; and reality 63; representational theory of 73; and skepticism 34, 67; tacit 53; and theory 72; and uncertainty 73
Kolakowski, Leszek 164–67
Kripke, Saul 59
Kuhn, Thomas 77

language: and beauty in the world 140; and behaviorism 142; construction of 142; and discourses 79; and ethical consciousness 61; in explanation and description 169; and God's creation 118; and God's existence 21; limitations of 24; and the mind 70; and negative theology 41; and nominalism 153; and the Ontological Argument 19–20; and postmodernism 75; pre- or post- 162–63; and Quine 176–77, 180; and referential delimitation 177; and the Self/Other distinction 58; and sensory particulars 60; and words and things 69
Lamed (L) 122
Leibowitz, Yeshayahu 119
Letter of Ramban (*Iggeret HaRamban*) 5–6
Levi, R. Joshua b. 27–28
liberalism 41, 43, 104, 193, 195; and Christianity 200; classical 1; and democracy 35, 140, 157; and the good 66; Hobbes and 33–34, 36, 195; in Levinasian perspective 33–38; Machiavelli and 33–34, 36; and modernity, 11–12; and neutrality 103; and politics 36, 65, 172, 188–89, 198; religious 49; and skepticism 197; and the state 34–35; and the Talmud 27
limitations of reason 14, 16
linguistics *see* language
literalism 82

logical atomism 80
lover and beloved 53–55
lowliness of mind (*Shiflut Ha'Daat*) 94–95
lowliness of spirit (*Shiflut Haruach*) 91–92
Lyotard, Jean-Francois 74

Mach, Ernest 164–65
Machiavelli: and Levinas 33–36; and modernity 11–12; and power 12, 33–34, 126–27
MacIntyre, Alasdair 103
Maimonides 7, 15–17, 214; *Code* 30–31; on freedom 194–95; and horizontal transcendence 41–44; and Levinas 43–46, 98–103; on the naming of God 120–21; and the Other 43–46
manna 135–36
masochism 115, 126
McDowell, John 69–71
means, interminableness of the 119
Meinong's Pure Object 19
Meir, Rabbi 181
memory (q-) and experience 58–59
metanarrativity 74
method 78, 132, 141, 151, 165
middle way 91–92
mildness 88–90
modal thought 171
modernity 11–12, 33, 38, 75, 103
moment(s): of action 215; diachronic 182; and flux 149; as mildness 88; next 199; originary 190–91, 198–200; of palpable containment 101; persistent stationary 38, 40; power as foundation of 128; pre-theoretical 189–91; present 36, 64; quintessentially human 157; of Revelation 204–8; Salvation 199–200; and the Self/Other 125, 190–91; as the only source of knowledge 133
monotheism 40–41, 157–59
morals *see* ethics
Morgan, Michael 175
Moses 181
multivalued logics 4
mundane and sacred, the 136
mysticism; and under-determination 3
myth 131–32
Myth of the Given 69–71

Nagel, Thomas 35, 75
Nahmanides 5–6

232 *Index*

narrativity and facticity 159
Natanson, Maurice 78
negative theology: and God 2; and linguistics 41; Maimonides on 13–14, 55–56; and paradox 3, 224; and skepticism 2–3; *see also* generalized agnosticism, skepticism
neutrality 35, 73, 84, 103
Nietzsche 1, 12, 53, 200; on Dionysus and Apollo 131; and generalized agnosticism 128; on knowledge 104; on Plato 78; on power 66, 77, 126, 133–34; and ressentiment 126–28, 184, 201; and the Self 128–31, 201; and skeptical idealism 129–30; and totality and infinity 127–28, 131–34
nominalism 20–21, 59–60, 82, 143–45, 150–55, 198
normalized contradiction 4, 51
normativity 79
noumenal selves 35

objectivism 115, 132–33, 147
One, the 52, 105, 146, 150, 158
ontological argument 19–21
Other: affirmation of 200–202; and being 189–93; metaphorical 109–11; and others 43–46; and the self 31–33; subordination to 6; *see also* Same/Other
otherwise than being 12–13, 22–24, 172, 182–83, 214
Otherwise than Being 2, 5, 18, 23, 57, 164, 170–71, 173–76, 180–81, 185, 193, 202–3, 205, 207
ought and can 67
Ovadia MiBartenura, Rabbeinu 92
overly meek person (Shfal-Ruach) 101

paganism 157–58
Paine, Thomas 133
paradigms 77
paradox: of creation 102; epistemological 99–100; of explanation 3, 39, 169; of knowledge 151, 153; in Levinas' thought 56; of monotheistic belief 4–5, 158; and negative theology 3, 224; and the One 52; of power 33; of reflexivity 148, 151; of skepticism 4–5, 98; in the theory of ideas 105; and Ben Zoma 224
Parfit, Derek 58–62, 65–67
Parmenides 146, 149–50
parsimony 167–68, 180, 183

particulars: discrete 143–44; and Form 105
passion 32, 131, 171–72, 188, 195, 218
passivity: Aristotle on 90–91; in Christian ethics 174–75, 180–85; in Levinasian ethics 174–75, 180–85, 188, 190, 196, 199, 201, 205, 208–9; phenomenological description of 164
patience *see* temperance
peace (Shalom) 136–38
performative contradiction 99
phenomenological description 46–48
phenomenology 78
philosophizing 14
philosophy 33, 173; analytical 176; beginning of 157; and categorization 11, 216; discourse called 159; discrediting of 21; limitation of 13; as modal thought 171; of science 77–78; 81–83, 104, 132, 166–68; and skepticism 181–82
Pirkei Avot *see* Avot
Plato: on beauty 104–5, 107–8; and circular mirrors 161, 202; circularity 140–41, 145–46, 157–61; *Cratylus* 106–7, 141–46, 150–53, 160; and Derrida 53–56; and dialogue form 104–5, 107–9, 149, 159–62, 202; elsewhere 159–61; and flux 146–49, 158; *Hippias Major* 104, 106–9; 140, 146; and infinity 53–55; 105–6, 109; and Levinas 53–56; and nominalism 144–45, 150–55; *Parmenides* 12, 52, 69, 105, 146, 149–50, 158, 202; *Phaedrus* 53–55, 89, 146, 151; and the political 160–61; and process and substance 106–7, 159; and reflexivity 104, 109, 116, 143–44, 147, 150–53, 155, 160; *Republic* 104–6, 140–41, 159–61; and the Same/Other distinction 24, 54; and skepticism 140–41; and Socrates as midwife 146, 155–57, 159; *Theaetetus* 106–7, 141, 146–59; and the Theory of Ideas 105–6, 140–41, 160; and the third man argument 69, 105, 202; theory and ideology 104–9; and the Western Tradition 1–2
pleasure and pain 32, 115, 195
plus and quus 59
political obligation 65
political theory 188–89
political, the 159–62
positivism 77, 168–69

postmodernity 73–75
power: abnegation of 184; as endless deferral 36; Foucault on 76–77; God's 157–58, 198–99, 220, 224; Hobbes on 32–34; human 198–99, 224; and inner strength 126, 128; knowledge and 82, 198–99; Machiavelli on 12, 33, 126–27; Nietzsche on 12, 66, 77, 126–28, 133–34; as virtue 216–18
pragmatism 69
pride *see* haughtiness
procedure *see* process
process 33, 67
process-being 49
psychologism 165
public and private sphere 33, 35, 129, 160–61

Quine, W. V. 19, 176–77, 180

Raba 6–7, 93
rabbit (gavagai) metaphor 176–77
Rashi (Rabbi Shlomo Yitzchaki) 6–7, 8, 28, 41, 92, 95
rationalism 41, 75–76
rationalization, total 131
Rawls, John 35
reason and imagination 158–59
redemption 110–11
reenactment 65–66
reflective equilibrium 203
reflexivity 25, 33–34, 40–41, 48, 60, 63, 75, 83, 140–41, 220, 225; and Derrida 50; dilemmas of 50–51; test of 69, 71–72, 74
relativism, 115–16
relevance and priority, criteria of 164–65
religion; and secularism 4–5, 36, 38
religious fundamentalism 103–4
repentance (Teshuvah) 127, 194–95, 214–15
ressentiment 126–28, 184, 201
resurrection of the dead 181
revelation 112, 119–20, 205
Ricoeur, Paul 56–58
right and good 33, 35–36, 103
righteous (the) (Tzaddikim) 211
rights 64–66
Ryle, Gilbert 104
Rytina, Steven 82

Same(Self)/Other 34, 51, 55, 89; and generalized agnosticism 63; and the golden rule 62; and haughtiness 98; and Levinas 31, 34, 62; and Plato 24; and the primacy of ethics 12–15; and projection 203; Ricoeur on 58; and the Talmud 27–30; and totality and infinity 23–25, 57
saying and said 3, 51, 161–62, 183, 204–5
science: philosophy of 77–78; 81–83, 104, 132, 166–68; role of theories in 3, 169; and truth 77–78
Self *see* Same/Other
self-abnegation 91, 184–85
self-affirmation 200
self-cultivation 98
self-identify 59–61
self-incrimination 6–7
self-knowledge 58, 82, 95, 129
self-realization 219
self-referentialism *see* reflexivity
Sellars, Wilfrid 69–71
Shesheth, Rav 210–11
Shils, Edward 38–39
Shneur Zalman of Ladi, Rav 121–22
Shoshani, Mordechai 177–78
Sica, Alan 73
skeptical idealism 66
skepticism: and Reb Chaim of Brisk 178–80; and endless deferral 46; and generalized agnosticism 3; and knowledge 34, 67; Levinas' 176–80; and Levinas' ethics 180–83; and liberalism 197; and monotheism 40–41; and negative theology 2–3; paradox of 4–5, 98; and Plato 140–41; and Popper 167–70; and Quine 176–78; as theme of *Cratylus* 141, 143–45; and totality and infinity 141; and transcendence 51, 130; and truth 172; *see also* generalized agnosticism, negative theology
Skvoretz, John 80–81
social contract theory 33, 35, 65, 189, 200
Socrates, as midwife 146, 155–57, 159; *see also* Plato
Soloveitchik, Reb Chaim 176–80
Spinoza, Baruch 170
state of nature 189, 200
state, the 189
Strauss, Leo 78
strength 126, 128, 216, 218–24
stuck to ourselves 128–29
subjectivism 13, 48, 75, 165, 171, 174, 195

234 *Index*

subjectivity 48, 174, 195
substantialization 176
substitution 170–74, 180–84, 190–92, 195, 201–2, 205–9, 214–15, 217

Tarfon, Rabbi 199
temperance 97
textualism 76, 79
theory 101–4; and ethics 27–31, 88–91; and fact 12; and ideology 4–5, 38–40, 71–73, 104–6, 109; limits of 73, 80–83, 88; of the mean 88–91; and practice 134–40; and the sacred 38–40; the Talmud on 27–31
Theunissen, Michael 13
thing (Cheftzah) and person (Gavrah) 178–80
things in themselves 169
Thirteen Rules (Middot) 117
Tosafists 179
totalitarianism 72
totality and infinity 11, 43
Totality and Infinity 1–2, 18, 57, 164
tradition *see* practice
transcendence: 35, 103, 121; horizontal and vertical 4–5, 18, 34–36, 41, 51, 192–93; self- 98; and skepticism 51, 130; and substitution 192
transcendental idealism 165
transcendentalism 13–14
transference 66
trust *see* belief
truth: concept of 166–67; endless deferral as 35, 59; foundational 76; and goodness 73; as incoherent 165; of induction 164; language as 80; pursuer of 54; philosophical 21; and politics 64; and the priority of process 146; Protagoras on 147–48; religious 112; in science 132, 166–68; and skepticism 172; transcendence of issues of 130; unconditional 137; will to 77
Turner, Steven 79
tyranny 196

uncertainty and knowledge 40
underdetermination 3–4, 9, 12, 56, 66–67, 168–70, 179–80
unsaid and unsayable 161–62
utility and truth 59
utopia 173–74

voluntarism 111–12

walk in the ways of God (V'Halachtah B'Drachav) 210–11, 218
weak messianism 55–56
willful destruction 42
wisdom 7
wise man (Chochom) 102, 217–18, 221
Wittgenstein, Ludwig 59
words and things 69, 73, 82, 104, 129, 142–43, 160, 182, 190, 202–5

Yavneh, Rabbi Levitas of 91–94, 96, 98, 101–2
Yishmael, Rabbi 117
Yochanan, Rav 102–3
Yohai, Rav Simeon b. 102
Yonah, Rabbeiu 91–93

For Product Safety Concerns and Information please contact our EU
representative GPSR@taylorandfrancis.com
Taylor & Francis Verlag GmbH, Kaufingerstraße 24, 80331 München, Germany